CONTEMPORARY

SEP 8 1975

PSYCHOLOGY

DYNAMIC PERSONAL ADJUSTMENT: AN INTRODUCTION

Herbert L. Sachs

Professor
City Colleges of Chicago
Mayfair College

Behavioral Publications, Inc.
New York

Dynamic Personal Adjustment:
an introduction

Herbert L. Sachs

DOWNS JONES LIBRARY
HUSTON - TILLOTSON COLLEGE

Library of Congress Catalog Number 74-8053
ISBN: 0-87705-165-8
Copyright ©1975 by Behavioral Publications, Inc.

All rights reserved. No part of this work may be reproduced or utilized in any form or by any means, electronic or mechanical, including photocopying, microfilm and recording, or by any information storage and retrieval system without permission in writing from the publisher.

BEHAVIORAL PUBLICATIONS, Inc.
72 Fifth Avenue
New York, New York 10011

Printed in the United States of America
56789   987654321

BF724
S24

Library of Congress Cataloging in Publication Data

Sachs, Herbert L

Dynamic personal adjustment: An Introduction
1. Adolescent psychology. 2. College students—Psychology. 3. Adjustment (Psychology) I. Title. BF724.S24   158'.1   74-8053

To my students, who have contributed so much
to help make this book possible.

67876

Contents

At the back of this book is included a unique Student Service Section feature whereby the student using this textbook may communicate directly with the author.

Students may use these pages freely. They are encouraged to do so. The views, opinions and comments of students are valuable. Each inquiry will receive a direct reply by mail. The author merely requests that the questions posed be specific, rather than general.

Preface

Our behavior is not always rational. There are causal factors outside the realm of consciousness that bear important influence upon what we do or do not do in our everyday lives. We may even know how we came to be what we are and why we behave as we do, but often we cannot seem to do much about changing our behavior—even those selected reponses which we want to change.

Usually, most of us are faced with genuine choices. We are not compelled to act in only one way, but rather we can select one choice of action over another. The process involves weighing the most desirable consequences of our choice as against the negative alternatives, as well as highly individual and unique factors. An understanding of our own psychological history and of the general principles of human behavior increases our control in this decision-making process.

Thus, for each individual, there are facts he cannot accept for use, and insights he cannot translate into changes in behavior. We are influenced by our conscious and immediate needs—the emotionality of a situation frequently dictates the direction of our actions.

Teachers and counselors frequently ask an individual what he wants, on the assumption that he knows what he wants. We teach and help others to know because we assume that this additional knowledge will help people to make wise choices in the modification of their behavior.

This latter premise is as false as the first. We must accept that there are large areas of behavior that are subject to rational control by the individual. In these areas, in particular, a basic knowledge of the principles of human behavior is essential.

Understanding the factors which influence human behavior greatly increases one's potential for success in working with others. By applying our knowledge we can be more productive, happier, and better adjusted people.

This book is written for those freshmen and sophomore college students who may or may not have taken the basic, general introductory course in psychology. It does not pretend to treat at length the topics usually found within the scope of the general introductory course. Even those students who have had a basic introductory course will find the basic principles of adjustment important to them in their college life: academic problems, dating and courtship, choosing a career, and looking ahead.

The author assumes:

—that students have problems and want to solve them.

—that most students want to be successful in both their academic careers and future vocational endeavors.

—that young people today are faced with major decisions in choosing a career, getting married, and having a family.

—that the highly sophisticated and well-informed youth of today want to know what lies ahead, and also want to know how they came to be what they are at the present time.

—that students want to do something about the problems which they are facing.

Of course, the idea that an understanding of human behavior can help one to better understand oneself is by no means universally accepted.

Authors of textbooks know that they are the expositor of the works of others. Thus, in the writing of this book, as in other basic texts, the author is keenly aware of the contributions of many authorities. The unique contribution, if any, of this book, lies in the clarity of presentation of the material and organizational utility.

Thus, for each chapter, a definite format has been followed:

 I. Outline of the Chapter
 II. Introduction to the Chapter
 III. Presentation of formal material
 IV. What We Have Learned
 V. What We Still Need to Learn
 VI. Suggestions for Further Reading

It is hoped that the materials presented herein will be both of general and specific value. If even one individual is aided in making wise choices, in seeing himself more clearly, and in gaining a better grasp of the essential nature of human behavior, then all of the effort which has gone into this work will have been magnanimously rewarded.

Herbert L. Sachs

Part I

LOOKING AT YOU
The College Student Today

1

Introduction

- Differences in adult behavior
- Basic psychological principles of behavior
- Motivation as a key factor in understanding behavior
- Typical adjustment problems in young adulthood
- Challenges facing today's generation
- Societal ambivalences and pressures on young adults
- The dependency role of the young adult in college
- The structure of this textbook
- Subdivisions and structure: Utilizing your textbook materials
- What We Have Learned
- What We Still Need to Learn
- Suggestions for Further Reading

PURPOSE OF THIS CHAPTER

In this chapter, the student will become aware of some basic principles of psychology, some adult adjustment problems, societal influences, and so on. Important, too, is gaining an awareness of the structure of each of the chapters. The student is urged to carry on a "dialogue" with the text. Do not accept statements at face value; see if the statement is relevant for you, for your friends, and for larger groups within your sphere of acquaintance. In this way, the material to follow will become more meaningful and relevant. For "Dynamics/Personal Adjustment: An Introduction" involves people . . . people trying to get along in this world . . . in very active, albeit very individual ways.

SOME BASIC PRINCIPLES

Adult behavior differs from that of the adolescent and the child in many significant ways. Yet, in spite of the differences, to be discussed in detail in the following chapters, certain basic similarities persist, and certain basic principles of human behavior may be applied to all stages of development.

What are these basic principles and how are they related to the problems of human adjustment? Although each individual is unique in terms of his particular heredity and experiences, human beings exhibit similar patterns of development. Given the opportunity, they grow, crawl, walk, speak, and manipulate objects. The environment in which the human being develops is the basis from which the individual's attitudes, values, and habits are formed. A basic postulate is that the environment is an extremely important contributing factor in human development.

All human behavior is motivated; that is, there are underlying reasons why we do what we do. While some behavior seems to defy rational explanation, it is assumed that probing deeply enough beneath the surface of the observable behavior will reveal motives in various forms, strengths, or disguises.

All humans have the same basic sense organs, but the nature of sensation for each individual is highly subjective. There are differences in how people perceive and interpret what they see, hear, feel, and taste, as is dramatically illustrated in so many courtrooms, movie houses, and rock sessions. Yet, despite the differences, we can recognize a commonness of response; for most people sweet is sweet and loud is loud.

Human beings are born with intellectual capacities which require environmental stimulation for their realization. Intellectual functioning may be enhanced by stimulation or curtailed by an impoverished environment. Indeed, few individuals ever realize their intellectual capacity, and fewer still utilize their intellectual attributes to their fullest potentiality. Each person, in the course of his development, finds unique and highly individual ways of approaching the learning process. One's "short cuts" may be quite unfathomable to others, but to a particular individual they may seem proper.

BEHAVIOR AS PROCESS

As indicated, all human behavior is caused (motivated). Behavior is purposive, although the individual may not be aware of the reasons for his actions at a given moment. Explaining behavior is not a simple matter, although people are prone to look for and accept simple answers. The causes of behavior may be far-reaching and tied in with a host of other factors, some of which seem to bear no relationship to observable behavior. Single factors are often isolated for study, but it is the totality of factors which must be considered in understanding behavior.

Behavior is a continuous process. Events which have happened years ago—in early childhood or adolescence—can have an important bearing upon present behavior, current problems, conflict, and anxiety.

ADULT ADJUSTMENT PROBLEMS

Studying the adjustment problems of young adults who are college students is a relatively new undertaking. While each stage of human development seems to have a set of problems all its own, until recently the adjustment problems of the college students drew little attention, having become somewhat "lost" in the emphasis upon the problems of childhood, adolescence, and old age.

The marked increase in college attendance has focused greater attention on the problems of the college student. Young adults are faced with problems which cluster about their life situations, such as the pursuit of educational goals, the need for self-reliance, the desire for independence, feelings of inadequacy, choice of vocation, and the selection of a marital partner. The extent to which an individual finds satisfaction in life depends largely upon his ability to cope with the adjustment tasks appropriate to each stage of development. This is as true in young adulthood as it is in the earlier stages of development.

Typical Adjustment Problems of Young Adulthood

Attaining Maturity	Obligations toward Military
Attaining Independence	Service
Fulfilling Adult Roles	Developing Political Interests
Ambivalences in Society	Challenging the Establishment
Societal Pressures	Student Militancy
The Generation Gap	New Identity Roles
Educational Choices	Facing a New Morality

Keeping the Student Role
Sexual Problems
Marital Adjustment
The Challenges of
  Parenthood
Vocational Choices
Economic Problems
Making New Friends
The Uncertainty of the
  Future
Changes in Interests
Regression toward
  Immaturity
Focusing Level of
  Aspiration
Environment—Ecology

Problems of Mental Health
Problems of Study
Course of Study Selection
Personality Modification
Challenging One's Family
Religious Decisions and
  Doubts
Racial Tensions and Conflict
Concern for the Poor
Career Choice and
  Preparation
Getting a Part-Time Job
Living Up to Role
  Expectations
Negative Self Concepts
Womens' Roles

ATTAINING MATURITY

Social and emotional maturity do not just "happen." Many parents rely upon the euphemism that their children will "grow up" or "grow out" of their immature ways of expressing themselves. And in the course of maturation, many children do. But in a psychological sense, some individuals never reach maturity. While physical maturity is more evident than other forms, social, emotional, and mental maturity are at least equally important facets of an individual's development.

What is "mature behavior" for the college student? The behavior which is deemed appropriate to one's era is often considered irrelevant in another era. In the 1930's many college students were enthusiastic in their support of "worthy causes." Compared to today, however, their participation in active demonstrations was extremely limited. In the 1940's college campuses reflected the era of the returning World War II veterans—an era of new academic intensity and purpose on the campus. In the 1950's, college students came to be known as the "silent generation"; they were believed to be apathetic toward the social and political issues of the day. The 1960's saw different forms of behavior in college students: protesting activists and those seeking radical reforms. These students challenged the establishment in many directions, employing vocal and sometimes physical confrontation. Current evidence indicates that most college students of the 1970's will continue to be interested in changing those social structures which they view as unresponsive to human needs, with an emphasis on human needs and ecological problems.

SOCIETAL INFLUENCES

Adding to the uncertainty of the college student as he seeks his role as an adult are the uncertainties of the society itself. Today's college generation has grown up in a period of revolutionary changes in all areas: social, political, economic, and technological. Every young person is aware of an infinite number of problems and crises, local, national, and world-wide. For the most part, there are no immediate and final solutions to these problems, and young adults have come to accept these realities. Society itself is not clear as to how it expects its young adults to respond to its demands.

Going to college has created its own unique kinds of pressures and problems. Many young adults object to spending four or more years in preparing "to be." But while college is not the "final answer" for all young people, society offers few acceptable alternatives.

AMBIVALENCES IN SOCIETAL STRUCTURE

The ambivalent nature of our society creates pressures upon its young adults. He is expected to look toward the older generation for guidance; yet when he does, he all too often meets with criticism, chastisement, rebukes or hypocrisy. He is aware of example after example of mismanagement, waste, negligence, and illegality. Thus he faces the dilemma of heeding a society which dictates: "Prepare yourself to take a place in the established order of things," while at the same time recognizing the weaknesses of that established order.

Society expects its young men and women to be independent and capable of making mature judgments based upon sound principles. Yet at the same time, society keeps them in a highly dependent state, partly due to the prolonging of the educational process, to economic dependency, and to insistence on adherence to a fairly rigid moral code. The ambivalent nature of the dilemma is obvious, and the young have found solutions to these problems, not all of which are totally accepted by the "established" population of adults.

Young adults, then, are often forced into highly dependent roles, and often experience psychological states of despair, depression, and guilt. If the individual can adjust to this situation with some degree of tolerance and future anticipation, he soon finds himself emancipated from the dependency role and accepted as an adult; at such time he can express his individuality, demonstrate his potentialities, and find greater acceptance for his real self. If he cannot adjust to a situation where his independence is curtailed, he may find himself confused, embittered, aberrant, or neurotic.

College students face another unique kind of societal-imposed ambivalence. Although cultural values dictate the necessity of a college education, many colleges are slow to adapt the college curriculum to meet the relevancy demands of today's college youth. Thus many young adults find themselves disenchanted with the college curriculum, or unable to meet its rigorous demands, or totally unmotivated towards completion of a sometimes long and arduous course of study. The problem of the high-school "drop-out" of the 1960's has become today's problem of the college "drop-out."

What We Have Learned

1. The adjustment problems of the young adult differ in several ways from the adjustment problems faced at earlier stages of development.
2. Each individual exhibits highly individual and unique adjustments to his environment.
3. All human behavior is motivated.
4. Environmental circumstances play an important role in determining the degree to which an individual may or may not reach his potential.
5. The causative factors explaining the behavior of any one given individual form complex syndromes.
6. Exploratory behavior begins early in life.
7. Each individual adopts highly unique and individual modes of expressing himself.
8. Behavior is a continuous process. Present behavior can be the result of previous experiences.
9. The materials in this book focus upon the adjustment problems of the young adult, more specifically, the young adult in college. The material is relevant for the junior (community) college student and the college and university student.
10. Young adults are faced with several unique adjustment problems today, some of which are created by the society in which we live.
11. The extent to which an individual finds satisfaction in life depends to some degree upon the extent to which he can make satisfactory adjustments.
12. The typical problems of the young adult today differ from the problems of previous generations in several respects.
13. Social and emotional maturity do not just "happen" as a part of the growth process.

14. College students reflect different levels of maturity in their behavior.
15. Society does not impose a definitive standard of conduct for the young adult today; rather the standards are highly ambivalent.
16. In America today, college education and the completion of college is considered a necessity.
17. Young adults today actively seek participant roles and enjoy working with others cooperatively.
18. Many young adults experience psychological conflict created by the dependency status of the college student role.

WHAT WE STILL NEED TO LEARN

1. As the text unfolds, the student will learn many details concerning the college student as he is today, how he came to be what he is, and his future as an adult.
2. This text attempts to broaden the scope of the student and to provide new horizons and frameworks from which the student may view himself and his future.
3. The need to be adaptable is a prime need in our modern, fast-moving, complex society. It is hoped that the material in this textbook will help the student in these perspectives.
4. College life as it is today will be examined, and several ways in which the beginning student can help in adjusting to college life will be indicated.
5. Several of the challenges faced by the young adult will be examined, and, as he matures into adulthood, making the necessary adjustments should become easier for the individual who has studied "Dynamic Personal Adjustment: An Introduction."

SUGGESTIONS FOR FURTHER READING

Atkinson, J. W., *An Introduction to Motivation,* Princeton, New Jersey: Van Nostrand Reinhold, 1964.

Bell, Norman T., et al., *Introduction to College Life,* 2nd Edition, New York: Houghton Mifflin Co., 1966.

Boroff, Judy, *What I Wish I Knew Before I Went to College,* New York: Pocket Books, Inc., 1966.

Dennis, L. E., and J. F. Kauffman, *College and the Student,* Washington, D.C. American Council on Education, 1966.

Garrison, R. H., *The Adventure of Learning* in College, New York: Harper and Row, 1961

Goldsen, Rose K., Morris Rosenberg, Robin M. Williams, & Edward A. Suchman, *What College Students Think*, Princeton, New Jersey: Van Nostrand Reinhold, 1960.

Hamsher, J. Herbert, *Psychology and Social Issues*, Riverside, New Jersey: The Macmillan Company, 1973.

Krasner, Leonard and Leonard P. Ullmann, *Psychology of Behavior Influence*, New York: Holt, Rinehart & Winston, 1973.

McNeil, Elton B., *Being Human: The Psychological Experience*, New York: Harper and Row, 1973.

Psychology Today, 2nd Edition, Del Mar, California: CRM Books, 1973.

Rivlin, Harry N., *The First Years in College: Preparing Students for a Successful College Career*, Boston, Mass: Little, Brown and Company, 1965.

Sachs, Herbert L., *Student Projects in Child Psychology*, Dubuque, Iowa: Kendall Hunt Publishing Company, 1967.

Stone, L. Joseph, and Joseph Church, *Childhood and Adolescence*, New York: Random House, 1973.

Wenar, Charles, *Personality Development: From Infancy to Adulthood*, Boston, Mass.: Houghton Mifflin Co., 1971.

2

The Concept of College

- Differences in college life
- Reasons for entering college
- Kinds of colleges and universities
- Living at home—Living away from home
- Courses of study in college—The need to make decisions
- The need for independent study in college
- Designations of college instructors: Professors are people
- Techniques of study
- Rights and freedoms of students
- Importance of record-keeping and following-through
- College grading systems
- The young adult begins to question the establishment
- What We Have Learned
- What We Still Need to Learn
- Suggestions for Further Reading

PURPOSE OF THIS CHAPTER

As adolescents leave high school and prepare to face the future, some will go to work immediately, while others will work for a short time prior to entering college. Still another group, rapidly becoming the

11

largest segment of the young adult population, will enter a community college, college, or university immediately upon graduation from the secondary school.

College life will be different, and the differences between the secondary school and the life of the collegian will necessitate several adjustments. This section examines some of the problems encountered by college freshmen, the differences between living at home and living on campus, and attempts to examine some of the usual modes of adjusting to the various problems encountered by freshmen in colleges.

Perhaps one of the most valuable sections of this chapter appears toward the end—the material on how to study and techniques of study. This section also examines the rights and freedoms of students in the perspective of the alert, questioning college student of today.

"The Concept of College" should be clearly in the mind of each entering freshman student. A tremendous advantage accrues to the student who enters with a positive attitude, with the self-knowledge that he knows what to expect, and that he is able to cope with the numerous adjustment problems he is about to encounter.

HIGH SCHOOL AND COLLEGE DIFFERENCES

Students entering colleges and universities for the first time soon become aware of one glaring fact: *College is different.* Just as each college is unique in its physical plant and to some extent in its organizational structure, so too, each student adapts in unique and individual ways to the changes and challenges which he faces in his new endeavor.

The freshman year in college is often a time of doubt, searching, and confusion. It is also marked by discovery, new awareness, and accomplishment. While secondary schools tend to be highly structured in the sense of strict adherence to time schedules and more or less repetitious routine, colleges are much less so. Students have greater freedom in course selection, time scheduling, and class attendance—choices which place a greater burden of responsibility upon the student.

One of the chief differences in high school vs. college life is the need for student initiative. In colleges, unless the student is actively interested and "reaching out," the extent of his learning is seriously impaired. Still, students come to college with a wide variation in both their home backgrounds and their academic preparation; and students come to the colleges for a wide variety of individual reasons.

Reasons for Entering College

It is the expected thing to do
To prepare for a professional
career
To be somebody of
importance
Parental desires
All of my friends are in
college
To get training for a job
A college degree is needed in
business
Prestige
To develop friends—and
possible future mates
To make good contacts
To get an education
To round out education
To get into graduate school
later

As an aid to maturation
To help others in this world
For social life on the campus
Because I don't know what
else to do right now
To find out what I'm best
suited for
Because a degree is required
to be a professional
To avoid a blue-collar level
type of job
To prepare for a future
career
To meet interesting people
To delay entrance in my
father's business
To learn more in a specific
subject area
Future financial reward

While there are many different reasons for entering college, each student has his own unique motivational framework which leads him to pursue a college education and a college degree.

While most high school students begin making plans for college entrance relatively early in their careers, they are still somewhat surprised at the abruptness of the end of their high school days. In a flurry of proms, parties, and graduation ceremonies, the high school student suddenly finds his senior class and classmates diminished in importance. Four years of loyalties and close ties have disappeared, and the student is faced with forming new loyalties, making new friends, and finding a place and role for himself in a new societal structure.

One of the first and earliest decisions faced by the future high school graduate is the question of cost of college. "Can I afford it?" is a primary question for many young adults. Other problems arise:

—Can I get into the college of my choice?
—Shall I live away from home or at home?
—Shall I attend a state or private institution?
—Shall I attend a community college or a four-year institution?
—Does the college have what I need for my career?
—What do I want to be?
—Will I be able to compete scholastically?

—Is the social life of the school what I want for myself?
—Shall I attend a co-educational school?
—Shall I attend a secular school?

KINDS OF COLLEGES AND UNIVERSITIES

There is a great diversity in kinds of colleges and in the programs which they offer, as indicated in the accompanying table. The anomaly in the situation is that while the entering freshman student is often uncertain about his future and has not made specific vocation or goal directed plans, he is faced with making decisions which may bind him in a given direction for two to four years or more.

Most high school students still dwell under the illusion that college programs encompass four years of their lives. In fact, business schools may vary in time from several weeks or months to years, community colleges generally offer one- and two-year college programs, while regular colleges and universities offer programs which may take four or more years to complete. Many colleges and universities today frankly admit that their so-called "four-year" baccalaureate program may take five years to complete, or may include the necessity for summer school attendance.

Colleges differ, too, in their time schedules. While high school students may have become accustomed to a semester plan or an annual plan in their neighborhood schools, colleges and universities may operate on the basis of:

Semesters—two terms per year and a summer session
Trimesters—three terms per year and a summer session
Quarters—three or four terms per year and optional summer session

Colleges also offer a diversity of summer scheduling, so that some schools have anywhere from four- to twelve-week summer terms. In some colleges it is possible to attend one, two, or no summer sessions at all, depending upon student desires, needs, and progress.

While most high school students become rapidly accustomed to a self-contained building with a rigid time schedule (daily attendance from 9 to 3, or 8 to 2), colleges operate both day and night, some including Saturdays, and classes often meet irregularly. Classes may meet one to three or more times per week, but rarely do they meet daily. Too, while in high schools classes for 40, 45, or 50 minutes in length, in college the classes may meet for one hour, seventy-five minutes, or longer. Most colleges and all universities have more than one building. In large universities classes may be several miles apart in various campus building locations. All of these differences create adjustment problems. Fortunately, the majority of college students find the adjustments not too difficult, and rapidly change their life-style to accommodate the differences in time and space orientation.

LIVING AT HOME—LIVING AWAY FROM HOME

Once the high school graduate has committed himself to attendance at a given college, he has also automatically made a commitment to living at home or living away from home. Perhaps the earliest consideration in this matter involves parental and family wishes and economic considerations. Often the student's choice is at variance with his parents', and often the variance centers about financial matters as well as questions of maturity and capability.

Most community (junior) colleges are commuter colleges, providing no resident facilities, and expecting that their students will live at home. While this eases considerably the financial burden upon the student and his family, residing at home while going to college poses other psychological problems for the college student.

Living at home may mean that the young adult faces a prolonged period of adolescence, often being treated by his family on a level more commensurate with the treatment accorded his younger brothers and sisters. Thus small family frictions quite suddenly become voluminous issues: "Where are you going?" and "Please take out the garbage" are viewed by the young adult as impositions on his maturity, while the family view them as part of the ordinary pattern of family living and responsibility.

Studying at home poses another psychological problem. Many college students express the desire to move out and be on their own, even when they have a room of their own within the family home. They express a desire to be more independent (to have to account to no one other than themselves for their behavior and whereabouts), and the need to be able to concentrate better on their studies. Of course, some college students living at home do not even have the luxury of a room of their own for study.

College students living at home face psychological pressures (some of which are of their own creation) in terms of seeing their former friends living away from home at universities, on campus. They sometimes become envious, and their reflective behavior may be sullen or depressive.

Yet living away from home has its attendant pressures as well: the college student is faced with the daily problems of maintenance: meals, laundry, finances, self-care, loneliness, writing letters, and adjusting to new roommates. Sexual challenges also present themselves as the college student, often away from home for the first time in his or her life, is suddenly exposed to a wide variety of diverse personalities and family backgrounds. Religious and moral challenges abound as the world of the college student broadens considerably in the short span between high school and college days.

COURSES OF STUDY

Choosing the correct course of study can be a difficult decision for the freshman student who is uncertain of where he is going. Even for the freshman with a definite goal in mind, the large university poses a number of course majors which may bewilder the unsophisticated and dishearten the undecided. In general, those students who are uncertain about their major course of study take a year or two of general education "core" or liberal arts studies. However, even these students find that somewhere before they reach their junior or senior year at college they must "declare" a major course of study which they plan to pursue.

While high school counseling has improved tremendously in the past several years, there are still enormous strides which need to be taken. The high school senior counselor today is too often forced to be content with offering some minimal form of college guidance. Much of his time is taken up with helping the student with his entrance examination, applications, transcripts, and recommendation forms. Rare is the high school which provides sufficient counselor service, time, and staff to adequately guide the young adult into an appropriate course of study. However, there is a need for this type of guidance, and, at the present time, it can only be hoped that enlightened high school administrations will take cognizance of the vacuum which has unwittingly been created.

THE NEED FOR INDEPENDENT STUDY

Supervised study halls and designated study times are part of the accepted pattern in the secondary schools of the United States today. These concepts are alien to the colleges and universities. There the student is expected to plan his own individual study time and locale, as well as method. Many college students find it necessary and expeditious to spend study time in college libraries, partly due to the convenience of access of research materials. It has been stated that the difference between the superior and the average college student is that the former is knowledgable about the use of the library and how to obtain the resource information which he needs.

College libraries, like everything else on the college campus, are changing rapidly. Perhaps within the next few years the term "library" itself will become obsolete; for more and more colleges and universities are designated libraries as "learning resource centers"; and, indeed, today's modern college library is a source of learning materials far beyond the concept of mere books. Journals, tape recordings, records, casettes, film strips, programmed units, television tape reruns, and teaching machines are all part of the repertoire of the modern learning resource center. It is a challenge for today's college student to master the use of these materials and to utilize them effectively, along with the traditional books, journals, reader's guides, reference materials, and other more traditional resource materials.

Academically-poor students often believe that attending class more or less regularly, taking some notes, and listening to lectures is all that is required to obtain an education. Nothing could be further from the truth. The excellent student is one who actively contributes to class, seeks further sources of knowledge, and knows how to utilize effectively the learning resource center on his campus. Too, superior students "read with a pencil." In studying materials and reading sections of texts, they underline, take notes, raise questions, and, in general, carry on a "dialogue" with their study materials.

The need for independent study extends beyond the formal course material. The student should methodically "study" the various course offerings and instructors available for the term to come. Most students are better at shopping than they are at course selection. And yet it is in the selection of teachers and courses that crucial decisions are made in the learning process. Students should be selective and exercise all of the choices available to them in course selection. Unfortunately, some students pick subjects on the basis of time convenience, e.g., "I took it because it fit into my schedule." More knowledgeable students would reject such a statement, sacrificing convenience of time to gain opportunity for learning. These students are better equipped right at the start of a course, because they know what to expect, having made a study of the professor, his methods, and, to some extent, the course content.

PROFESSORS ARE PEOPLE

Sometimes beginning college students are bewildered by the size of the campus, the seeming complexity of the schedules, the large numbers of students with whom they must compete, and the change from "teachers" to "professors." Professors are people. They are also teachers. Just as students in high school have had the experience of good and bad teachers, so too they can look forward to the experiences engendered by good and by bad professors. For the title "professor" does not automatically become the equivalent of "superior teacher."

Some of the college teachers in freshmen courses particularly will not be professors at all. Many will be graduate students, going to school themselves to complete required work for higher degrees, and teaching one or two beginning freshmen courses at the same time. In general, beginning students should be aware of the "professorial hierarchy," as follows:

Teaching Assistant (T.A.)	A graduate student who also teaches a class or helps in teaching a part of a class.
Instructor	A part- or full-time teacher; usually one who is relatively new at the college.
Lecturer	A part-time teacher or graduate student who is teaching one or two classes.
Assistant Professor	The lowest professorial rank, but higher than instructor or lecturer. The title designates mastery of material and teaching experience.
Associate Professor	The second highest professorial rank. The title designates recognized skills by fellow-teachers, a number of years of experience, and a record of publication.
Professor	The highest academic rank. The title designates a number of years of teaching experience and recognition of merit by fellow-teachers.
Visiting Professor	A teacher from another school who will be on campus for a limited time only.

All college professors have designated conference hours during which time they are free to consult individually and in small groups with their students. Often appointments have to be arranged, sometimes well in advance, and sometimes through their secretaries. The important point, however, is that these individual conferences are the student's responsibility. He generally initiates the request for the conference when he feels the need for help on a particular topic. Some beginning college students are unaware of this procedure; others shy away from it, feeling they do not wish to "impose" upon the professor's time. This attitude is fallacious. Most professors welcome a chance to meet with their students individually and are more than willing to help with particularly difficult sections of their course material.

Another type of adjustment for which the beginning college student needs to be prepared is the difference in teaching method in college as contrasted with high school. In high schools classes are usually in the 25 to 35 student range, and almost all classes fall into these categories. In college, while some groups may be quite small, others may be as large as several hundred. Some classes may be taught by more than one instructor: i.e., a lab instructor in chemistry class may not necessarily be the lecturer. Again, in college, the lecture method is the one chiefly employed. Opportunity for small group discussion may be restricted, if present at all, in some courses.

In high school, the student's English teacher may also be the student's French teacher or homeroom teacher. This is very unlikely in most colleges. First, there are no homerooms or divisions. Second, the college teacher is usually a specialist in one subject area, and stays pretty closely within the framework of his own field.

STUDY TECHNIQUES

One of the amazing and unusual facts about education is that most students spend from twelve to thirteen years in elementary and secondary schools, studying a large number of different subjects, and rarely, if ever, spend even five minutes in a formal way devoted to "How to Study." Some schools are now offering regular courses in this area, while others incorporate the material into special classes or group counseling sessions. However, it would seem a real necessity to have each student carefully and formally exposed to good study techniques early in his school career, considering the number of years he will need to utilize this information.

Most students spend some time in study. However, *how* they study and under *what* conditions, utilizing *which* techniques, as well as *when* the studying is done, are important factors which determine the effectiveness of the study procedures. In order to study effectively, the student must have a purpose or goal. The student's goal and the intensity of the desire to achieve will determine the amount of energy he devotes to study, how effectively he will study, and how valuable the results will be in terms of permanent learning or retention. The student's attitude toward study is equally as important as his aptitude for learning the material.

A positive attitude toward study begins with setting worthwhile, attainable goals for oneself. The next step is to establish a procedure for accomplishing the desired goal. There are many reasons for studying: (1) Teacher or parental pressure, (2) desire for good grades, (3) fear of failure or other negative consequence, (4) desire to achieve status among peers, and, (5) the need to acquire knowledge and mastery of a subject.

Self-confidence is important in study. Each time the student masters some of his material (achieves a stated goal) his self-confidence is enhanced; each time he meets with failure, his self-confidence is weakened. Some students have such negative self-attitudes that they virtually defeat themselves in their attempts to master a given subject. Neither apathy, complacency, nor frantic cramming are aides to effective study. For the mastery of subject matter is a planned, continuous, if somewhat rigorous process.

One of the major adjustments that beginning college students need to make is the tremendous increase in amount of study time and individual, independent work required as contrasted with their high school careers. A frequent complaint of college freshmen is that their high schools failed to prepare them adequately for the amount of time needed and the type of study required by the colleges. Perhaps this one factor alone accounts for a large number of freshmen failures in college. The attrition rate in college is greatest in the freshmen year and smallest in the junior and senior years; perhaps this is another way of stating that effective study process and adjustment to it have been achieved successfully by those who remain beyond their first year of college.

In utilizing the effective techniques required of students who are attempting to master new materials, the basic principles of learning, or the so-called "Laws of Learning," can be of assistance. Learning takes place in meaningful ways; it is more difficult to learn material until that material has some form of conceptualized meaning for the student. Thus, looking up the meaning of unknown terms and fixing these meanings is a positive aide in memorization and understanding.

Learning materials which are alien to students requires a process known as "overlearning;" that is, learning beyond the point of simple recall and to the point of instant recall without difficulty. In this regard, repeated practice and drill is often an aide to both the original learning and to the retention of learned materials.

Like every other human process, learning requires motivation. It is not enough to study because the student is faced with an examination; the motives must be examined more deeply. Learned materials, when related to past knowledge and when viewed as utilitarian in one's everyday life, become more readily mastered and more thoroughly integrated.

Learning requires time. Effective study can occur under conditions which lend themselves toward the mastery of materials. In this regard, the conditions under which the student studies become a factor in learning equal in importance to those stated previously.

Conditions for study should be optimal. This means that the student needs:

Adequate materials
A quiet place to work, uninterrupted
A positive mental attitude
Motivation to achieve a stated goal

Cited among college freshmen as a frequent reason for lack of study is the inability to concentrate. A quiet place is considered a prerequisite for the above, but, aside from this, the student must delineate optimal conditions for quiet concentration. This means no TV, radio, stereo, hi-fi, etc., while study is in progress. Concentration also involves freedom from anxiety, and the ability to put other problems and pressures aside for a designated period of time. Some students spend several hours in study, but do so only prior to exams. Shorter periods of regular study have been found to be more effective.

In setting his goals, the student should allow for periods of rest. Mental concentration is fatiguing work. Some parents do not recognize this fact, and chide their offspring with remarks implying that they haven't been doing anything in the way of work because they have been spending hours in study. Nothing could be further from the truth. The student who studies effectively for a period of time is apt to be at least as exhausted, if not more, than the laborer who spends eight hours a day in physical exertion.

A place for study is necessary. A room of one's own, along with one's own desk or table, should be designated for study and for little else. Some students use the college library for this purpose, although many complain of the distractions of other students moving about, so that in practice the library is utilized effectively by only a small percentage of students.

Avoiding distractions is one of the prime requisites for effective concentration in studying. Any influence which diverts attention is a factor which reduces efficiency. For most college students the prime distractor is their friends; friends dropping in to talk; friends calling on the telephone; friends with exciting future plans for parties or dates. While friendship is important and necessary for college students, the student needs the moral stamina to avoid these forms of distraction while studying.

A time schedule prepared in advance is often helpful in effective study procedures. The time schedule should be realistic; neither too rigid nor too demanding. A common freshman error is underestimating the time needed for the preparation of assignments and for studying for exams. A rule of thumb for most college students requires two hours of study time for each hour of class time. For the students spending fifteen hours per week in class, this means a minimum of thirty hours per week in study. The thirty hours, obviously, cannot be accomplished over the week-end.

While some students keep detailed activity and time schedules for study and leisure, many find it unnecessary to place these schedules into written form. The important thing is balance—allowing sufficient time for needed work and allowing time for relaxation and leisure. Some students try to "cheat" on the number of hours of sleep they get each night, in order to accommodate the above time schedules. Such cheating is unwise; it rarely accomplishes positive results, and has many negative effects. Likewise, the use of "pep" pills to help keep one awake is frowned upon because of the negative after-effects upon most individuals.

Study involves five steps:

S——Survey the assigned work
T——Think of possible questions
U——Understand everything you read
D——Demonstrate your understanding by self-practice
Y——You review the entire assignment upon completion

Begin by surveying the entire chapter or section you are about to study, instead of just beginning by reading the first line. Reading the section headings within the chapter can often furnish a comprehensive "quick overview" as to the chapter contents. Summaries at the end of the chapter, as well as tables, charts, and graphs within the chapter, should not be ignored.

As you read, think of possible questions the instructor may wish to ask you based on the content of the chapter. Who? What? Why? Where? and How? should be answerable for each section which the student has completed. Understanding what you have read is important. A dictionary should always be at hand for difficult terms, as well as scratch paper for noting parts which are not clear. Some students choose to underline important statements; others take notes of important items within the chapter. This is what is meant by "reading with a pencil." This stage in the study process—reading for understanding —is by far the most time-consuming. It pays, at this point, to prepare adequate materials for later review, since time usually does not permit a complete re-reading of the entire assignment.

The student must be satisfied that he understands the material and is able to retain it. This is something which is highly individual, and can only be known by each student himself. A simple method for testing one's understanding, knowledge, and comprehension of a chapter is to test oneself by answering possible questions, or by writing out clear and concise answers to self-imposed questions.

The final, and important, step in the study process is a review. What is done at this time is called "overlearning." Many students omit this vital step in the process, only to find later, perhaps on examinations, that what they had learned initially now is difficult to recall. The need for overlearning is crucial because we forget so much so quickly. Learning to the point of possible recall is not enough; one must learn to the point of easy, rapid, and immediate recall.

Mnemonic devices, "memory aides," are sometimes helpful for some students. Practically speaking, these are memorization aides, and can be of some help if they are not abused. Most students are familiar with the sentence: "Thirty days hath September, April, June, and November" as a memory aide in remembering the days of the year in which the four above stated months have thirty days; hence all others, except February, have thirty-one days. The pattern, the rhythm, and the ease of retention of the mnemonic device determine whether or not they have value for the student.

STUDENT RECORDS

In order to gain admission to a college or university, the high school student is asked to submit certain records. While various colleges differ somewhat in their requirements, in general the student will be asked to send his high school transcript; application for admission; and his A.C.T. scores or S.A.T. scores, or both.

The A.C.T. refers to the American College Testing Program scores, while the S.A.T. scores refer to the Scholastic Aptitude Test (sometimes referred to as the C.E.E.B., or College Entrance Examination Board Scores, or simply "College Boards").

In addition to the above, some colleges may request:

—recommendations from high school counselors, teachers, or principal
—recommendations from adults other than school personnel
—a physical examination report from an M.D.
—a fee for applying for admission (often non-refundable)
—results of the particular college's entrance tests

In light of the above, students should not be too surprised to note that once admitted to college, a new series of records and reports become part of his "file" indicating academic progress. Each course the student takes is recorded on a permanent record card; often, today, by means of computer codes. The final grade in the course, and, sometimes, the mid-term grade is likewise noted. College students are expected to take the initiative in certain aspects of their records, such as:

—applying for scholarships
—applying for financial aid
—applying for work-study programs
—withdrawing from a course
—applying for exemption from certain courses
—applying for graduation
—taking comprehensive examinations
—requesting transcripts
—requesting counseling services and appointments

Students should become knowledgeable as to when it is to their advantage to make certain applications. For example, each college has an official "course withdrawal date," during which time a student may officially withdraw from a course with no penalty. It is sometimes to the advantage of the failing student to withdraw from a course and either try it again at a later date, or take another course during a new term.

Each college has rules and regulations, usually published in the official college bulletin, describing its procedures. Student should be thoroughly familiar with these as often it is academically advantageous, and sometimes it is financially rewarding. Some students, for example, are eligible for veterans' benefits; others for social security payments; some for various kinds of scholarships. In general, the colleges leave the responsibility for the initiation of action in any of these to the individual student. Colleges do provide counseling services for students who need help in making decisions, for those who wish more information, and for those desiring personal guidance.

Each college establishes a grading system and a standard for academic performance. Students should familiarize themselves with the rules and regulations regarding minimum passing standards, class, attendance, grades, grade-point averages, probation, and exclusion. By having this knowledge well in hand, students can often act wisely and prevent possible academic difficulty.

In addition to the above, many colleges provide health clinics, mental health facilities, nursing offices, and other aspects of the campus plant facility. Here again, some schools require students to have yearly check-ups, while others rely upon the student's initiative in requesting help.

RIGHTS AND FREEDOMS OF STUDENTS

The late 1960's found the college campuses in the United States centers of controversy concerning the rights and freedoms of students. As students, individuals find themselves in positions with little or no authority; as citizens, they still maintain the rights and privileges of citizenship. Young adults attending colleges and universities have certain rights and freedoms inherent in their position as young adult citizens.

One of the first rights of the student is his before he ever enters the college campus: the right to choose the college he will attend. The college, however, also has the right to expel a student for academic or disciplinary reasons, as well as to reject candidates due to factors such as lack of available space.

While students should have the right to free expression of opinion within the classroom and on the campus, no matter how radical or different the opinion may be, the college has the right and obligation to protect other students from violence and must make the campus operable and available to all students who wish to pursue their legitimate educational interests.

Recently, grading systems in colleges have been challenged by students, parents, and some educators. Several plans have been offered as superior to the present classic A, B, C, D, F, W* grading system. Among these are:

—A pass-fail grade
—An A, B, or W grade
—A satisfactory or unsatisfactory grade
—No grades at all
—Exemption from classes by examination
—Student evaluators working with teachers in determining grades
—An interdisciplinary grading system where one grade might represent more than one course

When a student's record is forwarded to agencies such as graduate schools, possible future employers, and legal agencies, he should be

*Under this system, A is the highest grade, C is average, D is the lowest passing grade, F is failure, and W stands for officially Withdrawn from the class with no penalty attached.

consulted whenever possible and in any event informed. Ordinarily the student has the right to determine which agencies shall receive copies of his college record, and ordinarily the request that this information be forwarded is initiated by the student.

Students have the right to join and to form campus groups of a wide variety of diverse political, social, and ethnic philosophies. The delimiting factor here should be based simply on the fact that these organizations do not impinge upon the rights of others. Students have the right to publish campus newspapers, including editorials which may or may not agree with the administrative procedures of the school. These publications should be free from administrative censorship. This form of criticism has long been a cherished right in the United States (freedom of the press) and should not be denied to a person because of the fact that he is a student.

Students have the right to participate in campus government organizations, and in recent years have been demanding a greater voice in the operation of their institutions. In those cases where students are accused of violating campus rules (disciplinary matters), the student is entitled to face his accusers, to know what it is he is accused of doing, and to have a fair and impartial hearing at which time he may defend himself.

QUESTIONING THE ESTABLISHMENT

The late 1960's found college students questioning the rights of college administrators in a wide variety of directions. The violence of campus protest cannot be sanctioned, but the rights of groups of students to raise questions must be preserved. Students have challenged college administrations in a number of directions, among them:

—Does the college have the right to do research for military-industrial organizations?
—Does the college have the right to sponsor military or quasi-military programs in the name of education?
—Should the college displace poor people in acquiring land for expansion?
—Should military personnel be allowed on college campuses for recruitment purposes?
—Should private industrial concerns be allowed on campus for recruitment purposes?
—Should communist or fascist speakers be barred from the campus?
—Are minority groups given equal treatment in the colleges?
—Should students have a voice in the evaluation and selection of faculty?

—Should students have the right to demand new courses of study which the college does not presently offer?

—Should student groups have sole control over the budgets of student organizations?

These kinds of questions are raised by large groups of students and student organizations. Many of these groups have sincere motivations: to improve the colleges for themselves and for those to follow.

Individual students also have occasion to voice highly individual complaints concerning matters of teaching, grading, or what they consider to be unfair or inadequate treatment. Before turning to group protest, strikes, walk-outs, and campus building take-overs, the student should be aware that most colleges have established modes of protest. Usually at one level of the procedure or another, the issue can be resolved. At most colleges the procedures involve:

—Conference with the Instructor
—Conference with the Department Chairman
—Conference with a Counselor
—Conference with a Dean
—Appearance before a Hearing Board

The problems of the 1960's centered about the fact that many students refused to follow the above procedures; others claimed that the procedures led to no satisfaction or no action, and thus turned to more dramatic methods. Because the student of today WANTS TO BE HEARD, modern college administrations are providing the means, encouraging co-operative efforts, and welcoming students as equal partners in the pursuit of mutual educational goals.

WHAT WE HAVE LEARNED

1. The largest segment of the young adult population of the United States now attends colleges, community colleges, and universities, as contrasted with any other nation in the world.
2. College life is different in many ways from high school life, requiring a number of complex adjustments.
3. Students enter college for a wide variety of different reasons.
4. There are several different kinds of colleges, offering many different programs.
5. There is a formal procedure to follow in applying for admission to college.
6. Colleges vary in the number of years of required attendance, from one, two, four, or more years. Many so-called "four-year" colleges now admit freely that it will take longer to complete all requirements.

7. Students going to college face adjustment problems whether they live at home or on campus.
8. Choosing the correct course of study can be a difficult decision for the entering freshman.
9. Colleges demand a large amount of individual and independent study by students.
10. High school students are often not prepared for the change in the kind of work and the amount of time that successful college careers demand.
11. The methods of teaching on college campuses are often significantly different from the methods used in secondary schools.
12. There are definite techniques of study which can be of tremendous help to all students.
13. Colleges keep detailed records of students' academic progress.
14. Students have definite rights while attending colleges; their rights of citizenship cannot be abridged because of their student status.
15. In the late 1960's students raised serious questions concerning some of the long-accepted administrative practices on college campuses.

WHAT WE STILL NEED TO KNOW

1. We need to find a better way to prepare students in high school for the number and kinds of adjustments which they will face when they enter college.
2. We need to inform students of the variety of college choices which are available to them early in their high school years.
3. We need better counseling and guidance in the high schools so that having selected a college, the student can then make intelligent decisions about course selection.
4. We need to begin in the elementary schools to teach our young people about study techniques, such as how to read differing kinds of materials, how to take tests, how to take notes and how to listen to a lecture.
5. We still have not met adequately the problem of the rights and freedoms of students as against the responsibilities and obligations of college administrations.

SUGGESTIONS FOR FURTHER READING

Bell, Norman T., Robert W. Burkhardt, and Victor B. Lawhead, *Introduction to College Life*, Boston, Mass.: Houghton Mifflin Co., 1966.

Boroff, David, *Campus U.S.A.*, New York: Harper and Row, 1962.

Bronfenbrenner, Urie, *Influences on Human Development*, Hinsdale, Ill.: The Dryden Press, Inc., 1973.

Brown, J. S., *The Motivation of Behavior*, New York: McGraw-Hill, 1961.

Coleman, James C., *Psychology and Effective Behavior*, Glenview, Ill.: Scott, Foresman and Company, 1974.

Grebstein, Lawrence C., *Toward Self-Understanding*, Glenview, Ill.: Scott, Foresman and Company, 1969.

Havemann, Ernest and Patricia Salter West, *They Went to College*, New York: Harcourt, Brace and World, Inc., 1952.

Heath, Douglas, *Explorations of Maturity: Studies of Mature and Immature College Men*, New York: Appleton-Century-Crofts, 1965.

Johnson, Paul E., *Psychology of School Learning*, New York: John Wiley and Sons, Inc., 1971.

Keats, John, *Sheepskin Psychosis*, New York: Dell Books, Inc., 1966.

Lindner, R., *Must You Conform?* New York: Holt, Rinehart & Winston, 1962.

McClelland, D. C., *The Achieving Society*, Princeton, New Jersey: Van Nostrand Reinhold, 1961.

McDavid, John W. and Herbert Harari, *Psychology and Social Behavior*, New York: Harper and Row, 1974.

Sawrey, James M. and Charles W. Telford, *Educational Psychology*, Boston: Allyn & Bacon, Inc., 1973.

Stricker, George and Merbaum, Eds., *Growth of Personal Awareness*, New York: Holt, Rinehart and Winston, 1973.

Wise, W. Max., *They Came for the Best of Reasons: College Students Today*, Washington, D.C.: American Council on Education, 1958.

3

Utilizing the Resources of the College

- Resources available to the college student on campus
- College administrative personnel and their functions
- The role of the faculty advisor
- The office of student personnel services
- Counselors and their function: The counseling office
- How to obtain financial assistance
- Similarities and differences in stipends, loans, grants, and scholarships
- Vocational guidance for college students
- Taking tests: A part of the college student's role
- Kinds of tests and how to prepare for them
- Personal problems of college students
- What We Have Learned
- What We Still Need to Learn
- Suggestions for Further Reading

PURPOSE OF THIS CHAPTER

In this third chapter of *Dynamic Personal Adjustment: An Introduction*, the kinds and types of resources available to college students will be examined. This text takes the point of view that these services to students are at least as important as the teaching function per se, and together form a total picture of student life in college.

The informed student should be aware of the services offered by his college, when to utilize these services, how to go about making effective use of them, and which services may be of personal value for himself. While colleges will differ somewhat in the various titles of the officials offering these services, their function, nevertheless, remains similar.

The role of the college administrator, the faculty advisor, the student personnel officers, counselors, financial aide officers, and others will be examined in this chapter. Each of these individuals can offer valuable assistance to the informed college student, helping him make an easier and better adjustment to campus life, as well as gain the optimum in satisfaction and pleasure from his college days.

Let us proceed to examine the various ways in which students may find it possible to "Utilize the Resources of the College."

COLLEGE ADMINISTRATIVE PERSONNEL

Administrators in colleges are almost invariably former teachers. As such, they have had a number of years of experience with college students and their problems, needs, and demands. Most college administrators realize that their function can only be enhanced when they work co-operatively with individual students, groups of students, and student organizations.

While titles may vary considerably, there is a tendency to label all college administrators as "deans." Some may have considerably different titles, such as: chancellor, president, provost, vice-president, director, dean, assistant dean, registrar, business manager, financial aides officer, or co-ordinator.

The freshman student is generally somewhat overawed by the impressiveness of titles, or bewildered by the differences in terminology. The fact is that college administrators function to operate the college efficiently, give the school direction, and to provide services for both students and faculty.

While most students experience little or no direct contact with college administrative personnel, these individuals nevertheless have a direct and important bearing upon the lives of students. The decisions they make include:

> The number of students to be admitted
> The kinds of faculty to be hired
> The variety of programs to be offered

DOWNS JONES LIBRARY

HUSTON · TILLOTSON COLLEGE

The amount of housing to be made available
The amount of funds to be allocated for various student functions
The retention or dismissal of students who are weak academically
The retention or dismissal of students who have violated campus
   regulations

The chief function of a college administration is to provide optimal facilities and services so that each student has an opportunity to develop to the maximum of his given potential. College administrators recognize that what a student will be, he is now becoming. They are concerned, then, with more than his academic development; they are also concerned with matters of his stability and maturity.

Providing an educational program for students today involves more than the mere sphere of activity known as the college domicile. For, today, college campuses are part of a larger community, and the trend for the future is for more and more involvement, both directly and indirectly, with the life and problems of that community. College administrators are the ultimate resource for individual students and groups of students who have legitimate complaints, requests for change, and problems which need authoritative resolution.

The curriculum of the college is determined largely by these same administrators. Recently there have been numerous complaints, largely from students but also from educators, that present curricula do not adequately meet the needs of today's students. No curriculum, old or new, can really meet the needs of all students. Methods of instruction can only survive with administrative support.

Most college administrators support the contention that education is more than book learning and that the educated student has more than textbook knowledge. Education should give life a new meaning and a broader dimension, so that the educated individual has greater control over his actions, a broader attitude towards social issues, and an awareness of his capacity in the form of self-evaluation and self-realization.

THE ROLE OF THE FACULTY ADVISOR

Some students enter and complete their college careers without ever consulting a faculty advisor. These students, fortunately, are rare. For faculty advisors have an important role to play in a student's life. Their timely advice can prevent serious errors in course selection, in vocational aspirations, and in personal matters. Many faculty advisors, but not all, are also department chairmen in a field of specialization such as mathematics, English, or foreign languages.

DUWES JONES LIBRARY
HUSTON-TILLOTSON COLLEGE

Faculty advisors must recognize that they are working with young adults who are still changing in their thoughts and behaviors. The changes may even become evident from week to week, but are certainly apparent over a prolonged period of several years. Secondly, faculty advisors must realize that people today live in a changing world, a world which is rapidly narrowing, adopting new social codes, and increasing in its tempo and pressures. Finally, advisors must also recognize that educational structures themselves are undergoing rapid changes. Consider for a moment the concept of the one-room, self-contained schoolhouse. It has virtually disappeared from the educational scene in less than fifty years.

Faculty advisors sometimes express frustration because they have so many students to advise, so little time for each student, and, perhaps, a somewhat inadequate background for coping with the diversity of problems presented to them.

Perhaps, in the future, as colleges acquire adequate, capable counseling staffs, the role of the faculty advisor will diminish. At the present time, however, it is a vital, if somewhat unrewarding role. It is unfortunate that some students make only cursory use of the advice and services that can be provided by skilled, competent, and interested faculty advisors.

Faculty advisors play important roles, then, in the student development of what has been termed the psychosocial areas. According to this point of view, students need to develop along four basic areas:

(1) To achieve reasonable autonomy from parents
(2) To achieve a sense of identity
(3) To achieve a sense of intimacy
(4) To achieve a sense of responsibility towards themselves and towards society.

STUDENT PERSONNEL SERVICES

The area of student personnel services is one of the newest within the framework of college campuses. This area encompasses the functions of the college:

Counseling Centers
Psychological Services Centers
Admissions Offices
Registrar's Office
Business Manager

Essentially, the student personnel function is based upon a philosophy of helping the student make the various adjustments required by college life. The broad philosophy of most college student personnel offices is based upon the following tenets:

—Education is necessary for the maintenance of a democracy.
—Education is essential for the improvement of society.
—Education helps equalize opportunity for all people.

College personnel working in the areas of student personnel services have come to recognize that students are not only the objects of education, but its principle instruments. The institution may provide physical facilities, faculty, and counseling services, as well as a set of standards for conduct and behavior. But in a very real sense the primary environment of the student is other students. Students "set the pace" for each other; they learn from each other in direct and indirect ways in addition to the formal teaching done in the classroom itself. Enlightened college administrations have therefore provided means whereby students can participate more visibly in the making of decisions concerning their campus lives.

While student personnel services alone cannot solve all the problems and fears of young adults as they face a world of uncertainty, most college administrators, as well as the students themselves, agree that this is a step in the right direction. Today student personnel staffs are woefully inadequate in the number of personnel available and in the supply of trained specialists in various areas. This lack can be somewhat forgiven on the basis that these services are among the newest to be established by colleges. Students, however, are less forgiving. They want and need these services and they need them now. Providing adequate facilities and services in the future is of little comfort to those entering and leaving the college campuses at the present time.

Most educators conversant with the college's responsibilities to its students agree that student personnel services are indispensable to the functioning of the college. At the same time, they point out that these services as offered today have several serious shortcomings. For the most part these shortcomings stem from a lack of adequate planning and inadequate professional staffing.

In order to function effectively, student personnel service departments need:

—A favorable climate of opinion concerning their services from other faculty and from students;
—A college administration which is student-oriented;
—Qualified and skilled personnel trained in specific areas of student personnel services; and
—An efficient and effective mode of organization for the student personnel department.

Student personnel services have been recognized as a means not only of providing needed services for the student, but also of educating him. To be sure, the education is less formal, for it is not based upon regularly scheduled classroom attendance; but it is a means of broadening a student's horizon, and this has become a recognized goal for the educated man in today's complex societal structure. A college may provide a plant, a faculty, and a curriculum, but unless there is an orderly means for admitting students and for helping them with their problems once admitted, the college is in reality an empty shell masquerading as a place which provides a broad educational spectrum, whereas in reality it provides the mere outer facade.

Colleges have recognized that the transitional state from high school student to college student marks a significant change in a young adult's life, requiring changes in self-conception, adaptation of new roles, and, more often than not, needed help and guidance in making major new decisions. Thus student personnel services encompass an area on the campus which, while relatively new, has become rapidly vital. The future will see a vast expanse in this area in time, budgetary allotment, personnel of a more highly specialized nature, and administrative philosophy devoted to an increase and expansion of these services.

THE COUNSELING OFFICE AND THE COUNSELOR

It is difficult to realize that only a few short years ago counselors were not in existence in the secondary schools and colleges in the United States. Some high schools still do not provide counseling services, and too many of those that do do so with inadequate facilities and staff. Many high school students still view the counselor as the "disciplinarian" or the "prom sponsor" or as a "good fellow who is nice to talk to, but who can't do very much for you."

Counselors in colleges today provide recognized services for students. Among these are:

Vocational guidance and direction
Job placement
Testing
Academic counseling
Counseling concerning personal problems

Assisting the student to assess himself and his role in an uncertain society is probably a good capsule summary of the work of the college counselor today. In a society and world which is rapidly changing, counselors are charged with the responsibility for providing a sense of security for college students. This is no small task. Even in such long-established areas as vocational guidance, counselors are faced with a rapid expansion in knowledge and hence the creation of new jobs and job titles which did not even exist a few short years ago.

While some students make extensive use of the counseling office and its services (and here, too, there is a danger in that some students may become too dependent upon the counselor), others rarely use the counselor's offices, and some never do. The reason for the above is the uncertain image which counselors still have among various groups, including their own faculty and peers. All too often the campus administrative head views the counselor's functions as at least quasi-administrative; the faculty see the counselor as a special privileged category, since he often has a larger and more private office facility; parents are often wary of the degree of confidentiality with which he may be trusted; boards of governors view him as a necessity for accreditation; and students express a wide variance in the form of mixed opinions.

The term "counselor" itself has become hybridized, so that the man who finances your new car purchase calls himself a "financial counselor" as well as the man at the local loan; lawyers, psychologists, and psychiatrists boast about the "counseling" which they offer, and true college counselors add to the concept and often differentiate between "counseling services" and "guidance functions." Dr. Robert Williams has stated:

> The school counselor is engaged in an intensive search for identity and identification. He is clarifying an image of self that will enable him to make his most significant contribution to education and to youth.

At the present time, the nature of the counselor's role and function is not clearly understood by many students or their parents. Opinions differ and judgments vary considerably, and perhaps this is as it should be, because just as there are superior teachers and poor teachers, so too there are superior and poor counselors. Effective counseling requires that the counselor be sensitive to the needs and emotions of the students with whom he is working.

Students seeking counseling services have the right to expect that the counselor will be:

> qualified in his area of counseling;
> sincere in his respect for students;
> a practitioner of a code of ethics which includes confidentiality;
> sensitive to the problems of students;
> capable of offering positive help; and,

persistent in his responsibility to follow through on matters which
defy immediate solution.

Sometimes beginning college students simply don't know how or
when to see a counselor. They should see a counselor whenever they
feel the need for help, guidance, explanation, or information. How to
make an appointment is relatively simple; most counseling offices have
secretaries who will schedule appointments for a student during the
student's free time. However, the important point (and here, again, is
a big difference between secondary schools and colleges) is that seeing
a counselor remains largely a matter of student initiative. The student
must initiate the request for counseling services.

Effective counseling has "salvaged" many a student's college career, as well as helped him in his personal life. The counseling of the
future will be aimed at "preventive counseling." This means that more
elementary schools will have counselors, and that there is to be a
tremendous upgrading in high school counseling services. Dr. Clovic
Hirning, a well-known psychiatrist, has stated that: "I feel after so
many years of pulling people out of the river, that I'd like to meander
upstream and find out who's throwing them in." Dr. Hirning feels that
today's student is working under pressures and tensions which simply
should not exist. But the fact is that these pressures do exist, and it is
precisely for this reason that colleges offer counseling services for
students. Often the student is faced with a working day far in excess
of what his parents would consider acceptable if they themselves were
required to perform their job functions on that basis. Is it any wonder,
then, that students have emotional problems and need help?

While in the past counselors and counseling offices were considered to be of value only in the context of being able to assist a small
percentage of students (perhaps 10 to 25%), today more and more the
philosophy of the college dictates that counseling services by provided
for all. Dr. T. R. McConnell, in an address at the University of Minnesota, made the following comments about counselors:

> ... Perhaps instead of stressing the autonomy and separate orga-
> nizational status of counselors, it would be better to create an
> atmosphere in which counselors are thought of as ranging from
> teachers who have acquired considerable understanding of the
> dynamics of human behavior to highly trained professional coun-
> selors whose services are actually extensions of the services of
> their faculty colleagues. ...*

*Snoke, Martin L., Ed., *Approaches to the Study of Administration in Student Personnel Work.*
#9 Minnesota Studies in Student Personnel Work, E. G. Williamson, Ed., Minneapolis,
University of Minnesota Press, 1960. Reprinted by permission.

No educational program can function effectively without the support of students. No counseling program can be effective in its attempt to aid students unless students understand the role and function of the counselor and can easily and readily make use of the services of the counseling office.

FINANCIAL AIDS

Students and their families who were concerned about the high cost of a college education in the 1950's and 1960's now have real cause for concern. Like so many other costs, college costs have skyrocketed, and the outlook is that the trend has not as yet begun to peak. It is not uncommon for private college costs to reach as high as $16,000 for four years, including tuition, materials, room and board, while state colleges have reached a high of $10,000 for in-state students who are not living at home. Perhaps this is one of the reasons for the great growth in community and junior colleges across the nation, since their costs are markedly lower for the first two years of college.

The United States, as yet, has not reached the point where it is ready to pay students for going to college, a practice common in the Soviet Union, Denmark, Sweden, Norway, and Finland for several years. However, as America experiences critical shortages in key professional areas, more and more financial aid has become available to students pursuing certain academic goals. Today there are critical shortages in the United States of trained professionals in such fields as:

Special Education
Engineering
Advanced Computer Sciences
Scientific Technological Areas
Registered Nursing
Certain Areas of Teaching
Certain Medical Positions

In the ghetto, in other poverty areas, and among low-income wage earners, the chief deterrent for sending youngsters to college has been the high cost. As we approach the "college education for everyone" era, the financial burdens of getting a college education have been eased considerably by the number and kinds of financial aids which have been made available to students. The various kinds of financial aids are not the same. Some are based on the ability of the family to demonstrate financial need, while others make no allowance for the amount of family earnings.

The following kinds of financial aids are available at almost all colleges today:

Federal Loan Programs
State Loan Programs
State Scholarships
Local, County, or City Scholarships
Stipends and Grants-in-Aid
Work-Study Programs
On-campus Work Programs

Of course, the prime resource for paying for college work is still the support provided by parents, by the student's own financial savings, and by private loans. Wise parents begin college savings plans for their children at a very young age, although the effects of an inflationary spiral has partially offset this type of financial planning.

Loan programs provided by financial aid officers (and almost all colleges today have such specialists, whose sole function is to help students obtain the needed financial support to continue their educational careers) include the following:

—National Defense Education Act Loan (N.D.E.A.) providing undergraduates up to $1,000 per year, and graduate students up to $2,500 per year
—State guaranteed loans, provided through co-operation with local banks and providing up to $1,500 per year
—Loans provided by the college's own funds, which are usually relatively small amounts
—Community organizations, including religious groups which provide loans for college students

Many parents and students are reluctant to seek a loan to complete a college education, but it is a method of completing college and, additionally, these loans provide several features:

(1) The loan need not be repaid until graduation.
(2) The rate of interest is usually low.
(3) The interest on the loan does not begin until after graduation.
(4) Some loans have "cancellable" features, whereby some or all of the loan may be cancelled (not repaid).

As with so many other areas of student life in college, the student must initiate the request for the loan. This is usually done in connection with the college's financial aid officer, who is generally a part of the counseling office or student personnel services.

Almost all of the states in the United States today have a loan plan for students known as the State Guaranteed Loan Plan. Under this plan, a student with no financial resources (collateral) may obtain a loan from his local bank because the state guarantees the repayment of the loan to the bank if the student should default. These loans bear low interest rates, are relatively easy to obtain, and do not bear interest at all until after graduation, at which time repayment begins. Requirements for obtaining the loan, in general, are:

(1) The student is a United States citizen.
(2) The student is a resident of the state in which he is applying for the loan.
(3) The student is attending college on a full-time basis.
(4) The student demonstrates financial need through making application for the loan.

Scholarships differ from loans in several respects:

(1) They demand high grades.
(2) They need not be repaid.
(3) They are not always based upon financial need.
(4) They vary in time from one term to one year to all four years of college.

The kind and number of scholarships vary considerably from college to college. Some are based upon specific requirements (e.g., father must be a union member), while others are much more general (e.g., student must rank high in class). Many state governments have provided Scholarship Commissions which will award either monetary or honorary scholarships to students who have achieved high academic success. The moderate or middle-income family who is reluctant or ineligible to obtain a loan often seek scholarships for their youngsters.

In general, the more expensive the costs, the larger the number of scholarships which are available. The moderate priced state-supported colleges and universities usually provide a smaller percentage of scholarships, and the amount of the scholarship is often small (not enough to pay all costs).

A scholarship is often equated with the outright "grant," but they are not always the same. "Grants" or "grants-in-aid" may be provided by the colleges or by local, state, and private agencies to students pursuing particular kinds of programs.

"Stipends" are financial awards provided by the colleges, by private, state, or local agencies, to offset the college costs. They are similar to grants in that they are most often awarded to students engaged in certain kinds of programs, e.g., many states have provided "stipends" for students studying in Special Education areas, since teachers of Special Education are so desperately needed and the available supply is so small.

Most colleges today use the College Scholarship Service (C.S.S.) evaluation system to determine financial needs of a family prior to awarding scholarships, stipends, or grants. This system assures the non-partisan, non-biased awarding of scholarships to students. The College Scholarship Service is a non-profit agency, located at Princeton, New Jersey, and at Berkeley, California. This agency requires the family to complete a Parent's Confidential Statement, available at all colleges and most high schools. This statement asks for the amount of income which the family has reported on their Federal Income Tax forms. The colleges themselves make the decisions as to the actual awarding of the scholarships, grants, and stipends, but the impartial College Scholarship Service agency attempts to insure fair treatment for all who apply, negating the effects of local bias or possible prejudice in favor (or not in favor) of any one individual.

Most colleges today have what is known as "work-study" programs. In this program, the student is given an on-campus (or, at times, an off-campus) job which will fit into his schedule, and which will provide an opportunity for the student to work between 15 and 30 hours per week at a fair wage. This provides an opportunity for the student to meet his daily expenses through respectable work. The program is supported by federal funding, and the jobs are obtained through the college's job placement center, counselor, or student personnel services officer.

The picture of financial aid in colleges today is not quite as clear as has been presented herein. Most students in need of such aid find that their funds come not from one source, but rather a combination of these. For example, a student might have a work-study job for daily income and necessities, a stipend for a part of his tuition, plus some support through his parents or through a loan. This situation, while complex, is not at all unusual today. Perhaps in the next decade it will come to be more generally recognized that the need for trained professionals in the United States is so great that a new and better system for financial aid must be established. Such a system would pay for all college costs and also provide a monthly allowance for full-time students. Funding would come from the federal government, whose return would be an enormous increase in the level of education in the United States, a core of professionals trained in a variety of areas, and better services for the people of the United States in such areas as health, housing, and in government itself.

There are other, less well known and generally less widely available sources of financial aid for college students. These include:

athletic scholarships;
political scholarships;
military scholarships to those seeking careers as officers in the military services;
private industry scholarships (usually awarded to children of career employees);
religious scholarships (denominational scholarships awarded by religious organizations);
local college scholarships (e.g., faculty wives contribute to award a scholarship to a needy or deserving candidate);
Social Security benefits;
Veterans benefits.

It has been stated that financial need not be a deterrent to any student who genuinely seeks a college education. The relatively low costs of state-supported community colleges makes possible the completion of at least two years of college even for those in financial straits. These colleges also offer evening, and in some cases, Saturday programs for students who must work in order to complete their college careers. Thousands of students have completed their college careers which originally began in the community colleges. There are numerous examples, too, of enterprising students who have earned substantial amounts of money while attending college.

"G.I." or "veterans" benefits have provided financial aid in the form of full tuition plus monthly stipends to millions of young adult men and women who have completed military service. The benefits vary, depending upon the length of the individual's prior military service, from several semesters to thirty-six months of college. Many veterans have postponed the use of their "G.I." benefits until such time as they need the financial aid to complete their college education, choosing to pay for the first year or so of college by themselves. Other military benefits accrue to students participating in a full four-year college R.O.T.C. (Reserve Officer Training Corps) program, and planning on later military careers. These individuals may receive full tuition payments plus monthly stipends, as long as they remain active in the program.

The Social Security Law provides monthly benefits to youngsters when a parent on whom they were dependent dies or starts receiving Social Security retirement or disability benefits. Such benefits ordinarily end when a youngster reaches the age of 18, but they are continued in force until the age of 22 for youngsters attending college as full-time students. Students seeking these benefits should co-ordinate their efforts through two sources: the college financial aid office and their local social security office.

VOCATIONAL GUIDANCE

The seeking of vocational preparation and the training for needed professional service remain the basic reason for college attendance for most students in the United States. Some students have what is termed "impoverished" backgrounds; that is, they arrive at college poorly prepared and ill-equipped for the tasks which they are about to face. They have not read the books, they do not possess the study skills, and they have never learned to work independently, although the college assumes these characteristics of entering freshmen. The new student must adjust not only to the college world, but must also be prepared to face the problems of choice of vocational career, choice of major in college, and his future as an adult. Most colleges today provide vocational counseling by trained counselors, experts in the area of vocational guidance. They are charged with the responsibility of "keeping up" with the latest trends in employment and advising students about old and new career opportunities.

Choosing a career is a difficult problem. The need to make a choice often comes as the student is entering college, when more immediate problems of gaining admission and financing are present. Yet the college freshman must make a long-range commitment due to the pressures of his friends, his family, himself, the college itself, or any combination of these. Once the choice is made and the appropriate curriculum has been entered, it is often difficult, costly, embarrassing, or time consuming to start anew. Yet all too often a student's vocational choice is a rather haphazard decision, based on glamorous appeal, misinformation, family choice, or other factors rather than on a clear understanding of the job's demands and one's qualifications for these demands. All too often also the choice is an unrealistic one, with the student encountering unwise "levels of aspiration" (aiming too high or too low for a given occupation, as measured against his own ability level to succeed).

Some students are steadfast in their claim that they "know what they want," and they cannot be dissuaded in spite of evidence that they may be unsuited in their occupational choice. Later they will probably have adjustment problems to face; problems which might have been avoided initially had a wiser vocational choice been made. Some students base their career choice upon "images"; they see only the glamour and the ultimate goal, without realizing fully the preparation needed and the obstacles to be overcome in attaining their choice.

The world of work is undergoing numerous changes, including the availability today of many new technologies and a vast increase in automation. Vocational fields have arisen in the past few years which some students may never have heard of before, such as "prosthetics" (the fitting of artificial limbs to handicapped individuals) and "human space engineering" (the application of psychological principles to the operation of complex machines such as computers). Some older occupations have become obsolete.

Most colleges have counselors trained in the field of vocational guidance, and many of these use vocational interest inventories as an aid in helping a student to determine his special abilities and vocational interests. Two of the more commonly used vocational guidance instruments are the Kuder Preference Record and the Strong Vocational Interest Inventory. These instruments attempt to determine the broad areas where a student feels "comfortable" or where he would meet with little success (e.g., "likes to work with people" or "mechanically inclined").

Many community colleges face the dualism of eager students who wish to attain academic success while they have weak or impoverished backgrounds and vague notions about their future occupational choices. In general, a wise vocational choice can be made only after much investigation and after one has acquired factual information concerning the occupation itself. Many high school students profess to be interested in "psychology" although they have had no exposure to the subject other than some vague concepts of "Freud" and "a couch." When appraised of the fact that skilled psychologists need strong mathematical backgrounds they are often dismayed, disillusioned, or both. Even in such a broad field as "business," there are many subdivisions, such as:

clerical-stenographic-secretarial;
personnel management;
accounting;
data processing (computer sciences);
executive and corporate control (managerial positions); and
banking and finance.

Consulting the vocational guidance counselor, talking with individuals working in the given occupation (what, really, are the duties and job responsibilities of the chemist engaged in "quality control"?), as well as exploring one's own interests, likes and dislikes, and level of ability, can lead to a better occupational choice. The goal, in this respect, is to avoid the situation in which so many adults find themselves: to have prepared for a given vocation only to find that they are unhappy in their work, and, more often than not, unable to change occupations because of lack of needed training in other areas, and because, at their stage in life, it is "too late."

TESTS AND MORE TESTS

Most high school students have taken numerous teacher-made tests and several "standardized" tests. In order to apply for college today most college students find that they must take such tests as the A.C.T.; the P.S.A.T.; and the S.A.T. (C.E.E.B.)

Additionally, some colleges require their own entrance examinations for admission. The A.C.T., the American College Testing program battery of tests, covers the areas of mathematics, reading, natural sciences, and social sciences, as well as a "personal inventory" of student activities and student goals. It is an attempt to find out how much knowledge a high school student has internalized, as compared with his peers. Most often taken in the junior or senior years of high school, it is widely required by numerous colleges before an admission application can be acted upon. The test is also used in many colleges for placement in certain subject areas and in certain levels (e.g., remedial, basic, or advanced) within certain subject areas (commonly, English and mathematics).

The P.S.A.T. refers to the Preliminary Scholastic Aptitude Test (the Scholastic Aptitude Test is frequently termed C.E.E.B., or, College Entrance Examination Board Tests, or, more simply, College Boards). This test is a "practice" for students who are planning to take the S.A.T. (C.E.E.B.), that is, its results are given to the student for individual assessment, and are not sent on to the colleges.

The S.A.T., the Scholastic Aptitude Test, measures a student's ability in such diverse subject areas as chemistry, mathematics, foreign language, English, and social sciences. Here again the student is compared to his peers in terms of the amount of knowledge to which he has been exposed and which he has mastered.

Educational tests have several distinct purposes. They include:

Aptitude Tests	To measure the innate capacity of the individual to learn
Evaluative Tests	To measure the effects of learning, e.g., achievement tests
Diagnostic Tests	To provide the basis for the diagnosis of learning difficulties
Prognostic Tests	To make predictions about one's educational attainment in future

Vocational Guidance Tests	To suggest suitable occupational choices
Personality Assessment Instruments	To measure relative emotional stability or instability
Intelligence Tests	To provide a measure of an individual's intelligence
Special Interest Tests	To measure aptitudes in such areas as art, music, and clerical skills
Teacher-made Tests	To measure mastery of a limited amount of a specific subject area

These tests are generally of the "objective" or multiple-choice variety, using separate answer sheets in which the student indicates the choice of his answer by filling in a square or circle marked "A," "B," "C," or "D." Test-taking techniques and adequate preparation are important factors in helping the student achieve success on objective types of tests.

Some students find that retention of learned materials is difficult. They complain that they "know the work" but cannot remember the answers at exam time. They get "flustered" by the threat of the exam. Improving retention and memory for school subjects can be achieved by:

(1) Overlearning;
(2) Taking notes while reading;
(3) Testing oneself after reading; and
(4) Periodic reviews.

Test performance can likewise be improved by active participation in class discussion, by taking careful and orderly notes and reviewing same, and by adopting an attitude of "positive anxiety." It is not good for the student to be completely relaxed when he is about to take a test. A certain amount of tension or anxiety is desirable, if it is directed towards successful test performance. One should be concerned and one should want to do well on tests. This is what is meant by "positive anxiety."

There is a difference between the method for preparing and for writing an essay examination as compared with an objective examination. On essay exams, many students perform poorly because they write aimlessly. The best essays are those which are concise, precise, come directly to the point, follow a stated outline, develop a sequence of ideas and express same clearly, and seem to have an organizational goal which can be satisfied in the time allocated for the examination.

Objective examinations require a precise knowledge of specific facts. Recall is the all-important aspect of good performance on an objective test. Some general suggestions for helping to improve one's performance on objective tests include:

(1) Study on a regular schedule;

(2) Avoid cramming (last-minute preparation);

(3) Use previous examination questions and the questions at the end of a chapter as a means of testing your knowledge;

(4) Develop a system for review in the form of your own self-test;

(5) Survey all parts of the examination before starting any one section;

(6) Read the examination directions very carefully;

(7) Mark the examination time wise, so that you know when you are at the halfway and three-quarter point in the test;

(8) Answer first those questions of which you are sure, and then go back to the others;

(9) Review the answers to each question before turning in the test;

(10) Enter the exam with a positive mental attitude; you have studied; you are ready; you know your material.

When preparing for exams, students often fail to utilize all of the materials at their disposal. Laboratory manuals, lecture notes, term papers, written materials distributed by the instructor, and other reference materials should all be included in one's preparatory work prior to taking an examination. Some students try to "predict" which questions will be asked, and hence study only a part of their materials. This is a serious error.

Students perform much better on examinations if they have had a good night's sleep before the test. Staying up all night to study will effectively lower performance, rather than improve upon it. The use of drugs, pep pills, and alcohol have never been verified as aides to preparing for examinations; even if they were, the physiological and psychological after-effects would not be worth it.

PERSONAL PROBLEMS

Most modern college campuses offer resource personnel to students who have personal problems. These individuals may be counselors, guidance directors, psychologists, or psychiatrists. The kinds and extent of the personal problems of students vary considerably, from moderate to severe. Many students find that talking over their problems with a trained professional can give them several insights into aspects of a problem which they had not previously recognized. No college student should feel that his problems are so unique or so overwhelmingly complex that no one can help him. For many students the most difficult thing is to take the initiative in making the first step towards getting help. There should be no stigma attached to a student who needs help with his personal difficulties, for students are people —and people have problems.

College students face many problems, especially during their freshman year at college. Some of these are related to academic studies or choice of career; while still others are related to family, social, or emotional problems associated with student life. The realities of the college campus and of college life are often disappointing when compared to the dream and illusion. Long years of anticipation sometimes result in frustration and disappointment for the young adult.

Some students expect too much—they long for freedom and to be fully responsible for their own actions—only to find that one is never completely free to do as he chooses regardless of the societal structure, and further that one's own actions have important effects upon others. Some students find the pressures of campus life too overbearing or too disappointing, with concomitant anxieties and frustrations resulting.

One of the most challenging problems confronting the college student is to get to know himself realistically. Many students are not fully aware of their weaknesses and limitations, or of their strengths. and abilities. The matter of finding one's identity is important, or, in the terms of Erik Erikson, the "identity crisis" of youth is a crucial one.

College is often one of the first opportunities the young adult encounters for making independent choices outside of the family and home influence. Students must decide how best to spend their time and expend their energies; how to and how much to study; how to meet their sexual urgencies; as well as a host of other matters.

Clinicians, vocational guidance counselors, psychologists, and counselors can be of immense aid to students seeking self-identity and for those seeking solutions to their day-to-day problems. These trained individuals, provided by the colleges, can help students to achieve maturity and self-understanding, as well as meet the daily problems of campus life. Their services should not be underestimated.

AND ONWARD FROM HERE

The effective utilization of the resources of the college depends upon several factors. First, the student must know which resources are available to him. He must be aware that each college has unique features and services which differ slightly from all others. It is difficult to generalize with regard to each of these unique services, but the student should be forewarned that it is his responsibility to familiarize himself with the services of the college he is attending. (It is amazing to note that many college students complete four years at an institution without ever having referred to that institution's catalog!!) Only if he knows what is available can he begin to utilize functionally the services of the college for his own benefit.

Secondly, having become knowledgeable about the resources which the college offers, the student must decide what resources to utilize effectively for his own personal situation. Can he use some pointers on the use of the library? Does he need help with a personal matter? Can financial problems be eased through a loan or other source of financial aid? Can a department chairman or dean clarify the rules and regulations established by an individual professor? Should he participate more in social activities? How does he join the school newspaper (or other activity)?

Finally, each student must decide how much advice to accept. While most college personnel render their decisions with a view toward a student's self-improvement, it is the student himself who must make the effective determination to utilize, reject, or partially accept the information and guidance which he has received.

WHAT WE HAVE LEARNED

1. The so-called "auxiliary" services offered by colleges today have become very important in the life of the student.
2. College administrative personnel function to offer services to students and to operate the college efficiently.
3. Faculty advisors and department chairmen are specialists in given areas of the curriculum, and as such should be consulted for advice regarding a student's major subject area.
4. Student personnel services offer students counseling, psychological help, help in admissions and registration, and job placement.
5. College counselors can assist the student in self-assessment as well as with a host of personal, academic, and social problems.
6. Numerous sources of financial aid are available to students, including scholarships, loans, grants, and work-study programs.
7. Most college students attend college because they wish to gain the vocational preparation and background they will need in the pursuit of their adult careers.
8. Students can improve performance on objective tests if they are knowledgeable about the psychological methods for preparing for tests and test-taking techniques.
9. There are several distinct kinds of educational tests: diagnostic, aptitude, achievement, and prognostic.

10. Most modern college campuses offer resource personnel for students with personal problems.
11. The effective utilization of the resources of the college can help in the numerous adjustment problems which college students face.
12. College is often one of the first opportunities the young adult experiences for making independent choices outside of the sphere of family influence.
13. The decision as to which resources of the college can be most effectively utilized by the student remains a highly individual matter.

What We Still Need to Learn

1. Some colleges need to clarify the functions of their various officials, so that students can utilize their services more effectively, and so that duplicity and overlap in function can be prevented.
2. College administrative personnel need to find a way to get "closer" or "more in touch" with their students in order to understand their problems and meet their needs better.
3. We still need a tremendous elaboration and proliferation of student personnel services which are offered by most colleges, in order to help the student make a better adjustment, particularly in his first year of college.
4. The number of counselors available to students needs to be increased; even the present ideal counselor-student ratio of 250 to 1 (while not met at most colleges) needs to be lowered so that more students can have counseling services more readily available.
5. We need to find effective ways to make students more fully aware of the resources of the college at the time they enter, and even before they step foot on the campus itself.
6. We should embark upon a more enlightened system for getting financial aid to needy and deserving students.
7. Improvement in the techniques of vocational guidance will yield direct, positive results in the form of more satisfied, better adjusted adults.
8. We need to recognize the urgency of critical shortages in certain areas for obtaining trained and skilled professionals, and to implement new plans for meeting these needs not only for the benefit of the individual student, but, ultimately, for the nation and all of its people.
9. We need better ways of informing high school students about the multiplicity of new vocational careers from which they may choose.

10. We need to find ways to alleviate some of the mounting pressures on campus, so that students need not necessarily face some of the adjustment problems with which they are confronted today.

SUGGESTIONS FOR FURTHER READING

Bell, Norman T., *Introduction to College Life: A Book of Readings*, Boston, Mass.: Houghton Mifflin Co., 1962.

Conger, John Janeway, *Adolescence and Youth: Psychological Development in A Changing World*, New York: Harper & Row, 1973.

Crowne, Leslie Joan, *Adjustment Problems of College Freshmen*, New York: Columbia University Teacher's College, 1955.

Gordon, Richard E., and Katherine K. Gordon, *The Blight on the Ivy*, Englewood Cliffs, New Jersey: Prentice-Hall, Inc., 1963.

Hurlock, Elizabeth B., *Personality Development*, New York: McGraw-Hill, 1974.

Kronovet, Esther and Evelyn Shirk, *In Pursuit of Awareness*, New York: Appleton-Century-Crofts, 1967.

Lloyd-Jones, Esther M., and H. A. Estrin, *The American Student and His College*, New York: Houghton Mifflin Co., 1967.

McConnell, James V., *Understanding Human Behavior*, New York: Holt, Rinehart and Winston, 1974.

McConnell, T. R., "The Relation of Institutional Goals and Organization to the Administration of Student Personnel Work," in *Approaches to the Study of Student Personnel Work*, Martin L. Snoke, Ed., Minneapolis, Minn.: The University of Minnesota Press, 1960.

Resnick, William C., and David H. Heller, *On Your Own in College*, 2nd. ed., Columbus, Ohio: Charles E. Merrill Publishing Company, 1969.

Rivlin, Harry N., et al., *First Years in College*, Boston, Mass.: Houghton Mifflin Co., 1965.

Soldwedel, Bette J., *Mastering the College Challenge*, New York: The Macmillan Company, 1964.

Von Hoffman, N., *Multiversity: A Personal Report on What Happens to Today's Students in American Universities*, New York: Holt, Rinehart & Winston, 1966.

Warga, Richard, *Getting Personal*, Boston: Houghton Mifflin Co., 1974.

4

Academic Problems of the College Student

- Self-appraisal: Using one's abilities
- How to compute your grade-point average (G.P.A.)
- The overachiever in college
- Problems of the underachiever
- Underprivileged minority groups in college
- Educational Innovations: Some Suggestions
- Personality factors as they affect scholastic progress
- Modes of individual expression
- Selecting the right courses
- The need to achieve: Motivational factors
- Adjusting to the student role in young adulthood
- Preparing for examinations
- Essay examinations and objective examinations
- What We Have Learned
- What We Still Need to Learn
- Suggestions for Further Reading

PURPOSE OF THIS CHAPTER

As students begin their college careers a realistic self-appraisal can be a valuable asset in setting their goals during the college years and for future vocational aims. The purpose of this chapter is to help the student to understand himself better.

Using one's abilities involves several concepts, as well as those individual and unique personality factors which come to have an effect upon the scholastic achievement of the individual. These concepts will be examined in this chapter, as well as the problems of the under-achiever, the overachiever, and the underprivileged. In each of the above examples, unique adjustment problems will be examined.

Some students find it difficult to adjust to the role demanded by their college. These adjustment factors will be examined in the section titled: "What Is A Student?"

In the latter section of this chapter, the all-important task of se-lecting the right courses will be examined. The student will also find in this section some helpful hints on how to prepare for various kinds of examinations.

The central thesis remains: The better informed and the more aware a student is, the better his performance as a student, and the more satisfactory his adjustment as a person. Not all students will encounter all of the problems detailed in this chapter. All students do not face the same kinds of academic problems and adjustments, be-cause of their unique individuality. However, all students should ben-efit from a reading of the "Academic Problems of the College Student."

USING ONE'S ABILITIES

It is important that college students recognize their limitations as well as their abilities. They need an opportunity to explore the various areas where they have natural talents and academic interests, as well as those areas where they have less skill and perhaps meet less aca-demic success. In those areas where students find the work difficult, it is of great help if they can utilize the learning skills which they have acquired in other areas. This is the concept of "transfer of learning," whereby useful knowledge acquired in one subject area can be utilized effectively in another.

Transfer of learning is facilitated by following the dictums of the several principles presented below:

1. Learn material in a meaningful way. Avoid rote memorization.
2. Integrate isolated facts with basic principles.
3. Attempt to see, wherever possible, the practical application of the learning material. Using examples from everyday life and applying these examples to oneself is of help in this regard.
4. Use previously acquired study skills in mastering new materi-als. The old, familiar, "tried and true" methods which the

student has adapted for himself, can act as a positive aid in the learning process when applied to the new learning material.

5. Overlearn. That is, learn beyond the point of bare recall, to the point of immediate, free, and easy recall.

As Katherine and John Byrne wrote: "You are going to have to live with yourself for the rest of your life, no matter what, so you may as well enjoy the experience."*

Assessing one's own abilities, skills, and interests involves the concepts of personality, self-study, and evaluating the opinions of others. It is admittedly difficult to be objective about oneself. What are your goals? What are your objectives? Where do you plan to be five years from now? How will you achieve these goals? What is your general philosophy of life? These kinds of probing, soul-searching questions should help a student in gaining a more realistic self-appraisal.

Several current studies have indicated that there is a positive relationship between personality and success in school. (For purposes of simplicity, personality is used in terms of an individual's total reaction to himself and to his environment). Some students experience what has been termed "academic anxiety." This syndrome appears when students have a powerful, pervasive fear of academic failure because of the disgrace which may accrue to their families, as well as to themselves. The general reaction pattern is one of escape, inability to concentrate, and a wide variety of attempts at withdrawal. Such students sometimes experience difficulty in their relationships with authority figures, often finding themselves in positions where college administrators exclude them from the campus (which, in itself, is a form of withdrawal).

Students who have confidence in their ability to succeed take positive actions, are capable of making decisions, and are generally free from academic anxiety. Their relationships with others does not suffer, and they are said to be goal-oriented, actively pursuing, successfully, their stated goals.

Often a school counselor can be of help in assessing one's own abilities. An impartial, objective evaluation by a trained counselor can give the student new insights into his positive traits and into his areas of weakness. The student can help himself, too. One such method is to keep a careful record of academic achievement through a calculation of one's grade-point average. This can be done at the end of the first college term, and should be done for each term thereafter. Some students are totally unfamiliar with the simple mathematical process.

*Katherine and John Byrne, "You and Your Abilities," Chicago, Illinois, Science Research Associates, 1959.

In the standard grade-point average calculation, one type of which is illustrated herein, the highest grade (A) is assigned a grade-point value of "4," the next highest grade (B) is assigned a grade-point value of "3," the average grade (C) is assigned a grade-point value of "2," the lowest passing grade (D) is assigned a grade-point value of "1," and a failing grade (F) has no grade-point value (zero). Some colleges assign different grade-point values to the various grades (a frequent variation assigns the highest grade a point value of "5," and so on from there, to a grade-point value of "1" for a failing grade). The student proceeds to calculate his grade-point average as follows:

Calculation of Student Grade-Point Average

Letter Grade	Point Value	Hours of Credit	Total
A	4		
B	3		
C	2		
D	1		
F	0		

Total Credit Hours_____

Total Point Value for Hours of Credit _____

Calculation of Grade-Point Average:		Notes:
Total Credit Hours	Total Point Value for Hours of Credit	_____
		_____

Date of Calculation:_____19_____

Grade-point average for: Student's Name _____

Grade-point average includes grades for term ending_____19_____

Step One	Make a list of all courses completed, the grade for each course, and the number of credit hours received for each course.
Step Two	Insert the correct number of hours of credit for each grade received, counting first the total number of "A" grades, next the total number of "B" grades, etc.
Step Three	Multiply the number of hours for each letter grade by the point value as indicated on the calculation form.
Step Four	Total the number of credit hours and the number of point values, so that you have two separate totals.
Step Five	Divide the total point value by the total number of hours of credit. This answer is the student's grade-point average.

A realistic self-appraisal of academic progress can now begin with the interpretation of one's academic progress in light of the grade-point average one has factually received. An example of the calculation of a student's grade-point average follows:

Step One:

Student: Joe College   *School:* Big City Community College

Courses Completed	Grades	Credit Hours
Rhetoric 101	B	3
Social Science 101	C	3
Biology 117	A	5
Speech 100	D	2
Art History 115	A	3

Total Credit Hours Earned: 16

Step Two: Re-arrange the student's grades as follows:

Letter Grades	Point Value	Hours of Credit
A	4	(5 plus 3) 8
B	3	3
C	2	3
D	1	2
F	0	0

Step Three: Multiply the point value for each letter grade by the total numbers of hours of credit listed at each of the point values, under "Hours of Credit," as follows:

Letter Grades	Point Value	Hours of Credit	Total
A	4	8	32
B	3	3	9
C	2	3	6
D	1	2	2
F	0	0	0

Step Four: Total the number of hours of credit earned and the totals obtained in the last column, to obtain two separate figures, as follows:

Letter Grades	Point Value	Hours of Credit	Total
A	4	8	32
B	3	3	9
C	2	3	6
D	1	2	2
F	0	0	0
		TOTALS: 16	49

Step Five: The final step in the process for the calculation of a grade-point average involves the division of the total obtained for the hours of credit into the total in the last column, as follows:

$$
\begin{array}{r}
3.06 \\
16 \overline{\smash{\big)}\ 49.00} \\
48.00 \\
\hline
1.00 \\
.96
\end{array}
$$

An analysis of the above would indicate that the student has an overall grade-point average of 3.062, or slightly better than a "B" average, in spite of his poor grade in Speech 100 (D). He appears to be an above-average student, capable in some subject areas of doing superior (A) work.

THE OVERACHIEVER

Some students seem to do well in college with a minimum amount of effort. Other students often envy those who never seem to need to study and who still make excellent grades on examinations. The overachiever is the student who is working to the maximum of his capacity. This requires constant effort, conscious striving, and the expenditure of great amounts of energy in each step of the learning process. Overachievers earn their grades, and they do so through a method of continuous and consistent hard work.

Overachievers operate at a high level of energy expenditure. While conforming to academic pressures, the overachiever seems able not only to control but to direct his anxieties into productive channels. Overachievers are able to resist pressures from peers in order to attain academic excellence (they will often forego social events in order to spend time in study). There is apparently little conflict in this regard, and the typical overachiever exhibits few guilt feelings.

In a study of overachievers, it was found that they view themselves as efficient and hard-working students. While studies vary concerning relationships with parents, the typical overachiever attempts to create a favorable impression and to please authority figures; he seems to like most of his instructors. In general, too, he tends to like other students, is accepting and feels accepted, and generally feels that he belongs in the college community, even though he may not participate in its events as fully as he might.

Overachievers are usually very dependable and reliable students who carry out assigned tasks to the letter of the assignment, and who perform required functions adequately. The outstanding characteristic of the overachiever is his highly motivated sense of direction toward academic achievement. His assignments are completed punctually, he derives satisfactions from his academic achievements, and desires adult approval. Often this type of student sacrifices originality because he places too great an emphasis upon conforming exactly to instructions in completing his assignments. High grades are important to the overachiever, and they provide enough impetus to hold him to his self-imposed standards of perfection in future assignments and examinations.

Overachieving college level students generally set their own goals for self-improvement; they carry out activities with vigor and pursue educational activities to completion. They are often deeply disappointed when desired results (high grades, parental approval, scholastic recognition, high test scores, etc.) are not immediately forthcoming. The overachiever enjoys praise.

THE UNDERACHIEVER

Many students with high potential fail to meet academic success in college, satisfying themselves with mediocre performances. Other capable students are excluded from college because of poor grades, although studies have indicated that they have the potential to perform capably. These students, known as "underachievers" tend to fall into two categories:

(1) Students who could be superior but whose performance is only average or less, and,

(2) Students who should perform at an average level but who do not manage to meet even minimum academic standards.

Underachievers operate at variable levels of energy expenditure. Their performances are erratic, and, more often than not, poor. They tend to conform to the pressures of peer groups, resisting academic demands, performing minimally whenever possible, thus incurring greater anxiety with concomitant lower level of ability to control the anxiety. It is a vicious cycle. Lack of academic achievement leads to anxiety, which in turn demoralizes personal and academic activity, leading to further lack of academic achievement.

Underachievers, as a result of the above, have trouble concentrating in the classroom and at home while trying to study. Much of their efforts are expended in trying to control the results of their anxieties. They often feel restricted, hemmed in, deny their shortcomings, and have an overwhelming and pervasive fear of failure. Some youngsters in this state become self-derogatory, depressed, morose, and contemplate acts of self-destruction. These youngsters, categorically, have a poor adjustment. They need outside help from counselors and psychologists. Family and parental aid is usually to no avail, since parental relationships often have deteriorated and become another source of anxiety.

Underachievers in general have feelings of hostility toward authority figures. These feelings may stem from attitudes toward parents, because there generally is overt or covert conflict between parents and the underachiever. These family conflicts are carried over into other aspects of the individual's life. Underachievers usually feel that they are "left out," that they have "missed" many things in life, and that there are many things which they deserve to have but which they have been unable to obtain.

Often the underachiever is critical of others, thus further antagonizing his peers, and thus further compounding his own difficulties in relationships with others. Some underachievers attempt to negate the effects of their all-encompassing anxieties through:

(1) Overt aggression;

(2) Acts of rebellion;

(3) Withdrawal from social relations; and

(4) A wide variety of deviant behavior.

Underachievers tend to operate on impulse and on the basis of wish fulfillment. They are often sorry for their actions, but seem unable to make amends, or apologize for them. They attempt to obtain satisfaction in areas other than the academic. They are interested in immediate rewards and self-gratification. They enjoy the support and identification which they may receive from group membership.

Underachievers have many conflicts causing them to be unsure about their goals. As college days progress, the underachiever experiences stronger and stronger self-doubt and uncertainty. He becomes more and more indecisive. It is as if his approaching future brings to the surface more and more his deep, underlying anxiety about himself. He begins to realize that many of his goals are unattainable and unrealistic. A better-oriented individual would be able, at this point, to reassess himself and his goals and to re-direct energies into positive channels of action. This is very difficult for underachievers to accomplish, and many enter adulthood and live their entire lives in a state of indecision, uncertainty, and maladjustment.

PROBLEMS OF THE UNDERPRIVILEGED

The culturally disadvantaged young adult faces numerous school problems as he begins his college career. Many youngsters today, particularly those in large urban areas and those in relatively isolated rural areas, grow up in an environment which is impoverished both economically and socially. Despite the existing educational opportunities, they often receive substandard elementary and secondary school education, combined with a lack of motivation which is so necessary if learning is to be accomplished. To an outside observer unfamiliar with the problems of the ghetto, it may seem ironic that these individuals negate the very avenue which has the means to free them from their lives of poverty and frustration: a strong educational background which qualifies one for a professional-level position, with its accompanying benefits of salary, social position, and prestige.

Underprivileged, impoverished, poverty-area, and ghetto youth comprise several ethnic groups in the United States which include: black youth; Puerto Rican youth; Appalachian whites; and other minority groups.

Many of these youngsters come from homes in which self-perpetuating poverty and alienation from the mainstream of society has been accepted as an inevitable way of life. Hopelessness, despair, and lack of motivation become constant companions. These youngsters lead lives which are in sharp contrast to those of white, middle-class, urban, and suburban youth. Often they become resentful, bitter, and outwardly aggressive. They often enter college fearfully or skeptically, and with fatalistic attitudes.

Middle- and upper-class youngsters, by contrast, more often enter school willingly and with positive mental attitudes. Taught by teachers who themselves have similar attitudes and standards, they come to expect certain kinds of behaviors and standards. Culturally disadvantaged youth are far less able to learn profitably from the usual kind of lectures and demonstrations, and abstractions are almost meaningless when compared with the stark realities of their lives. Middle-class homes have a "hidden curriculum" built into their walls; learning and education are held as worthy goals to be attained and strived for; study and school work is held in high esteem. But among the impoverished, these values are often negated by the reality of the need for immediate funds and survival.

Impoverished youth do not necessarily value the college years and the need for college preparation in the same way as middle- and upper-class youth. The incentives of grades seem like artificial rewards, and impoverished youth often wonder if it is all worthwhile. The culturally deprived actually show a decline in academic progress as they proceed through the elementary and high school years, necessitating remedial (non-credit) kinds of classes as they enter college. Many of these youngsters attend community colleges because they cannot meet the financial and academic standards of the larger universities, and because they must, of economic necessity, live at home.

A report by the National Advisory Commission on Civil Disorders has indicated that conditions of life in a racially segregated ghetto area are strikingly different from life as depicted in middle-class, white America. The ghetto areas have startlingly high mortality rates, high incidence of reported crime, more forms of major illness, lower availability per person of existing medical facilities, and generally poorer quality schools. Life expectancy is lower for non-whites in ghetto areas; admissions to mental hospitals is higher.

Educationally, the National Advisory Commission on Civil Disorders has stated that:

> The black record of public education for ghetto children is growing worse. In the critical skills—verbal ability and reading ability —Black students fall further and further behind white students with each year of school completed. . . .

The result of the above is that in poverty areas, fewer students strive toward college education and fewer students are eligible for enrollment in the colleges as they are now structured. In the metropolitan areas of the midwest and northern cities of the United States, the high school drop-out rate is more than three to one, when comparing underprivileged youth with middle-class youth. Many of these high school drop-outs are ill-equipped for employment of any kind, and they soon become a part of the "hard-core unemployed." In a few years many of them realize the need for an education, but find it difficult or impossible to begin all over again. The contribution of an inadequate educational preparation toward unemployment, while not quantified, seems substantial and is indicative of the need for drastic changes in many of our present educational procedures.

Some colleges are presently making earnest attempts in this direction. They are admitting students from poverty areas, even though the student does not meet the admission standards of other students. This has led to criticism, as it would seem then that there is a "double-standard" for college admission. Some colleges have made a start in the direction of providing special programs of education for those with impoverished backgrounds. However, more and more there is the realization that these students cannot be offered "more of the same." They need a different type of education; a different format; a different structure. In this regard, some colleges have adopted plans for impoverished youth which encompass all or some aspects of the following educational innovations:

(1) Admitting students regardless of standards of past achievement (or lack of achievement);
(2) Providing special courses with small group teaching;
(3) Financial subsidies to alleviate economic problems;
(4) College course work combined with on-the-job training;
(5) The off-campus, or field college, which goes out to the youth, instead of being centered within the classroom;
(6) The interdisciplinary approach to learning;
(7) The non-theoretical, practical approach;
(8) An emphasis upon vocational-technological education rather than the usual liberal-arts academics;
(9) Special tutoring services; and
(10) Increased counseling in small groups and for individuals.

Nevertheless, there is still a long way to go. More needs to be done to prevent the cycle of lack of education, unemployment, welfare roles, further lack of education among progeny, etc. It is only when an enlightened population can realistically approach many of the present social problems in America that we can begin to meet many of the crying needs for better hospitals, schools, and jobs.

PERSONALITY FACTORS AND SCHOLASTIC ACHIEVEMENTS

Psychologists have recognized that there are marked differences between individuals in their ability to learn, and that some of these differences stem from factors other than native intelligence, school background, and academic preparation. Personality factors have been recognized as aids to learning, and, in some cases, as impediments to the learning process. Environment, culture, and sub-cultures all play important roles in personality development. Whether or not an individual will reach his given potential, and whether or not he will have an opportunity to utilize effectively his skills and abilities in his personal life are matters which may largely be attributed to personality manifestations.

Personality (simply defined here as the organization of the individual's behavior) develops from many experiences and situations. Biological factors, the home, the family, the environment—all play an important role in the development of one's personality.

No one is a *born* leader. Personality development is the result of both biological and social forces. Some students in their personality expressions are self-defeating. They impede their own academic progress through negative attitudes and hostility. While individuals in the course of their development have both "common" and "unique" experiences, for some individuals experiences which are common are uniquely interpreted. Society dictates roles to which an individual must conform, e.g., the feminine role, the male role, the parent role, and the student role. Each has its unique attributes.

It is generally agreed that the basic pattern for personality expression in young adulthood and adulthood is formulated in the childhood years. By the time an individual reaches college, his personality has largely been formed. However, new modes of expression and new directions appear as the world of the young adult broadens considerably through college campus contacts with a broad range of individuals of varying backgrounds and cultural experiences.

Data from large-scale psychological studies has indicated that the relationships between parents and their children have a marked effect upon the personality of the developing individual. Parental influence reaches its peak in the development of attitudes among the young. An attitude refers to an individual's "set" or "readiness" for action as focused upon various aspects of life. Attitudes are usually general, focusing around institutions, concepts, and theories. They may be directed more specifically at individuals or events.

Some attitudes are rational, intellectual, and matter of fact. Others are emotional, negative, and irrational. Attitudes toward college, toward education in general, toward the need for study and toward the importance of self-improvement are important factors in determining the extent to which an individual can make a satisfactory college adjustment. Successful adjustment to the college community involves several factors which are directly effected by one's personality. Among these are:

(1) Doing reasonably well in one's work;
(2) Having some social relationships;
(3) Self-satisfaction; and
(4) Achieving one's goals.

John Donne's succinct statement: "No man is an island" seems to summarize in capsule form the need for the expression of one's personality among peers. The purely "academically oriented" college student generally feels that he is "missing something." And he is. College is more than study, exams, and grades. It is also a matter of affecting positive social relationships, and it is within this frame of reference that one's personality manifestations are paramount.

The student's successful adjustment to the college community is closely related to his level of maturity. The concept of maturity includes autonomy, independence, responsibility, emotional control, adaptability, benefitting from experience, and social participation.

Various individuals experience unique personality problems in their attempts to adjust to the college community. These "unique" groups—minority students, foreign students, etc.—have problems which are indigenous to themselves or to the group to which they belong.

Many minority group students begin college with vague feelings of uncertainty and isolation. Sometimes they rebel against a "system" which attempts to keep them as part of a minority group; other students find fitting into the life of the campus a relatively easy adjustment.

In some college communities, women are still looked upon as "intruders." Some families still persist in the notion that college is for the male offspring, since the female is going to get married anyway. Nevertheless, more and more women continue to embark upon college careers, and they are entering or planning to enter fields of employment which were previously closed to them.

Married college students experience unique adjustment problems in terms of their problems of finance, housing, and social lives. For a number of years now (particularly since the end of World War II) colleges have been providing resident facilities for married college students. Some find that coping with the problems of the campus and the problems of starting out in married life simultaneously places a great strain upon them. Others find that the additional stability of the marriage tends to foster increased maturity and better academic performance.

Today, veterans of the Viet Nam war comprise a greater and greater percentage of students on college campuses. These students sometimes find it more difficult to adjust to the student role. Their

previous experiences having tended to mature them in a more sober-
ing way, they may have little or no patience with some of the younger
students' antics. Veterans, both male and female, tend to perform well
on the college campus. As a broad, general statement, they are mature,
serious students, with definite goal-orientations. They are often impatient, eager to "get on" with the serious business of their education,
and long for the day when they can assume a more adult (self-supporting) role in society.

Foreign students on college campuses face the problems of adjusting not only to the college community, but to possible language
barriers, ethnic group prejudice, and a feeling of isolation. These
students are often "clannish," existing in a somewhat self-imposed
isolation. They are generally quiet, often tend to get "lost in the
crowd," and express the desire to "cause no problems." Most foreign
students are so grateful for the opportunity to be on a college campus that they are overly cautious, not wanting to risk in any way the
danger of removal. Perhaps this stems, at least partially, from
the present "visa" system in the United States. Revocation of a student visa is a calamity which no student from a foreign country
wishes to chance.

A relatively new phenomenon on college campuses throughout
the nation is the presence of older students on campus. Many of these
individuals, often in their late forties and early fifties, are married
women whose children are now in college, or are married and self-
supporting. They may have already had some college background, but
perhaps it was twenty or more years ago. Some colleges have special
programs for the older student returning to complete their college
education. (The "D.C.P." program of Mundelein College, Chicago,
Illinois, is an example of the above. The "D.C.P.," "Degree Completion Program," is especially tailored for the married, mature, older
college woman returning to complete her college education. A unique
requirement is a minimum age of twenty-six for entrance into the
program. Classes are scheduled at what most regular students would
consider to be odd hours, i.e., late afternoons, evenings, and Saturdays. Students in this program have an opportunity to earn "life experience" college credits, for work performed in such areas as foreign
languages, mathematics, and the social sciences.) As these students
sometimes feel alienated from the usual campus social activities, some
colleges have provided social activities particularly geared for the
older student. These students tend to be very mature, sincere in their
desires to complete their college educations, somewhat uncertain of
their own ability levels, anxious to complete required courses, and
impatient with anything on the campus which they consider to be a
"waste of time."

Some of the problems of students from impoverished areas have been previously discussed. Often these students come to the campus with negative and openly hostile attitudes. Their adjustment problems are compounded by weak academic preparation, and lack of adequate financial support is often an ever-present problem.

The academically weak college student has the ever-present fear of failure. He may be on academic dismissal, academic warning, or academic probation. His need to achieve is heightened considerably by the pressure of needing good grades to stay in college. Often these very motives can be self-defeating, causing the student to perform poorly, and thus increasing his anxiety level. Many colleges have adopted special counseling for students who are on academic probation. These students are guided in effective study habits, the correct choice of courses, preparing for exams, study skills, etc. On some campuses these students are seen individually; on others, group guidance techniques are utilized.

SELECTING THE RIGHT COURSES

"What courses shall I take?" is a frequently asked question among college students. All too often their selection is based upon the "grapevine" analysis by other students of which courses are "good" or "easy" or have "nice profs." While colleges have a certain percentage of required courses over which the student has no control and little or no choice, more and more colleges today are increasing the number of "elective" courses which students may select, and hence the importance of proper course selection by the student has become enhanced.

Students often select courses simply because they fit conveniently into their particular time schedule. This not uncommon practice is probably the poorest way to select courses. Community college students who need to work while going to school use this method almost exclusively. An even more frustrating and sometimes anxiety-inducing situation occurs when students have selected courses wisely and judiciously, only to find that they do not fit into their time schedules (the courses conflict, or are offered at the same time), or that the courses are closed. Some students select courses because of the subject matter they expect; others follow a particular professor, taking as many of his classes as they possibly can fit into their schedules.

The registration procedure on college campuses has become a source of friction for students, faculty, and administration alike. Long lines, closed classes, and what seems to be interminable waiting are often characteristic of the registration period. Some colleges have sought to eradicate these problems by pre-registration conferences which are held long before the term actually begins. Often these sessions are held individually or in small groups. When schedule conflicts arise, students can be consulted, again, long in advance of the start of the term. With these procedures, students know exactly which courses they will have at the start of a new term, and can study their future schedules and plan accordingly. Some students purchase their books and study for the new term in advance of its beginning.

Suggested procedures for students planning their program of studies for a new term include all of the following:

(1) Conferences with faculty advisors;
(2) Consultation with teachers of selected courses;
(3) Referral to the college catalog;
(4) Discussion with fellow students; and
(5) Advice from counselors.

Unfortunately, time often does not permit the student to follow the suggested procedures. Selection may be based on some minimal advice from any one of the above sources, or worse, based on what courses happen to be available. The astute student selects his courses as carefully as he would when he is about to make a major purchase. He shops. He compares. He discusses. He gets facts. He looks into all possible ramifications before making a decision.

The ultimate decision belongs to the individual student. It is his choice, and his alone, for he must "live" with his selection for several months. Some students follow a regular practice of "over-enrolling." That is, they sign up for one more course than they plan to take, knowing that they will drop one or another course after having had some minimal exposure to all of their selections. This practice cannot be condoned nor recommended, because:

(1) On crowded college campuses it "blocks out" other students who might wish to take the class;
(2) It leads to procrastination and poor work habits;
(3) It is expensive in terms of time and expenditures for books and materials;
(4) It leads to an attitude of escapism; and,
(5) It prevents the student with a serious intent to achieve from enrolling.

THE NEED TO ACHIEVE—MOTIVATIONAL FACTORS

The need to achieve is a strong psychological motive. It is not inherited; hence it must be acquired, or learned. It has been classified as a "secondary" drive, but nonetheless it is a powerful force in deciding an individual's actions. The need to achieve directs the individual toward striving for excellence in performance. Acquiring this need begins in early childhood. Different cultures view the need to achieve from different perspectives. Americans are among the most achievement oriented individuals in the world. Motivation is a key concept in any attempt to explain human behavior. In the preface of this text, it was stated that all behavior is caused. The direction which that behavior assumes depends to a large degree upon the type and extent of an individual's motivation.

Academic achievement is a fundamental motivational factor in the life of the college student. Parents, peers, and the community at large hold this value in high esteem, and the individual who achieves prowess accrues the respect of these groups. Students direct their energies toward academic achievement for several reasons:

Self-satisfaction in accomplishment
Praise from parents
Competitiveness with peers
To "prove a point"
To demonstrate their "self-worth"
To maintain scholarship requirements
To be eligible for further education (graduate school)
To be able to enter another college (community college transfer
    students, and four-year college students who plan to enter pro-
    fessional schools upon graduation)
To gain a position in the business world

The "primary" motives in human beings include the need for food, sleep, water, air, warmth, and sex. Secondary motives include the need for esteem, social position, companionship, and the satisfaction of needs. Sometimes we are not fully aware of why we behave as we do. Our motives, nevertheless, are operative, and our behavior corresponds to the kind and degree of motivation, whether or not we are consciously aware of the reasons behind our behavior.

Motivation is one of the essentials in attempting to understand the dynamics of adjustment. The term itself means to "move" or to "activate." In this sense, anything which initiates activity, whether internal or external, may be viewed as a motivating force. Psychologists are most often concerned with "internal" motivation, and, as such, these factors form the basis for the essential source of human activities.

Underlying the behavior pattern of each student is a combination of forces directing his behavior along certain lines. All people have drives and needs which direct their energies into observable actions. Adjustment is a constant process of attempting to meet our inner needs and the demands placed upon us by our physical and social environment.

As motivational devices, praise, approval, and encouragement have been found to be of positive value. Contrariwise, reproof, rejection, and punishment are far less effective in getting an individual to respond and indeed may be detrimental. This basic connection between motivation and the need for reinforcement underlies much of the philosophy of the academic world. Students enjoy tasks well-done. Grades are a form of reward or praise for their efforts. Further action and activity are enhanced by pleasant results and the feeling of accomplishment engendered by academic successes.

Some students seem to lack motivation or to have poor motivation. In these instances, a little research will usually elicit the fact that the student really doesn't want to go to college. He is attending for any one of a number of "negative" reasons, such as:

> His parents want him to go to college;
> He wants to get away from home;
> He doesn't know what else to do; and
> His friends are going to college.

A small minority of students have a great deal of hostility toward college, teachers, and the "establishment." They come to college to prove that it is not worthwhile; or to change the existing structure. These students, though a small percentage on college campuses, are often loud and vocal. Their demonstrations have reached national prominence (not all demonstrations can be so explained; some demonstrators have good cause for their demonstrations and are attempting to effect what they see as much needed improvement).

Many students are highly motivated at the start of their college careers, only to find it difficult to sustain their original drive. They become disillusioned when what they see as hard work results in mediocre accomplishments, or they become dissatisfied with the kind of education which they are receiving. Other students begin with poor attitudes because of a past history throughout the secondary school years of lack of academic achievement. Various colleges have different schemes to maintain student motivation. Honors programs, scholarships, awards, recognition assemblies, father's days, and the like are all forms of motivation-incentives.

Recently some business and industrial concerns have offered their employees free tuition in colleges if they will take night school courses leading to an improvement in their job performance. Some companies offer full tuition payments if the student receives an "A," half tuition payment for a "B," etc. This too can be viewed as an artifically contrived, though strong, motivational incentive. Many individuals require this type of stimulation for effective performance; others seem to be able to motivate themselves effectively.

ADJUSTING TO THE STUDENT ROLE

Many students find it difficult to adjust to the "student role" when they reach young adulthood. One of the chief complaints directed at community colleges is to be found in the fact that students feel that the school is not a college at all, but a "glorified" continuation of their high school days. Even when students are given a voice in campus affairs, the nature of that voice is still one of subservience. This is perpetuated by the fact that most students are not self-supporting; some live at home, which increases their family dependency status. Students are faced with the problem of postponing marriage in order to complete their educational goals, of conforming to school rules in order to remain in good standing at college, and in general of expressing their opinions only when called upon to do so.

In the late 1960's students across the nation began to rebel against the stringent demands of the student role. In various nations in the world, notably Latin America and certain parts of Europe, college students have long been an important political force. It is only recently that students in the United States have reached out in this direction. In the 1968 and 1972 presidential elections, students played an important part in national politics. They began to demand certain changes in the structure of the "establishment."

Young adults, so much in need of freedom of expression and a "voice that counts," sometimes are faced with tremendous pressures in making decisions with regard to morality, how actively to participate in campus protest movements, and whether or not non-participation means alienation from peers.

Disagreeing with a college instructor can be a hazard. Some students have no qualms and proceed to voice their opinions freely, but others are inhibited. They do not wish to appear offensive. They fear reprisals in the form of lowered grades. Too many elementary and secondary school teachers punish pupils by doing just that. Past experiences of this nature contribute to the conflict college students face as they attempt to meet the demands of the student role as viewed on campus.

Colleges too are facing the challenges of new roles. The diversity of educational opportunity in the United States is a source of wonder to many foreign students. Many colleges have diversified because of student demands. Today most colleges view themselves as an integral part of the community, as witness the very name and concept of "community colleges." Colleges which were formerly limited to special classes of students (including the wealthy) now find a diverse student population with new needs, challenges, and demands. Successful college administrations have changed with the times, while all too many still lag behind the times, forcing students into pre-cast molds.

Another relatively recent trend on the college campus that has had an important effect upon the nature of the student role is the increase in the number of years required to complete a program of professional training. The old concept of the "four-year college" is in many respects a myth. The prospective physician faces not four years of college, but, in reality, much closer to ten or twelve. This means the high school graduate of eighteen or nineteen must now adjust to facing the student role for an increased number of years—an increase which postpones the full assumption of adult responsibilities well past the age when other young adults have acquired those responsibilities. The concomitant conflict for some individuals is great. Postponement of the more natural adult role and maintenance of the more artificial student role over a prolonged period of years has created many difficulties on campus both for individual students and for campus administrations.

The college student of the 1970's is more openly expressive, and has little patience with those who challenge this position. Because the young adult is "caught" in this conflict between an adult and student role, he often assumes adult attitudes and positions, even though he does not have the same equivalency in adult responsibility. The result is a student population which is highly critical of artificially established standards and patterns of behavior.

Today's college student is better informed and more aware than any other previous generation. Having this fund of knowledge, it is only natural that he is challenged to utilize it. He is often highly critical of what he considers to be administrative lag, inefficiency, and waste. He cannot understand why many of today's social problems still exist. Some college students have "given up" on trying to conform to the modes of our present society, and have even "given up" on trying to effect changes. These students may become social outcasts in their attempt to reject the values of current society and to establish a society more in keeping with their own value systems.

"Students today are different:" This can be either a factual statement, or a lament, depending upon who's doing the talking. Many young adults today find the sexual codes of yesteryear to be outmoded, hypocritical, and unrealistic. They are not inhibited in the way that youth of yesteryear was inhibited. They are candid and open about their actions, and see no reason to conform to what they consider to be a "double-standard" of artificially imposed sanctions. Thus unmarried college students live together openly; others, a bit more reserved, experiment with various aspects of sex with fewer guilt feelings and inhibitions. This is not a sexual revolution, but rather the results of a sexual evolution which finds its supporters in young adults on today's campuses. Only time will tell if the newer standards and modes of conduct will lead to fewer frustrations, aggressions, and to a better social world.

PREPARING FOR EXAMS

Students succeed or fail as a result of their performance on tests. Much as colleges try to stress the importance of research, discussion, or term papers, in the long run it is the examination which tells the tale. Some college students find it difficult, at first, to adjust to the concept of "mid-term" and "final" exams, having all of their knowledge measured in these two tests of ability by themselves. Because of this, some college instructors offer a number of variations in their examination procedures, such as "hourly" exams, quizzes, quarterly exam, or outside-of-class exams.

However, when all is said and done, a test is a test, and student test performance remains a key factor in determining his final course grade, and hence his academic progress and standing. Thus any knowledge which will help him improve his test performance is valuable knowledge.

Some students when taking a test persist in continuing their errors. For example, in writing the essay examination, the student should *never* begin to write immediately. He must first be able to answer at least two questions: (1) What type of question is being asked? and, (2) Which approach will I use in answering the question? After answering these two questions the student should make a brief outline (on scratch paper) of his proposed positions, and then proceed to answer the essay question.

There are generally three types of essay questions. In the first type, the student is asked to deal with a situation. The question may ask him to "discuss," "trace," "compare," or "evaluate" but the thesis is the same: he is asked to answer with all of the pertinent factual information on the given topic. A second type of essay question begins with an interrogative: "Why," "Who," "What," "How." This question demands a limited amount of discussion and a more direct and precise kind of answer. A third type of essay question asks the student to "pretend," such as "What if you were . . ." or "Imagine that you are . . ." This type of question is less frequently used in colleges. The answer demands some uniqueness, novelty, and the justification of the student's position.

Understanding the type of essay question being asked is only half the battle. Before the student begins to write, he must decide upon which of several approaches to use. Usually, because of time limitations, only one or two approaches can be adopted. This is a very important choice, and once made, should be adhered to throughout the exam. A student can answer an essay examination question from one or two of several different approaches. These include:

(1) The development of a central thesis.
(2) An introduction to the thesis.
(3) Presenting a body of factual information.
(4) Stating some definite conclusions which re-affirm the student's central thesis.

Essay examinations may be answered chronologically, argumentatively, categorically, or through the presentation of stages of development, depending upon the nature of the material. The entire point of writing the superior essay examination is to convince the reader (professor) that: (1) You know what you are doing, (2) you have a carefully planned and well-organized paper, and, (3) you know your material well enough to take a position and defend it.

Objective examinations differ markedly from essay examinations in content as well as format. They therefore require a somewhat different kind of preparation. As objective examinations demand a knowledge of specific facts, including small details, the ability to recall is often more important than the ability to make broad generalizations.

There are several different kinds of objective examinations. Some are mixed, using parts of any of the following kinds of format:

(1) The multiple-choice test;
(2) The matching test;
(3) The fill-in the blank test (completion);
(4) The true-false test; and
(5) Unique and individual teacher-made objective tests; these include puzzle formats, cryptograms, etc.

The multiple-choice objective examination is by far the most common type, and the most widely used. Generally, the student must choose the correct answer from four choices which are presented to him. The answers are all there in front of him. He must have enough knowledge to be able to recognize the right one. Lacking this knowledge, he can still get the correct answer by eliminating all but one or two choices, and then reducing these to a true-or-false query.

The preparation of multiple-choice questions has developed into a highly skilled area of educational psychology. Astute test construction often includes a series of answers which are "close" to the right answer, or "misleading." That is why it is important to look to *all* of the choices before settling on one. Some students find it easier to answer the multiple-choice question by looking for reasons why all other choices save the correct one are in error, thus following a process of elimination, and, in a sense, double-checking the worth of their choice of answers.

An example of a multiple-choice question with somewhat misleading choices for each of the answers is:

"How many oranges can one purchase at seven cents apiece if you have a total of $1.68?"

ANSWERS: (A) 23 (B) 24 (C) three dozen (D) none of these

Answer "A" is misleading if one makes an error in his arithmetic. Answer "B" is, of course, the correct answer. Answer "C" introduces the additional concept of "dozen," and one must know that there are twelve in a dozen in order to eliminate this choice. Answer "D" can be chosen only if one cannot solve the problem correctly or if one makes an error in arithmetic and arrives at the wrong answer.

In answering the multiple-choice type of questions, students should:

(1) Analyze the exact meaning of the question, reading it exactly as stated (many students misread this type of question, and hence arrive at the wrong answer).
(2) Eliminate all choices which are obviously incorrect.
(3) Examine the remaining choices and choose the correct one on the basis of one's studies and learning.

Matching questions are presented in two columns. In this type of question the student is usually given minimal information, upon which he must use his fund of knowledge to match the correct pairs. Matching questions usually have more answers available than are needed, and usually each answer is to be used only once. An example of the matching type of examination question is:

Match the book titles with the author

Books	Authors	Answers (Insert Letters)
1. *Brave New World*	A. Caldwell	1.
2. *Farewell to Arms*	B. Huxley	2.
3. *Huckleberry Finn*	C. Kipling	3.
4. *Jungle Boy*	D. Hemingway	4.
	E. Steinbeck	
	F. Twain	

The fill in the blank, or completion type, test requires that the student answer by inserting a word or short phrase into a question such as:

"Laws are made by _____."

In some completion tests the student must choose the correct insertion from a series of possible choices, such as:

"Laws are made by the _____."
Congress—Senate—President—Courts

This type of question really becomes a multiple-choice question, and the same rules as detailed previously will apply. The advantage of the latter type of question is that it eliminates a wide range of student choices in the answer. In the illustration above, "Congress" is the correct answer; but some student might insert: "elected senators and members of the House of Representatives."

The true-false test is an example of the alternative-response question. It may be an "agree-disagree" choice, or a "yes-no" choice, or something similar. This type of examination has been severely criticized, because random guessing can result in about 50% accuracy. Some instructors therefore institute a right minus wrong grading system when using this type of examination.

All in all, however, nothing can help a student taking an examination, regardless of type, as much as:

(1) Thorough preparation;
(2) A positive mental attitude and self-confidence;
(3) Motivation to perform well; and
(4) A history of past success in previous exams.

CURRENT FINDINGS—RECENT VIEWS

Colleges are changing and they are changing rapidly. With these rapid shifts are accompanying changes in the academic problems of the student. We have previously indicated that students today are demanding more of a voice in college affairs. Educators are cognizant of these facts, and are acting in these directions.

Samuel B. Gould, the Chancellor of the State University of New York, has recently written:

America's institutions of higher learning must do more than change their curricula or allow students and faculty to create their own new programs. They must do more than change their committee structures or their organizational arrangements. They must do more than make piecemeal concessions to change. They must do more than merely defend themselves.

They must *take the initiative*, take it in such a way that there is never a doubt as to what they intend to achieve and how all the components of the institutions will be involved in achieving it. They must call together their keenest minds and their most humane souls to sit and probe and question and plan and discard and replan—until a new concept of the university emerges, one which will fit today's needs but will have its major thrust toward tomorrow's. . . .

In 1940 only 8%, or roughly 190,000, of America's 22-year-olds graduated with baccalaureate degrees. In 1960, 18%, or approximately 400,000, of the nation's 22-year-olds completed four years of college and received their baccalaureate degrees. In 1970, a little over 25% of the nation's 22-year-olds, or roughly 875,000, graduated with the baccalaureate degree. Predictions for the 1980's indicate that at that time over one million young adults will graduate from four-year colleges and universities with baccalaureate degrees!

That colleges and universities will change in the near future is inevitable. The powerful surge of social forces in the past few years has made such a conclusion inevitable. The direction and nature of the changes to occur will affect the lives of those youngsters currently in the elementary schools across the country. But even more importantly, these changes will reach the very core of our nation.

WHAT WE HAVE LEARNED

1. Adjusting to the student role requires a reassessment of values and goals and a positive self-concept.
2. Students should learn, wherever possible, with a view toward transfer of learning.
3. There is a positive relationship between personality and academic success.
4. Self-appraisal, though admittedly difficult, should be part of the learning process of every college student.
5. Characteristics of overachievers include the enjoyment of competition, relative freedom from anxiety, self-imposed standards of high academic achievement, great expenditures of energy, and striving for academic excellence.
6. Characteristics of underachievers include poor motivation, dislike of competitive academic pressures, work performance at a minimal level, low energy expenditure, and pervasive presence of anxiety.

7. The problems of the underprivileged present unique demands when compared to the ordinary college student, enhancing the need for a satisfactory school adjustment, while, at the same time, making this goal more difficult to achieve.
8. Psychologists have recognized that there are marked differences in individuals with regard to their ability to learn.
9. The basic pattern for personality expression is formulated in childhood and adolescence.
10. The selection of the right courses for each student is an important aspect of college life.
11. The need to achieve is a strong, acquired psychological motive.
12. Many students find it difficult to adjust to the student role as they reach young adulthood.
13. Preparing for examinations is a vital responsibility of students.
14. The college of the twenty-first century will reflect the vast social changes currently beginning in America.

WHAT WE STILL NEED TO LEARN

1. As colleges face the challenges of the twenty-first century, they will need to formulate new and better methods of evaluating student progress. The present academic grading system will probably be replaced, and more effective methods of evaluation will develop.
2. New methods need to be developed to help the underachiever in his formative educational years, before he gets to college.
3. Ways must be found to "reach" the underprivileged and help alleviate many of the pressing problems which they face, so that college adjustment will not be made more difficult than it is for any other student.
4. We need to develop methods for getting more information to college students before they plan their course of study for each new term. The "communications" gap is a serious one.
5. As educational requirements in the various professions become extended so that more and more mature adults are faced with life as students, we need to adopt methods for helping individuals to adapt to the student role.
6. Leading educators across the nation agree that higher education will change dramatically in the next few years. We need to find ways for the leaders and administrators in these fields to take the initiative in formulating plans and forging new directions as America faces the challenges of a changing social order. Higher education must find the way to lead society into avenues which will provide a better life for all.

SUGGESTIONS FOR FURTHER READING

Anderson, Ralph E. and Irle E. Carter, *Human Behavior in the Social Environment*, Chicago, Ill.: Aldine Publishing Company, 1974.

Becker, Howard S., *Making the Grade: The Academic Side of College Life*, New York: John Wiley and Sons, Inc., 1968.

Bugelski, B. R., *The Psychology of Learning*, New York: Holt, Rinehart, and Winston, 1956.

Byrne, John, and Katherine Byrne, "You and Your Abilities," Chicago, Illinois: Science Research Associates, 1959.

Duck, S. W., *Personal Relationships and Personal Constructs*, New York: Wiley-Interscience, 1974.

Feldman, Kenneth A., *The Impact of College on Students*, San Francisco, California: Jossey-Bass, 1969.

Fitch, Stanley K., *Insights Into Human Behavior*, Boston: Holbrook Press, Inc., 1974.

Hall, J. F., *Psychology of Motivation*, Philadelphia, Pa.: J. B. Lippincott Co., 1961.

Hamachek, Don E., *Encounters with the Self*, New York: Holt, Rinehart, and Winston, 1971.

Severin, Frank T., *Discovering Man in Psychology: A Humanistic Approach*, New York: McGraw-Hill Book Co., 1973.

5

The Mature Student in College

- Attaining satisfactory adjustments
- The problems of young adults
- Kinds of conflict
- Misguided and deviant behavior
- Sexual deviations
- Kinds of drugs and their effects
- Social deviations
- Goal-directed behavior
- The adjustment mechanisms
- The challenges of peers
- The challenges of the social world
- Relaxation as a part of the life of the student
- Choosing a career: making long-term decisions
- Planning a course of action in college
- What We Have Learned
- What We Still Need to Learn
- Suggestions for Further Reading

PURPOSE OF THIS CHAPTER

"The Mature Student in College" completes the fifth and final section of the first major section of the text, "Looking At You—The College Student Today." In this section some of the problems of young adults and some of the realities of campus life will be examined.

There are many ways in which individuals seek to attain a satisfactory adjustment in their lives. Regression, aggression, sublimation, substitution, rationalization, projection, and identification are some of the commonly operative psychological defense mechanisms which will be explored in this chapter. How the individual uses or misuses these mechanisms will be a part of the investigation.

Choosing a career and planning a course of action are vital components of the college student's life. Helping in these decisions, this chapter will present material relevant to making these decisions.

What is maturity? What is meant by the "mature" student in college? These questions will be discussed in this section of the text, as well as the challenges of a changing social world and some of the misguided behaviors that have been evidenced in recent years.

As some of the challenges of peers and adjustment problems of college students are explored, the student should be able to see more clearly the need for a mature approach to the various issues, and to obtain a better understanding of what is meant by the "Mature Student in College."

THE PROBLEMS OF YOUNG ADULTS

Just as much of the behavior of childhood is carried over into adolescence, so too some adolescent patterns of behavior carry over into the young adult years. All along the natural course of development, behavior patterns are reinforced, modified, strengthened, eliminated as being too immature, and new patterns and modes of expression are attempted. College students in their young adult years need the opportunity to experiment, to explore, to decide which of their former behavior patterns will be retained, which will be reoriented, and which will be eliminated. As they are presented with new challenges, they need the opportunity to attempt new modes of behavior, more mature and responsible actions, and behaviors which are more commensurate with the ending of their teen years.

The effectively functioning, or mature, personality has autonomy, a term Abraham Maslow described as "self-actualization." An autonomous individual is relatively free from the demands of either the physical or social environment. He has attained a degree of maturity wherein he seems to be able to function autonomously—in his own way—tolerant of any social rejection and true to himself and his ideals, aspirations, and standards. He can adapt critical attitudes toward the sacred cows of his own cultures. Carl Rogers has emphasized a movement by the mature young adult in the direction of autonomy, self-direction, and an increased freedom from adherence to the expectations of others.

Not all young adults, of course, are so self-sufficient, so self-functioning, and so autonomous. Most have numerous adjustment problems, and the fact that young adults do meet difficult kinds of adjustment as part of their campus lives is not unusual.

Although individuals experience a wide variety of adjustment problems, they can be broadly categorized as follows:

Problems of self-perception;
Problems related to the environment;
Problems of frustration; and
Problems of immaturity.

The well-adjusted person must have a clear perception of reality and how he fits into the "picture." Many college students are very unsure of themselves; they don't know if they will be able to "make the grade." The fact that there is tremendous pressure in this direction does not make the adjustment easier. Some students do not really know their capabilities and weaknesses. Some delude themselves, while others become negative and derogatory toward their own self-images and self-constructs.

American society and culture is success-oriented. From an early age students are urged to do "well," and implicit in this concept is a tendency to urge them in the direction of conformity to existing value systems. The image of the young man or woman who attains position, prominence, and prestige has been foistered from an early age. But what about the reality of the fact that not all young men or women will succeed in such goals, and, what about the reality that not all young adults strive in these directions? How far can we proceed in demanding "success" when we risk breaking the spirits, hearts, and minds of those who do not attain these levels?

Students beginning their college careers .encounter numerous problems connected with establishing themselves as individuals. They must cope with the daily problems of obtaining food, study, performing assigned and required tasks, balancing social life, sexual pressures, and the need to succeed academically. These are problems related to their immediate environment. Community college students find it difficult to adjust to living at home, and the need to "move out" into an apartment of one's own is a common young adult syndrome. Some college students find it difficult to verbalize this need to their parents; many parents are overwhelmed or crushed when the request is presented, taking the matter as a personal affront, and wondering where they have "failed."

The problems of frustration and anxiety that confront the college student may be summarized in three categories:

(1) Approach-approach conflicts
(2) Avoidance-avoidance conflicts
(3) Approach-avoidance conflicts

In the first, or approach-approach type of conflict, the individual sees two mutually attractive goals, and would like to achieve both. However, the conflict arises because it is not possible to do both (e.g., two events at the same time—which to attend?). This type of conflict has also been termed a positive-positive conflict, since the individual is positively attracted to each of the goals. At first thought, one might feel that there should be no conflict, since regardless of which goal one chooses he has attained something which is both positive and desirable. But this is not so, for in the process of making a decision or choice there is always the nagging doubt that the alternative choice might have been the better of the two.

In the avoidance-avoidance conflict (which has been termed a negative-negative conflict), the individual is faced with two mutually unattractive goals. He really does not wish to choose either, but by force of circumstances, he must (e.g., to do one's homework, which may be a long arduous task, or to suffer the consequences of the failure to do the work, such as poor grades, chastisement, the risk of being assigned even more work, etc.). Facing the decision in an avoidance-avoidance type of conflict is a sign of maturity. Some individuals simply cannot make this type of decision, and withdraw from the situation in order to avoid making it (e.g., If I am sick, I cannot work; or, If I quit school I will not have these problems).

In the approach-avoidance conflict (which has sometimes been termed a positive-negative conflict), the individual must choose between an attractive or positive goal which he knows is wrong for him, and a negative, much less appealing goal which is the right thing to do. This kind of choice involves an even greater type of mature behavior —doing what is right because you know that it is the right thing to do, and not because anyone else is forcing you. (While dieting, for example, food is most attractive, but one knows that abstinence is a necessity and the right thing to do if one is to keep to the rules of the diet.)

Many beginning college students experience the problem of persistent immature patterns of behavior. They do things for which they are later ashamed or feel guilty, or they fail to do things which are expected of mature young adults. Effective college adjustment requires that the individual be able to cope with his environment and with himself. The immature student finds difficulties in both directions. Often he is handicapped by his unrealistic and impractical armamentarium of skills, insights, and self-concepts.

There are many barriers, pitfalls, and difficulties in the framework of the typical college campus structure. Schools are not necessarily tailored to meet the needs and demands of unique personalities. The individual must learn to adjust to other people—to their needs, demands, frustrations, expectations, resentments, and competitiveness.

The adjustment problems of the immature college student are further compounded by the fact that motives do not express themselves singly, but appear in complex syndrome patterns. Students are often motivated in two or more different directions at the same time. One of the problems of young adults is making sound decisions and then sticking to them.

AGONY ON THE CAMPUS

Volumes have been written about the torment of youth. While many adults express the desire to be young again or refer to the "good old days," few would realistically wish to return to the days of late adolescence and young adulthood, for most would not want to live through the trials and difficulties of this particular stage of development. "Neither fish nor fowl" is a capsule description of the young adult college student: he is too old to behave or to be treated as a child, and too young to assume the full responsibilities of the adult.

Not too many years ago, the goal of a college education was sought only by the academically elite and financially wealthy. This situation has changed drastically today. Many young adults find themselves on college campuses even though their academic background is weak and their financial resources extremely limited. A potentially explosive situation has been created which lends itself to a great deal of torment and soul-searching on the part of many young adults.

The wave of student discontent on campus in the late 1960's manifested in the drive for student power and in the take-over of student buildings, riots, picketing, and the formation of "new left" and "radical" student groups was a reflection of student torment on campus. The fires did not suddenly arise, but had been smoldering for years. Too many college administrators held to the attitude that "It can't happen here," or that "My students don't do these kinds of things; it is all caused by off-campus, non-student radicals." Writing in "Ramparts" magazine, Tom Hayden, an S.D.S. (Students for a Democratic Society) leader stated: ". . . What is certain is that we are moving toward power—the power to stop the machine if it cannot be made to serve humane ends."

Today's college student is better informed and more keenly aware of social problems and the value systems of the society in which he lives. He wants to take an active part and a leadership role in major public issues. Problems of the environment, inadequacies in housing, the problems of the poor, racial discrimination, corrupt political machines, and administrative rigidity and lag are part of the "business" of the young adult on campus today. He has made these various social issues his problem, and wants solutions for them. He has involved the college community in the lives of the larger community, and wants the college to assume a leadership role. Some college administrators, somewhat bewildered by the chain of events, still cling to the outmoded notion that the problems which are causing so much campus agitation are not the college's responsibility and that there is no real need to become involved and committed.

If oppression is non-existent on the college campus—a case students do not find very often, they often see oppression in the communities surrounding the campus. Many students experience great conflicts of conscience in trying to decide whether or not to participate in campus demonstrations. A part of the problem can be seen in the fact that the line between serious intent to improve existing structures and revolutionary intent is a fine line, often blurred and tenuous.

To date, campus administrators have reacted to the rising tide of student discontent in one of three ways: by ignoring it; by suppressing it; or by reconciling some of the issues. More and more, however, enlightened college administrators are taking leadership roles and asking the students to join *with them* in the resolution of recognized problems in the social and the campus community.

MISGUIDED BEHAVIOR

In Chapter 10, Section II, the concepts of "normality" and "abnormality" will be discussed. Social behavior of the college student which is deviant, unusual, or provocative will be discussed in this section.

Not all individuals agree on which behaviors are unusual. In resolving conflicts such as the need to achieve, the desire for independence, the pressures toward sexual exploration, and resentment of authority, some young adults adopt unusual and provocative modes of behavior. They call it "doing their thing," and point out that an open expression of behavioral patterns is more honest than hidden or hypocritical behaviors.

Young adults naturally experience sexual needs. Sometimes the pressures become so great that they engage in sexual intercourse, as well as lesser forms of love-expression and love-making. The sexual problems of the young adult cover a wide range of behaviors. Young adult males experience their peak of sexual pressure, and young adult females rebel against passivity in their roles. In general, their sexual problems center about: heterosexual modes of expression; feelings of homosexuality; autoerotic practices; sexual and moral code ambivalences; and perversions.

Most young adults enjoy the company of the opposite sex and have passed the earlier adolescent stage of being uncomfortable in the presence of the opposite sex. For the most part they actively seek the company of the opposite sex in wholesome social activities. Some young adults are randomly sexually promiscuous, but this is far from the common practice on college campuses today.

Young adults experience heterosexual adjustment problems as they begin going "steady," begin to get serious about one individual, and begin to plan for engagement and marriage. The necessity for the postponement of sexual practices over a long period of time because of extended educational careers often increases the sexual pressures upon the individual. Too, college campuses today offer more opportunity for intimate contact, as dormitories are open at all hours to both sexes, as colleges experiment with co-ed dorms, and as the use of the automobile on campus increases.

Some students live together without the benefit of wedlock, defying convention and openly expressing their right to individuality and freedom of choice. This new morality is a phenomenon which at first upset college authorities, causing some to ban students from the campus. Whether or not one condones these actions, one must at least admit that the young adults are being candid.

Many students are unsure about their sexuality. Some express concern that they may have homosexual tendencies, and others proceed into experiments including physical intimacies with members of the opposite sex. The fallacious argument: "How will I know unless I try it?" is illogical; one can know and appreciate the presence of electricity and atomic energy without being executed to prove its presence!

Although studies of homosexual practices on college campuses have been minimal, and more research is needed in these areas, there is some information on the subject. The tendencies first begin to exhibit themselves at an earlier stage of adolescence, in self-doubts, seeking the companionship and comfort of members of the same sex, and in poor parental images. Irving Bieber and others have made several investigations into the problem of homosexuality, and have reached several conclusions, among which are:

Homosexuality is a psychological problem and should be treated as such.
Homosexuality exists in a latent and overt form. In the latent form the individual is not presently engaging in overt homosexual activity.
The problem of homosexuality is probably more widespread than is presently recognized.

Autoerotic practices, or self-sexual stimulation, range from sexual stimulation from the stray touching of one's body to overt masturbation. The problem is generally more common among males than females, and it not indigenous to college campuses. Prisons and the various branches of the military are faced with similar kinds of problems. The real problem lies not in the action itself, but in the psychological feelings of guilt, inadequacies, shame, self-doubt, and the need to hide the practice which accompanies the act. Some individuals who engage in masturbation for prolonged periods of time find that making a heterosexual adjustment is more difficult, and later in life have difficulties fulfilling traditional sexual roles. Some college campuses have had problems with groups of individuals of the same sex engaging in mass acts of self-stimulation and autoeroticism. Many of these individuals find that satisfactory sexual outlets can only be achieved by engaging in further acts of sexual deviation such as fetishes, exhibitionism, sadism, and masochism.

There are many forms of sexual perversions. In some societies, that which we consider "perversion" is the normal mode of sexual expression. Even within the framework of our own society, some sexual activity of a few generations ago which was regarded as extreme, abnormal, or provocative, are accepted modes of practice today. (Witness the advent of the bikini, the monokini, the miniskirt, the see-through, and the topless fashions of recent times.)

Some common sexual deviations include promiscuity, incest, prostitution, homosexuality, fetishism, masochism, sadism, exhibitionism, pedophilia, rape, and voyeurism. These practices are socially taboo, and society currently provides legal penalties against these engaging in these practices. All individuals may experience stray or random thoughts in any of the above directions; it is the overt practice which is forbidden. Many sexual topics still remain in the realm of forbidden subjects today, and college students feel that this is wrong. As a result some campuses have experienced student demands for practical, real-life courses in sex, and are now offering these classes. Sex education in the elementary and high schools has been instituted for several years now, although there is still some public opposition and controversy concerning the merits of various programs.

There is some evidence to indicate that young people who have been raised in very strict home environments, with accompanying censure of all sexual matters, have a tendency to turn toward sexual activity which may be harmful to themselves or to others. Some young adults are merely following the sexually provocative patterns they have observed in the various segments of our society. One such phenomenon is the rising presence of group sex. These practices, to the sexually naive individual, can be traumatic experiences; even to the sexually experienced young adult, they can raise serious questions of guilt feelings and moral doubts and uncertainties.

Another form of misguided and ill-advised behavior occurs on the college campus when students begin to use drugs. Although the majority of students experiment with various drugs to see the effects upon their bodies, all too often, they ignore the possible effects upon their minds. There is a difference of course between the college student who uses drugs infrequently, the habitual drug user, and the addict. The student who occasionally uses a drug may be responding to social pressure or to a challenge from his peers. He may actually be afraid of what he is doing, but is more afraid not to take the drug because of peer ridicule. His mental attitude however is quite different from the habitual drug user or the addict.

The young adult who habitually takes drugs does not do so to impress others. The use of drugs may have become a routine. He does not feel addicted, and feels that he can stop at will. He does not necessarily boast about the use of drugs to others. If the process continues, he may slip into addiction without realizing it. The addict has a compulsive craving for a particular form of drug. His ultimate dependence comes with the increased psychological and physiological pressures brought on by drug use. Unlike the habitual drug user, the addict needs larger and larger doses in order to sustain himself. Addicts exhibit painful withdrawal symptoms when they cannot get the drug, when they cannot get enough of the drug, or when they cannot get the drug soon enough.

In order to obtain funds for the purchase of drugs, some young adults will perform a variety of criminal or illegal actions. Young female addicts often turn to hustling, prostitution, peddling narcotics themselves, and shoplifting to support their habit. Male addicts more frequently commit such crimes as armed robberies. Some addiction may stem from an original medical prescription, prescribed to relieve pain, but overused and abused by the patient.

There are many different kinds of drugs, and each has its unique effect. Young adults have been known to use any of the following:

Alcohol	Tranquilizers	Gasoline vapor
Cocaine	Nasal inhalants	Paint thinner vapor
Barbiturates	Amphetamines	Hasheesh
Opium derivatives	Pep pills	Heroin
Marijuana	Reducing pills	Banana weed
L.S.D.	Airplane glue	

The use of L.S.D. has become a popular "fad" among some young adults. Recent tragic suicides have shown that the drug has a lengthy period of "after-effect." That is, even several months after discontinuing the use of the drug, the individual may take a "bad trip." The use of L.S.D. and most other drugs in its category has been prohibited by law. However, this has not stopped the illegal drug traffic in the United States, and most college students seem to have no difficulty in obtaining drugs.

A final form of misguided behavior is exhibited by those individuals who have decided to "drop out" of society. Some textbooks classify them as "psychopathic deviates." They adopt modes of dress which are shoddy, unkempt, or bizarre in appearance, tending to alienate them further from the mainstream of a society which they have rejected.

Most psychopaths are nonconformists. They resist the "establishment" and the "power structure." They choose to live as they please, ignoring the tenets of morality and legality. Some hold no regular employment and some attempt to form a society of their own. They may not necessarily break any laws, but their behavior is anti-social.

GOAL-DIRECTED BEHAVIOR

Feelings of security comprise perhaps the most basic and fundamental aspect of good adjustment. One feels secure when he knows who he is, what his capabilities are, where he is going, and what his goals are. He has some feeling of accomplishment, and a certain amount of satisfactory social relationships. Feelings of security are often defined as feelings of "belongingness"; the feeling of being accepted by others and by oneself.

Many college students are sure about their goals. They want to be engineers, teachers, business executives, artists, musicians, lawyers. But while their goals are well-fixed, they experience doubts as to whether or not they can achieve their goals and whether or not the goal is worth the effort which must be expended. Some young adults attain their desired goals only to find afterward that it is not really want they want at all. Some students change their major mid-point in their college careers, often necessitating taking courses to make up for deficiencies in the newly-chosen area.

Through childhood and adolescence, most individuals undergo a series of experiences which lead them to a stated level of productivity. This becomes their standardized "work pattern." Ideally, the individual student should be able to assume the major share of the responsibility for his learning by the time he arrives at college. He should know the appropriate resources of the college, and when and how to utilize them effectively. He should be able to identify those problems which he considers to be important and know how to proceed in their resolution. On his own initiative, the goal-oriented student should be able to give serious attention to his studies in an effort to reach an ultimate long-range objective.

But not all students are so well adjusted. Many experience adjustment problems along the path of their collegiate days, causing their goals to become clouded, distorted, out-of-proportion, or lacking in value. These students frequently use any one of a number of "adjustment mechanisms."

THE ADJUSTMENT MECHANISMS

Almost all adults use certain devices to retain their psychological equilibrium. These devices are generally known as "adjustment mechanisms." While many are commonly employed by most individuals, some are used less often; the excessive dependency on any of the mechanisms can lead to further adjustment difficulties. The "adjustment mechanisms" include:

Rationalization	Identification
Projection	Reaction-formation
Substitution	Dissociation
Withdrawal	Repression
Sublimation	Compulsive behavior
Selective forgetting	Compensation
Procrastination	Over-compensation

Sometimes the "adjustment mechanisms" have been termed "defense mechanisms." Regardless of terminology, these modes of behavior stem from the framework of Freudian or psychoanalytic psychology.

Rationalization is a process whereby the individual invents excuses to justify his behavior. The excuses are usually perfectly acceptable, rather logical, and untrue. When a teacher asks a student why he missed class, the student may find it difficult to say: "Because I dislike the class and the teacher." Such a response may be true, but simply is not socially acceptable. Hence, the student may feign illness, which is more socially acceptable, and, in the process, use the psychological mechanism known as rationalization.

Projection involves a process of blaming others for one's difficulties. When the instructor asks why a student is late he may project by stating: "The bus was late" or "The alarm didn't ring." This absolves the individual from some of his responsibility and shifts the onus for behavior onto someone or something else.

Substitution involves redirecting one's goals into different channels. When one cannot afford a Cadillac he may purchase a Chevrolet.

There is nothing unusual about this, unless the individual feels it necessary to explain to all that he really doesn't want the better car, and then explains numerous reasons why. Convincing oneself that alternative choices are one's true wants is the basic mechanism of substitution.

Withdrawal means leaving. It is an escape mechanism. When the "kitchen gets too hot" we can alleviate the discomfort we experience by leaving the kitchen. When the academic pressures mount many college students solve the problem by withdrawing from school, often to the bewilderment and puzzlement of their parents. There are numerous forms of withdrawal, including daydreaming, forgetting to meet responsibilities, and feigning unawareness of assigned tasks. An extreme form of withdrawal involves aspects of amnesia.

Sublimation involves the subtle re-directing of one's energies into similar, but perhaps less demanding, areas. For example, when sexual pressures cannot be overtly released through intercourse the individual sublimates by engaging in some other activity: reading a magazine, going to a movie, engaging in vigorous sports, etc. Perhaps the entire idea behind "diet" foods is to satisfy the sublimated motives of the dieter. He cannot have the food he wants because of the higher amount of calories, so he accepts similar food, perhaps not as satisfying, but lower in calory content.

Selective forgetting is an unconscious mechanism. The individual is rarely aware that the mechanism is in operation until after the process has been completed. Hence, he remembers an unkept dental appointment only after it is too late to keep the appointment. He is really saying that he consciously fears going to the dentist, or dislikes the eventuality. Other examples of selective forgetting are failure to keep a stated appointment (when one really didn't want to meet the person involved), failure to turn in an assignment ("I didn't know it was due today!"), and forgetting to write home ("Has it really been that long since I've written?").

Procrastination is delay. The temporizing approach is easy to use, and many individuals do so commonly. "I'll do it later" is a form of procrastination. The term means putting things off, and implies that what we are putting off is unpleasant. Efficient people face unpleasant or difficult tasks first, because they are fresher and their energy levels are then at their peak. Procrastination is so common that some individuals develop the habit, which then becomes difficult to break. The habit of procrastination usually increases the kinds of adjustments which the student must face.

In the process of *identification*, hero images are used by the individual as models for his own inadequacies. The student may respond: "No, I don't know the answer, but I'll ask my brother—he's good at math." This kind of statement is a form of identification. It is a face-saving mechanism, because, even though the student cannot solve the problem himself, he can at least respond with a source which he admires and respects and which is capable of solving the problem for him.

Reaction-formation occurs when we take the opposite posture of our real needs and wants. It is childlike behavior in some respects, but it is used often by many adults. When we respond: "Keep your old book —I don't want it anyway," when in reality we would very much like to have the book, we are using a defense mechanism known as reaction-formation. In the throes of reaction-formation the individual may develop deeper forms of rejection, such as: "I wouldn't take the book now even if you begged me to take it!" Reaction-formation as an adjustment mechanism is usually self-defeating, because the problem hasn't really been resolved, and alienation of others often accompanies the process.

Many college students go through periods when they experience mild *dissociative reactions.* In this process the individual temporarily loses "track" of the time, or the date, or an assignment, or who he is, or what he is doing, or what he was planning to do. Such temporary states are usually quite fleeting, but can cause considerable concern. Many students become excessively alarmed, wondering if they are mentally ill, if they are losing their minds, or if they are abnormal. In reality, dissociation is only of concern in cases of mental illness. It seems to be a physiological-psychological mechanism for the temporary relief of pressures, tension, and anxiety.

Repression is common among students who are shy, reserved, withdrawn, and "loners." They hide their true feelings, sometimes never expressing them at all, or only in very mild, or altered forms. Continuous repression of strong feelings and emotions can, over a long period of time, cause psychosomatic disorders. As a temporary defense mechanism it is used quite often. "Discretion is the better part of valour" expresses the psychological concept of repression.

Compulsive behavior is sometimes also called obsessive-compulsive reaction. While this behavior is characteristic of certain forms of mental deviation, it is also commonly used by individuals who want to "play it safe." They follow the same routines day after day in an attempt to avoid problems. These individuals like to do things in the same way, or at the same time, or with the same person. Compulsivitiy also takes the form of wanting all doors closed, all window shades drawn to the same height, and all assignments completed perfunctorily. It avoids scoldings, naggings, and punishments, thus accomplishing a form of adjustment for the individual.

Compensation and *over-compensation* occur when an individual fails to succeed in any one given area of endeavor and channels his energies into an area where he can be a success. There are many biographical examples of compensatory and over-compensatory behavior. (Over-compensation is similiar to compensation, varying chiefly in degree.) Handicapped individuals, e.g., blind persons, find it necessary to compensate for their handicap by the more effective use of other sensory organs. College students compensate for poor progress in one subject by striving for a high grade in others.

There are limitations on how effective our adjustment mechanisms can be for each of us. Often we are unaware that we are utilizing adjustment mechanisms, and hence are powerless to prevent their use. (Can we ever see ourselves as others see us?) Strong self-identification emotionally with ourselves makes it difficult to understand why we are using a particular adjustment mechanism, even when we become aware that we are using it. Finally, force of habit has become so ingrained by adulthood that it is difficult to change behavior patterns which we have become accustomed to using over a long period of years.

Ordinarily the use of defense mechanisms leads to rational conduct. But the abuse of the mechanisms can lead to peculiar, disturbed, irrational, or neurotic patterns of behavior. An individual who is too compulsive may be mentally ill.

THE CHALLENGES OF PEERS

Friends are wonderful; all of us need them. Friends can also be the source of problems, either in attaining friendship, in maintaining friendships, or in breaking up of long-standing friendships. College students have reported that the temptation of joining with friends in various social events—parties, meetings, get-togethers—often interferes with good intentions toward study. On the other hand, the college student with no friends may lead a very singular, lonely life.

H. G. Wells once remarked that all of man's history is a race between education and catastrophe. This is particularly true in the United States, because we follow the rule of democracy and obey the will of the majority. But this situation sometimes causes problems of a peculiar nature for the college student. When all of the "guys" are going to the big game it is hard to be left out. It takes will-power to be able to say "No," and even more will-power when the need to say "No" is prompted by the need to study. The student who can so perform finds that all too often he cannot concentrate satisfactorily anyway, and then reproves himself for not joining in with the others.

Too, some students can be ostracized if they fail to join with the others at social events.

Education develops the individual and teaches him to think. However, he must learn to think critically, and one of the critical thoughts and actions which become part of a student's life involves the need of maintaining a satisfactory, balance between friendships and the demands of the academic world.

One of the great unseen tragedies on campus is the waste of talent which occurs when able college students fail to maintain their academic standing because of an overactive social life. The situation, unfortunately, is not uncommon.

College students today live and mix with all races and creeds and come to know people in ways which previous generations could not, if only for lack of exposure. As this present generation reaches full adult maturity and assumes adult responsibility, it is to be hoped that the fervor and ardor which they express regarding many of the present social problems besetting our nation will be translated into mature forms of actions which will be of benefit to all. At the present time, such evidence, while limited, points to the contrary. It seems that once graduation has been accomplished, and often even before, disinvolvement occurs. Among young adults who pursue graduate degrees, this seems to occur also, but to a somewhat lesser degree.

Wide social contacts are important as part of the broad liberal education which college students should receive. If students are to be educated in the democratic tradition, then equality must be a central thesis. Another fundamental concept is that of the dignity of man and the value of human life. Many centuries ago Epictetus pointed out that "only the educated are free." Today it is recognized that education involves more than the academics. The social value of an education can no longer be ignored.

The holding power of a college is related indirectly to the social tenor of the campus. In addition to supplying academic challenges and supportive services for students, the college community today must also supply a balanced social atmosphere in which all students can freely participate. Colleges have moved in this direction in their attempts to integrate faculties and students, and to provide "student activity directors" or "student affairs" deans.

Erik Erikson has described what he terms the "psychosocial stages of development" in man. According to his thesis, each stage of human development presents its psychological and social challenges to the individual, which he terms a "crisis." Some individuals meet the challenge of these crises satisfactorily, and hence are ready to move on to the next stage in mature development. Others fail to make satisfactory adjustments and continue in immature adjustment patterns, perhaps throughout their lives. In the area of psychosocial development for mature young adult students, Erikson has delineated four main tasks:*

(1) Achieve reasonable autonomy from parents and from the older culture.
(2) Achieve a sense of identity, i.e., to know who they are and where they are going.
(3) Achieve a sense of intimacy, i.e., the ability to relate themselves to others.
(4) Achieve a sense of responsibility toward society and toward themselves.

In adult life meaningful relationships are important. The doctor-patient, lawyer-client, teacher-pupil relationships, are only a few of the more obvious ones. College students who feel secure in their relationships with others will become adults who can assume social responsibility in meaningful and effective ways.

The challenge of peers, then, is to develop not only the intellectual side of the student, but his emotional and social aspects as well. No one needs to like everyone. But everyone needs to like and be liked by someone.

THE CHALLENGES OF THE SOCIAL WORLD

Man, by his very nature and since the time of his earliest existence, has been gregarious. Even in today's complex, highly technological, and somewhat impersonal world, man remains a gregarious creature. People like to be with people, and people need the companionship of their fellow-man.

The educational system is slowly changing to meet the changes evidenced within the society. The emergence of the community college as a potent factor in higher education is one example of this type of change. Some educators have predicted that in the future virtually all high school graduates will enter community colleges, and thence into junior-senior-graduate institutions of higher learning.

Writing in the Chicago *Daily News*, syndicated columnist Carl T. Rowan states that:

> The public schools of America's cities are in a mess. And growing worse:
> They are populated by children who do not or will not learn and burdened by teachers who cannot or will not teach.

*E. Erikson, Chapter Four, Late Adolescence, in *The Student and Mental Health: An International View*. Report of First International Conference on Student Mental Health, Princeton, New Jersey, 1956, and also World Federation for Mental Health and International Association of Universities, New York and London, 1959.

They are plagued by racial and ethnic hostilities and by violence flowing out of an assortment of emotions.

In some big city schools three out of four graduates cannot truly read or write and are utterly unprepared to go on to higher education or to cope with the problems of earning a living.

Almost 600,000 (in 1969) of the nation's 16 and 17 year olds (or about one out of every twelve) have found high school so boring, so irrelevant, so uninspiring, or their total environment so devoid of hope, that they have dropped out.

The social world presents many challenges to the educational world. No longer can education withdraw into the cozy niche of the world of the academic and remain in isolation from the social world and social values systems which surround it. Dean Theodore R. Sizer of Harvard's graduate school of education has stated categorically that: "school systems are, particularly in large cities, close to collapse." While the National Education Association (N.E.A.) has charged that urban schools: "perpetuate the cycle of poverty, the merry-go-round of despair and frustration. They consciously or inadvertently continue to discriminate against the poor and the powerless."

In light of the above, is it any wonder that there have been "student protest movements?" Indeed, the wonder would be if there were not! The student protest movement should be viewed not as disruptive, then, but rather as a means to jar complacency. While no one can rationally condone some of the methods utilized by radical student protesters (e.g., subversion or physical violence), the fact is that these young adults have become a powerful force in education, causing movement in the direction of social change. Glenn T. Seaborg has stated that he believes we are entering a new phase in our society; not merely a continuation of the Industrial Revolution, but, rather, a new stage which he terms the "Third Revolution." In this stage of social change, society must accept the challenge to implement the huge scientific advances of the past several years. Education must upgrade its course offerings and be creative enough to implement new programs in keeping with the challenges of the new technological advances.

Although the present social system dictates that all young adults should go to college, educators are aware that college is not for everyone. It is only for those who are able to profit from college experiences, and for those who are willing to work hard in order to obtain profitable experiences.

As John Stuart Mill wrote: "Men are men before they are lawyers or physicians or manufacturers, and if you make them capable and sensible men, they will make themselves capable and sensible lawyers and physicians."

The dichotomy exists because we are attempting to upgrade academic standards while at the same time attempting to provide more time for leisure and contemplation. By the 1980's the four-day work week for adults will have become a reality. What will happen to the traditional work week for college students? Are we moving in the direction of increasing the number of days and hours of schooling required. Or are we moving in the direction of decrease, as seen in other aspects of our society? The question, to date, remains unanswered.

ALL WORK AND NO PLAY

College students need time for leisure. Mental work can be as fatiguing as physical work, and students need time to release pent-up energies. Most colleges provide rather extensive club and sports programs. On campus sororities and fraternities provide further outlets for social activities, although not all students find that they are able to belong to these groups. However, there is a form of leisure suitable for each student, and each student adapts his own individual mode of relaxation. For some, this amounts to loafing or "rapping." For others, additional sleep is required, or solitude. For most, leisure-time activities involve being with others, either as passive observers or as active participants. All students can't make the team, but all can enjoy the activities by participant observation.

Many college students have schedules far in excess of the traditional forty-hour week, combining in-class work, after-class homework, study time, and part-time jobs to make a schedule which allows little or no time for leisure. Such students often find that they suffer periods of fatigue, depression, discouragement, or general unrest. They need a "break" in their routine. Many adults would rebel against the kinds of schedules that some students face on a daily basis for four or more years.

Through a frenzied competition for high grades and the maintenance of academic standing, some students risk the possibility of poor physical and/or mental health. Colleges, as presently constructed, are not the ideal model for the fomenting of mental health in their clients; rather they tend in the opposite direction. The need for suitable wholesome outlets for students becomes a vital need, and many institutions of higher learning have taken steps to alleviate the situation through provision of student lounges, "play" areas, smokers, card rooms, bowling alleys, gymnasium facilities for use at "off" hours, and the like. Some students, even while relaxing, are plagued by guilt feelings, thinking that they are wasting time, and should be studying instead. This tends to negate the value of the recreation period. Almost all parents of all college students are concerned about the academic progress of their offspring and inquire regularly as to how their youngster is "doing," implying are they "passing?". Very few parents have been known to inquire with the same degree of frequency or intensity as to whether or not their college-age youngster is spending enough time "relaxing" and enjoying the college years.

CHOOSING A CAREER

Many students today hold part-time jobs while going to school. Some even engage in full-time work while attempting to complete their college education. Most jobs both on and off campus involve the type of work that the student really does not want to do: the jobs tend to be menial, underpaid, and nonchallenging. Very few part-time jobs actually prepare students in the direction which they are going, leading to further resentment on the part of the student and lack of job satisfaction.

The choice of a suitable vocation has much to do with man or woman's happiness. The greatest portion of one's adult years are spent in working. How one spends these hours and how much he enjoys them may very well reflect the fact that his relationships with his family are good or poor, his feelings of self-esteem are adequate or inadequate, and his attitude toward his friends is positive or negative.

Because success on the job is so paramount to adulthood, it is a terrible tragedy to fail, either actually or in relation to one's expectancies. In order to prevent such failures and to insure proper choice of vocation, parents' concerns are directed toward channeling their youngsters into suitable educational programs. Parents try to influence their youngsters' choice of schools and the kinds of programs they will undertake, often using economic power as a controlling weapon in this matter. Most parents believe they are acting genuinely for the youngster's own good. They may not realize that what they are doing may to some extent be a compensation for their own failure to achieve. Nor do all young adults want the same occupational choices as dictated by their parents. Indeed, many young adults adopt fatalistic attitudes because they "know" they are destined to take over "Dad's business" regardless of their own vocational aspirations.

Too many adults harbor resentment because they have been directed into vocations not of their own choosing. Many outwardly successful professionals are extremely unhappy with their given vocation. Some adopt a variety of hobbies to compensate; others merely remain discontent throughout their vocational careers, perhaps never accomplishing as much as they might had the choice been of their own direction.

Family attitudes toward work play a large role in the vocational choice of the adult. The family may place various jobs on a hierarchical scale, valuing some highly and others not at all. In some parts of the United States, for example, teaching is still viewed as the vocation of women. (The advancements of the past several years make it difficult for the family to be aware of the multiplying number of vocational opportunities which have been created since their own school days, and difficult for the young adult to become aware of all of the possible job choices with which he is faced. *The Dictionary of Occupational Titles* lists over 40,000 different occupations. It is next to impossible for any one individual to be an expert in more than a small percentage of these).

Many studies have highlighted the influence of the father's profession upon the choice of the son. Although some young people rebel, even when the young adult chooses a vocation quite in opposition to that of the father, the influence of the parent's thinking, outlook on economic matters, recreational pursuits, and value systems still prevail to some extent. Many young adults are faced with a dualism in occupational choice: their own, and that of their parents. Whether or not their own occupational choice is the correct one, and whether or not they can attain it, is a problem further compounded by the question as to whether or not their job or career choice will be acceptable to their families.

Young adults are not unaware of the social prestige value of various occupations. Many *young men* would like to be salesmen, but find the job title not "professional-sounding." Business and industry have attempted to upgrade the titles of many of their low-level occupations in order to attract employees, recognizing the social-prestige value and importance of job titles. Thus "clerks" become secretaries (and even this title has been further refined, e.g., "private secretary" and "executive secretary"), and garbage collectors become "sanitation engineers."

Making the correct vocational choice is probably one of the most important decisions of the college student. Vocational counselors are available at most colleges, and often these counselors will use various testing devices along with past records, hobbies, and interests of students in trying to assess the vocational level of aspiration of the individual along with his probability for accomplishment. One of the most difficult problems facing these counselors is the realignment of vocational aspiration (when it is too high or too low) with the realities of an individual's capabilities.

The choice of vocation by a student is often an expression of the degree of his adjustment or maladjustment, his maturity or immaturity. Students build up attitudes so that they view certain occupations as worthy goals, making the expenditure of energy over a protracted college career worthwhile in their eyes. In our present society it is difficult for the son of a physician to aspire to be a semi-skilled worker, and this problem becomes self-defeating. For progeny sometimes "give up" in their attempts to be like their parents or to surpass them, feeling the goal is unattainable or not worthwhile. The psychologically well-adjusted person is likely to be a vocationally well-adjusted person.

Poor adjustment is a frequent cause for job dismissal. Although poor performance is often the visible cause for losing a job, the underlying cause is often expressed as "He's too hard to get along with," or, "He can't get along with his fellow-workers." Coping simultaneously with the pressures of emotional, social, and academic adjustment and the need to make a vocational decision, the young adult often faces a series of conflicts which demand resolution at the very time when such resolution is most difficult. He may not only be confused about his present status, but his dreams of the future may reflect unrealistic goals and unstable attitudes. It is not uncommon for college students to reshape their thinking academically and vocationally and to change the choice of their career aspirations. Although a student may spend a great deal of time in discussing his ambition (e.g., to be a lawyer), his grades may be a realistic reflection of the fact that he will never succeed in either entering or staying in law school.

What is not always realized is that vocational decisions are not made spontaneously, but rather are they made continuously throughout life. Even the individual who aspires toward a specific goals, say that of a physician, may find that after many arduous years of preparation, on attainment of his goal he is still faced with vocational decisions with regard to a multitude of possible specialties within his chosen field. No single decision determines an individual's vocational future, but rather a series of changing decisions occur throughout one's lifetime. Many young adolescents aspire to occupations of which they have only the vaguest notion; others are not even cognizant of the meaning of many of the job titles and the type of work entailed. How can a youngster aspire to be an "osteopathic surgeon" or a "human space engineer" if he does not know what the terms mean?

The tragedy of poor vocational choice lies in the gap between expectation and reality, resulting in dissatisfaction and discontentment, or, what is known as the "maladjusted" individual.

PLANNING A COURSE OF ACTION

In light of the foregoing, planning a course of action becomes a problem of paramount importance for the college student. It is no easy chore. Just as high school days come to an abrupt halt and the decision to enter college is upon one, so too college days end in a relatively few short years and the individual is faced with the decision of entering the job market or continuing his education with graduate school work. Actually, this type of decision needs to be made at least one year before graduation because of the necessity for applications for admission, recommendations, transcripts, credentials, etc. More and more, today's college graduates are seeking further graduate study, and graduate schools are overcrowded, short of facilities, and, hence, selective.

The higher one goes in education the more severe the competition. Just as college adjustment is more difficult because college students are of a higher academic level (the academically less able students have not been admitted), so, too, in graduate schools across the nation the competition becomes more stringent. Graduate schools select top-ranking students. The academic pressures are therefore greater. Many graduate schools have the policy, openly stated, of eliminating any student who receives two or more "C" (average) grades in any class; other graduate schools "count" only grades of "A" or "B."

In regard to graduate school, once again the need for decisions concerning a course of action often comes at the wrong time. Many students realize that graduate education is vital, only to further realize that their finances have been exhausted or that they themselves have been physically and mentally exhausted by the rigors of the collegiate career. Many students plan to work for a while after graduation and then return to complete their graduate work. This plan, however, can be misleading and should only be adopted if absolutely necessary. Numerous studies have indicated that it is much more difficult to "come back" to education than to continue one's educational progress. (Many college graduates find that they must go to work immediately upon graduation, and continue their academic careers on a part-time basis while working full time. The difficulties in this plan are evident, though not insurmountable.)

Many business and industrial firms, including the teaching profession, have offered a variety of incentive plans to encourage their employees to continue with their studies. These include financial reward, job promotion, payment of the costs of education, greater job security, and individual employee promotion and prestige.

New adjustments face the college student planning for further education. Most probably he must cope at the same time with self-financial support, marriage and the problems of starting a family, establishing his own residence, adjusting to in-laws, keeping the student role while at an even higher level of maturity, and the like.

Yet despite the evident difficulties and numerous problems which must be faced, the student has certain advantages. He now knows the "system" because he has been through it. He has faced numerous prior adjustments and adopted modes of behavior in response to problems. He has adopted a mode and pattern of study and learning which he feels secure with and which he can rely upon in pursuit of further study. In short, he has matured considerably.

Once again a positive mental attitude is a vital component, for the greatest difference between graduate and undergraduate work lies in the degree of autonomy required. Much graduate education today remains self-education. The individual is expected to work independently, with minimal guidance, and to produce some original research of his own. It is assumed that graduate level students are prepared for this type of challenge, but not all of them are so prepared.

Another distinct advantage for the college graduate who pursues further educational goals lies in the degree of specialization possible. The graduate student chooses his given field of endeavor, and specializes in a very particular area. The number of required classes outside his field of choice is minimal, while the number of "required" courses within his field of specialization is usually high. However, the big difference here lies in the fact that the student himself has made the choice of continuing his education; the motivational factors therefore stem from within the individual, rather than from the artificial pressures exerted by parents, peers, and college administrations.

WHAT WE HAVE LEARNED

1. The effectively maturing and functioning personality maintains a degree of autonomy.
2. In the process of becoming an adult, many college students express feelings of self-doubt; they are often very unsure of themselves.
3. A part of the maturation process of young adulthood involves establishing oneself as an individual.
4. Frustration and anxiety are expressed in the three basic kinds of conflict: approach-approach, avoidance-avoidance, and approach-avoidance.
5. College campuses across the nation have felt a rising tide in the quest for "student power."

6. The chief misguided behaviors of the young adult involve sexual adjustments, social adjustments, and temptations from peers.
7. While goal-directed behavior is desirable and many college students have very definitive goals, some young adults need re-orientation and re-direction because they will never fully attain goals which they view as desirable.
8. Individuals use numerous adjustment mechanisms in their daily lives, including such devices as repression, sublimation, substitution, compensation, identification, rationalization, projection, withdrawal, and selective forgetting.
9. The social problems of the community have become the social problems of the campus.
10. Public education in America's large cities faces a crisis.
11. College students need a balanced social life. They need time for leisure and time to relax.
12. Choosing a vocation is a vital task of the college student, and many colleges today provide counselors to help with this very important decision.
13. As the choice of college careers multiplies, the student faces the problem of continuing graduate studies or terminating his academic career upon receipt of the baccalaureate degree.
14. The higher one proceeds in an educational career, the more severe the competition, because the less academically able have not been admitted.
15. Many business and industrial firms encourage their employees to achieve higher educational status by offering a variety of incentive plans.

WHAT WE STILL NEED TO LEARN

1. We need to find methods of avoiding situations on campus which contribute toward conflict and frustration within the individual.
2. New methods for reaping the harvest of student concern need to be adopted, so that the "threat" of student power and student revolt can be channeled into productive ends for the student, for the college as a whole, and for individuals within the college community.
3. The community must become a part of the campus and the campus must become a vital force in the life of the community. We need to find ways in which the college can take effective initiative and leadership roles in this regard.
4. We need to develop a better understanding of some of the newly formed student groups and of their code of the new morality. It

is only when these groups are better understood that we can begin to work with them effectively.

5. Much psychological research has already been done on the problems of the addict and drug user, but more answers are needed to questions such as: "Why do youngsters begin to experiment with drugs?" and "How can we help the drug user to break his habit?"

6. We need to find ways to meet the challenges of the large urban areas of America. Education needs to be revitalized as a dynamic force within the urban areas if it is to continue to function effectively.

7. Colleges need to recognize even further the need for wholesome leisure-time activities for students and the value of social relationships, and to make provisions in greater ways for each of the above.

8. Students need more vocational guidance than they are presently receiving, and, along with the quantification of the above, improvement in the quality of that counseling.

SUGGESTIONS FOR FURTHER READING

Bernard, Harold W., *Dynamics of Personal Adjustment,* Boston: Holbrook Press, Inc., 1971.

Blaine, Graham B., and Charles C. McArthur, *Emotional Problems of College Students,* New York: Appleton-Century-Crofts, 1966.

Coleman, James C., *Contemporary Psychology and Effective Behavior,* Glenview, Ill.: Scott, Foresman, 1974.

Erikson, E., "Late Adolescence," Chapter Four in *The Student and Mental Health,* Report of the First International Conference on Student Mental Health: Princeton, New Jersey, 1959.

Garfield, Sol L., *Clinical Psychology: The Study of Personality and Behavior,* Chicago, Ill.: Aldine Publishing Company, 1974.

Hutchins, Robert M., *Education for Freedom,* Baton Rouge, La.: Louisiana University Press, 1943.

Jacob, Phillip, *Changing Values in College,* New York: Harper and Row, 1958.

Kagan, J., and H. A. Moss, *Birth to Maturity: A Study in Psychological Development,* New York: John Wiley and Sons, Inc., 1962.

Lazarus, R., *Personality and Adjustment,* Englewood Cliffs, New Jersey: Prentice-Hall, Inc., 1963.

Leon, Gloria, *Case Histories of Deviant Behavior,* Boston: Holbrook Press, Inc., 1974.

Levy, Ronald B., *Self-Revelation Through Relationships,* Englewood Cliffs, New Jersey: Prentice-Hall, Inc., 1972.

McGuigan, F. J., *Biological Basis for Behavior: A Problem*, Englewood Cliffs, New Jersey: Prentice-Hall, Inc., 1963.

Munn, Norman L., *The Growth of Human Behavior*, Boston: Houghton Mifflin Co., 1974.

Pickunas, J., and E. J. Albrecht, *Psychology of Human Development*, New York: McGraw-Hill, 1961.

Resnick, William C., and Herbert L. Sachs, *Dynamic General Psychology: An Introduction*, Boston, Mass.: Holbrook Press, Inc., 1971.

Sanford, Nevitt, *College and Character*, New York: John Wiley and Sons, Inc., 1964.

Part II

LOOKING BACKWARD
How You Came to Be What
You Are Today

6

The World of the Teen-ager

- Developmental factors in young adulthood and adolescence
- Kinds of social structure: The sheltered environment
- Kinds of social groupings
- Self-concepts and psychological needs in young adults
- Emancipation: The process of attaining independence
- Individual responsibilities: Some unforeseen adjustments
- The competitive nature of the collegiate atmosphere
- Sexual challenges to young adults: Heterosexual adjustments
- Physical, social, mental, and emotional development in young adulthood
- Adolescent experiences: Common and unique experiences
- Attaining adulthood: The appearance of new problems
- What We Have Learned
- What We Still Need to Learn
- Suggestions for Further Reading

PURPOSE OF THIS CHAPTER

In this introductory chapter of the second section of the text, "The World of the Teen-ager," some of the developmental factors which have led to the status of the college student today will be examined. Chapter Six concerns the nature of the environment of the adolescent and some of the problems he encounters in attaining independence and emancipation from that environment.

Some college students live at home, attending classes in community colleges or in colleges in their areas; others live on campus, often great distances from home; while still others attend colleges in the vicinity of their homes but choose to live away from home in college campus facilities or in private apartments. The problems involved in adjusting to each of these situations are several and they will be examined in this chapter.

The sexual challenges of the young adult also comprise a section of this chapter; adjusting to the opposite sex and developing a moral code of one's own are part of the adjustment problems of young adults which will be investigated.

What is an adult? How does one attain adulthood? These questions will be of concern in the latter part of this chapter; for the world of the teen-ager is a many-sided world. The complexities of his society, the adjustment problems which he must face, and the family situations which are common to the young adult will be examined in this sixth chapter of the text, as we attempt to expand our knowledge of the "World of the Teen-ager."

THE SHELTERED ENVIRONMENT

Young adults do not just "happen." In the United States, they come from environments which, for the most part, are sheltered or protected. While not all youngsters come from what has become the stereotypic image of the sheltered environment of white suburbia, most young adults evolve from environments which have been carefully planned with a view toward the protection of the young.

The United States today has shifted radically from the social structure of the 1900's–1930's. The patriarchy of that era has virtually disappeared. In its place is an environment which some term matriarchal, others term pedarchal, and still others term equalitarian. The kinds of social structures are:

Patriarch	Strong, dominant male and father figure; father dominates all important decisions in the family structure

Matriarch	Strong mother and female image; mother assumes dominant figure in family structure; mother makes important decisions.
Pedarch	Child-centered society; all aspects of family life revolve about the protection and well-being of the child; family decisions are based on the welfare of the offspring.
Equalitarian	Both mother and father hold equal positions of importance and responsibility in family matters; children are often brought in for conferences where important decisions are to be made.

There is little point in arguing over semantics. However one describes the current family structure within the United States today, the era of the dominant father has virtually disappeared. Mother has assumed a more prominent role as have the children.

Another recently observed phenomenon in the United States is the trend toward being "middle class." Middle-class standards have virtually dominated the thrust of those in poverty; indeed, even the wealthy want their children to be "red-blooded American," "typical as apple pie," or just "one of the boys." Perhaps this is one of the problems in present society: everyone wants to be middle-class. Perhaps society is trying to fit too many square pegs into pre-rounded holes.

Until the past several years, there was a reluctance to discuss "class" positions as is openly discussed today. The old European concepts concerning social position were considered unacceptable. Today, however, such terminology as the following is commonly used in describing various social classes:

Lower-Lower	Poverty and ghetto dwellers; little education; little hope for the future.
Lower-Middle	Poor people who are trying, often desperately, to live a decent, if impoverished life.
Lower-Upper	Those who are very near middle-class standards; about to purchase homes; have some savings, etc.
Middle-Lower	Usually urban dwellers who rent or own modest quarters; may have a car; usually finance purchases; struggle to make ends meet.

Middle	The great American ideal: father works, mother may or may not; own their own home and car, although may be paying them by means of financing; have many appliances; children attend public schools.
Middle-Upper	A bit above the middle class in earnings and personal acquisitions, they may have two cars; suburban dwellers; children attend parochial or private schools.
Upper-Lower	The newly acquired wealthy family; may have some servants; own their home; usually live in suburbs; have many personal belongings.
Upper	The long-wealthy group; often their wealth is inherited, although it may be of relatively recent acquisition.
Upper-Upper	The elite or aristocracy; lineage goes back to Mayflower days; belong to many private clubs; family wealth inherited over long generations.

Regardless of family finance and social position, most American parents want to see their children "succeed." Even in areas of extreme poverty, parents want their children to do well and thereby attain a status higher than their own. Parents who are totally unconcerned about the welfare and future of their children are the rare exceptions.

American children are not necessarily "spoiled." They are accustomed to having their needs met. Food, shelter, and the protection of family are accepted as their due. Few American youngsters work in their self-support prior to adolescence. This image is in contrast to the patterns which may be found in much of the world. All of the foregoing tends to lessen the self-sufficiency of the youngster up to a certain point in his development, when he is rather suddenly told that he is now old enough to take care of himself and must meet many of his needs individually.

The sheltered and protected environment has many advantages, but it also has several disadvantages. The sheltered environment must eventually become the unsheltered environment; the young must grow up, and with maturation comes the acceptance of new roles and responsibilities. Too many young adults are wholly unprepared for these kinds of changes.

Of course, not all youngsters are so protected. Ghetto areas tend to foster early maturation in vocabulary vulgarities, in the realities of the unpleasantness of many aspects of life, and in the necessity to fend for oneself. These youth have been emancipated far ahead of the usual age for emancipation attributed to their middle- and upper-class peers. They have missed something along the way—something which can never be made up, for life can be lived only once, and the ultimate law is that there is no going back.

IDENTIFICATION VS. EMANCIPATION

Human beings experience the effects of complex motivation in operation simultaneously with needs, wants, desires, and energy directed toward the attainment of goals. Some of these motives are biological in nature: the need for food, air, water, sex, avoidance of pain, and shelter. The need for identification and emancipation are not biological needs; they are social needs, or as they are sometimes called, "acquired needs."

Social motives are probably more highly individualized than biological motives. Certainly the mode of expression for the social motives becomes a very unique individual expression. Some people love while others destroy. Some seek approval while others rebel against all authority figures. Some seek to achieve while others strive to outdo their neighbors. Social motives involve others. They are a part of the complex process known as interpersonal relationships. Identification and emancipation fall into these categories.

In Abraham Maslow's attempt to list a hierarchy of human motives, his classification included:

Physiological Needs	hunger, thirst, air, etc.
Safety Needs	freedom from threats and danger; the need to be secure.
Belongingness and Love Needs	the need to allay oneself with the familiar and the secure.
The Esteem Needs	achievement, strength, competence, status.
Self-Actualization Needs	the need for self-fulfillment; to realize potentials; to become what one is capable of being.
Cognitive Needs	curiosity; the need to explore the unknown.
Aesthetic Needs	the need for symmetry, order, system, and structure.

The essence of self-identification is encompassed in Maslow's concept of self-actualization. As the individual reaches toward maturity, several different aspects of self are identifiable:

> The real self;
> The future self;
> The social self; and
> The idealized self.

The "real self" is what we are, as only we can know ourselves. It includes our innermost secrets, that which we are ashamed to reveal to anyone else. Of course, since the real self is how we see ourselves, it may or may not be an accurate perception. The "future self" is what we believe we shall become in the next five, ten, or twenty years. It is the self as we visualize our future roles: manufacturing executive, criminal trial lawyer, skilled surgeon, etc. Most individuals picture their future selves in somewhat rosy terms, only to become somewhat disappointed or disillusioned in middle age by the perceptual reality. The "social self" is how we appear to others. It includes the concept of the extrovert and introvert; the outward-going personality as opposed to the shy, withdrawn personality. Some individuals live two "selves"—how they appear to others and how they hope to appear to others. The "idealized self" is an inner fantasy or fiction which each person creates. He imagines that if he were given an opportunity to do so, he could be the movie-hero type, an image in which one commands admiration from others. The imagery of the idealized self rarely coincides with reality; few individuals ever realize the realities conjured up by the imagery of the "idealized" self. When the concept persists into later adulthood it is, at best, a form of immaturity. It can also be a form of mental illness, if the fantasy becomes excessive.

Emancipation occurs in stages. It begins with a greater degree of self-sufficiency and autonomy in adolescence and continues into young adulthood. Sometimes during this phase of maturity the individual reacts in a sullen way, and the process is difficult, requiring several family adjustments. But the process is also inevitable, and the mistake made by many parents to stop or slow it down can backfire. Just as a mother couldn't believe that her son was ready to cross the street at age five, or drive the car at fifteen, so too it is difficult for her to realize that he is now old enough to date, to have sexual relations, and to assume the responsibilities of a young adult. It is as if some parents were saying: "You can't be that old yet—if you are, then I must be very old indeed" (and who wants to admit that they are getting old?).

The normal process of emancipation from family ties leads to the attaining of independence. It is a strange psychological phenomenon. The very thing that parents have been working toward and hoping for

for over twenty years has occurred. Yet most parents are extremely reluctant to accept the fact that their youngster is now a mature, capable, and—yes—independent individual. The parent is no longer needed in the same ways that he has been accustomed to being needed for the past twenty years. This process is an adjustment that some families find extremely difficult; others never make a satisfactory adjustment, alienating their offspring for life.

ATTAINING INDEPENDENCE

In primitive societies and cultures the attainment of independence is a natural phenomenon which occurs early in the individual's life. This is not true in the American culture. It is a uniquely human process to be born into a culture whose values, mores, and modes of living have been inherited over a tradition of hundreds of years of successive generations. Cultures vary considerably, and practices and standards of one may be strange and different in another. Eskimos are amazed at the American practice of embracing, kissing, and preoccupation with the sexual nature of the female breast. Americans cannot understand fully certain aspects of the Eskimo culture. Any given culture changes slowly, over a long period of time. One of the phenomenons of the past twenty years has been the attempt by young adults to introduce rapid changes into the culture and value systems of the United States.

Subcultures exist within the various cultures. If you were asked to write a term paper or do a research project on the degree of independence among the young adults of any given large metropolitan area, you would have a great deal of difficulty, for you would need to account for the variations of a huge number of subcultures to be found within the larger urban culture. You would probably find a great deal of variation within the framework of the structure of each subculture.

Americans are raised in an atmosphere of rich materialism. Youngsters are exposed to TV, radio, hi-fi, stereo, refrigerators, jet planes, and other materialistic concepts at an early age, so that by late childhood they accept these values as part of their culture. Many other societies strive to attain, but have not as yet attained, a great number of material possessions which Americans take for granted as part of their natural heritage.

The process whereby young adults attain independence, then, is a culturally determined pattern. The process begins in early infancy and childhood, as youngsters are indoctrinated with the feminine or the male role. Conformity to societal dictum highlights the elementary school years, and it is not until the end of these years that the first glimmerings of independence appear in what is termed early adolescence. The adolescent actually passes through four stages of development: pre-pubescence; pubescence; post-pubescence; and late adolescence or young adulthood.

While there is variation in the characteristic behavior patterns which have been established for each of the above phases of development, there is a commonality too. Not until the final stage of late adolescence and young adulthood, for example, does the individual begin to show marked signs of attaining independence. There is a great range of individuality within a culture and even within a subculture. No two individuals have the same history or environment.

In the process of attaining independence, adolescents face decisions involved in identifying with new peer groups. The adolescent seems to be trying to "find himself." In this attempt he finds comfort and companionship in peers with similar interests and problems. Growing youngsters also face the problem of changing interests. Suddenly girls are no longer to be avoided, but hold a strange, new, mystifying, and appealing interest for the adolescent male. Some youngsters find that they must narrow their range of interests, for high school years do not allow enough time for all of the hobbies and games of childhood.

As the adolescent gains more and more independence he finds he must re-organize his schedule, his life-pattern, along with his friends and his interests, in order to meet the new challenges and demands which create new adjustment problems. New work and school patterns are gradually evolved. With the use of the family car, the world of the teen-ager broadens tremendously.

The adolescent seeking the normal path of self-direction soon finds that making decisions is not easy, and often he makes the wrong decision in his attempt to attain maturity. This is the dilemma of adolescence: he is expected to assume more and more adult responsibility, while at the same time he is still being treated essentially as a child and being forced into childlike roles of dependency. There is generally considerable anxiety associated with the emergent independence of American youth, because of the uncertainties of future, vocation, marriage, and whether or not the youngster will be able to "make it."

LIVING ALONE—INDIVIDUAL RESPONSIBILITIES

Young adults pass through a stage where they need to assert their independence by living away from their parents and family structure. If the college student is going to live on campus, this at least partially resolves the pressure of the need to live alone, although new problems appear in its place. Often this is the first experience the young adult has had in living away from home. The glamour and the advantages soon fade as the realities assert themselves. College students living on campus may do so in any of a number of ways: university-approved housing; private housing; fraternity-sorority housing; or self-supported apartment living.

Students not only live away from home, but many attempt to support themselves entirely during this period of development. It is no small accomplishment. Many students work full time as waitresses, bus boys, sales clerks, messengers, and in a host of other jobs while attending school full time and attempting to manage a residence of their own. The student often ends up mentally and physically exhausted because of the vicious cycle in which he finds himself. He needs to be "on his own" so that he can study better, away from family disturbances. But being on his own means working to pay for the rent and utilities to support a place of his own. This takes precious time away from his studies. He needs to spend time maintaining his residence, if only minimally, but this again takes time away from studies. When he does study, he finds it difficult to do so because of simple fatigue, the pressures of economic worries, and self-doubt, wondering if he is doing the right thing and if it is all worth it.

University-sponsored housing is probably the most economical for students. There are dormitory facilities and also rooms where two, three, or four students may share the costs and responsibilities. Compatible roommates are a very important factor in this first college living experience. Most colleges attempt to provide some supervision through dorm and room supervisors (these may be young adults working full-time at this job; more often they are graduate students performing the function to earn money themselves), board in the form of two or three meals a day, and some minimal rules and regulations, e.g., hours to be kept, amount of cooking which can (or cannot) be done in the room, etc. Because the cost is nominal compared to the cost of other housing, colleges often have long waiting lists for this type of housing.

Many colleges maintain lists of private residences where students may obtain room and in some cases board. These vary from apartments, to a room with a private family, to a private room in the "Y." Some students living in large urban areas use this kind of facility even though they live in the city. Their schedules make traveling to and from home inconvenient or impossible; also, as stated previously, there is the need to leave home and be on one's own, even though it may mean returning home each weekend.

Some colleges provide five-day-a-week residences for students who then return home for weekends. These are usually colleges located in large urban areas. Community colleges generally provide no resident facilities, although counselors often try to help place students in need of lodging in off-campus facilities.

Fraternities and sororities on campus provide an opportunity for living away from home in private housing with other students with similar interests and problems. They also provide an incentive to study, a varied social life, some sense of security and belonging, and a sense of status. On the negative side, these groups are usually difficult to join (one must be selected), expensive as compared to other forms of housing, and somewhat self-centered rather than total-college-centered. Often these groups have an ethnic or religious orientation, and sometimes they derive some of their financial support from ethnic organizations and religious institutions.

Much has been written about the pros and cons of the college fraternity and sorority. Many freshmen find the "hazing" or "initiation" period too much to cope with; indeed, colleges have attempted to regulate some of the fraternities and sororities in this and other areas. Let it suffice to say that for some students the arrangement is fine; for others it is unsuitable.

Married students attending college find that today's colleges provide them with residential (apartment) facilities, but here again there are often shortages as this type of facility is in great demand. Economically, the rental costs are much lower than comparable private apartment facilities, the housing, in effect, being subsidized to some extent by the colleges. Some young adults live in apartments off campus, sharing the facilities and the costs among two, three, four, or more persons.

The problems of living on one's own are small problems, when taken individually, but collectively they can mount to a proportion where some young adults find it is too much with which to cope. Problems of cleaning, laundry, cooking, and day-to-day housekeeping routines can seem overwhelming, especially when these duties are added to the full-time student role: study, preparation of assignments, and homework.

Communication with parents and family is often another problem for the college student living away from home. The need for some financial support is evident, yet the stigma attached to accepting that support can lead to psychological feelings of dependency and inadequacy. Young adults gain in maturity by being on their own; they face new problems of adjustment; they must re-adjust when, for example, in a summer session, they return to live at home once again. Often the adjustment is a difficult one, and parents report that they find it hard to communicate with their youngsters under these circumstances. The young adult commonly expresses the "Greta Garbo complex"—wanting to be left alone as much as possible.

SOME UNFORESEEN ADJUSTMENTS

Not all young adults attend college away from home. Many attend community or four-year colleges located close enough to their homes so that commuting is feasible. This situation may, at first, seem ideal, but it is not necessarily so. There are numerous adjustment problems entailed with living at home while attending college, for young adults have the need to be more independent and flexible in their schedules.

They often find that while attending college as a young adult they are still being treated as if they were in high school. The family claims that they make few demands: take out the garbage, sit with a younger sibling on occasion, let us know where you are going and when you'll be back. But to the young adult these demands imply conformity and a compliance which is excessive. As a result he or she rebels, and family friction blooms like a daisy.

While living at home, young adults in college often find it difficult to study. The routines of family life interfere with concentration, and some college students do not have a room of their own in which to study, further complicating matters. The need to "burn the midnight oil" is not uncommon while in college. Yet some families cannot understand this "staying up to all hours." College students rebel when parents want to know what they are doing, if their homework is done, where they are going and with whom, etc. They consider these inquiries to be infringements upon their maturity.

College students are exposed to a host of individuals from every conceivable racial, ethnic, political, and philosophical background. Often these new relationships cannot be accepted by the "closed mind" frame of reference of the family. Inter-racial or inter-religious dating, or associating with radical individuals often pose problems in adjustment for the college student. He first may try to conceal these associations from the family, but he soon realizes that this is difficult or impossible, or he soon rebels at the necessity for doing so.

Some college students respond to these new challenges by experimenting in various ways which are anti-social. The individual who sets himself apart from the mainstream of his fellows soon comes to distrust them. He may become isolated or "a loner" or he may seek out groups which are more akin to his way of thinking or mode of living. He may become a hippie, a radical, or a drug user. Most college students experiment in some ways with alcohol, whether in the form of beer, wine, or hard liquor. While the vast majority of students can keep these challenges in perspective and balance, a few cannot, and go "overboard" in one direction or another. This relatively small percentage of students has recently received a great deal of publicity, probably all out of proportion to their number

The present generation has grown up under circumstances of continuous "cold war" policy, which has often erupted into "hot war" fighting. These pressures affect all college students. They cause frustration because they involve larger world events over which the student has little or no control.

Many college students face uncertainty as they near graduation, because of the dilemma of continuing their education in graduate school, or trying to find a job in a very crowded and tight job market.

No one can really foresee all of the adjustments which a college student must face. Some are totally unexpected. A family tragedy, such as death, financial crises, or divorce, can easily cause unanticipated adjustment problems for the young adult. Under these stress situations, many individuals simply abandon college careers; others find academic progress made much more difficult and are barely able to keep up with their studies. Some students have attended college in order to prepare for professional school, only to find that they cannot gain admission, or lack the necessary finances to continue. In some cases, marriage and the start of one's own family causes a change in plans.

College students today are faced with a decision concerning campus activism: how active to be, how fully to participate, and where to draw the line. Each student must decide for himself, and his decision must be one that he can live with, even though it may not be accepted by family and friends.

Peer influence is important in the course of college careers. No one can make exact predictions about the final choice of peers, for much of what occurs is on the basis of chance or happenstance. However, college students are exposed to a greater range of attitudes and values, as they meet new people and gain new friendships. The wisdom of their choices remains a matter for future evaluation.

COMPETITION FROM PEERS

Youth is a highly valued period in the American culture. Many aspects of society actually cater to the young. Youth is regarded as a time of peak strength and vigor, a period of creativity and spontaneity, and a time of happiness. The idealization of youth found within the American society is by no means universal. Other societies cherish the older person and assign special roles to these individuals.

As young adults enter college, many of their childhood associations disappear. High school friends may or may not persist in their friendships; as new roles become necessary, new friendships are formed, and some of the old associations die of neglect, disuse, and the very fact of separation in time and distance.

The college scene differs from the high school atmosphere in several respects. There is a greater degree of individual autonomy expected; there is a wider range of mature behavior demanded; and there is greater competition from peers. College students, by virtue of their admission to the college, have become a select and hence more stratified group. Generally they are superior students academically, having been refused admission unless they have a certain rank and level of A.C.T. scores, etc. There is more competition socially, too, as young adults seek peer group identification.

Rejection is a common malady among many college students. They don't make the team or the fraternity; they fail to get the expected high grades; their social lives reflect a greater degree of competition from peers in dating and in group activities. Young adults on campus are beginning to face the realities that not all can be successful; not all are leaders; indeed, the aura of the "outstanding" goes to the very few. Often these students feel very hurt or very much "left out" at the start of their college careers.

Freshmen in college face additional adjustment problems. Their lives have not yet settled into a pattern which they are willing to accept. Everything is new and happening all at once. The inability to cope with the various aspects of college life can cause many a freshman student to give up.

In light of the above, many students seek peer groups in which they can find suitable social outlets for tension, and in which they can gain security in group membership. These groups may or may not be a suitable basis for the satisfaction of their needs. College groups themselves may be very demanding upon the individual, requiring various degrees of loyalty and conformity.

Although many students gain a sense of affiliation from group memberships, some do not. These latter feel the need for a closer, more intimate relationship with peers, and turn to the natural process of dating or going steady, forging strong emotional ties with a selected individual of the opposite sex. So college careers often lead to romance and marriage, as well as to scholastic achievement and vocational preparation.

SEXUAL CHALLENGES

Adolescents face sexual challenges, and the process of development is a fairly well-documented pattern. The sexual pattern of development affects every aspect of their lives. The usual pattern goes from self-assertion before the opposite sex to crushes, and thence to dating, going steady, engagement, and marriage. From about ages ten to eleven there is still some evidence of antagonism between the sexes. Boys are afraid of being called "sissy" and girls wish to avoid the "tomboy" label. In the early teens girls become interested in boys and there is evidence that they are more aware of the natural stages of physical development. The adolescent girl is generally considered to be a year or two ahead of the boy in sexual development and awareness in the early stages of adolescence.

In middle and late adolescence, dating, groups going out together, and double-dating among couples is the usual practice. There is, however, a wide variation within age groups and some youngsters do not reach these stages until much later than others.

The heterosexual adjustment of the adolescent proceeds in the direction of recognition of the opposite sex in positive terms; suddenly the opposite sex holds attraction instead of negativism. The youngster seeks opportunities to meet and be with the opposite sex in socially approved roles. "Crushes" and vague sexual sensations from stray stimuli are commonly reported at this stage.

In the college years, young adults date and enjoy the company of the opposite sex. Since some experiences in behavior with the opposite sex have been obtained in earlier adolescence, the young adult is somewhat more sophisticated in the matters of dating and courtship. Many young adults today report that the pressure for physical contact and sexual stimulation is great. Young adult females are more sexually aware in today's generation than in any previous generation, and young adults want to express their feelings and emotions rather than to inhibit them. The resultant petting, or as today's youth use the term, "making out," sometimes leads to strong emotional involvement and actual physical intercourse. Not all college youth are promiscuous. Various studies have indicated that there is probably no more active sexual involvement on campus today than in previous generations; but they are more vocal and open about it.

Pre-marital sexual intercourse in young adulthood often creates further adjustment problems. The couple may experience shame or guilt. Breaking up and going each other's way is often made more difficult. Unless marriage is seriously contemplated, premarital sex may have the effect of driving the young couple apart, rather than bringing them closer together.

With the advent of modern chemical contraceptives (the "pill"), the fear of pregnancy has been all but removed as a problem in sexual intercourse. The real problem today is one of morality. Many young adults feel it is hypocritical to expect the male to be sexually experienced and the female to be chaste. They justify their behavior as being more natural or more honest. Psychologically, however, there are still conflicts, moral doubts, shame, guilt feelings, and uncertainties. The very fact that there is fear that "someone may find out" points to the psychological uncertainties accompanying the new morality. Many young adults, completely independent on the college campus for the first time in their lives, mistake physical attraction and sexual urgencies for love. They often regret their behavior, but find that there is no way to eradicate their actions. Discussions with family become difficult or impossible, and the "generation gap" moves one notch further apart.

Another aspect of the rather free sexual behavior of today's college youth may be seen in the decline in influence of religious institutions. Today's youth do not want to be "told"; they want to form their own opinions based on fact. Since much in religion is based on faith and acceptance rather than fact, the religious institutions are a somewhat less powerful influence in the lives of many of today's young adults.

ADOLESCENT DEVELOPMENT

The United States stands alone among the civilized nations in the world in that it fosters the longest period of adolescence among its young. Today's youngster experiences a ten-year period of adolescence in slow stages of development, and the tendency in the United States is to prolong that development. In general, the longer the educational period lasts, the more prolonged the period of adolescence and the longer the delay prior to the assumption of adult responsibilities.

The start of adolescence is often equated with the start of puberty. A. Kinsey stated that puberty begins in the male with the first ejaculation, and in the female with the first menstruation. The concept of "adolescence" today encompasses more than the physical stages of development. The adolescent today is one who thinks and acts at a given level of maturity. Adolescence is a recognized psychological stage of development between childhood and adulthood. During this period of development the youngster undergoes tremendous changes in all aspects of his life: physical, social, emotional, and mental.

Psychologists agree that there are wide cultural variations in adolescent development. Many of the adjustment problems of the adolescent are indigenous to the culture in which he finds himself. In addition, he also undergoes numerous physical changes, some of which are obvious to the casual observer, and some not.

The physical changes which adolescents experience include: the development of secondary sex characteristics; the functioning of the endocrine glands and sex hormones; the onset of the menstrual and estrous cycles; an increase in height and weight, and a shaping of the body into adult-like proportions. Internal physical changes include the refinement of muscular coordination, changes in rate of respiration, changes in the circulatory system, changes in the bone structure, and glandular changes. These physical changes have ramifications upon the behavioral patterns of the adolescent. Indeed, it would be a strange phenomenon if they did not.

The mental development of the adolescent includes an increase in reasoning, the ability to concentrate for longer periods of time, the ability to memorize, the use of vivid imagery, and an increase in verbal skills. The vocabulary of the adolescent has increased, and with the increase there is an increase in verbalization. Adolescents seem ready for the challenges of the secondary school curriculum, with the changing of classes and the experiences of a wide variety of teachers and teaching methods.

Social and emotional development accompanies the above, as adolescents increase the range of their friendships, begin to question limits placed upon their behavior, display an interest in new events and worldly matters, and assume new responsibilities. Social-emotional development becomes evident as the adolescent is able to see the point of view of those who differ from him; as he becomes a bit more objective in self-evaluation; and as he begins to select realistic college goals.

ADOLESCENT EXPERIENCES

All human beings in the natural course of development from childhood to adulthood experience two kinds of events: common experiences and unique experiences.

Common experiences are those which seem to happen to almost everyone. Falling down and bruising a knee or elbow; feeling foolish because of an inept physical action; learning the proper table manners: these and many other events are called "common" experiences. Some common experiences become unique because of the way in which the individual interprets his experiences. Thus if a youngster falls and scrapes his knee (a common experience), the action may become unique if he goes into a catatonic state, becomes paralyzed with fear, and demands hospitalization, sympathy, and attention.

Unique experiences are those which do not happen to all individuals in quite the same way, or at all. For instance, not all people experience surgery as part of their development; the experience is a unique one with many psychological overtones. So, too, the death of a parent when one is young, a traumatic fire, unusual sexual experiences at an early age—are all unique experiences which effect the development of the adolescent and to some extent determine the kind of adult he will become.

It has often been stated that "Adolescents today are different." If they are, it is largely because they live in a society which is different from that of previous generations. Adolescents today have matured in an era of world unrest. They see change everywhere, some for the better, and some for the worse. They have known nothing but a cold war state since birth. Many of today's youngsters really aren't sure at all who the "enemy" is that we seem to be fighting. They have some vague conception of communism, but have had little or no formal exposure to its chief political, social, and philosophical tenets.

Young people today are concerned about the environment, social issues, ecology, poverty, race relations, the plight of urban areas, the energy crisis, the schools, and their futures. They are better informed and more aware than previous generations, and they are anxious and eager to help in the effecting of needed changes in the societal structure. They have lived through the dramatic shift from rural to urban life, and have begun to experience the effects of megalopian society. Theirs is an urban-suburban generation.

Young people today are not cognizant of the prejudice toward women of a few generations ago. They largely accept women as equals. Young adolescent girls experience a broader range of freedom than any previous generation. Adolescents have also grown up in the automobile age. The family car is an accepted reality, instead of a goal to be attained. Many adolescents have their own cars, and with it a greater sense of freedom and a wider range of possible activities.

Friction between parents and adolescents is common. We have come to relegate this friction to a part of what has been termed the "generation gap." Many sources of parental friction remain in the social area. Parents feel their offspring should be doing one thing, or should not be doing other things. Adolescents feel that they are ready and capable of choosing their own actions and activities. The differences in opinions and ideologies often remain unresolved.

ATTAINING ADULTHOOD

Adolescence has been described as a period of transition from childhood to adulthood, and we have indicated that this is a normal or usual stage in an individual's development. We have further indicated that the course of adolescent development is largely culturally determined. There are no sharp, definitive dividing lines between childhood and adolescence, or between adolescence and adulthood. Each stage merges imperceptibly with the next, and many of the behavior patterns of the earlier stages of development persist at least for a time into a later stage.

Just as there are differences in children and in their levels of maturity, so too there are differences in adults and in their levels of maturity. The biggest difference is that adulthood extends throughout one's lifetime. Even here, however, there are stages in adulthood which have been recognized as: early adulthood; middle age; old age (senior citizens); and senescence.

In general, early adulthood or young adulthood extends from ages twenty-one to forty; middle adulthood from ages forty to sixty (middle age); and old age from sixty on. Senescence occurs when the individual outlives the normal life expectancy. A whole field of psychology is devoted to the science of senescence and geriatrics which concern the problems of aging. Each phase of adulthood has its own adjustment problems, many of which cannot be fully appreciated by youth.

From the psychological point of view, adulthood can no more be said to begin at age twenty-one than adolescence at age thirteen. For just as adolescence is a characteristic way of behaving and thinking, so too adulthood is characterized by certain behavioral modes. The young adult faces the problems of marriage and adjusting to the husband-father, or wife-mother, role.

As adolescents mature into adults they face new responsibilities and challenges. They must now begin to plan for a home and family of their own, and it is sometimes at these stages that the young adult becomes aware of his philosophical weakness. Most young adults today plan for marriage and family. Percentagewise, the number of single adults has declined in the past several years, although there has been an increase in the number of divorces and separations. Perhaps the two factors are related, for the American ethic is still that of marriage and family.

People who reach the climacteric stage of development (old age) prefer the title of senior citizen. They object to being cast aside, and want to play an active role in their families and in social affairs. They long for the status which American society has to date denied them— that of wise advisor or respected senior citizen. This is a stage of adjustment as are all other stages in human development. The loss of physical prowess, changing family patterns and roles, the shift from parenthood to grandparenthood, loss of ambition, and the facing of the retirement years are all common adjustment problems of the elderly.

The end of adolescence used to be signalled by marriage. This is no longer true today. More and more today young people are judged to have reached adulthood when:

close family dependencies are severed;
the individual lives apart from family;
the individual becomes self-supporting;
the individual makes free and independent decisions.

A formerly held axiom stipulated that the ability to learn declines sharply in the adult years. The major deterrent to factual investigations of the relationship of age to the learning process lies in the fact that learning conditions for the adult are rarely, if ever, the same as they are in adolescence. Adults who are in school face difficulties in learning due to the necessity of maintaining a household and a family, economic responsibilities, worries over progeny, and other problems of day-to-day living. These concerns interfere with the learning process and the ability to concentrate making it difficult to measure the speed at which an adult learns. Many colleges have successful adult education programs; some, as indicated previously, have instituted special programs for mature adults returning to college to complete their educations or to take courses necessary for vocational advancement and training. At any rate, there is little or no evidence to support the conclusion that adulthood signals an abrupt decline in learning. Because of higher motivation and past experiences, many adults even surpass the young students in school achievement.

With its emphasis on youth and with an increasing young adult population, new trends are apparent in the United States. The demand for shorter work weeks and more leisure time is an example of these new trends. Also there is a trend in the United States today for younger marriages, more working women (marriages where both partners are employed on a full-time basis), and marriages where both members attend school in order to complete their education.

Young adulthood has traditionally been viewed as a time of achievement. It is the time when many young people marry, begin to raise a family, embark upon vocational careers, and face the problems of home management. In each of these phases of development, young adults face adjustment problems. The choice of marital partner, or the decision to marry itself, the choice of vocation and the difficulties in getting started, decisions with regard to having a family, and the problems of home management all require adjustments on the part of the young adult.

There is variation among adult development just as there is variation in children and adolescents. Psychologists have demonstrated that emotional maturity is not reached at a fixed point in time, but varies considerably with each individual, his experiences, his problems, and his methods for resolving problems. Adults do not simply reach adulthood and stagnate thereafter. People are constantly moving forward, away from the past, and toward the future. That is what it means to be alive.

WHAT WE HAVE LEARNED

1. Many young adults have been raised in sheltered environments, and college is often their first attempt to live on their own.
2. American society has been variously classified as patriarchal, matriarchal, pedarchal, and equalitarian.
3. The era of the patriarchal society in the United States has virtually disappeared.
4. Culture plays an important role in the development of the adolescent. Culture consists of many subcultures and these vary within a given environment.
5. Although Americans are generally reluctant to admit the existence of social classes, they do exist, and their composure and organization is complex, ranging from the lower-lower to the upper-upper class.
6. Most parents are concerned about the welfare of their children: they want their children to succeed; they want their children to attain a status higher than their own.
7. Most Americans are absorbed with "middle-class" standards of behavior and morality.
8. American children are generally sheltered and protected. They become accustomed to having their needs met, and take the presence of material belongings as a matter of fact.
9. The needs for identification and emancipation in adolescence are acquired, or social, needs.
10. The mode of expression for social needs is a highly individual and unique format.
11. Maslow's concept of self-actualization is an expression of the need for self-identification.
12. There are actually four "self" concepts: the real self, the future self, the social self, and the ideal self.
13. The emancipation of the adolescent in the process of maturation occurs in stages.
14. The process of emancipation leads to independence and self-sufficiency.

15. The American ethos tends to prolong the period of adolescence.
16. Adolescence has four definitive stages: pre-pubescence; pubescence; post-pubescence; and late adolescence or early adulthood.
17. In the process of maturation, new challenges and situations create new pressures and demands on the adolescent, causing the need for further adjustment.
18. Not all of the adjustments needed in college can be foreseen; many individuals experience unique and unusual situations which cannot be predicted or anticipated.
19. College students gain security and status from peer group associations; the affiliation motive is strong in young adults.
20. Heterosexual adjustments in adolescents proceed in the direction of greater attraction toward the opposite sex.
21. Adolescence and adulthood are defined in terms of psychological levels of behavior, rather than in terms of chronological ages.
22. Individuals experience both common and unique experiences; some common experiences can become unique because of individual interpretation.
23. Young adults today are more informed and concerned about social problems within the nation.
24. Adulthood has four stages: early adulthood; middle age; old age or senior citizen stage; and senescence.
25. Adulthood begins with economic independence, the severance of former family dependencies, marriage, and the start of one's own family.

WHAT WE STILL NEED TO LEARN

1. The American family is undergoing a rapid series of changes. The evolutionary process is moving away from a patriarchy toward an equalitarian family structure. New formats need to be developed for the effective functioning of the family unit within this frame of reference.
2. Social class distinctions and barriers need to be overcome so that all young adults have an equal opportunity, regardless of race, religion, or place of birth within the United States.
3. The family and the maturing adolescent must learn how to develop an effective dialogue in order to prevent the kinds of alienation seen today in the "generation gap."
4. Adolescents maturing into adulthood need to attain a more prominent position within the societal structure. They need a voice and an opportunity to display their positive talents.

5. Young adults need to be better prepared for some of the more commonly experienced problems as they attempt to live alone for the first time in their lives as part of campus life.
6. Traumatic events within the family of an unforeseen nature can cause havoc in the life of the young adult. Maturing adolescents need to be better prepared for the unexpected; they need to develop an attitude and a means to cope with tragedy.
7. High school graduates should be better prepared for the much stronger competitive nature of peers in college, both academically and socially.
8. The present state of evolving morality leaves many young adults confused and perplexed. Some definitive posture along the lines of sexual development for young adults needs to be taken.
9. The older generation need to accept youth as they are, not as they would like them to be; for youth today is different, and trying to fit them into preconceived molds simply will not work.
10. There is a need to recognize that there are stages in adulthood, and that adults encounter numerous adjustment problems, just as do adolescents.

SUGGESTIONS FOR FURTHER READING

Berelson, Bernard, and Gary A. Steiner, *Human Behavior*, New York: Harcourt, Brace and World, Inc., 1964.

Bindra, D., *Motivation*, New York: The Ronald Press, Inc., 1959.

Brown, J. S., *The Motivation of Behavior*, New York: McGraw-Hill, 1961.

Byrne, Dann, *Introduction to Personality*, Englewood Cliffs, New Jersey: Prentice-Hall, Inc., 1966.

Cantwell, Zita M. and Pergrouhi N. Svajian, Editors, *Adolescence: Studies in Development*, Ithaca, Ill.: F. E. Peacock Publishers, Inc., 1974.

Crowne, Lesile Joan, *Adjustment Problems of College Freshmen*, New York: Columbia University Teacher's College, 1955.

Dennis, L. E., and J. F. Kauffman, *College and the Student*, Washington, D.C.: American Council on Education, 1966.

Douvan, Elizabeth, and J. Adelson, *The Adolescent Experience*, New York: John Wiley and Sons, Inc., 1966.

Garrison, Roger H., *The Adventure of Learning in College*, New York: Harper and Row, 1959.

Goldstein, Joseph, Anna Freud and Albert J. Solnit, *Beyond the Best Interests of the Child*, Riverside, New Jersey: The Free Press, 1973.

Gorlow, L., and W. Katkvosky, *Readings in the Psychology of Adjustment,* New York: McGraw-Hill, 1959.

Hall, J. F., *Psychology of Motivation,* Philadelphia, Pa.: J. B. Lippincott, 1961.

Lindner, R., *Must You Conform?* New York: Holt, Rinehart & Winston, 1962.

Lugo, James O. and Gerald L. Hershey, *Human Development—A Multidisciplinary Approach to the Psychology of Individual Growth,* Riverside, New Jersey: Macmillan Publishing Co., Inc., 1974.

Reisman, David, et al., *The Lonely Crowd,* New Haven, Conn.: Yale University Press, 1950.

Rokeach, Milton, *The Nature of Human Values,* Riverside, New Jersey: The Free Press, 1973.

Streib, Gordon F., Ed., *The Changing Family: Adaptation and Diversity,* Reading, Mass.: Addison-Wesley Publishing Company, 1973.

Ziller, R. C., *The Social Self,* Elmsford, New York: Pergamon Press, Inc., 1973.

7

The Nature of Adolescence and Young Adulthood

- The psychological view of adolescence and young adulthood
- Adolescent development: Physical changes
- Physique and temperament: Physical body types
- Changes in adolescent behavior: Sources of conflict
- Sexual problems of the developing adolescent
- The disturbed adolescent: Kinds of psychological treatment
- The problem of adolescent suicide and suicidal attempts
- Moving from adolescence to adulthood: The concept of adescence
- Recent trends on the American scene
- The concept of adulthood: Some adult problems
- What We Have Learned
- What We Still Need to Learn
- Suggestions for Further Reading

PURPOSE OF THIS CHAPTER

The psychological view of adolescence and adulthood differs in several ways from the popular conceptions held by many individuals. In this chapter some of the theories of adolescence which attempt to account for the numerous developmental changes typified by this stage of development will be examined. The physical changes in adolescence will be detailed along with the expected behavioral changes.

The major problems of the maturing adolescent will also be discussed. Included in this chapter are the problems involving his sexual maturation, plus a discussion of the suicidal adolescent and the deviant adolescent, from a point of view which will indicate the typical behavioral patterns of a disturbed young adult. As the adolescent approaches adulthood, some of the adjustment problems indigenous to this stage of development will be examined, as well as some of the more recent trends on the American scene.

The concluding portion of this chapter will examine the question: "What Is an Adult?" from the point of view of the maturing adolescent who is becoming an adult. The dynamics and the psychological adjustment mechanisms will be examined in order to help explain the behavior of the maturing adolescent and the young adult by way of looking further at the "Nature of Adolescence and Young Adulthood."

PSYCHOLOGISTS VIEW ADOLESCENT DEVELOPMENT

Psychologists attempt to explain the nature of the changes which occur during adolescence on the basis of several different theoretical constructs. While the theories differ in several aspects, most psychologists agree on several principles:

(1) The chronology assigned to the adolescent years is somewhat artificial, since there is a wide variation in development and maturity.
(2) Most psychologists consider adolescence as starting at approximately age ten or eleven and terminating anywhere from ages eighteen to twenty-one, depending upon the psychological maturity of the individual.
(3) The adolescent stage is characterized best as a manner of thinking and behaving.
(4) Adolescence is transitional in nature, reflecting the period of years between childhood and adulthood.

While adolescence is a universal phenomenon, its format and characteristics vary considerably from culture to culture, and within a given culture in the various subcultures indigenous to the given environment.

Historically, one of the earliest attempts to explain the changes and nature of adolescence was that of G. Stanley Hall in the late 1800's. (Of course, one could go back to the ancient philosophers such as Aristotle and Plato, and excerpt some of their precepts concerning the state of adolescence, as well as turning to literature, such as Shake-speare; however, only a few of these theories which seem to have had a profound and lasting effect within the United States in the past half-century are presented here.) Hall's theory is known as the concept of "Ontogeny Recapitulates Phylogeny." In brief, this concept has it that in the development of the individual may be seen a repetition of the history of the entire human race. Thus, in early adolescence, the individual is roughly analagous in behavior to the cave-man: he is wild, untamed, uncivilized, and dominated by physical needs. It is an era of the survival of the fittest. Hall likens young adulthood to the more modern era of civilization. The theory is little accepted today, and is presented here for historical perspective. Nevertheless the pioneer work of G. Stanley Hall did lay the groundwork for other theories to follow.

William McDougall believed that adolescence and adolescent be-havior represented an instinctive phase of development, so that all adolescents could be expected to behave and respond in identical fashion. The theory has been discredited largely by the evident facts of differences in adolescent behavior as observed in various parts of the world.

Myers and Sidis felt that adolescence represented the "ripening" of a new self; somewhat related to the child as the caterpillar is related to the butterfly. While one cannot spring from the other without the former stage of development, they felt that the emergent individual was so different from the former as to be a "new self." Modern theories of adolescence hold that the relationship between childhood and adolescence is a much stronger and closer tie.

Eclectic theory is a synthesis of the several elements found in other theories. Modern day humanistic psychologists are eclectic; that is, instead of holding to one theory or another they accept elements from each, rejecting various aspects of each theory, and formulating a compounded theory made up of the selected aspects of the other precepts.

The individual-social-cultural-hypothesis is a developmental the-ory of adolescence which is widely held today. This theory states that the individual is responsible for his actions and behavior, albeit he is conditioned by the facts of his environment and culture. The theory is the most widely accepted in psychology today. There are other theories of adolescence, such as the Psychoanalytic theory, Role the-ory, and Behaviorism, but suffice it to say that psychologists have attempted an objective interpretation and analysis of adolescent be-havior with some degree of agreement and success.

Most psychologists also agree that girls mature earlier than boys, that puberty signifies the beginning of the physical changes in adolescence, that the more civilized the culture the longer the period of adolescence and that the end of adolescence is signified by the assumption of adult responsibilities rather than by a stated chronological age. The profound and numerous changes which occur in adolescence include physical, social, emotional, and mental changes.

PHYSICAL CHANGES IN ADOLESCENCE

The physical changes the adolescent undergoes are generally observable and have a distinct effect on his behavior. One has only to consider the behavior of the individual who is ill as contrasted with the behavior of the same person when he is at his physical prime to acknowledge how dramatic a part one's physical condition plays in behavioral manifestations. With the numerous physical changes which occur in adolescence, it is small wonder that there are concomitant behavioral changes.

The less-evident internal changes in adolescence include glandular changes, changes in the circulatory and respiratory systems, increase in lung capacity, refinements in manipulative skills, the development of greater muscular co-ordination, the acquisition of permanent molars, and changes in bone structure.

The more obvious changes in physical structure include the lowering of the voice, the onset of pubic hair, the development of the sex organs, the development of the secondary sex characteristics, the onset of the menstrual cycle, an increase in height and weight along with a shaping of the body to adult contours, and the obvious increase in physical capacity to perform for longer periods of time as indicated by athletic skills and the lessening need for sleep.

Physical changes in adolescence ordinarily occur in girls somewhat sooner than in boys; boys tend to "catch up" to the girls in late adolescence and early adulthood. Until recently, certain physical changes in adolescence (e.g., the lowering of the voice) were "reserved for males only"; other changes were thought to occur in girls only (breast development and menstrual cycle). Yet while the breasts of boys do not develop in the same way as in girls, there is nevertheless a "breast" development in young males in terms of the loss of baby fat and in the development of the masculine chest.

While one does not ordinarily think of the menstrual cycle in terms of the male, psychologists have indicated that the accompanying emotional overtones can often be found in the male—tension, nervousness, anxiety, irritability, and tenseness—in a cyclical pattern which parallels that of the female.

Psychologists William H. Sheldon and Ernest Kretschmer have attempted to classify individuals on the basis of their physical structure (body type) and to relate these factors to personality. Thus we have the concepts of:

The fat person (overweight)	= pyknic	= endomorphic body type
The thin person (underweight)	= asthenic	= ectomorphic body type
The mixed body type	= dysplastic	
The perfect body type	= athletic	

These categories, and the popular interpretation associated with them, have contributed much toward confusing the lay public. The old cliches about the fat man being jolly and the thin man being nervous have led to a further broadening, so that popularly the red head is equated with being fiery tempered, etc. Almost all of these interpretations bastardize the original theory, and have tended to overextend it fallaciously.

Some of the accompanying physical development of the adolescent have overtones for definitive behavioral patterns. The need for sleep in early adolescence, the nervous supply of energy later, the ravenous and then finicky appetite, the active participation in sports (although in the United States girls are still encouraged to be observers rather than participants), and the more acute muscular refinements leading to higher skills such as automobile driving and scuba diving, are examples of behaviors which stem rather directly from newly acquired physical prowess and development.

As the reader can readily note, there are many physical developments in adolescence. Still, we have not as yet touched upon one of the most important: acne. The facial blemishes and pimples associated with adolescence virtually dominate the life of certain adolescents today. His diet is watched carefully (common foods such as chocolates and peanuts are avoided), his skin is carefully cleansed, numerous ointments and creams are purchased and used profusely, all in an attempt to control the problem of acne. The interpretation of the seriousness of the condition is highly individual. Some adolescents adjust fairly well, while for others the condition makes life close to unbearable.

Related to physical and mental development in adolescence is the awakening of sexual drives. In the male, the hormone testosterone becomes active: the male is now capable of reproduction. In the female the hormone estrogen becomes active and ovulation occurs: the female is now capable of reproduction. Along with the primary sex characteristics, secondary sex characteristics develop: pubic hair, underarm hair, lowering of the voice, etc. Each male has a small amount of female hormone, and each female has a small amount of male hormone. This is a natural state, but has led some to the false conclusion that homosexuality and other forms of sexual deviation are simply the result of hormonal (endocrine) imbalance. The problem is not so simple. Indeed, if it were primarily a physical problem, hormone treatment might be an effective cure. But the problem is both physical and mental, as are most sexual aberrations.

CHANGES IN ADOLESCENT BEHAVIOR

Just as there are vast and profound physical changes occurring in adolescence, so too there are numerous behavioral changes occurring concomitantly. Important as these changes are, they should be kept in proper perspective. Profound changes in behavior occur in all stages of human development. Consider the changes in infancy as the youngster learns to walk and talk, two tremendous achievements; or the changes in childhood, as the child learns to read; or the changes in limited physical capacity which occur in senescence—all of these have tremendous impact upon the life-style and behavior of the individual. In short the tremendous impact of change in adolescence is largely a myth; changes occur in all stages of human development.

Adolescents develop their own unique form of communication, or language. In every decade in American history, adolescents have developed their own form of communication with its unique vocabulary and meanings. It is as if they were trying to shut out the adult world from their world. Consider the "zoot suiters," the "beeboppers," and the "beatniks"—all had their own special language. Not surprisingly, adolescents today also use a form of communication with each other that most adults find difficult to comprehend. Yet with the passage of a relatively few short years, a new generation will appear on the horizon and a new vocabulary will develop. The phenomenon occurs with regularity.

Each generation of adolescents has its own unique characteristics and behavior patterns. It has been said that the current generation is "different." Of course it is, and this is a good thing. The present generation is different from previous ones because they have matured under different circumstances, have different problems, and different points of view. The adolescents of the 1930's were the products of a depression; this generation is not. The adolescents of the 1940's were the products of a world at war; this generation is not. The adolescents of the 1950's were largely silent and unconcerned; this generation is not. The adolescents of the 1960's, particularly the late 1960's, became vocal, demonstrative, and concerned. No doubt future generations of adolescents will have, as a group, their own unique characteristics and attributes (the "streakers" appeared first in 1974).

Young adults and adolescents today are the product of a tremendous urbanization which has taken place in the United States in the past several years. The trend for the future is toward more and more centralization in large city populated areas. But we have not begun to solve many of the problems of the cities: lack of energy sources; air and water pollution; slum areas; poor schooling; high taxation; racial prejudice; political inequities, etc. The present generation of adolescents is not only concerned about these matters and seeks to do something about them, but they are in a hurry. They want changes and they want them now.

The present generation of adolescents have lived through a decade or more of "cold war" which most of them do not understand and think unjust. They are products of world unrest, world tension, and rapidly changing global conditions. They have accepted the realities, but not the necessity for the existence, of many of these situations. They seek change; they want a voice in their own future; they are more interested in politics, local and international, and they have a kind of altruism missing from previous generations.

The status of women, including adolescent girls, has undergone radical changes in the past several years, comparable perhaps only to the changes which occurred as women were given the franchise (the right to vote) in the 1920's. Today's adolescent girl undoubtedly has more freedom than her predecessors. Although some women still feel there is inequality in the treatment of the sexes, more progress in the direction of freedom and equality has been made in the past generation than in the past half-century.

Adolescents of the present generation have matured in an age of rapidly changing moral standards. Indeed they themselves have contributed to the accelerated pace of these changes by their insistence upon being more candid and honest in matters concerning morality and ethics. They have also spearheaded the drive toward more open and natural sexual expression. Evidence of this can be seen in the movie industry, clothing styles, manner of speech, and rebellion against oppressive rules and regulations. Every social institution—the church, politics, and the schools—has felt the wave of the new morality and its effects.

Adolescents of today, then, reflect in their behavior patterns many of the changes within our socity. They are: more alert and responsive; better informed and knowledgeable; concerned about others; altruistic; and impatient.

The physical and social changes that have been described here do not occur in isolation, but are accompanied by emotional and intellectual changes as well. There is an increase, or broadening, in many of the mental capabilities of the adolescent, comparable to the tremendous mental accomplishments of reading and writing a language in early childhood. Yet too often the mental development of the adolescent is overshadowed by the obvious physical changes and the changes in social behavior.

Adolescents find that they are in possession of new-found mental capabilities, and that some of their former childhood abilities have changed. For example, they can concentrate for longer periods of time, but are subject to being more easily distracted; they can memorize more material, but often dislike the chore; their reasoning and imaginative powers are increased; and they are more verbal, although often this is directed toward peers; their attention span is increased, although here again they can be readily distracted.

By the time a youngster reaches adolescence most parents find that physical means of punishment (hitting, slapping, spanking) are no longer effective. Simply put, the youngster is physically too large. One of the anomalies of adolescence is that just at the time the parent is turning to verbal means of discipline (reasoning), the adolescent himself has reached a stage where *his* powers of reasoning have increased to the point where he is perfectly willing to argue with his parents, debating small and large issues, and often logically out-reasoning the parent.

Adolescence is a stage of "positive-negativisms." By this it is meant that behavior fluctuates from the positive to the negative and from the negative to the positive in rapid sequence. Behavior is at one moment poised and self-confident and at the next inadequate and self-doubting. In other words, behavior fluctuates fairly rapidly from maturity to immaturity, reflecting the "in-between" nature of this stage of development—neither yet an adult, nor any longer a child. These kinds of changes make an adolescent's adjustment in his home and school life more difficult for himself, his parents, and his peers. Many of the problems encountered result in frustration and conflict which is ordinarily resolved in adolescence, but which may persist in various forms into adulthood.

MAJOR SOURCES OF CONFLICT IN ADOLESCENCE

While the adolescent is undergoing the physical, social, and mental changes which have been enumerated, he is also experiencing a series of emotional changes coupled with the mental changes which often result in conflict and frustration. While each developmental stage has its own crises or conflicts, the adolescent stage is unique in that its conflicts, if not resolved, will persist into adulthood and perhaps on into the rest of the individual's adult life, causing further difficulties and adjustments. Often school counselors, church officials, and family (adult) friends can be a source of aid and comfort to the adolescent trying to resolve these tensions. Certainly all too often the parent is the last to be consulted for advice and help.

Some of the more typical adolescent problems include the desire for independence at a time when the adolescent is still very much dependent upon his family for physical support and his daily needs; the desire for sexual experiences at a time when society states that this is immoral, illegal, or unacceptable; the feeling of resentment toward authority figures when he is at a stage of exposure to more authority figures than in childhood (teachers, police, parents, school officials, etc.); and the need for adult guidance and direction when he is least willing to accept that advice.

Adolescents commonly experience sexual arousal from stray stimuli, and are often perplexed at their own bodily reactions to these sensations. The problem is compounded by lack of factual information and a confusing standard of behavior. The interests of the adolescent are changing in heterosexual directions, including dating, dancing, parties, and club activities. These wholesome interests require direction on the part of the adolescent, and taking a direction requires decision. Often the adolescent is ambivalent as to the proper course to pursue. He likes to date, but may feel awkward and uncomfortable in some situations; he doesn't know how to proceed sexually although he is interested in the opposite sex; he enjoys club activities but may become involved instead in gang membership; he enjoys group participation but sometimes feels like staying away from the group; and he likes going to parties but sometimes feels bored when he is there. The ambivalent nature of adolescence is a factor in adolescent conflict.

The adolescent is faced with the need to abandon immature ways of behaving and expressing himself, but often he doesn't know how. He must face the problem of re-organizing himself as he is faced with new challenges in school, new time schedules, and new demands upon his time and himself. He must begin to assume some of the adult responsibilities on his own, but he isn't quite certain that his behavior is proper.

As the adolescent nears the end of his secondary school years, he is again faced with a series of potential conflicts. Making decisions regarding college, making vocational and career plans, and other such decisions all come at a time when the adolescent is in a crucial stage of maturation. For he is not yet an adult, and often his behavior regresses to a very childlike level. Perhaps the regression, usually only fleeting, is an expression of escapism from the tensions and pressures he is facing as he faces maturity.

The ambivalent nature of adolescent behavior is often confusing to parents. One moment they are talking to a young adult who wants to use the family automobile; the next minute the youngster is playing with some childhood toy and behaving in other immature ways. In these circumstances, parental discipline of the adolescent often becomes erratic, compounding the adjustment problems of the adolescent himself.

Some of the more common day-to-day problems which face the adolescent (and, therefore, even if indirectly, his family) include:

Problems of dress and appearance	School problems
Forming friendships	The use of leisure time
Dating	Family inter-relationships
The use of the automobile	Sibling rivalry
The need for money	Day-to-day routine disagreements

SEX PROBLEMS OF THE ADOLESCENT

The sexual problems in adolescence cover a broad spectrum as youngsters find themselves undergoing an "awakening" of new-found sexual attractions and interests. The former antagonism between the sexes, so characteristic of childhood years, rapidly dissipates and is replaced by an uncomfortable feeling of enjoyment in the presence of the opposite sex. Much of the myth of adolescent awkwardness and clumsiness stems from inept social posture at the start of heterosexual relationships. In general, girls mature earlier than boys and become sexually aware and interested in boys before boys have achieved a similar status. The fourteen-year-old girl is probably more woman-like in appearance than child-like, but the counterpart in the boy is not true. The fourteen-year-old boy in appearance is still very much a boy.

The sexual development of the adolescent passes through stages. While not all adolescents experience each phase, the general pattern is:

Pre-adolescence	Antagonism between the sexes
Puberty-adolescence	Girls more interested in boys than vice versa
Post-adolescence	Group parties; some dating; antagonism between sexes beginning to disappear
Young Adulthood	Dating; going steady; making future plans

Adulthood	Engagement and marriage; raising a family

While the problems of sexual adjustment are by no means unusual in adolescence, individuals may experience deep concerns over real or imagined sexual problems. Many adolescents experience self-doubt; they think themselves "abnormal," "queer," "homosexual," or "perverted" because of feelings and actions which they have experienced. While talking about sexual matters is no longer a social taboo, many adolescents find it difficult or impossible to communicate their repressed feelings to others.

The sexual adjustment problems of adolescents today differ in several respects from the problems of previous generations. In general, adolescents today are:

Exposed to sexual matters at an earlier age
Less inhibited by social mores and tradition
More communicative with their peers
Maturing at a faster pace than previous generations

The heterosexual adjustment of the adolescent proceeds from a recognition of the opposite sex to attraction to the opposite sex to feeling secure when in the presence of the opposite sex, and, finally, to actively seeking opportunities to join with the opposite sex in social situations.

Many factors have combined in the past several years leading to the more sexually stimulating and provocative situations in which adolescents and young adults find themselves. There is more open acceptance of public expressions of sex, such as hugging and kissing; boys and girls who are more knowledgeable and informed in many other areas tend to seek sexual activities at an earlier age today than in previous generations.

Most adolescents pass through a phase in their sexual development where self-doubt about their sexuality is common. Young men wonder if they are effeminate or homosexual; girls wonder if they are feminine enough. Common too is a feeling of perversion when stray sexual stimuli arouse feelings that are difficult to control. The problem of autoeroticism or masturbation in adolescence is more indigenous to the male than to the female. Societal taboos against several sexual practices make it difficult to discuss these matters and the adolescent finds himself living with guilt feelings, self-doubt, and anxiety.

Notwithstanding all of the so-called "modern" approaches to informing the adolescent on sexual matters, it is still true that adolescents are misinformed or ignorant about many sexual matters. There is surely a connection between the fact that the chief source of sexual information for the adolescent comes from his peers and the increasing spread of venereal disease in the United States.

Sexual pressures and taboos are largely societal pressures. Great Britain recently repealed its legal sanctions against homosexuality, and today treats the problem as a medical problem, so that the "offender" receives treatment instead of imprisonment. Unfortunately the United States is still far from an enlightened approach in the treatment of adolescents classified as "sexual deviates." (Recently, however, some mental hospitals instituted departments to treat the psychological problems of the sexually disturbed adolescent.)

In the process of sexual maturation on college campuses, young adults find new experiences and new challenges. Often they must face the test of their own moral standards. They make up their own minds about inter-racial dating or dating those of other religions and philosophies, as well as decide for themselves how much sexual activity in which they will engage. The former deterrents to actual intercourse—fear of pregnancy, religion, and lack of opportunity—are now largely removed.

Contraceptive devices are widely available to young adults. With the advent of the automobile, the widespread availability of motels, apartments, and on-campus living quarters, there is ample opportunity for sexual practice. The matter, then, becomes one of individual choice. The question "Do I have the sufficient moral fiber to resist the physical pressures and sexual stimulation to which I am exposed?" is a very real one.

Many young people today feel that active engagement in premarital sex is a part of life, no different from going to school or working. The problem is the guilt feelings and anxieties one may experience after engaging in these activities. Further, the actual act of intercourse under these circumstances is often performed furtively, because of fear of discovery, leading to disappointment and disillusionment. The active engagement in overt sexual practices prior to marriage often drives young people apart; where it does not, there are often nagging, lingering doubts, tensions, and anxieties which persist.

THE DISTURBED ADOLESCENT

The student may be somewhat surprised to learn that only recently have we become aware of the existence of disturbed adolescents and their need for help. For a long time their problems and themselves, as a group, were totally ignored. The symptoms of disturbance were largely attributed to broad categories such as immaturity, lack of experience, or delinquency. The fact that an adolescent could have emotional and mental problems was simply not taken seriously. Today, however, there is a growing awareness that there are disturbed adolescents and that they do need psychological help. Yet the facilities for aiding these young people remain inadequate.

For years the difficulty lay in the fact that many of the symptoms of emotional disturbance were so similar to the patterns of usual adolescent development that it was difficult or impossible to separate the two. It is true that many of the patterns of the disturbed adolescent resemble closely those of the adolescent who is not disturbed, but there are differences in quantitative and qualitative aspects. Disturbed adolescents are categorized today as "exceptional youth" and it is recognized that they need psychological help.

The symptoms of the youngster with problems sufficient to warrant professional help are varied. They include physical, mental, emotional, and social patterns which can be described as "deviant." The physical symptoms include such behaviors as refusing to eat, nausea, vomiting, frequent headaches, extreme changes in weight, tics, extreme fatigue, speech disturbances, fainting, and dizzy spells.

While any of these symptoms, in isolation, may at one time or another appear in any adolescent, it is their continued or prolonged appearance, in combination, and with regularity of occurrence that leads to the conclusion of disturbance.

Emotionally, the disturbed adolescent may find it difficult to communicate; have few or no friends; rebel against authority to the point where he sees no reason for any limitations being placed upon his behavior; and undergo a lack of interest, which results in apathy. Apathetic behavior, or complete lack of interest and lack of response, is one of the key emotional symptoms in diagnosing disturbance in adolescence.

Socially, the adolescent who is disturbed may be very shy or withdrawn (or the opposite can occur, as in gang memberships). The youngster also may be preoccupied with the use of scatalogisms, he may fail in school, cutting classes or even dropping out, and he will probably refuse to accept responsibility. Mental patterns of abnormality are also in evidence: he is easily distracted, unable to concentrate, or may experience any one of a number of "manias" or "phobias" (e.g., kleptomania or phonophobia—fear of speaking outloud), and even partial amnesia, agnosia (inability to perceive relationships clearly) and aphasia (partial blockage of speech and thought patterns).

None of the above stated symptoms occur in isolation, but rather in combination, to form patterns which have been termed "syndromes." These patterns are quite diverse, so that it is not possible at the present time to say that a given set of symptoms will cause a given type of disturbance. Prognosis is still in the infancy stage.

The first step in helping the disturbed adolescent is recognizing the fact that he needs help. Often the youngster himself will deny the situation or resist assistance. In this case, it is up to the parent, the school official, the family physician, relatives and friends, or sometimes even the court to recognize the young man or woman's need. The family must be willing to get professional help.

Professional treatment centers are often found in connection with universities or hospitals. More and more large universities have centers for the treatment of youngsters with problems, and more and more large hospitals have formed psychiatric departments. Treatment proceeds along the lines of diagnosis, treatment, prognosis, and follow-up care. The person helping may be a psychiatrist, psychologist, or trained counselor. There are many forms of treatment to aid disturbed youngsters. While the specifics of each form of treatment will be discussed in more detail in Chapter Ten, the chief aim of each form of therapy may be briefly stated:

Family Therapy	A re-orientation of each member of the family group, in some cases involving in-laws and grandparents.
Psychotherapy—Individual	An intensive look into the development of an individual over an extended period of time.
Psychotherapy—Group	A gaining in positive mental attitude through insights into the behavior and problems of others.
Drug (Chemo) Therapy	The use of tranquilizers and other drugs to achieve a desired physical status.
Electrotherapy	Employed with limited usefulness, and not in general, the technique involves electric shocks.
Somatic Therapy	Through diet and bodily care, a building up of the physical in order to control the social, mental, and emotional states.
Adjunctive Therapy	The use of games, vocational tests, machine shop work, occupational and recreational therapy.
Occupational Therapy	The teaching of useful and employable skills.
Physical Therapy	The use of water treatments, swimming, exercises, etc., in order to im-

	prove the overall physical tone and to change the mental and emotional outlook.
Recreational Therapy	A form of release therapy wherein one can release tensions and anxieties in socially approved recreation such as golf, tennis, and swimming.
Educational Therapy	A development of mental skills in specific areas to overcome handicaps and disabilities.
Work Therapy	A change in occupation involving new skills and techniques which will be less harmful to an individual.
Milieu Therapy	A change of habit, social patterns, and family living or structure; sometimes requires a re-location into new neighborhoods.

There are other forms of therapy which have not been mentioned, such as behavior therapy (a change in specific kinds of action-modification), hydrotherapy (alternating warm and cool baths to sooth and calm the individual), and sensitivity groups (a group structure where the individual may lose some of his inhibitions and feelings of self-doubt and self-recrimination), logotherapy and primal therapy.

Probably the two most common forms of disturbance in the adolescent concern rebellion against authority (See Section III, Chapter Thirteen) and depression. Adolescents who are seriously disturbed sometimes become very seclusive and depressed. They keep to themselves, refuse to leave their rooms, become apathetic, morose, and brooding. Their thoughts remain unto themselves; they often contemplate or attempt suicide. (Until rather recently, the problems of potential suicide, suicide attempts that are unsuccessful, and the adolescent who actually does commit suicide have been relatively ignored.)

ADOLESCENT SUICIDE

Adolescence is a time of decision and a time of anxiety. While many adolescents worry too much, and some worry needlessly, others become moody and brood. The youngster who habitually is joyless, brooding, irritable, and morose may or may not be a potential suicide. The symptoms overlap between the deviant and the usual forms and patterns of behavior. This makes the anticipation of the problem arising even more difficult. All too often the signs are not recognized until after the fact of suicide. But then, of course, it is too late.

Depression is a common symptom of the potential suicide. The youngster may be morose for a long period of time, brood about relatively minor incidents, become apathetic, choose to spend most of his time alone, and express a great deal of self-doubt and worry. Part of the problem may be his lack of achievement; part of the problem lies in the necessity to postpone success until some future time. Many adolescents feel incapable and inadequate; all too often they meet nothing but negativism from their teachers at school and their parents at home. The constant nagging of which adolescents complain is frequently a simple "putting down" process which many parents are not fully aware of doing.

Adolescents frequently worry or express concern over such problems as school achievements, school marks, problems with peers, sexual matters, self-consciousness, inabilities to achieve in athletics, lack of ability (real or imagined lacks), and guilt feelings. Often the youngster becomes very angry and expresses this anger by directing it inwardly. The ultimate form of this anger is the attempt at suicide or self-destruction.

Many investigators in the field of adolescent suicide believe that the adolescent never really intends the act to cause his own death, but uses it as an extreme measure in his attempt to gain attention and help for his anxieties. Other explanations for attempted adolescent suicide center about guilt feelings, the need to be with a deceased parent, the need to punish oneself for felt or real guilts, and the psychotic reaction to imaginary voices commanding attempted self-destruction.

Studies have indicated that school concerns and school pressures create a climate conducive to attempts at suicides by adolescents and young adults. Various colleges have conducted studies which indicate that attempts at suicide increase at final examination time. Other investigators have indicated causative factors such as home and family problems, economic problems, and self-inadequacies.

Many research investigators point out that adolescent suicide is rarely a spontaneous action; often the adolescent has been thinking about the matter for some time prior to the initial attempt. Many feel that the suicidal adolescent is neurotic, or even a borderline, if undiagnosed, psychotic. Recent attempts at coping with the problem have included the establishment of suicide control centers, where "hot lines" are available twenty-four hours a day, and adolescents and young adults contemplating suicide can telephone for help. The staff of these centers include religious and psychological personnel, and personnel trained in counseling and psychiatry. Most of the centers are staffed on a voluntary basis, although some have local funding and municipal support. The United States is in the process of establishing a National Suicide Prevention and Control Board. Part of its duties will include research on the problem, so that perhaps a better and more accurate indicator of the action which is about to occur before the act is performed can be obtained.

The general consensus seems to be that the problem of the potential suicide can largely be prevented with positive action. The first step involves the recognition of the seriousness of the problem by family and school personnel with whom the adolescent is in contact. Counseling and therapy hold promise for treatment and, if the youngster is willing to accept treatment and his family is willing to co-operate, prognosis is good.

The tragedy of the loss of human life by suicide is compounded when the loss of that life is a young person, whose productive and useful years lie beyond him. Who knows how many potentially productive individuals have been lost through the tragedy of suicide? Statistics are unreliable, for they cannot include the unreported attempts at suicide, the suicides which are not reported as such, but instead are listed as "accidents," and the suicides which are attributed to factors such as disease and illness when in actuality they were acts of self-destruction.

FROM ADOLESCENCE TO ADULTHOOD

The process of going from adolescence to adulthood is a slow, meticulous, almost agonizing series of imperceptible changes. The youngster goes from immaturity to maturity through a series of advances and regressions. The parent sees hopeful signs of positive behavior, only to realize that the youngster is not as mature as he thought when the childlike behavior characteristic of immaturity re-appears. There are several recognized stages in going from late adolescence to adulthood. These stages include: Pre-pubescence; pubescence; post-pubescence; late adolescence or young adulthood; and adulthood.

There may be yet another stage heretofore unrecognized. This state, occurring between late adolescence and adulthood, might be termed "Adescence." The young adult in this "in-between" stage is an "Adescent." Such a person is well into the young adult years, but is not yet an adult. Characteristically he is still vacillating; the stage of maturity characteristic of adulthood has not become finalized or definitive; and he often lapses into adolescent-like patterns of behavior.

These lapses are a natural part of development, although they are often frustrating to parents and confusing to the young adult himself. For if adolescence is a period of transition or change, so too is the period from adolescence to adulthood. The term adolescent itself comes from the Latin, meaning literally "to ripen." Its modern meaning has been interpreted as "growing up." If the adolescent is growing up, he is growing up into adulthood. Just as the infant must learn to creep and crawl before he can walk, and even then there are times when he falls uncertainly, so too, the adolescent must advance into adulthood by small steps and imperceptible changes, with some accompanying uncertainties.

In the United States, the period between adolescence and adulthood is extended by the prolongation of the educational process in college, combining economic dependency, the postponement of the assumption of adult responsibilities, and, in many cases, the postponement of marital plans. The student should not be misled into thinking that once adulthood has been attained life's problems are thereby terminated. Each stage has its own unique adjustment problems, and adults have their own unique set of problems with which to cope. Adults must face, among other problems, those of marriage, adjusting to new family relationships, starting a family of their own, vocational success or failure, economic problems, sexual adjustments to mates, religious problems, and problems of involvement with society. Ultimately, they face problems of waning physical vigor, a leveling off of aspirations, and being satisfied with the status quo.

There are a great many individual differences in adulthood, just as there are individual differences in all other stages of development. From the psychological point of view, some people never attain adulthood, regardless of their chronological age. For adulthood implies a level of maturity which some persons never reach. Although legally one is considered an adult at a given chronological age, psychologically they may remain forever adolescents. Although adulthood extends throughout the rest of one's lifetime, it too has stages. Individuals vary in their degree of acceptance of adult responsibilities and relationships, some slipping into "second childhood," others refusing to admit the onset of middle age, and still others reacting in considerably more mature fashion.

THE AMERICAN SCENE—RECENT TRENDS

The developing adolescent is at least partly a product of the social forces surrounding him, forces over which he has little or no control. Recent years have seen a shift in the direction of emphasis upon higher education. When one considers that fifty years ago the goal of the adolescent was to leave school as soon as possible and enter the job market, then one can begin to appreciate the dramatic shift in trends in some of the recent developments which surround the maturing adolescent of today. Today, the adolescent "drop-out" is considered to be a serious social problem; some years ago his behavior was the norm.

Recently, too, there has been a shift in the direction of college education for all. Community and junior colleges have grown all over the country as a partial answer to the tremendous need and emphasis in the direction of higher education. Today's society believes that education holds the answer for all of its evils and all of its problems. If there is a traffic and automobile accident problem, the answer is to teach driver education to all high school students. If there is a sex and venereal disease problem, the answer is to teach sex education in the schools. If there is an unemployment problem, the answer is to teach more vocational skills and to offer more vocational education to more individuals. Eventually, however, we must come to the realization that the schools cannot do the entire job by themselves, nor can they reasonably be expected to carry out these new roles with an outmoded structure and organization.

One of the more flamboyant aspects of the current American scene has concerned the social deviation form of protest adopted by young adults throughout the United States. The wearing of bizarre hair styles and clothing, adopting a mode and pattern of life not in conformity with the rest of society, and seeking new sexual and moral codes of behavior are patterns of protest wherein the young express their displeasure and discontent with the present social order. Of course, if enough young people adopt these patterns of behavior, then what has been termed "social deviation" will no longer be considered different or deviant; it will become the accepted norm, as have certain patterns already.

Experimental colleges are not a future hypothesis; they are a reality of today. There is a seagoing college where students study while they travel around the world; a non-credit college and non-graded college, where students study and pass examinations without the usual class rank, grades, and promotional system. Open admission policies, where college is available to all who apply, are a commonplace reality in community colleges across the nation. Interdisciplinary programs, and using the entire city as a campus, are also accepted innovations. All of the above are attempts to meet the new and different social needs of a new generation, as the colleges of America have virtually exploded with young people who are thirsting for knowledge but who at the same time are angry at the current state of social affairs, and are demanding immediate change. Some of the experimental colleges have been successful, others less so; the programs need to be evaluated on an individual basis, and no sweeping generality can do justice to the concept of the experimental college in the United States. The outlook for the future, however, is for the advent of more experiments in higher education. The trend is far from reaching its peak.

Colleges are faced with challenges by their communities, and the concept of the college as a part of the community is now an accepted reality. Colleges today are more concerned with the welfare of people. The cloistered "ivory tower" concept has virtually disappeared from the realm of higher education as realistic college administrators and teachers seek to become a part of the involvement of their students. Altruism in the young has found its roots in reality, as more attention is being paid to the needs of minority groups, and as young adults foist their intense awareness upon the older generation.

One of the trends in the future will lean in the direction of the "paid" college student. Students will be given tuition, books, lodging, plus a small salary or stipend and in return will be expected to complete their college educations, and thereafter give service to country and community in their chosen areas of work, becoming meaningful and productive members of society. There is a trend in the direction of an "educational corps" of young adults who are prepared and qualified to help others in the areas of teaching and education, and assist the needy, the poor, the indigent, the hungry, the illiterate, and the medically disabled. These socially conscious young adults will be termed "paraprofessionals."

Finally, treatment facilities and centers for disturbed adolescents and young adults will be much more readily available and accepted in the future. They will probably be as common as the corner drug store. People seeking help for mental and emotional and social difficulties should have this help readily available, and there should be no stigma attached to the process. In future, just as hospitals and doctors are available to those with physical problems, these treatment centers, probably functioning as community mental health facilities, will be readily accessible. Some will be municipally financed; others will be private; still others will be offered in conjunction with the services of community colleges, colleges, and universities. Their widespread acceptance is just a step around the corner as the stigma of mental illness disappears and the realities of mental pressures, anxieties, and frustrations become more evident.

WHAT IS AN ADULT?

Adulthood has been described as a logical step in the progression of development toward maturity. Legally, one is an adult at a given chronological age, but this concept has been rejected as being psychologically unsound. An adult is one who has passed through a series of developmental stages and arrived at a plateau of economic and family independence, self-sufficiency, and maturity. The adult faces the problems of marriage, employment, · ·ting a family of one's own, and developing political and social p.ilosophies and objectives. These problems differ from those found in adolescence and childhood.

The adult is also an individual who has reached his full physical potential. The growing years are past (although in adulthood the development of certain physical organs, such as wisdom teeth, still occurs. Traditionally the adult years are viewed as the most productive years in one's lifetime, but there are numerous adjustment problems which adults must face, too. The problem of waning physical powers and the overall concept of "aging" is an adult problem known as "middle age."

A key concept in adulthood is one of acceptance by fellow-adults. An adult is one who feels adult, behaves maturely, and is accepted by his fellows on adult terms. Society shapes adulthood every bit as much as it shapes all other levels of development. Adults in different societies play different kinds of adult roles. In the American society the male is traditionally aggressive and dominant; the female recessive and less aggressive. There is evidence that these roles are undergoing some degree of modification.

Adult adjustment problems include the decisions to get married or to remain single, reconciling religious views of one's family and oneself, political and social philosophies, getting a job, completing one's education, starting a family of one's own, starting a new residence, getting along with in-laws, adjusting to the sexual needs of one's mate, making plans for children, and making future plans. The problems are different from the problems of adolescence in degree of complexity and in kind. Many adults need help in adjusting to the adult role, and counseling services and psychologists can attest to the urgency of their needs.

Adults find their interests considerably narrowed. They develop a pattern or "life-style" in which they will spend the major portion of their adulthood. This is one of the reasons that later adjustment to retirement is difficult for many adults. The life-style pattern is so easy to get used to, and the adult has engaged in this pattern for so many years, that further re-adjustment in the waning years is especially hard.

The change from young adult to husband or wife, and then from that to father and mother requires further adjustment. Some young husbands assume their wives can manage a household as well as their mothers; some young wives expect their husbands to be as capable as their fathers. Adjustments are required in each stage of marriage and parenthood.

Most adults are viewed as being "stable." And indeed their vocational, religious, political, social, and leisure-time activities do not tend to fluctuate greatly. They are "settled." They have reached the stage described as "maturity."

WHAT WE HAVE LEARNED

1. While psychologists disagree about certain aspects of adolescent development there are several areas of fundamental agreement.
2. There are several psychological theories which attempt to explain the changes during the adolescent stage of development.
3. While many of the adolescent's physical changes are self-evident, others are less obvious.
4. The adolescent changes physically, socially, emotionally, and mentally. These changes are an expected part of human development.
5. Adolescent girls mature earlier than boys.
6. The problem of acne for the adolescent has social, mental, and emotional overtones.
7. Changes in adolescent behavior reflect changes in the current social atmosphere.
8. Adolescents develop a vocabulary of their own, partly as a means of communicating and partly as a means of forming a close-knit circle with peers from which adults can readily be excluded.
9. Each generation of adolescents has its own unique forms of expression and behavioral patterns.
10. The adolescents of the current generation are "different" from those of previous generations in several positive and significant ways.
11. The status of women, including adolescent girls, has undergone some radical changes in the past several years.
12. Today's adolescent is more alert, responsive, better informed, more aware, and more deeply concerned about social problems than ever before.
13. The ability to reason reaches adult proportions in adolescent developmental stages.
14. Adolescence is really a series of stages: Pre-pubescence; Pubescence; Post-Pubescence; Early Adulthood; Adescence; and Adulthood.
15. The term adescence has been proposed to describe a developmental stage prior to adulthood and immediately following late adolescence, or young adulthood.
16. Adolescents face numerous adjustment problems which are compounded by simultaneous physical development.

17. Adolescents are often expected to behave as adults while they are treated as children.
18. Sexual problems in adolescence are probably unique to this particular stage of development.
19. Many of the symptoms of the disturbed adolescent are similar to those of the normally developing adolescent, differing mainly in degree or in manner of expression, making diagnosis of the disturbed adolescent more difficult.
20. For a long time the problem of the mentally disturbed adolescent was largely ignored.
21. Numerous forms of professional treatment and therapy are available today for disturbed adolescents.
22. The problem of adolescent suicide is related to pressures and anxieties. It is a serious problem in the United States and throughout the world.
23. Adulthood is characterized by stages such as: Young Adult, Adescent, Adult, Middle Age, Old Age, and Senescence.
24. The period of time between adolescence and adulthood has increased due partially to the prolongation of the process of higher education.
25. The college of the future will be a part of the community; the college campus will need to adopt many new procedures and organizational changes in format and structure in order to meet the needs of today's youth.
26. An adult is a person who has reached his full physical development, has matured, and is ready to assume the responsibilities of self-support, marriage, and starting a family of his own.
27. Adulthood has its own set of unique adjustment problems, including vocational success, marriage, children, family problems, and becoming involved in political and social realities.

WHAT WE STILL NEED TO LEARN

1. We need to know more about the subtle psychological effects upon the developing adolescent brought on by the physical changes that most young people undergo.
2. We need to know why some adolescents form socially acceptable groups and clubs and others go in the direction of gangs and delinquency.
3. We need to develop a better form of communication between the generations to prevent the tragic consequences of the prolongation of a "generation gap."

4. The developing adolescent frequently encounters sexual problems; we need to find a better means for coping with these problems.
5. We need to be able to better diagnose the disturbed adolescent.
6. We need to know more about the developmental stage termed "adescence."
7. We need better means of treating the adolescent with problems.
8. The problem of preventative measures as regards adolescent suicide is one that requires much attention and more extensive research.
9. We need to recognize that adults have serious adjustment problems which are peculiar to and characteristic of the adult stages of human development.
10. We need to better prepare society for several of the changes on the horizon; those changes that can be foreseen through an analysis of recent trends.
11. There is a tremendous need for re-education concerning the adolescent and young adult seeking help for mental and emotional problems so that these young people will not be stigmatized or ostracized by a cold and unfeeling society.

SUGGESTIONS FOR FURTHER READING

Allport, Gordon W., *Pattern and Growth in Personality*, New York: Holt, Rinehart & Winston, 1961.

Baller, W. R., and D. C. Charles, *The Psychology of Human Growth and Development*, New York: Holt, Rinehart & Winston, 1961.

Dennis, Wayne, Ed. *Readings in Child Psychology*, Englewood Cliffs, New Jersey: Prentice-Hall, Inc., 1963.

Gross, Nancy E., *Living With Stress*, New York: McGraw-Hill, 1958.

Guilford, J. P., *Personality*, New York: McGraw-Hill, 1959.

Hall, C. S., and G. Lindzey, *Theories of Personality*, New York: John Wiley and Sons, Inc., 1957.

Horrocks, John E., *The Psychology of Adolescence*, New York: Houghton Mifflin Co., 1973.

Hunt, J. McV., *Intelligence Quotient: Infancy to Maturity*, Boston, Mass.: Houghton Mifflin, Co., 1961.

Jersild, A. T., *In Search of Self*, New York: Columbia University Teacher's College, 1952.

Jourad, S. M., *Personal Adjustment*, New York: The Macmillan Co., 1958.

Kagan, Jerome, and H. A. Moss, *Birth to Maturity: A Study in Psychological Development*, New York: John Wiley and Sons, Inc., 1962.

Lazarus, R., *Personality and Adjustment,* Englewood Cliffs, New Jersey: Prentice-Hall, Inc., 1963.

Leeper, R. W., and P. Madison, *Toward Understanding Human Personalities,* New York: Appleton-Century-Crofts, 1959.

Patterson, C. H., *Theories of Counseling and Psychotherapy,* New York: Harper and Row, 1973.

Pikunas, J., and E. J. Albrecht, *Psychology of Human Development,* New York: McGraw-Hill, 1961.

Resnick, William C. and Herbert L. Sachs, *Dynamic General Psychology: An Introduction,* Boston: Holbrook Press, Inc., 1971.

Resnick, William C. and Herbert L. Sachs, *Student Workbook to Accompany Dynamic General Psychology: An Introduction,* Boston: Holbrook Press, Inc., 1971.

Rimm, David C., *Behavior Therapy: Techniques and Empirical Findings,* New York: Academic Press, Inc., 1974.

Sachs, Herbert L., *Student Projects in Child Psychology,* Dubuque, Iowa: William C. Brown Book Company, 1967.

Stone, L. Joseph and Joseph Church, *Childhood and Adolescence,* New York: Random House, 1974.

8

Social Problems of a New Generation

- Why students go to college
- Societal views toward college
- College student organizations: social challenges
- Fraternities, sororities, and fratorities
- Societal pressures on college students: The need to perform
- Societal attitudes toward college students: The need to conform
- The concept of student power
- Student revolt on the college campus
- Student unrest: The radical student groups
- Cultural values and cultural differences in youth
- Developing a philosophy of life
- What We Have Learned
- What We Still Need to Learn
- Suggestions for Further Reading

PURPOSE OF THIS CHAPTER

The decade of the 1960's has become known as the years of "thinking young." Surgent, vibrant youth emerged from the shell of the 1950's into positions of prominence in the United States social structure. Whereas the students of the 1950's wondered if they could get into college, the students of the 1960's tried to take over the college. The students of today seriously question the value of a college education

155

as it is presently structured. The influence of society is pervasive, but at this time in the history of the United States, young adults are influencing society and effecting change in many directions. This chapter will examine some of the changes effected by young adults and explore some of the modifications in the social structure that have resulted.

Student dissent, student revolt, and student power was a phenomenon of the late 1960's which carried over into the early 1970's. These are relatively new concepts in America, although they are not new in other parts of the world. This chapter will discuss some of these phenomenon, along with the concept of the social deviate, the causes for deviation, and the behavior of individuals who rebel against societal values and structures.

In the final portion of this chapter, the social influences on personality will be explored. The importance of developing a sound philosophy of life for the young adult will be detailed. What attitudes should a young adult have? Which set of values are the correct set? What moral, ethical, and religious philosophies should the young adult adopt for himself? These are some of the challenging considerations which will be examined with regard to the "Social Problems of a New Generation."

REASONS FOR GOING TO COLLEGE

There are many reasons why students attend college. Some of the reasons are of their own making, while others reflect the choice of persons other than the student himself. All of these reasons, however, taken collectively, reflect some degree of social pressure, social influence, and social status.

This entire discussion could be terminated by simply stating that students come to college "to learn." But this oversimplification is hardly acceptable to anyone who is the least bit knowledgeable about the college student of today.

In comparison with the rest of the world, America is a prosperous land. Its citizens value education, and have freely chosen to invest much money, time, effort, and energy in the education of their young. The days when a young person had to go to work as soon as he was able have past. Today the tendency is to give every youngster, male and female, as much education as possible. In short, one of the chief reasons for going to college is the fact that society dictates this need. Society states that education is necessary for respect, professional employment, self-sufficiency, and status.

Many students enroll in college with very little idea of why they are there. They say that "it is the expected thing to do," or that "all of their friends are going." But in fact they have little or no real reason for attending, and are uncertain about education's values.

Many students enter college with unspecified vocational goals. They feel that college is a necessary evil, prior to assuming vocational roles. They feel that college is a path toward economic security. Others feel that going to college affords them prestige, or status. Typical student comments when asked their reasons for going to college include the following:

> My parents want me to go to college.
> They say that college is good for you.
> All my friends are going to college, so I am too.
> College graduates can get better jobs.
> My father is an engineer and wants me to be one too.
> Money counts, and the way to get money is with a college degree.

These comments reflect a certain degree of immaturity and uncertainty. They are completely unrealistic as concerns the serious business of studying to gain knowledge for self-improvement, and to be qualified to perform professional duties and obligations. Other students express more mature, serious, and realistic attitudes. Some of their typical comments reflect their degree of maturity and seriousness:

> —College contributes to building one's mind and fund of knowledge.
> —I want to get ahead in this world, and to do so I must be educated.
> —College is the best way to prepare to meet the responsibilities of adult citizenship.
> —I want to be able to help people and I need preparation and training to do so.

Some students come to college for the social aspects of campus life, and others, frankly, are seeking a husband or wife. The saddest situation of all is the student who states: "I don't know why I'm going."

In short, students come to college for a wide variety of reasons. And some come for no reason at all that they can clearly pinpoint. Small wonder, then, that many entering freshmen never complete their college careers. Of course, some of the attrition may be due to marriage, economic problems, entering the job market, lack of ability, and family problems. But some, no doubt, is due to a lack of clear purpose and motivation upon entering.

The reasons for going to college may be generally summarized under several broad categories:

1. Because it is the expected thing to do (family influence).
2. To prepare for a professional career.
3. To achieve social status and prestige.
4. For socialization and to meet other young adults (marriage)
5. To avoid the need to begin work (a negative motive, but still a motive).
6. To get a better education (self-satisfaction).
7. To gain adult maturity.
8. To be able to help others (altruistic motive).
9. To have fun before assuming adult obligations (social motives).
10. Because they don't know what else to do.

The societal influence in each of the above seems self-evident. Society in America has indicated that education has a high premium and that young people who graduate from college are to be more respected than those who do not. Statistics, too, bear out the fact that college graduates earn more money, achieve greater social prestige, and are generally more widely accepted in society.

The influence of society on the new generation of young adults is an important concept. It must be considered not only in terms of college entrance, but in terms of the dynamic influence upon the young adult in all aspects of his life.

SOCIETAL INFLUENCES

Many students attend college because of the active social life offered on college campuses. Participation in campus activities is largely a matter of individual choice, and most students find themselves attracted to one or another of a large number of clubs, activities, and events connected with college life. Large urban universities have proportionately more and diverse activities for students when compared to the smaller colleges.

A typical grouping of social and activity groups would include some or all of the following:

Campus Political Groups
Campus Social Groups
School Service Groups
Special Interest Groups
Literary Groups
Performing Arts Groups
Military Organizations and
  Clubs

Ethnic Groups
Religious Groups
Honor Societies
Professional Groups
Fraternities, Sororities,
  and Fratorities

These broad categories are very flexible. Some schools tend to have more of one type of group than another. Under each category listed above there are usually several slightly different types of organizations.

Campus political organizations might include any of the following:*

>Anti-Junta in Greece Committee
>Brothers (Black Students) at University of Illinois
>Council on International Relations and United Nations Affairs
>Friends of SNIC (Student Non-Violent Co-ordinating Committee)
>The Group (Black Students)
>Militant Labor Forum
>Socialist Discussion Club
>Students for a Democratic Society (SDS)
>Young Americans For Freedom
>Young Democrats
>Young Republicans

Of course, not each college and university will have all of the above listed political clubs and organizations. Some will have fewer; some will have quite different organizations.

Some of the groups listed above, and some of those listed in the material to follow, have "factions." That is, they exist as one group made up of several diverse groups within their overall structure. For example, the S.D.S. (Students for a Democratic Society) is composed of such diverse factions as the "Weathermen," the "worker-student alliance," the "revolutionary youth movement," the "labor committee," and the "independent socialist clubs," all of which, collectively, form the parent organization.

Probably most people have heard of R.O.T.C. (Reserve Officers Training Corps) on college campuses. But many college campuses have several other military-type organizations which have received much less notoriety. Included among these are such organizations as:

"Aiguillettes"	a women's R.O.T.C. organization which acts as hostesses for military events, balls, etc.
"Cadet Association"	promotes extracurricular activities for R.O.T.C. members

*The material in this section is based upon the University of Illinois offerings of social activities for freshman students, as listed in the January 1970 Handbook, and also based on information published in "Comment," the University of Illinois student newspaper.

"Pershing Rifles"	a national military organization for the development and maintenance of military honor.
Society of American Military Engineers (S.A.M.E.)	a national organization for the purpose of fostering co-operation between military and civilian engineers

College military organizations have come under scrutiny as groups which do not properly belong on the campus. On most campuses, membership is optional; but on a few—notably the military colleges—membership is required. The question of which organizations should be allowed on college campuses is a fiery one, still largely unresolved. For example, should colleges sponsor or allow clubs such as The Young Communist, the Fascist Club, or the Group to Overthrow the American Form of Government?. If not, who is to decide where to draw the line? Or is it within the realm of academic freedom to allow all divergent points of view to exist in a collegiate atmosphere, and to let students discover for themselves the values offered by each of the various organizations?

Ethnic groups may be found on virtually all college campuses. They meet the needs of people who share the same ideologies and want to be together, pray together, or follow the same religious traditions in the manner in which they have been reared. Some typical ethnic-group organizations on large urban campuses include the following:

Organization of International Students	Jesus Freaks
	Lutheran Association
Chinese Student Association	Muslem Student Association
Campus Crusade for Christ	Newman Community
Hillel Foundation (Jewish)	(Catholic)
Inter-Varsity Christian	University Christian
Fellowship	Movement

Each of the above serves a special interest group, helping students of a given national origin and religious background to maintain their identify in a diverse campus population. Membership in these organizations is usually voluntary. Some groups are much more active than others, and carry on keen rivalries with their fellow groups. Some are in direct opposition to others, but most tend to co-operate and get along well with each other.

Campus social groups comprise a diverse kind of club and organizational structure. Some typical social groups are listed below. The reader will note that these groups are really "special interest" groups, because they serve the needs of students interested in a wide diversity of social activities and events.

American Institute of
  Architects
American Society of
  Mechanical Engineers
Bioengineering Society
Business Administration Club
French Club
German Club
Hellenic Club
Institute of Electrical
  Engineers
Israeli Student Organization
Italian Club
Mayso Student Organization
Lambda Lambda Delta
  (Pre-law club)
Lituanica Club
Omega Beta Pi (Pre-medical
  club)
Organization of Arab
  Students
Oriental Students Association
Pars (Iranian) Student
  Association
Polish Students Club
Society of American Military
  Engineers
Society of Automotive
  Engineers
Spanish-Speaking Students
  Club
Student Education
  Association
Society of Women Engineers
Ukrainian Club
Young Adults Club
Zoological and Biological
  Society

School service groups comprise groups of students who are usually employed on a part-time basis by the college or university. They also include student volunteers who perform a wide variety of service functions for the school, ranging from public relations to office work to acting as student guides for freshmen, etc. These groups are composed of both formal and informal organizations. Typical student service club organizations include groups such as: Campus Kadets; Help (for inner-city youths); Orientation Committes (for freshmen); Rogers Park Car Pool; Skokie Car Pool; and Wheels, Inc.

So-called "special interest" groups on campus reflect a wide variety of social organizations. They include groups with political, ethnic, religious, and service orientations. They might include any of the following:

Amateur Radio Club
Astronomy Club
Bowling League Club
Classics Club
Geography Club
Geology Club
Karate Club
Sailing Club
Skiing Club
Students Sociological
  Association
Student Section of
  ORSA (Operations
  Research Society of
  America)
Veterans Club

Administrative-student groups are a part of the newest type of campus organization, stemming at least partially from the recent wave of student unrest and student protest. These organizations are attempts to give students a voice in those administrative matters which directly affect their lives. They are usually composed of a small percentage of students, a representative of the administration, and sometimes faculty, parents, or community groups. In some groups the students have an equal vote; in others their role is advisory. Typical administrative-student group type of organizations might include the following: Engineering Advisory Board; Inter-Fratority Council; Interorganizational Council; Senior Class Council; and Student Government Association.

Publications, literary, and performing arts groups are comprised of students who enjoy working on school newspapers and school literary magazines, students who are studying drama and theatre arts, speech, and radio and television broadcasting.

In honor societies students usually must qualify by scholarship and invitation. Membership is often by invitation, based on academic standing, grade-point average, class rank, and sometimes faculty recommendation and service to the school. Typical honorary groups include: Activities Honor Society, Alpha Lambda Delta, and Phi Eta Sigma. "Professional groups" is really a misnomer, for student members are not, as yet, professionals. However, these organizations are composed of students who aspire toward various professional careers. Included among such clubs are: The American Chemical Society, Society of Future Physicians, American Institute of Aeronautica and Astronautics, as well as numerous other similar organizations.

Fraternities (clubs for men only), sororities (clubs for women only), and fratorities (mixed sex memberships) are often restrictive. Membership is by invitation, and usually one must be "sponsored" by a student who is a present member. On many campuses fraternities and sororities offer students food and housing in addition to a wide variety of social activities. The value of the fraternity and the sorority have been widely debated, both pro and con, in the history of higher educational systems. Recent years has seen the emergence of the "fratority," groups composed of mixed-sex memberships.

The influence of society in the organization of student clubs and groups can be seen in the titles of their organizations and in their day-to-day activities. Society directs the goals of the various groups, the kinds of activities they may engage in, and the extent of their participation. Society also brings pressures to the college campus. All is not fun and games: the social structure demands productivity of its students. Yet the influence of society, while pervasive, is probably not as great as the pressures which it exerts upon young adults (e.g., the pressures toward conformity, attaining academic success, and others which will be discussed in the section to follow).

SOCIETAL PRESSURES

Social institutions exert pressures upon young adults in many different ways. Some of the means are subtle, psychological means, while others are more direct and observable. One such pressure comes in the form of resistance to change. Some members of the older generation see little or no value in the reforms demanded by the young adults on today's college campuses; they follow a "hard line" of resistance, adhering to established principles and practices, even when better ways may be clearly needed or indicated.

One of the demands placed upon the young adult by the established social institutions is for conformity—conformity in manner of dress, hair style, and manner of speech. Often the young adults capitulates to these demands, but often too they rebel. Conformity is aided by a demand for dependence. Society says the student role is one of dependence and even subservience. But college students today are more independent than ever before, because they are more mature and better informed, and because they stay in college for a proportionately greater number of years. It is difficult for many of these young adults to conform to the demands of what they consider to be outmoded and outdated social institutions and establishments.

As society exerts its pressure, there are several possible reactions:

conformity, or yielding to pressure;
partial yielding with some hostility;
open hostility and rebellion; or
escaping from the situation and creating new social structures free
   of these pressures.

Yielding to the pressures of adult demands is a form of solution to the problem, but it is not a satisfactory solution, because the basic problem still exists. Further, the act of yielding carries with its feelings of recrimination which contribute to psychological conflict. Many young adults adopt a compromise position, that of partially yielding while maintaining some of their position and dignity. These two forms of conformity have been supplanted recently by two forms which solve the problem for the young adult but create new problems for society.

Open hostility and rebellion against society's moral codes and dicta have characterized many of the young adult's actions in recent years. These young people defy accepted codes and traditions and often form societies of their own—societies in which the only rule for conformity is that there be no rules at all, where each individual can live as he chooses with no social regulation. But this form of escapism is not truly satisfactory to either the younger or the older generation, for each recognizes the differences between the two, and the fact that no reconciliation has been effected.

Societal pressures have attempted to regulate student hair styles, student dress, student coming in and going out from their place of abode, sexual behavior, and behavior in general on the college campus. Many of the recent protests have been a reflection of the pressures on the campus both from within and without. Student rebellion is a reaction, somewhat equivalent to the law of physics: "For every action there is an equal and opposite reaction." For every form of societal pressure, young adults react, although possibly not equally (indeed, sometimes they overreact) and often not in exactly opposite directions.

The college student finds himself in an unenviable position. He is generally not accepted by adult society, but he is too old to be a member of adolescent society. He is thus a member of an "in-between" societal structure which is at once not of his own making and is also somewhat artificial in structure, organization, and operation. Unlike other parts of the world, students in the United States lack status and prestige. Americans cannot accept, still, the political role which the American college student has begun to play, although this role has been widely accepted as commonplace in other parts of the world (notably in Latin America and Asia). The American ethic is still one of insistence upon the attaining of high grades and graduation as the chief concern of the college student. Only later may he concern himself with the larger political and social issues of the world. Societal pressures and the pressures of daily campus life have led to the demand for student power on the campus. The use of drugs, the breaking of moral and social taboos, adoption of new standards of conduct, new patterns of sexual behavior, and the new vocabulary of youth are all forms of rebellion worth one overwhelming message to adults: We will not be coerced; we will not yield to subtle forms of psychological pressures; we will not conform to artificial standards which are not of our own creation; we will not abide by what we consider to be outdated and outmoded standards of morality. In their music and in song, young adults are crying out; they want to be heard. As the drive for student power increases, the old forms of resistance to change will yield to newer standards and concepts, not all of which will be negative, and many of which will supplant or replace the former standards.

STUDENT POWER ON THE CAMPUS

There has been a swelling tide of dissent on college campuses which can be seen even by the casual observer. The majority of students still tend to conform in a wide variety of ways, but a growing vocal minority openly complain and want changes to occur now. Even among the majority who do conform, there are many who sympathize with the goals, if not the methods, of those students who seek a greater voice in university affairs. This is not a silent nor an apathetic college generation. Quite the contrary. The current wave of social unrest throughout the world has served to reinforce the position of students. These are changing times. For example, in the past decade many churches have instituted more changes than in the past several hundred years. And still the outcry is for more change.

The communications media have helped the cause of radical students by giving publicity to their demands. While in the past vocal and outspoken students chose to remain anonymous for fear of reprisal, this is no longer completely true today. Student leaders often try to make a name and reputation for themselves on a national and even international level. While the tactics of confrontation differ on the various college campuses, the goals are very similar. Students want a voice—a real voice—in matters which affect their lives on campus. They seem apprehensive about the future if change does not take place, and they sense a responsibility for effecting change. At no previous time in American history have students played so vital a role as a driving force in social change.

Some students, but by no means all, agree with the militant element in the student body: to effect change will require dramatic and often violent action. Most students feel that they can work within the framework of the given structure to effect the changes which they see as necessary and desirable. They seek a life which is different from their parents. They seek a world free from hunger, a world at peace, equal opportunity for rich and poor, a more involved college community, attention to the problems of racial inequities, a change in the living conditions in the ghetto, better forms of communication and understanding, and improvement in the environment and conservation of energy.

Students today believe that to achieve these goals, colleges must become vital forces in the community. They believe that it is their responsibility and challenge to help effect the desired changes, to move the college off the directed status quo and into a plane of dynamic change.

The generation gap is evident in the attitude of some parents. Some feel the colleges are directly responsible because they are too permissive; others look upon all of this as "campus cut-ups" or as a passing phase which they hope will not go too far. Some are afraid of student attitudes towards drugs and sex; most express a feeling of powerlessness.

Student power probably had its origins with in-campus complaints. The classes were too large, boring, or irrelevant. The students wanted changes in their immediate circumstances which led to a larger sphere: change in the social life of the community and the nation. Most students today enjoy an increased freedom as compared with students of yesteryear. They are faced with numerous decisions and must live by their own decisions. One of these decisions involves how active one should be in the participation of the various demonstrations demanding student power.

The drive for student power has led to campus demonstrations, picketing, building take-overs, riots and violence, sit-ins, live-ins, be-ins, and love-ins.

These are new concepts for college administrators. They require new approaches and philosophies to prevent the kinds of violence which became all too commonplace in the recent past on college campuses. Student unrest will not "go away." It is a phenomenon which will cease only when certain fundamental issues are resolved.

Student unrest is not new, but its forms of open demonstrativeness are. The world is changing rapidly. One can deplore student unrest, attempt to live with it, ignore it, or harness the energies behind these forces for positive good. But one cannot simply ignore it in the hope that it will dissipate; it will not.

Seeking the causes of student unrest and the drive for student power, psychologists find multiple factors. Frustration at what appears to be a lack of progress and a surge for independence created by a dependency status are two of those factors. The general overall condition of social unrest and the drive toward change is still another. We are living in an era where changes have not stabilized. As theologian Carl Michalson has stated: "We live between the time of the theology that no longer makes sense to us and the time of a theology which has not yet clearly dawned."

The term "theology" in the above quote may well be replaced with such terms as "philosophy," "education," or "moral sense of values."

Those who are critical of today's youth are likely to seek causes for the drive toward student power in various explanations which point in the direction of a weakening in the fibre or moral values of today's young adults. They cite factors such as emotional disturbance, permissive attitudes, callousness, lack of values in youth, and a general overall pattern of corruption. These explanations are hardly acceptable.

As Dr. Terry O'Banion, Professor of Higher Education at the University of Illinois, stated in a 1970 speech:

Student unrest expressed as a healthy concern for the improvement of society should be encouraged and praised. There is a distinction between student unrest and student protest.

O'Banion believes that there is an urgent need for an education which is "robust and rowdy." Students must come to know what it is to become human. To this end, Dr. O'Banion has offered a theory of student personnel work called "seductionism"—a way in which counselors can get to know and influence the student. It offers six basic tenets:

1. Seduction is easier when threats are removed (e.g., doing away with entrance tests). There are no zeros in human nature.
2. Seduction is often more possible in a group than on an individual basis. (Often groups can relate to each other.)
3. Seduction may have to occur in their room rather than in yours. (We must go to where the students are, not wait for them to come to us.)
4. Seduction must begin at a very basic level. (We must provide remediation where students require it.)
5. Seduction becomes easier when the seducee becomes involved in seducing others. (Students must play active roles in the college.)
6. Seduction has a more lasting effect when it is more than a physical relationship. (We must reach our students emotionally and psychologically, instead of treating them as physical entities or numbers).

STUDENT REVOLT ON THE CAMPUS

Students are young, and youth is impatient. Often when the drive toward student power has failed, students take what they consider to be the next necessary step—revolt, revolution, and violence, in an effort to press forth their demands. Some students totally reject the values of society and of their own past, and will not relent in their quest for change until reforms are instituted. They will not settle for tokenism. Both activist and alienated students on campus have difficulty relating to the older generation.

Students activists are those who have rejected partially or totally the values of society and seek to form a new society with new values. Generally they are on the border of despair, since all other means of communication seem to have failed. Their methods include mass picketing, shouting, pressing forth their claims to demand change with no justification required for their positions, and they have resorted to or been driven to taking over campus buildings, ejecting campus personnel, and violent confrontation with police and campus officials.

Many of these students justify their conduct by indicating that they are in the forefront (leadership) of a revolution, and no revolution is peaceful. They point out that in all past history great changes have occurred only after violent actions and violent confrontations with authority figures. They are not entirely correct in their logic, nor are they entirely wrong in their aims and goals.

Student revolt is often aimed at specific school policies. Students have objected to such policies as:

    College co-operation with military complexes
    College co-operation with industrial firms producing wartime
        products and products which cause death
    Campus military recruiting
    Graduation requirements which seem unfair
    Unrealistic or harsh rules imposed by the college
    Unfair treatment of minority groups
    Firing of radical teachers

Some of the explanations offered for student revolt include a wide variety of themes, ranging from family affluence to lack of student responsibility. These explanations cite the existence of an overly permissive society, a reaction to an overcritical older generation, the deterioration in the quality of life hypothesis, a protest against a "cold war" establishment, altruistic motivation, the fault of the mass media, and a general feeling of individual hopelessness to explain student action.

One positive outcome of student revolt has already happened: a re-examination by society of its established policies and procedures, and a re-examination of long-established values and goals.

The drive for student power and the resultant revolt on the part of some students have led to reactions by the conservative right-wing organizations in the country, many of which are seeking retribution. The polarization of student groups into right-wing conservatives and left-wing radicals has resulted in more political activity on the college campuses today than ever before in history. Part of the reason for this is that students are often older, and are of voting age. Many students (as many as 20% to 30% on some college campuses) are married. Graduate students tend to be more mature, and more students are in graudate schools today than ever before in the history of American higher education.

Radical student groups have become highly organized structures as a direct result of student unrest and the quest for student power.

Generally they belong to left-wing elements, proudly calling themselves members of the "new Left." While it is not entirely correct to
call these groups socialist or communist, they have been so labelled.
Accusations that they are communist-inspired or communist-financed
remain largely just that—unfounded or unproven accusations.

Probably the best known of the radical campus organizations on
the national level is the S.D.S. the "Students for a Democratic Society." This group, existing on many college campuses, has faculty spon-
sors, leadership representation, and national affiliation. In recent
times they seem to have disbanded, or gone "underground."

STUDENT UNREST: THE RADICAL GROUPS

Probably most college students and many adults have heard of the
Students for a Democratic Society. Most people, however, are not
aware of the type of organizational structure of the group, its purpose,
and its factions. The S.D.S. is a nationwide campus organization composed of individual and highly independent groups of students. Their
chief purpose is to effect change both on and off campus in order to
provide more equality for all. They are radical, sometimes revolutionary, and some factions encourage and promote violence as a means of
effecting change.

The five factions of the original organization of the S.D.S. are:

1. Revolutionary Youth Movement (R.Y.M), often known as the
   "Weatherman" faction
2. Progressive Labor Party-Worker-Student Alliance (W-S.A.)
3. Revolutionary Youth Movement II (R.Y.M.II)
4. Labor Committee Group
5. Independent Socialist Clubs

While the factions are autonomous, they have much in common.
They have their own forms of leadership and support, and differ with
each other on matters of origins, slogans, and positions on major
social issues. Some factions are more radical than others, but all have
one common goal: change.

The origins of each faction are somewhat different. The R.Y.M.
was founded at Columbia University and midwest campuses in 1968–
1969. The Independent Socialist Clubs are descendants from old-line
anti-communist groups. These groups have taken positions on such
social matters as the war in Viet Nam (in general, their attitude was to
get out at any cost, but to get out immediately); racial matters; communism; sex; education; taxes; and the need for revolution in the United
States. Their exploits have been documented on radio, television, and

in the newspapers. It should be clearly understood that these students comprise a distinct minority of students on college campuses. The various factions of the S.D.S. do not always agree with the intent and goals of the other factions. There is also disagreement on purpose and methodology.

There are several other radical groups of organizations on college campuses. Collectively, their chief contribution has been to make the nation aware that all is not right on the campus, that students are concerned, and that changes are needed. Some of their actions have been met with negative opinions and reactions. The groups have been labelled, by some, as subversive, detrimental to society, and communist-inspired and sponsored. It remains for the future to determine the lasting contribution of the radical groups, and to determine if the groups themselves will gain permanence.

There are those who believe that the two diverse groups of students—the radicals and the conservatives—cannot continue to exist, but that one or the other must "win out." Both groups can exist; there can be a conservative and radical element on college campuses; we are simply becoming more aware of the needs and demands of these groups as colleges begin to play an important role in community life. No doubt the future will see some blending or meeting in the middle as the conservative elements de-radicalize the radicals and the radical elements de-conservatize the conservatives. Perhaps a third group will be formed, composed of the less conservative and less radical elements of each of the two. The point is that presently neither group can be ignored. Both need to be heard and a means needs to be established for non-violent expression of their opinions. A way needs to be established for the equitable handling of just student demands and for the instituting of needed reforms. At the present time, these methods have not been satisfactorily developed.

SOCIAL DEVIATIONS

With the tide of unrest and drive for student power, the presence of radical groups advocating violence as a means of protest, and the worldwide sense of urgency in the direction of change, social deviation is a more or less expected outgrowth. College campuses have seen a wide diversity in social behavior in the past several years. Most of the social deviations are so classified because they break with tradition and form new standards of their own.

Social deviations can be seen in such areas as:

the use of drugs
sexual behavior

clothing and hair styles
non-conformity as a means of protest
the development of new music, art, and language forms
the change in accepted mode of life-style
free and public use of scatologisms
forms of protest such as "love-ins"

The use of drugs and other narcotics is widespread on college campuses. The problem is so acute that federal and state agencies have introduced the use of "Narcs" on college campuses. ("Narcs" are young-adult undercover agents enrolled as students in college whose function is to report student drug use to federal and state agencies.) Consideration has been given to change the existing laws and to make the use of certain drugs legal. Nonetheless, the use of drugs by young adults is a form of social deviation, a form of social protest, and a form of rebellion. The young adult is saying, in effect, that it is his body and only he can decide how to use it; society cannot dictate to him what he will eat, drink, or smoke. Drug-use has become a problem because many young adults, when under the influence of drugs or alcohol or both, are not in possession of reason, and perform acts which are detrimental to themselves or to others.

The range of sexual behavior on campus has undergone tremendous change in the past several years. There have been changes in the rules about visiting in dormitories and rooms and about hours for coming and going, and the phenomenon of unmarried couples openly living together in defiance of social and moral regulations has radically increased. Here again, the young adults seem to be saying that it is their lives and their bodies; no one can dictate the rules regarding their sexual codes and standards. These young adults claim that they are less hypocritical and more honest and forthright in their behavior than their parents. They point to divorce, infidelity, double standards of sex behavior, and many other sexual immoralities which exist within the conservative sphere of the older generation.

The clothing and hair styles of the younger generation are often unacceptable to the older generation. Short skirts, tight clothing, provocative styles, long hair are expressions of individuality and protest to the younger generation. It is still another form of non-conformity in which young adults express their need to be recognized—to be a group of their own with their own identity and standards of conduct.

The forms of social deviation of the young adult can be seen in the performing arts, in art itself, and in the expression of new patterns of language. The general approach is toward one of a different life-style for the young, one which they can accept and understand, and one which tends to alienate or exclude the older generation. There is a sense of security and belongingness (the psychological concept of the gregarious nature of man) in forming diverse social groups which are apart from those which traditionally have existed. The "beatnik," the "hippie," and the "yippie" all advocated the abandonment of traditional rules of social and moral behavior.

Social deviation has also moved in the direction of open and public use of scatologic speech (continuous unabashed use of vulgarity). Four-letter words are no longer thought of as scandalous. Along with this has come the "love-in" and the "happening," in which young adults participate in open, uninhibited and sometimes public expression of their feelings. Nudity, fornication, and other forms of challenging social behavior are the accepted mode or pattern at many of these gatherings. Many members of the older generation find much of the above difficult to understand. The goldfish swallowing or panty raids of their youth seem pretty tame in comparison. The older generation may be correct in saying the present generation has gone "farther" than their generation would have dared; but the younger generation point out that they are simply being more honest and open in their actions and activities.

SOCIAL INFLUENCES ON PERSONALITY

There are several different theories of personality. Older theories held to the biological construct, purporting that personality was largely the result of body size, shape, or structure, or the result of endocrine gland activity, or, more simply, inherited. Modern-day theories acknowledge the importance of heredity and biological factors, but they also tend to de-emphasize this aspect of personality formation and to favor the influence of environment and social forces upon personality formation.

Personality (broadly defined here as the individual's unique organization of his behavior) develops partly as a result of experiences and partly as a result of environmental factors. The home, the school, the neighborhood, the family, the church, and the totality of the culture all play an important role in shaping the individual's personality structure. Equally important are the ways in which each individual uniquely interprets his experiences.

Most contemporary personality theorists acknowledge the importance of social influences. No one is born a leader or a criminal. He is molded instead by various aspects of his environment. Environment, learning, and training all interact and play a vital role in what we have come to view as the "personality" of the individual. The culture, the subculture in which one lives, the individual's unique experiences and how he interprets them, together with numerous developmental changes which occur in the course of human development all play an important role in personality formation.

Basic patterns of behavior which have been long accepted, such as the roles played by men and women in our society, are culturally determined. American society has determined for instance, that the male is dominant and the female recessive (this is not true in all societies; in some the roles are reversed). Many people have come to accept this pattern so fully that they believe that men and women are born that way. (Quite possibly the next wave of unrest sweeping the nation may be due to the subservient role which has been forced upon women.)

Margaret Mead, the American cultural anthropologist, found that Samoan girls do not suffer the adolescent and young adult conflicts typical of American girls. She came to the conclusion that local customs and traditions play a key role in shaping the personality. Ruth Benedict, another cultural anthropologist, found that differences in cultural patterns result in different personality formation among young adults. Thus whereas the people of New Guinea were found to be competitive and somewhat deceitful, the people of New Mexico valued conformity and the lack of individual initiative. Culture, it would appear, is a key factor in the emergent personality of the young.

Within the same general culture, there are wide variations. Various parts of the United States offer wide differences in school opportunities, values, attitudes, and positions regarded as socially important. Home and family relationships, too, cannot be ignored as contributing factors in shaping the personality. The conclusion seems evident: a barren culture leads to a personality which is less rich than an environment which offers wide choices of cultural opportunity.

Data from large-scale psychological studies have shown that the relationships between parents and children have a marked effect upon the developing personality. The scars left by an incompatible marriage on a child's personality do not heal quickly, if ever. Since the child has a relationship to both parents, parental conflict and antagonism may well reflect itself in the child's personality through weakness and future maladjustment. Other studies have indicated a strong positive correlation between the disharmonious home and delinquency. Further, children of unhappy marriages are often unhappy themselves in their own marriage.

Harry F. Harlow, working at the University of Wisconsin Primate Laboratory, has investigated the effects of early maternal deprivation on the developing personality of the monkey. At birth, he separated monkeys from their real mothers and raised them with surrogate monkeys made of wire mesh and cloth (substitute images). When the young monkeys were freed and able to choose between relating to the surrogate monkey and the real mother monkey, they invariably chose the real mother. The need for warmth, comfort, and social relationships could not be provided by the surrogates. Tendencies toward aggressive behavior and unsocial actions were diminished or disappeared when the infant monkeys were reunited with the real mother.

That the social effects on the developing personality are profound seem clearly evident. But it has been stated that not all individuals have optimal environments (whatever these may be). Some individuals are raised in what has come to be known as "culturally deprived" environments, and the effects upon these young people are profound.

CULTURAL DIFFERENCES IN YOUTH

While in the past textbooks simply differentiated between "poor" people, "average" people, and "wealthy" people, today the term "culturally deprived" people is used to indicate the effects of such deprivation upon the developing individual's personality. Belonging to a minority group which is discriminated against may have considerable effect upon one's personality. Some individuals may be forced into aggressive behavior as a means of self-defense; others become openly suspicious and distrustful, recalcitrant, or reluctant to participate in social events.

Socially disadvantaged or culturally deprived youth are born into and grow up in subcultures which are outside of the mainstream of American middle-class life. They include underprivileged Caucasians (Appalachian Whites), Puerto Ricans, Mexican-Americans, and Indians. They comprise a considerable proportion of the population. In 1970 fully one-half the children in large urban public schools were culturally disadvantaged. These young people have many things in common: poverty, debilitating physical environments, poor family stability, disparaging outlook for the future, and generally poorer quality schools.

The current mode and standard of operation found in the urban public schools, based on a philosophy developed in the 1850's, seems totally unsuited for the education of culturally disadvantaged youth.

The Report of the National Advisory Commission on Civil Disorders (also known as the Koerner Commission Report) has indicated that the conditions of everyday living in a racially segregated ghetto area of a large urban city population differ strikingly from those in which most Americans live. The ghettos have startling high mortality rates, a higher incidence of crime per percentage of population, unbelievably crowded living conditions, and less availability of medical and educational facilities.

Almost all human behavior is learned behavior, and much of that learning is a process of socialization. But in culturally deprived areas, many of the ordinary kinds of learning simply do not occur. Not only must children learn who they are, but they must learn what they want. In culturally deprived areas, neither of these two tasks are satisfactorily accomplished, and the young adult is often confused, perplexed, and troubled, if not openly hostile and aggressive. He is taught to accept certain values, which the society that taught him then denies him. For example, underprivileged children of various backgrounds find that educational and vocational opportunities are restrictive due to their inadequate backgrounds. The skills and abilities may be there, but they go untapped.

The national waste produced by such a system is a concern to political leaders and college students alike. The social psychology of the ghetto is a field of study in itself, a new field of study within the framework of psychology, and one which is emerging as a very important area in the study of human behavior.

Opinions, attitudes, and beliefs are formed early in life. Probably no parent purposefully and willfully teaches prejudice to his children in a formal way, yet prejudice is learned largely at home in a very indirect manner. By actions, speech, and attitudes of acceptance and rejection, as well as subtle innuendo, parents teach their children to associate with certain kinds of children, to avoid others, to accept and reject certain values, and generally to reflect their own prejudices. These early learnings are important, because they form patterns which persist into young adulthood. When young adults in college are faced with having social relationships with minority group members, their early learning patterns come to the fore. Often the prejudices which they had learned as children prove to be unfounded in real-life situations; thus they have a value judgment to make: to accept and keep the teachings of parents or to internalize the findings which they have themselves objectively evaluated at close hand.

Young adults want and need the opportunity to think for themselves, to form their own friendships, to develop their own ideological philosophies and life-styles. The development of a sound philosophy of life in a young adult is a challenge which is at once unique and individual.

DEVELOPING A PHILOSOPHY OF LIFE

The development of a sound philosophy of life is one of the basic challenges facing the young adult. He must decide what he wants to be, what he wants from life, what his values and goals are, and what is to be his personal, religious, and moral behavior. Some people go through their entire lives without ever making these decisions. Others make the decisions and have goals and standards which are set so high that they cannot possibly attain them. Still others make realistic self-evaluations and develop sound philosophies of life.

College students face several moral problems on campus. The problem of drinking, the use of drugs, problems of sex, problems of cheating, stealing, and vandalism, all demand a sound basic philosophy if the young adult is able to live with himself. Many students experience personal turmoil in their attempts to resolve these and other philosophical problems. For many, this is the first time in their lives that they have been faced with the necessity of making personal and individual decisions which reach to the very core of their innermost selves.

Nearly all college officials agree that college students today are much more serious about study. Indeed, some college professors complain that today's students are too serious. They can't seem to relax; they have a kind of nervous tension about them which they cannot or will not shed. Possibly this is a result of there being more mature students on campus—graduate students, older seniors, (chronologically) and married students, as well as the presence of returning adults. Experiences change behavior, and the mature students are more intent about their college careers because they have begun to develop a philosophy of life—a philosophy which values education, placing it high up on the list of desirable achievements and priorities.

Psychologically, the individual emerges out of a social process in which he picks and chooses those values and attitudes which he internalizes as part of his essence and being. It may be a casual form of learning and development, but it is nevertheless an important part of one's education. For the adult knows who he is, what his limitations are, what he can do successfully, what is beyond his range, what he values, what is right, and what is wrong.

Personal change and development are a part of the college curriculum. It is not generally taught in any formal course of study; it is a process. Many parents complain that they no longer "recognize" their college-age youngster and lament about what college experience has done to their offspring. They are correct in the sense that their child is no longer a child, that he or she can no longer be regarded in a juvenile fashion; they have matured. Part of the process of maturation and development is the forming of a philosophy of one's own, a philosophy that may differ markedly from that of the parents. As a result parents, too, often face a process of adjustment as their young adults mature into adulthood with ideals and values of their own, ideals and values which may be contradictory in some or all respects to those of the parental generation.

Finally, part of personality development lies in attainment. The young adult, having achieved the goal of a college education, emerges as a person in his own right, a person with ideals and values and a philosophy of life. The philosophies of the college graduate, to be sure, will undergo some change as he enters the adult roles of work, family, marriage, and the assumption of new responsibilities. But most importantly the philosophy has begun, and this is a lasting contribution of college which is all too often ignored.

No one can develop a philosophy of life for another. Parents can hold forth certain values and standards, but in the end it is the individual who must accept or reject these values and standards, modifying some, supplanting others, and perhaps rejecting several. In developing a philosophy of life, a person changes; he becomes something other than what he once was; a new self has emerged from the old. Some of the elements of certainty from the past will surely be retained; but new elements will enter into the total construct of the person.

WHAT WE HAVE LEARNED

1. For the first time in the history of the United States, college youth are having a profound effect upon the political, social, and economic establishments both within the campus community and in the larger social sphere.
2. The thrust for student power, the phenomenon of student unrest, and the presence of revolt on the campus are facets of student behavior new on the college campus in the late 1960's and early 1970's.
3. The influence of society and culture on the developing personality of the young adult has been recognized as significant.
4. Students come to college for a wide diversity of reasons.
5. The overall philosophy of the United States is one which places high esteem upon the value of college education, and thrusts students in the direction of completion of college via graduation.
6. There is a wide diversity of social groups on college campuses today. Belonging to most of the groups is a matter of individual choice and option.
7. Social life on campus is an important part of the developmental process in the life of the young adult.
8. Society and social institutions exert pressure on young adults in the direction of conformity and maintenance of the status quo.
9. Students seem to be caught in a vise between societal pressures and campus pressures.
10. The college student finds himself in the unenviable position of being too young to be accepted as a member of the adult society

and too old to belong to adolescent society; he sometimes finds a solution for the dilemma by forming a society of his own.

11. There is a swelling tide of dissent evident on the college campus today. Some forms of dissent lead to violent confrontations.
12. The causes of student unrest and dissent are multifaceted.
13. Student activists and college militants generally belong to radical groups which advocate vast and sweeping reform.
14. One of the most widely known radical groups on campuses throughout the nation is the Students for a Democratic Society (S.D.S.).
15. Social deviations occur in the form of the use of drugs, sexual aberrations, hair and clothing styles, manner of speech, and non-conformity to social regulation.
16. Many psychological theories of personality emphasize the importance of societal influences and cultural and subcultural factors on the developing person.
17. Many of the basic patterns of behavior are culturally determined.
18. The relationship between parent and child, both positive and negative, has a profound effect upon the personality of the developing young adult.
19. Behavior patterns learned in childhood, including attitudes and prejudice, are often carried over into the adult years.
20. College students face the problem of developing a philosophy of life and a life-style of their own; during the course of this development both parents and the young adult face several problems of adjustment.
21. Socially disadvantaged and culturally deprived youth face problems which lie outside the mainstream of American middle-class values and ethics.
22. Most human behavior is learned behavior, reflecting the values and standards of the family and the culture.
23. College students today are much more serious than students of previous generations.
24. As students leave college and enter the adult world, they must face new problems of adjustment.
25. Developing a sound philosophy of life is part of becoming an adult.

What We Still Need To Learn

1. Methods need to be found to deal effectively with the thrust for student power.

2. Secondary school students need better guidance and counseling before entering college.
3. Young adults need better college orientation in their freshman year in order to be able to choose intelligently from the wide range of social activities on campus.
4. The social roles of fraternities, sororities, and fratorities are in need of clarification.
5. Ways need to be found to ease the pressure on students, in order to insure a more balanced life and to prevent mental breakdowns.
6. Methods need to be found to give students some of the power they request and yet to avoid the outright revolt and campus takeovers experienced in the late 1960's and early 1970's.
7. Radical and militant student groups need to be brought back "into the fold," or into the mainstream of college life.
8. Effective means need to be developed to deal with the wide variety of social deviation to which young adults are attracted.
9. Parents need to be better informed about the lasting effects upon their youngster's personality of friction, family dissent, divorce and separation, etc.
10. Young adults need to be better informed with regard to developing their own sound philosophy of life.

SUGGESTIONS FOR FURTHER READING

Allport, J. W., *Becoming A Person*, New Haven, Conn.: Yale University Press, 1955.

Blaine, Graham B., and Charles C. McArthur, *Emotional Problems of College Students*, New York: Appleton-Century-Crofts, 1961.

Coleman, J. S., *The Adolescent Subculture*, New York: The Free Press, 1961.

Freud, A., *The Ego and Mechanisms of Defense*, London, England: Hogarth Press, 1937.

Gardiner, John, *Self Renewal*, New York: Harper and Row, 1963.

Horney, Karen, *Our Inner Conflicts*, New York: W. W. Norton Co., 1945.

Lehner, George F. J., *Explorations in Personal Adjustment*, Englewood Cliffs, New Jersey: Prentice-Hall, Inc., 1957.

Lehner, George F. J., and Ella Kube, *The Dynamics of Personal Adjustment*, Englewood Cliffs, New Jersey: Prentice-Hall, Inc., 1964.

Lloyd-Jones, Esther M., and H. A. Estrin, *American Student and His College*, New York: Houghton Mifflin Co., 1967.

Lundin, R. W., *Personality*, New York: Macmillan Co., 1961.

Martin, W. E., and C. B. Stendler, *Child Development: The Process of Growing Up in Society,* New York: Harcourt, Brace and World, Inc., 1953.

Millon, Theodore and Reneé Millon, *Abnormal Behavior and Personality,* Philadelphia, Pa.: W. B. Saunders Company, 1974.

Rogers, Carl R., *On Becoming A Person,* Boston, Mass.: Houghton Mifflin Co., 1961.

9

Changing Values of Youth

- Relationships between the younger and older generations
- Student unrest: Causes and ramifications
- The concept of the establishment
- The younger generation: New standards and new concepts
- The college students of today: New experiences and new views
- Learning new identity roles
- Sexual revolution or sexual evolution
- Socially involved young adults: Current social problems
- The new morality: Youth speaks out
- What We Have Learned
- What We Still Need to Learn
- Suggestions for Further Reading

PURPOSE OF THIS CHAPTER

In this chapter, the dynamics of the relationship between the younger and older generation will be examined. The college student of today is our chief concern. Is he really a violent person? Is he more mature than his earlier counterparts? Is he a radical? A dissenter? Does he have emotional hangups? Is he better or less prepared for college studies and college life? These are some of the important concepts and problems which will be discussed in this section of the text.

In what ways do college experiences change the behavior of the young adult? In what ways are non-college-bound young adults different from those who do go to college? Are there differences? If so, what are they? These questions and others in a similar vein lead to an examination of the young adult as he seeks a new identity role in the process of what has been termed "maturation."

Is there a sexual revolution on the campuses across the nation? Are young adults more promiscuous than those of an earlier era? What are the actual sexual behaviors of the contemporary college student? These problems will be discussed along with the concept of the "new sexual morality" on college campuses today.

In the latter section of this chapter there is a discussion of the problems of "youth speaks out" in an attempt to answer the question: Are young adults today more outspoken? Without doubt, they are different. Perhaps we will find out why as we read about the "Changing Values of Youth."

STUDENT UNREST RE-EXAMINED

Chapter Eight detailed some of the problems which have led to the present state of student unrest on college campuses throughout the nation.

The divergent attitudes and beliefs of the older and younger generation remain one of the chief underlying causes for student unrest and dissent. Probably the resolution to the conflict lies somewhere in compromise: the more stringent demands of the student need to be curtailed, while the so-called "establishment" needs to become more flexible. To date, the basic problems have not been satisfactorily met or resolved. Accepted political and social values continue to be promulgated by the older generation and still remain largely questioned by the younger. As long as students maintain their marginal status, or semi-adult status, this state of affairs is likely to persist.

The fundamental underlying factors seem to be a misdirected sense of values, and pressures out of proportion to achievement between the two groups. Students tend to be committed to ideals, rather than to institutions. The evident differences between ideals and reality are a source of conflict on the campus and throughout society in general. Universities and colleges tend toward idealism and liberalism. In free discourse, subjects such as racial inequality, freedom of speech, the right to dissent, poverty, and the problems of ghetto areas are proper topics for discussion. But discussion leads to talk of action. And action is harder than words.

The immediate overt response pattern of students toward society's problems is a clamoring for rapid and sweeping change; but reforms do not come easily, and educational reforms have traditionally been among the most difficult to institute. Parents, too, contribute to the slowing of the process of change, as they often insist their children receive an education in the same manner in which they themselves were educated. Nor is all change successful; sometimes change for the sake of change leads to more difficulty, in which case conservative elements adopt an "I told you so attitude," or a "Let's go back to the good old days" philosophy.

An example of the above in recent years has been the widespread use of the computer in education, banking, and large industrial concerns. Many employees and students will readily attest to the fact that the first attempts at instituting these changes were characterized by what might best be termed organized chaos. It took much effort to iron out the "bugs." Today, however, even relatively small banks utilize the computer, as its value is recognized over former methods. Indeed most large colleges and universities are themselves "computerized" to some extent.

New concepts and new ideas may be readily and widely accepted by students before they can see the long-term implications and possible complications. Thus in recent times students have demanded a non-graded college system, automatic promotion, the right to choose professors, etc. While some of these ideas have aspects which are meritorious, their long-range results could be disastrous for the students themselves. Students need the advice and guidance of an older, more experienced, and better established generation. The concept of the "establishment" as the enemy of the new generation is a false concept. In reality, the two must work together, particularly on the campus, if progress for either group is ever to be satisfactorily attained.

THE OLDER GENERATION: THE ESTABLISHMENT

Can we ever see ourselves as we really are? Psychologists say that self-analysis is one of the most difficult of all types of analysis, even for those with years of training in the field. The meaning of events, in a similar fashion, is subject to the interpretation of the individual viewing these events. Older people perceive things differently from younger people. It is the interpretation of the behavioral event, rather than the event itself, which forms the crucial basis for the difference between the older and younger generations.

The younger generation of college adults has labelled as "the establishment" those people (mainly over thirty) who have set roles to play within the societal framework. Whether the adult is employed in a government agency, private industry, at a college, or what have you, he is considered part of the "establishment" if he follows societal standards and finds it somewhat difficult to agree with or to understand the actions of the younger generation. By labelling the older generation as the "establishment," certain significant attitudes are implicit:

1. The younger generation uses the term with derision.
2. The term implies fixed, set, and outmoded ways of doing things.
3. It implies inflexibility; unwillingness to adapt to new ideas and changes.
4. It indicates a fixed or set pattern of behavior which is not necessarily the best or right way of doing things.
5. It indicates a lack of understanding or communication with the young.
6. It sets the younger generation apart and polarizes the thinking of the two groups.

Several symbolic events have occurred in recent years which have tended to set the two generations another step apart. Labelling all law enforcement officials as part of the establishment makes them enemies, or, at least, on the "opposite side of the fence." The use of terms such as "fascist," "racist," and "pig," is an openly derisive expression directed at those who run governmental agencies. It is an indication that the goals of the two groups differ; their philosophies differ; their mode of response differs; their very concerns and priorities differ.

The values of the older generation are in many respects miles apart from those of the young. The suburban ideal of the middle-aged American is not often the ideal of the young adult. The acquisition of values is not simply a matter of learning, of motivation, or of adhering to the teaching and tenets of one's family. Value assumptions involve a total concept of personality. It is a problem wherein the individual comes to discover meaning for himself. The meanings valued by the younger generation are altruistic, self-sacrificial, and in fairly direct contradiction to many of those held by the older generation.

To a man of sixty, one of thirty is a young man. To the young adult, a man of thirty is suspect as being a part of the establishment, or is flatly labelled as the establishment. What the student must remember is that knowledge is but one determinant of human behavior. Learning may be defined as the acquisition of personal meaning. In this context, the young adults may not have had sufficient experience to effectively pre-judge the behavior of others. Indeed by the time they gain this experience, they may be a part of that very establishment which they have been rebelling against.

Traditionally, as one matures he becomes more sure of himself and more settled in his ways. He follows the established practices of society as a matter of course, or as a matter of least resistance. The candidness of expression of the young adult stands in direct contrast to all of the above. He claims to be more honest and less hypocritical; he eschews the double standard of sexuality he sees in the older generation; and he strives to improve society by encouraging broad changes in established practices and procedures.

Certain basic attitudes effect behavior. Attitudes are partially emotional (affective) and partially intellectual (cognitive). The attitudes of a person reflect what he values, what he believes in, what he feels is right. The attitudes of the older and younger generations reflect differences in these basic concepts and philosophies. The older generation (the establishment) feels threatened when it must change those attitudes and beliefs which it holds and values as correct. When the older generation is challenged, its reactions include fear, tenacity (holding more firmly to beliefs, even in the face of evidence that they may be wrong), and reaction (an attempt to stop the challenger from raising these unwanted doubts).

New experiences are a prerequisite for being a fully functioning person. The older a person gets, the less he welcomes new experiences, and the more he views them as a challenge to his established positions and practices. Young people, by contrast, welcome new experiences, though they may be a challenge, as a source of adventure and learning, and a means of breaking out of established practices and traditions. Thus the "generation gap" between the younger and older generations is born.

There is nothing basically new in the fact that the two generations have a lack of communication or a conflict of ideas. What is new is the expressiveness of the present generation. A generation of young adults which have grown up having their physical needs cared for, and most of their well-being taken care of by the parental generation has suddenly realized that things in the real world are quite different from the view they perceived as children and adolescents. They have suddenly realized that there are people who are starving, people whose medical needs are not cared for, people who are discriminated against, and people who have not had the benefits to which they have become accustomed and that they have taken for granted. They want all of this changed, and find it difficult to understand why they should be frustrated in this want, when all of their previous wants were so readily accommodated.

What they may have forgotten is that many members of the older generation have been busy with the cares of daily existence, making a living, caring for the home, and in general, just trying to "survive." The members of the younger generation do not have these problems; their needs have been cared for. Why, then, they ask, can't the needs of those less fortunate than they be cared for by government, by the members of society, and by the "establishment"? If the established offices cannot function effectively and properly to take care of these needs, why not institute new practices and organizational structures which can deal more effectively with these problems?

The answer to these questions, of course, is that life is not so simple. For the older generation, previous practices functioned effectively. They see little or no reason for the dramatic changes of the kind envisioned by the younger generation. They cannot or will not accept the new standards of behavior and morality offered by a surging, powerful, dynamic generation of young adults; they cannot accept the imperative nature of these demands.

THE YOUNGER GENERATION: NEW STANDARDS

The decade of the 1960's saw many changes in the standards held by young adults. Some of the changes were materialistic, others were moralistic, and still others were in the realm of social values. There were many changes as the young adult population virtually exploded with greater numbers, more challenging ideas, and new standards for behavior and new ways of doing things. Some of the new standards proffered by the younger generation include such behavior and practices as:

> The use of drugs
> Questioning established administrative procedures
> New sexual morality
> A concern for the underprivileged
> Revolt against oppressive prejudice
> Institutionalization of new educational policies and procedures
> A change in life-style
> Differences in modes of dress and hair style
> New art forms; new music; new forms of theater
> Concern for the environment

The surge toward change has affected virtually every aspect of life. Some young adults feel it is no more wrong to use drugs than it is to use alcohol. They feel that just as an excessive use of drugs can lead to individual problems and violation of the law, so too does an excessive use of alcohol. Equating the two, some young adults feel that the use of drugs, or the choice not to use them, is as much their individual right as the adult choice regarding the use of alcohol. Many young people have never used any form of drug; others have seen parents using various kinds of pills from their earliest days. Some college students point to the effectiveness of certain drugs in helping them to study; others mention the ecstatic feelings of freedom as they take a "trip."

The questioning by young adults has also extended to standard practices in administration in both schools and municipal agencies. Because young adults are in closer contact with the colleges, the schools have felt the impact, to date, more so than the local, state, and federal administrations. The new generation questions doing things because they have been done that way before. Certainly some of the established practices need questioning.

Probably the most provocative concept forwarded by the young adult is that of the new sexual morality. Promiscuous fornication, intercourse without wedlock, living together on college campuses, naked public appearances, and other matters which fall into the realm of sexual behavior are difficult for the older generation to grasp, to understand, or to accept. Indeed many adults will not even acknowledge that there has been a change. The change is one of evolution, rather than of revolution.

The current generation of young adults has a genuine concern for the underprivileged. They cannot accept prejudice, the existence of the ghetto, racial strife, hungry children, and inequity of treatment for the poor. They are altruistic, and their altruism leads to specific behaviors. They feel the older generation has absolved itself of the responsibilities in many of these areas, and that if anything is going to be done, it is their responsibility to do it.

Perhaps the most dramatically visible change instituted by the new generation has been the change in their life-style patterns. Some have "dropped out" of society altogether, living the life of the hippie or yippie, while others have remained on the fringes of society but have insisted upon their own modes of dress and hair styles. The "unisex" concept in dress, long hair for the male, see-through clothing, and other such innovations have largely been youthful innovations.

Theater-going crowds have long been thought of as the wealthy, the mature, the sophisticated—practically anything but the young. This has changed as young adults have developed their own new form of theater. Nudity, the frank discussion of heretofore forbidden themes, and "happenings" are now a part of American culture, as the drive for change in all aspects of life has permeated the theater. Certainly the movies, the stage, and other media have been in the forefront of the recognition of the interest and appeals to youth; some claim they have gone too far in their efforts at accommodation, falsely flattering the young audience in an effort to win their approval.

THE COLLEGE STUDENT OF TODAY

The contemporary college student has been described as a "new breed." He is different from students of other generations in many respects. Many college students today begin their educational careers at a two-year community college, planning later to transfer to a senior institution. With the open-door policy, higher education has become available to more young adults, and college campuses have felt the thrust of a population explosion. At the same time, many private institutions are economically handicapped in their attempt to compete for students and funds with the public institutions.

In addition to the relatively new concept of the community college (the older name "junior" college is rapidly disappearing), many communities are now experiencing the growth of a new type of college: the senior institution. These are colleges which offer only the third and fourth years of college work; some have, additionally, graduate school facilities. These senior institutions have been established partly because of the growing number of community colleges. Most universities and colleges now have special departments within their counseling staffs and admissions offices to deal specifically with the transferring community college student and their concomitant problems. It is somewhat difficult, for example, for these students to develop an allegiance or loyalty to a particular institution, due to the rapid change (virtually, every two years) in schools.

Many students remain on campus for a much longer period of time, pursuing graduate studies. This, coupled with the fact that there are more mature and married students on college campuses today, has led to the presence on campus of many students in their mid- and late twenties. These students are different from the typical seventeen-, eighteen-, or nineteen-year-old college freshman of a few generations ago.

Today's students are much more serious about their academic work and about their social lives. Knowing that there are many years of education ahead of them, many hesitate to enter into permanent dating and engagement patterns. Since marriage and family must be postponed, there is in this area, again, less loyalty, less to which to adhere.

The great thrust of college activity in recent times is in the area of community service. Many colleges have already instituted programs where graduation requirements include some form of community service. The academic-type "peace corps" has arrived. These young adults are interested in helping others, wish to contribute to the welfare of mankind, and seek an earnest position as part of a "team." Here, too, a new kind of college student is emerging.

Those students entering fields such as medicine, architecture, engineering, and teaching often strive to be an active part of a "team" rather than an individual performing the entire function on his own. The impact of technology is partly responsible for this change in attitude, as well as the need to belong to a group.

Today the adult community as well as the college community is desirous of having the campus become the "problem-solving" center for many social ills. Making colleges more accessible to the poor and underprivileged is a thrust in this direction. The campus today has on its frontier the potential for great social change. The mere presence of many more "marginal" students who a generation ago would not even have been admitted to the campus is a challenge for all educators. Newer teaching methods and administrative procedures must be developed in order to facilitate the educational progress for these students.

The contemporary college student has many dichotomous qualities. On the one hand, he is often a rebel, an activist, and a questioner. On the other hand, he is more mature, more serious, more intent, and more dynamic than his previous counterpart. Many more college students today find that they are in need of the services of the college, services ranging from financial aid to counseling and guidance.

Another phenomenon in many large public colleges is the presence of full-scale remedial programs. Although many high school students today enter college with better backgrounds and more adequate preparation, others do not. In the past colleges would simply not admit those who were unqualified. Today, recognizing the needs of many of the educationally disenfranchised students, colleges are providing one- and two-year programs of remediation aimed at overcoming these students' educational handicaps.

EXPERIENCES CHANGE BEHAVIOR

Why do young adults behave as they do? Is behavior a matter of chance or coincidence? Are actions random, spur-of-the moment things, or are they carefully thought out? Are there reasons for the things that we do, or is it pure happenstance? Are there reasons, too, for the things which we avoid doing? The causes and ramifications of human behavior are not simple. No one statement can suffice to explain all of human behavior. However, we do know that all human behavior is motivated; that is to say, there are reasons for the things we do and reasons for the things we avoid doing. Behavior is caused and it is purposive.

Most psychologists acknowledge that behavior is influenced by society and that experiences change behavior. As one grows older, childhood behavior patterns disappear (although there are periods of regression); adolescent actions and behavior no longer suffice in adulthood, although here again there are periods of regression. Youth is told that they must learn some things the "hard way," that is, by experience. Much learning takes place by doing; we often learn what not to do having done it once the incorrect way. But not all learning can take place in this fashion. One doesn't learn the dangers of electricity by experiencing a lethal shock; nor should one learn the tragedy of an error in crossing the street by being hit by a car.

Motivation is an important concept. Actions do not occur, nor can they be readily changed, without it. Motivation acts as a goad to behavior—one doesn't achieve unless one wants to achieve.

People differ in their behavior. Each individual finds a unique way of expressing himself. For a long time in the field of psychology every kind of behavior was explained by the concept of "instinct." Various areas of the brain were charted and pinpointed and thought to be the source for certain kinds of actions. Following the Renaissance, Rene Descartes described man's behavior as "intelligent" as contrasted with animal behavior, which was called "instinctive." Today, as a result of much work within the field of psychology, we believe that humans are born with a "generalized emotional" state, and that almost all behavior is learned (with the exclusion of some reflexes). The work of cultural anthropologists further pointed out the importance of society in directing an individual's behavior into certain socially-approved channels.

America is probably the most achievement-oriented nation in the world. To succeed, to do well, to win praise, have long been held up as standards of the American ethos. From early childhood the youngster is indoctrinated in the direction of achievement-motivation. Not all people, however, do well; not all people are successful (depending on what one holds to be success); and not all people really want to partake in the achievement "race." Psychologists see many people who feel that they are failures because they have not been able to attain some goal which they or their loved ones held as worthy.

Young adults have academic motivation, that is the need to succeed in school. They also have social motivation—the need to be a success in one's interpersonal relationships with others. It is this latter social motivation that has recently come into the forefront of the campus scene, as young adults realize that somehow in their elementary and secondary school education they were not taught how to get along well with others.

As young adults learn new patterns of behavior and encounter a wide variety of experiences, their values, attitudes, and beliefs are changed. With the changes occurring in these basic areas, the young adult must answer the questions:

"Who am I?"
"What do I really want?"
"Which values do I consider important?"
"When did I become what I now am?"
"How can I change some of my ways of thinking?"

In other words, the young adult must seek a new "identity image." He must answer these questions to his own satisfaction, so he will be able to live with himself as well as with others.

NEW IDENTITY ROLES

During the course of one's lifetime the individual is expected to play many roles; the role of child, adolescent, and adult each carry with them certain requirements and specificities of behavior. So too, during the course of each day, one plays many different roles: elevator passenger; motorist; pedestrian; student; part-time worker. Each role has its own prerequisite behavior patterns. Identity roles dictate what one will wear, how one will behave, what one will say and to whom, as well as what not to do. If one appears in street clothes at the beach he is out of his role; conversely, beach apparel in the classroom doesn't fit the identity role usually associated with the concept of "student."

Children typically identify with "hero images." Through the changes in the social structure, the hero images of the child have changed. At one time, the President of the United States was the typical hero image, at another, a cowboy or movie star; sometimes parents or older siblings become hero images in the process of identification and self-identity formation. From childhood on, society dictates the nature of the masculine-feminine role for each individual. Thus small children are given "masculine" or "feminine" toys. When a boy shows a tendency with dolls or buggies, parents quickly correct his play activity. Later, children learn student and work roles. Here, too, there are feminine and masculine-type roles. Thus the young adult male who aspires toward what are considered "feminine" kinds of occupations (nurse, secretary, beautician) and the young adult female who aspires toward the typical "male" role (executive, plumber, greasemonkey) may be chastised or ostracized by society.

Societal-dictated sex roles are sometimes the cause of sexual problems in the young adult. Not every young male is aggressive, tall, strong, and "masculine," just as not every young female is recessive, passive, shy, recalcitrant, and "feminine." When young adults face the reality of societal demands vs. their own self-images, the disparity in roles often becomes painfully evident. Later in life, young adults must adapt to the roles of husband or wife, mother or father, and later still, the aging adult. Each role requires a new adjustment, as circumstances change for the individual and for the totality of the society in which he lives.

Through maturation and experience the individual acquires the basic techniques for adjusting to new roles; learning helps one to discover these new techniques; after this, a combination of several factors allows the individual to choose his own mode of adjustment. Often the young adult engages in some strange behavior in seeking his new identity role. To gain attention, experience, or both, he may end up acting in outlandish fashion (e.g., dressing provocatively, drag-racing the family car, getting drunk or "high"). Adults consider this process to be a part of "growing up"; psychologists view it as one of identity-formation.

Habit, custom, and tradition dictate the nature of various identity roles. Rebelling against these roles, many young adults attempt to create new roles of their own choosing; often they themselves do not like the roles, but cannot admit this to others, or stay with their choice because it is at least different. American society is witnessing the emergence of new feminine roles for women and less-masculine roles for men. As young adults rebel against the pre-cast stereotypic roles assigned to the sexes by previous generations, they seek new forms of sexually responsive behavior, not all of which has been accepted, to date, by a rapidly changing social order.

SEXUAL REVOLUTION OR SEXUAL EVOLUTION?

The change in sex roles of the young adult male and female has been a process of slow and lengthy evolution. In America, it started in the middle 1800's, when women were relegated to extremely passive roles, and men were the dominant masculine prototypes of today's male. At the turn of the century, the evolutionary nature of the process turned a notch as women won the right to vote, to hold employment, and to appear in public meetings with men. Today, the situation has evolved where women are considered to be almost equal to men—almost—in social judgment and social value. Many women today feel discriminated against in the areas of equal employment opportunity, in educational circles, and in many other work and social spheres.

Nonetheless, contemporary women are much more capable, aggressive, and dominant than at any other time in the history of American society. With the increasing employment of women on a full- and part-time basis, and with the availability of higher educational opportunities, more men have sought refuge in recessive roles. The United States is still far from a position of equality in the treatment and accord given to women and men. The traditionally masculine role of dominance and superiority persists in many areas with a vengeance.

In the physical development of the child and adolescent, sexual matters and topics are often taboo. Middle-class morality is rather restrictive in matters of sexual information and expression. As an unfortunate result, repression, inhibition, and curtailment have been the lot of most of the present generation in matters related to sex. With the recent wave of unrest and drive toward change, sex has become a logical target for differentiating reality from theory. Today's young adult feels that openness and expressiveness in sexual matters is in keeping with his request for openness and expressiveness in politics, in college, and in the community affairs around him.

The sexual changes of the 1960's were best noted for their gradual and then rapid reversal of trends. From a close-knit hush-hush morality, sexual matters are now freely and openly discussed among most young adults. The evolutionary process is best noted for the fact that it accomplished more change in ten years than in the past one hundred, leading some to believe in the concept of sexual revolution rather than evolution.

The sexual changes of the new morality go beyond the surface. The casual adult observer sees nudity and promiscuity, the use of vulgarity and freedom in sexual activity and is somewhat repulsed or shocked by it all. Beneath the surface, however, new important forms and patterns of sexual behavior are slowly emerging. Many men now feel that doing housework and taking care of the children is a proper part of the masculine role; not at all a slur on their masculinity. Women freely discuss matters of finance, choice of family automobile, banking, and politics—without growing hair on their chest.

As this new sexual pattern changes and emerges, a healthier attitude and concept of sex will probably evolve. Hopefully the future will see a more balanced view, lying somewhere between the present double-standard of middle-class morality and the standards of the new generation. Somewhere between the middle-class standard of "Every female a virgin and every male an experienced sexual partner" and the younger generation's standard of "engaging in intercourse prior to marriage to see if the partners are sexually compatible," lies the sexual code of the future. The present drive toward change will probably lead to a better, more balanced, and more psychologically sound code of sexual behavior for young adults. The liberalism of today's youth, followed by a temporary period of conservative reaction, will hopefully end up in a more balanced view for all.

It is less necessary today for the male to be aggressive, dominant, and unyielding; he has not compromised his masculinity by becoming gentler, less pugnacious, and more verbal. So too it is less necessary today for women to prove their femininity by keeping their conversation on the level of cooking, sewing, and housework. The next generation will probably improve upon the sometimes clumsy attempts of the present one; progress comes slowly, and the process of change requires adaptation.

OUR INVOLVED YOUTH

One of the significant differences between today's college students and those of the past is in their degree of involvement in current political, economic, social, and academic issues. Today's youth want to know; they want to know reasons for not doing things; they want to know if there are better ways of doing things; they want to know how they can become a part of a society in which they feel alienated and ostracized.

As higher education has become more widely available to the poor, the disadvantaged, the underprivileged, the ghetto resident, and the high school graduate in general, more people are learning to think, to reason, and to philosophize about the great social problems of our day. Young adults are concerned about problems which yesterday's generation never even heard of—problems such as: pollution; inflation; prejudice; social change; starvation; overpopulation; and the energy crisis.

One of the reasons for the greater involvement of today's youth is the fact that so many college students are working part-time or full-time. As employees they are subject to the abuses of the employer, they become more aware of problems of transportation and earning a living, and they are more concerned about the welfare of the underprivileged. One of the big changes in today's college student is the fact that so many are working to help pay a part of their college expenses. Many campuses report that as many as 80 to 90% of their students work in some capacity. (To be sure, most college students find the kinds of jobs which are readily available, fit their student hours, and do not require too much in the way of transportation; these jobs tend to be in the service category, and thus do not usually provide the kind of satifactory outlet that work experiences provide for adults.)

One of the changes which needs to be instituted in the near future is the provision for on-the-job training on a paid basis for college students in areas where they plan to spend the major portion of their adult vocational lives. These kinds of experiences, could they be successfully provided, would help to dissipate the excess energy and dormant hostility of many young adults, living in a world in which they feel alienated and only marginally belonging.

YOUTH SPEAKS OUT

One of the significant changes that has occurred is the tendency of young adults to speak out and be heard. The "silent" generation of the fifties has been replaced with a robust, vocal, and outspoken generation of young adults. Some of their vocalizations have tended toward the vulgar, and this shocked the older generation. Ironically, it was in terms of this shock that the younger generation found its moving power. The use of descriptive exclamations, vulgarities, and emotionally-exciting language in general is characteristic of the present generation of young adults. Their language has a purpose.

Hidden behind protective screens for many years, the emerging young adult wanted the world to know of his dissatisfactions. The use of outspoken and direct language accomplished this purpose. Speaking out on many topics which were heretofore banned—sex, drugs, social inefficiencies and waste, prejudice, and the miscarriage of justice —young adults have asked questions which the older generation has been hard-put to answer.

In addition, for the first time in the history of the United States, black youth have demanded equal rights, the right to be heard, and a voice in the representative form of government which this country professes to offer. Black youth have shocked the nation with some of their verbal demands, complaints, and criticisms; but as the shock has worn off, actions are being taken to respond to many of their statements. Reforms, long overdue, are being instituted in many aspects of life in the United States—academic, social, and political. Still the outcry of the young adult can be heard across the nation. The present generation is not satisfied with tokenism. In a nation which determined to successfully land a man on the moon before 1970, and which accomplished this task regardless of cost, the younger generation feels that an equal determination by the establishment can lead to an end to prejudice, slums, and other forms of inequalities.

THE NEW MORALITY

Because today's outspoken youth find that their demands cannot or will not be met, or are being met too slowly, many have "dropped out" of society, and have instituted new societal codes which they feel are more in keeping with their needs. The new morality is based largely upon the concept of individual freedom: freedom to do as one wishes, in any way one wishes. Thus we find young adults engaging in a wide variety of activities which are anti-establishment and anti-societal in nature. The new morality embraces not only sexual activity, but virtually every aspect of human behavior.

While one aspect of the new morality forbids the strict delineation of rules and regulations, there are nevertheless certain basic tenets upon which the new morality is based. These unspoken and unwritten commands are a part of the society which the young feel closest to—a social order which differs in many respects from the present social establishment. Some of the chief principles of the new morality include a belief in the following:

> Equal rights for all
> Acceptance of people as they are
> Banning of all prejudicial forms of behavior
> Ending the double standard of sexual behavior
> Complete freedom of expression
> Revolt against authority
> Openness in sexual matters
> Complete individuality of expression
> The value of individual choice

In seeking to live out the above code of ethics and standards, many young adults engage in sexual activity and other forms of behavior which the older generation cannot condone or accept. The use of drugs, promiscuity, the use of vulgarity, and the sometimes violent protest of authority are tactics which the older generation see as unacceptable. The young see these actions as expressions of honesty—a necessary prelude to the establishment of a better world, an expression of their antagonism toward the present social structure.

WHAT WE HAVE LEARNED

1. The divergency in attitudes and beliefs of the older generation as contrasted with the present generation is one of the chief causes of student unrest.
2. Students today are outspoken in their criticism of the false values and standards of society.

3. The immediate overt response pattern of students in general has been a clamoring for vast and sweeping change.
4. Students today are very receptive to new concepts, new ideas, and new challenges.
5. Students view those over thirty as part of the "establishment."
6. The establishment includes all governmental, academic, and social agencies and institutions of long standing, where policy and procedure has been formulated by the older generation.
7. The values of the older generation are not necessarily the values of the present generation.
8. Any change poses certain psychological threats both to individuals and to institutions.
9. New experiences are necessary if a person is to function fully.
10. The generation gap is not a new phenomenon; we are simply more acutely and keenly aware of the differences in the generations today.
11. The present generation have established standards of their own; standards which have been loosely described as part of the "new morality."
12. The college student of today is different in many respects from students of previous generations.
13. Behavior of the young adult has been influenced by the society in which he was reared; experiences change behavior.
14. All behavior is motivated behavior; whatever we do or do not do, there is a reason for the behavior.
15. Individuals find unique psychological modes of expressing themselves.
16. America is probably one of the most achievement-oriented nations in the world.
17. As young adults encounter new experiences, they must adjust to new situations, and their behavior reflects this adjustment or adaptivity.
18. Young adults today are learning new identity roles.
19. Habit, custom, and tradition have dictated the nature of identity roles; the young adult is rebelling against this pre-cast mold and refuses to be placed into it.
20. The sexual revolution is a misnomer; what has occurred is a sexual evolution.
21. College students today are more involved in the social problems of the community and of the nation.
22. College youth are more outspoken than youth of previous generations.
23. As young adults have had a tremendous impact on morality; the older generation finds it difficult to understand or appreciate some

of the more obvious forms of behavior patterns which have emerged.
24. The new morality is a refutation of the older generation's standards and values.

WHAT WE STILL NEED TO LEARN

1. We need to learn ways of preventing student unrest before it erupts into confrontation.
2. We need to channel the energies and concerns of young adults into positive actions of social value.
3. We need to re-examine our goals and values and to re-align some of the misdirected efforts of the nation and the society.
4. We need to bring the younger generation into wholesome forms of dialogue and communication with the establishment.
5. We need to provide realistic job-training for college students in careers in which they will spend the major portion of their adult vocational lives.
6. We need to end frustration on campus and in society.
7. As a first step, we need to recognize that the college student of today is truly a "new breed" for whom old methods of instruction will be largely ineffective.
8. We need to better understand the challenges of the young as they seek new identity roles.
9. Rather than condemn the new morality as evil, we need to try to understand some of its underlying psychological aspects.
10. We need to be more realistic in accepting the fact that we are in the midst of a changing sexual morality—a process of evolution which sees new modes and patterns of behavior emerging.
11. We cannot continue to isolate the young adult from the real problems of society; ways must be found to incorporate the young adult meaningfully in helping to solve the problems of communities and the nation.
12. We need to be more accepting and tolerant of the fact that as youth speaks out and searches for a new morality, some of his behavior may be unacceptable and antagonistic; that does not affect the validity of his goals.

SUGGESTIONS FOR FURTHER READING

Atkinson, G., *An Introduction to Motivation*, Princeton, New Jersey: Van Nostrand Reinhold, 1964.

Berelson, Bernard, Ed., *The Behavioral Sciences Today*, New York: Basic Books, Inc., 1963.

Erickson, E. H., *Childhood and Society*, New York: W. W. Norton Co., 1963.

Hall, J. F., *The Psychology of Learning* Philadelphia, Pa.: J. B. Lippincott, 1966.

Maier, N. R. F., *Frustration: The Study of Behavior Without A Goal*, New York: McGraw-Hill, 1949.

Maslow, Abraham H., *Motivation and Personality*, New York: Harper and Row, 1965.

McClelland, D. C., Ed., *Studies in Motivation*, New York: Appleton-Century-Crofts, 1955.

McGuigan, F. J., *Biological Basis for Behavior*, Englewood Cliffs, New Jersey: Prentice-Hall, Inc., 1963.

McKinney, F., *Psychology of Personal Adjustment*, New York: John Wiley and Sons, Inc., 1960.

Mowrer, O. H., *Learning Theory and Behavior*, New York: John Wiley and Sons, Inc., 1960.

Murray, E. J., *Motivation and Emotion*, Englewood Cliffs, New Jersey: Prentice-Hall, Inc., 1964.

Rethlingshafer, D., *Motivation As Related to Personality*, New York: McGraw-Hill, 1963.

Ruvlin, Harry N., et al., *First Years in College*, Boston, Mass.: Houghton Mifflin Co., 1965.

Sherman, Julia A., *On the Psychology of Women*, Springfield, Ill.: Charles C. Thomas, 1973.

Sussman, Marvin B., *Source Book in Marriage and the Family*, Boston: Houghton Mifflin Co., 1974.

Turkel, Studs, *Working*, New York: Random House, Inc., 1974.

10

Adjustment and Maladjustment

- The concept of normality
- Adjustment and maladjustment
- The normality-abnormality continuum
- Kinds of neurosis
- The neurotic individual
- Neurotic patterns of behavior
- Psychosis: Serious mental illness
- Kinds of psychosis
- Psychotic behaviors
- Psychopathic personalities: social deviations
- Personality exceptionalities
- Kinds of phobias
- Psychosomatic disorders
- Drug and sexual deviation
- Situational stress disorders
- Problems of mental health
- Treatment for the disturbed individual
- The well-adjusted individual
- Help on campus for the troubled young adult
- What We Have Learned
- What We Still Need to Learn
- Suggestions for Further Reading

PURPOSE OF THIS CHAPTER

Many individuals wonder if they are "normal," or if there is something wrong with them. In this chapter we will examine the concepts of "normality" and "abnormality," "adjustment" and "maladjustment," as they have relevance for the young adult in college today.

More important than the concepts themselves, the student is probably most concerned with the "degree" of adjustment or maladjustment which is characteristic of his own behavior. This concept will be discussed in this chapter as we examine the behavior of the neurotic individual, the psychotic, and the psychopathic deviate. The problems of maintaining good mental health and a "balance" are not new to college students, because they have been and are subjected to tremendous pressures.

What exactly is abnormal behavior? What is meant by the term "nervous breakdown"? As we examine personality deviations and the problems of mental health we will be concerned about these and similiar topics. In the last part of this chapter we will investigate the sources available on campus for students who have real or potential mental problems.

Abnormal behavior has long been one of the most fascinating and challenging aspects of psychology. The role of the clinician is probably one of the most striking within the field of psychology. In this chapter we will examine the concepts of "Adjustment and Maladjustment" with a view toward the self-improvement of the individual.

THE CONCEPT OF NORMALITY

In previous chapters we have recognized the fact that each individual is unique in many aspects of his behavior and personality. How then can we arrive at a concept of "normality"? To state this in a more meaningful way, how do you know that you are normal? Of course, most of us think that we are normal. We admit to certain peculiarities and idiosyncracies, but are confident that these are minor deviations and that the totality of ourselves falls well within the range of normality. But if everyone so believes, then how can anyone be "abnormal"?

What was normal behavior at one time may be considered at another as abnormal. The usual mode of behavior today might have been considered abnormal a few years ago. In short, the concepts of normality-abnormality are relative, partially dictated by the tenor of the times. The concepts of normality and individuality and uniqueness seem to clash, as indicated above. Do they? Normality implies the existence of a fixed standard or scale by which one may judge the behavior of others. Traditionally, this standard was judged to be inflexible and unalterable; our views, however, have changed considerably in this regard.

The concept of normality as a fixed set of standards by which to judge others has changed to the concept of the average or usual mode of behavior. Partly the contribution of psychologists working in the field of statistics, and partly the contribution of cultural anthropologists, the concept of normality today has wide application and is flexible and adaptable. Statistically, the perfectly average or normal man probably does not exist. He is a mathematical average, a composite of many traits and behaviors. He falls between two extremes of behavior on any given scale—he is a "middle-of-the-roader."

The concept of normality involves the concept of "extremes." Much behavior which is perfectly acceptable becomes unacceptable if carried on in excess, involving the idea of "bizarreness" or "strangeness." The concept raises certain very disturbing questions. By its promulgation, virtually any kind of behavior can be considered as "normal" if enough people do it. The judgment of normality-abnormality depends on several factors, such as:

   the mode of expression of the action;
   the tenor of the times;
   the degree of expression of the action;
   the appropriateness of the action; and
   the time, place, and age of the person performing the action.

If everyone followed the exact course of action in all behavior, there would be no deviation from the norm, no such concept as "normal curve," and we would have a very mediocre world, indeed. Most persons fall within the normal range of behavior. Social groups apply pressure toward conformity. All living things must adjust to their environment, or perish. So-called "normal" adjustments can be made by each individual in a particular society, as a means of effectively functioning. Thus the emphasis has shifted from what most or the majority of people are doing, to the unique way of doing things which the individual develops for himself. The motivation for adjustment lies in dissatisfaction. If we are perfectly content with things as they are, there is little need for change. Too, the society changes, and that with which we are now satisfied may not be at all satisfactory tomorrow. If any pair of traits are plotted on a linear scale, from very negative to very positive, or from abnormal to normal, most individuals will fall in the center of the scale. Few individuals will fall at the extremes. The differences between the two groups, however, is one of degree, and not of kind, if we are measuring similar traits. Within each area of normality, however, there are deviations. Individual "X" may be on the "normal" end of the scale, but relative to individual "Y" he may be more toward the "abnormality" scale. The difference, here again, is one of degree.

The person who behaves in a bizarre fashion is stigmatized by society. His behavior receives no sympathy, little understanding, and a general lack of acceptance. Thus people with physical handicaps often receive help, care, and sympathy, while those with mental abnormalities find that they are often the subject of scorn and derision. While much progress has been made in terms of public acceptance of the problems of the mentally ill, much still needs to be done to gain public understanding and acceptance for those so afflicted.

The concept of normality is a changing one. Behavior considered normal in one society may be considered deviant or "abnormal" in another. There is what is termed a normality-abnormality continuum, which helps to explain the nature of abnormal behavior. It is an indicator of the changing nature of normality and the fact that much of normal behavior, under changing conditions, could readily be viewed as abnormal.

THE NORMALITY-ABNORMALITY CONTINUUM

As we have seen, the terms normality and abnormality are relative terms. The differences between the two are a matter of kind of behavior, degree of behavior, amount of interference with self and with others, and a matter of timing and societal acceptance. Indeed, the similarities between normal and abnormal behavior are often greater than the differences. The similarities and differences form a continuum, or progression. There are no sharp lines of differentiation; the borderline between the two forms of behavior is often imperceptible.

The normal person may deviate from the range of given normality in some respects, and still fall well within the range of normality. So, too, the abnormal individual has certain aspects of normality; rarely is a person abnormal in all traits and functions. The normality-abnormality continuum helps us to understand the bizarre behavior often characteristic of the abnormal; it also helps us to understand the sudden deviancy of an individual heretofore considered to be in every way normal.

THE NEUROTIC INDIVIDUAL

We have noted the difficulties in delineating the normal from the abnormal. There is no clear and definite line of demarcation. Still, individuals who are neurotic exhibit behavior patterns and symptoms which are in some ways different from the normal. Usually the neurotic individual does little or no harm to others (except perhaps his closest loved ones); he is generally not considered to be a "menace" to society. His behavior is harmful to himself and to his closest family. Sigmund Freud classified the various kinds of neurotic behavior as follows:

Hysteria
Psychasthenia
Neurasthenia
Anxiety-type neurosis
Hypochondria

The hysteria-type neurosis is characterized by various forms of paralysis and loss of sensitivity; the patient may be unable to walk, move an arm, or see. The symptoms are very real, although there are no known physical causes for the disabilities. The classification of psychasthenia has been largely replaced today by more specific terminologies; in Freudian terms, it includes those individuals who display phobic (fear of an irrational nature) or compulsive symptoms. The number of phobias is almost unlimited. While many normal individuals have fears, the fears tend to be controllable and usually well-founded. The neurotic fear or phobia is pervasive and uncontrollable. Compulsive reactions are developed as a form of security or safety. By performing the same action in the same way, the individual feels he will cause no hostility and experience no anxiety. The difficulty lies in the fact that it is almost impossible to do the same thing in the same way at all times; thus the compulsive neurotic sets out on a self-defeating pattern of behavior.

Neurasthenia is what most laymen think of when they think of a neurotic person. The symptoms are diverse, including extremes of fatigue, aches and pains, bodily complaints, and a wide variety of other complaints. The neurasthenic is a difficult patient to diagnoses; the first step in curing him is the elimination of possible physical causes. Many physicians report that as many as half of their patients have no physical basis for their complaints; they are neurotics of the neurasthenic variety.

The anxiety-type neurosis is characterized by a fear which is irrational, disturbing, worrisome, and carries with it a presentiment of evil about to occur. The anxious individual often does not know specifically the cause of his anxiety; he sometimes does not know what is worrying him, what he fears, or what it is that he thinks is about to happen. He does know that he is edgy, nervous, can't sleep, can't relax, and has a feeling of foreboding.

Hypochondriacs are individuals who exhibit an abnormal over-concern about their physical condition. They exhibit a wide variety of symptoms, take pills and medication readily with the least provocation, are constantly concerned about their well-being, and often have imaginary illnesses which they feel no physician is qualified to treat. They go from doctor to doctor hoping to find one who will understand their problem well enough to prescribe the one miracle drug they are seeking; they are neurotic individuals.

The neurotic is in contact with reality, although his perceptions may be distorted. He can generally function in society, hold a job, and live peacefully with his family. When his symptoms become severe enough, he seeks help, but he usually finds it difficult to find the kind of psychiatric or psychological help he is seeking because his perceptions of himself in relationship to others are so distorted. Neurotic individuals need family understanding and support.

THE PSYCHOTIC INDIVIDUAL

The distinction between neurosis and psychosis sometimes is a difficult one, comparable to the problem encountered earlier in differentiating between the normal and the neurotic. The psychotic is generally believed to cause more harm to himself and can be potentially dangerous to others. This does not mean that all psychotics are "dangerous," but rather that the individuals so afflicted require a more profound degree of care and treatment. Unlike the neurotic, psychotic behavior may require institutionalization. The generally accepted classification of the various forms of psychosis include the following:

Functional Psychosis	Paranoia
Schizophrenia	Organic Psychosis
Manic-Depressive	Alcoholic Psychosis
Psychosis	Senile Psychosis

The functional psychotic is one whose bizarre actions cannot be traced to any known existing organic or physical condition. Functional psychosis is considered to be psychogenic in origin. Symptoms include delusions, hallucinations, a loss of contact with reality, and general withdrawal into a "world of one's own." Legally, the psychotic is considered insane, in that he cannot successfully be responsible for or manage his own affairs. Functional psychosis includes schizophrenia, manic-depression, and paranoia.

Schizophrenia is a form of functional psychosis which includes several different types:

catatonic states;
hebephrenic states;
simple schizophrenia;
paranoid forms of schizophrenia; and
schizo-affective and childhood schizophrenia.

Schizophrenia is probably the most common form of psychosis. Certainly it has received the most widespread popularization, and thus there are many misconceptions surrounding this form of illness. Not all schizophrenics are "split" or "dual" personalities; nor are all schizophrenics dangerous to others. There is, however, a greater incidence of schizophrenia among the general population than any other single psychotic disturbance. The catatonic form of schizophrenia is probably the most dramatic form since it involves paralysis, and since it becomes readily clear to the family that their loved one needs professional attention.

The hebephrenic form of schizophrenia is characterized by silly behavior, giggling, laughter, inappropriate expressions, the use of jargon, mutterings, and continual smiling. The strange mannerisms of the hebephrenic are entirely out of context with the surrounding circumstances. The term "simple" schizophrenia is a gross misnomer. There is nothing "simple" about it. The term is used to describe a form of mental deterioration which cannot be classified as hebephrenic, catatonic, or paranoid, but which includes overall behavior which places the afflicted individual out of contact with reality. Simple schizophrenia may include some aspects of the behavior usually attributed to the hebephrenic, catatonic, or paranoid; it is a complex combination of behaviors, and could probably better be termed "complex schizophrenia."

The paranoid schizophrenic differs from the individual suffering from true paranoia, but here again, several of the symptoms may bear strong resemblances to each other. The paranoid schizophrenic suffers delusions and hallucinations; he may hear voices and act in response to these imaginary "commands." He often tells of detailed plots or plans, sometimes formulated against himself, or in which he is a conspirator. Some of the bizarre mental schemes become quite detailed and elaborate; some become fixed obsessions. Many paranoid schizophrenics feel that the world is against them and that people are planning to do some harm to them; no particular reason or justification is necessary. Schizo-affective reactions, involutional forms of schizophrenia, and childhood schizophrenia are less common forms of the illness, usually afflicting specific age groups. Involutional and schizo-affective forms of schizophrenia usually affect people under extreme emotional stress; the illness may come on suddenly, but it is actually the result of many years of the internalization of problems.

Manic-depressive psychosis is a debilitating mental state wherein the individual goes through a series of stages from unnatural happiness to unnatural depression. The stages may take only a few moments between each successive phase, or may take several days, weeks, or longer. No one seems to know, at present, why the manic-depressive psychotic proceeds from one stage of the illness into the next. "Triggering" factors and incidents have long been suspected, but never factually substantiated. Manic-depressive psychosis has several stages:

Involutional melancholia (extreme depression);
Depressive stupor;
Hypoactivity (Depression);
Hyperactivity;
Mania; and
Hyperacute mania.

The phases of manic-depressive illness cause physical deterioration as the body is racked with the exhaustion of the mania stage and deterioration due to lack of eating and sleeping in the depressive stage. Prognosis for those afflicted with manic-depressive psychosis is not good. Some manic-depressive patients exhibit one phase or stage only; whether or not they will ever fluctuate from this stage to another becomes a highly individual matter.

The paranoid psychotic has a system of highly fixed and systematized delusions which control his thoughts and actions. He seems to have lost contact with the "real" world and entered a world of his own; a world in which he receives commands, plays a role, and is often the victim of bizarre forms of persecution or torture. Unfortunately the nomenclature of paranoia is often confused with the problems of the paranoid schizophrenic; although the two illnesses are not the same, many of the symptoms are similar, adding further to the difficulty of separation of the two.

The psychotic individual can be helped in today's society. Early recognition of symptoms and early treatment help greatly in the prognosis for recovery. A willingness on the part of the patient and his family to receive the necessary aid is essential. Treatment is often long-term; sometimes treatment can be given on an out-patient basis. Unfortunately, there are still many mentally ill individuals who spend the major portions of their lives in institutions.

PSYCHOPATHIC PERSONALITIES

The behavior of the psychopathic deviate is among the most perplexing in the entire field of psychology. His behavior is characterized by anti-social actions, strange and unusual patterns, and non-conformity. Often the individual seems quite normal in almost all respects—except for his particular forms of social deviancy. The psychopath often voices deep concern for his behavior, promising to cease his particular form of activity, but invariably breaks his promise. Psychopathic personalities have been known to perform criminal acts, acts which make no sense to ordinary people, and are generally in defiance of authority. They seem to enjoy their status, and the harm that they do accrues mainly to their families, many of whom disown them in disdain.

Few psychopaths seek treatment willingly. Most are extremely reluctant to receive aid, even when forced to seek help by court order or by their families. They feel there is nothing wrong, if only the rest of society will leave them alone. Many have long histories of repeated contacts with the law. Many more are simply not "caught," and many are protected by their families through fear or shame.

Each psychopathic personality seems to develop his own unique form of deviancy, and it is difficult to generalize about the entire group. Overall, they seem unwilling or unable to form stable relationships with others, have few friends of long duration, and seemingly trust no one. They often scorn all forms of authority. Although their nonconventional behavior is a matter of choice, there does seem to be evidence of some compulsivity in their behavior.

Although the dynamics of psychopathy are not as yet fully understood, several theories have been advanced to explain the behavior. One such theory relates to an over-indulgent and over-protected childhood, including a parental attitude strongly voiced that "my child can do no wrong." Another theory holds that organic factors may be responsible. Other investigators point to the fact that the psychopath is rebelling against society in his own unique fashion. However, he rarely joins groups, is not a leader of rebels, and remains an individual objector. Still another theory points to a lack of love in early childhood, for which the psychopath seems to be searching as an adult, never really being able to find happiness and contentment.

At the present time, prognosis for a complete or even partial modification in the behavior of the psychopathic personality is poor. The difficulty is that the psychopath seems to have no motivation or inclination to change his actions; he resists all forms of therapy, and resists attempts to form close relationships with others. He seems to enjoy his status and difficulties, even while realizing that they cause problems for himself and his family. He often voices sorrow for his actions, only to proceed shortly afterward to perform similar actions which lead to similar difficulties.

OTHER PERSONALITY EXCEPTIONALITIES

There are numerous other personality deviations which do not come directly under the category of "neurotic, psychotic, or psychopathic deviate." These personality exceptionalities represent problems for the individual, for his family, and often for society. They range in degree of seriousness from mild to acute, but rarely require institutionalization; that is, the individuals can function in society, with the exception of their particular kind of problem. These deviations include:

>   Non-incapacitating phobias;
>   Mild dissociation (dissociative reactions);
>   Compulsions;
>   Depressive reactions;
>   Psychosomatic disorders;
>   Alcoholism or drug addiction;
>   Sexual deviations; and
>   Situational disorders.

Phobic reactions are fear reactions. Of course, it is normal to fear certain things; children are taught to be afraid of strangers, matches, crossing the street, etc. But phobias are uncontrollable, often illogical fears. Most people can live with their particular phobia or phobic reactions, while some find their influence so disturbing that they cannot function effectively. Some common phobias include:

Claustrophobia	Fear of closed places
Hematophobia	Fear of blood
Misophobia	Aversion to dirt
Zoophobia	Fear of animals

There are literally hundreds of phobias. Some people attempt to hide their fears from others, while some are quite outspoken about their problem. Usually the phobic individual tries to avoid all situations where he might be exposed to his particular fear-producing stimulus. Most phobias are of the non-incapacitating nature, and while they may not be eradicated completely, much can be done to curtail their effects and bring the reactions of the individual under control.

Many individuals have experienced temporary and relatively mild forms of partial dissociative reactions, as evidenced by lapses in memory, not knowing the time, forgetting the date, or temporarily being confused in time and spacial perception. Air travelers commonly experience disorientation on a temporary basis due to having traversed thousands of miles in a few hours or entering new time zones. These reactions are generally very temporary and not too disabling.

Compulsive behavior is adopted by some persons as a habit-pattern of reaction to situations which may cause conflict. The compulsive personality must have everything "just so." The problem may be mild, reflecting itself in a desire to have all doors closed, or all shades drawn to a certain height, or everything in its exact place; or the problem can be severe, causing a great deal of anger and upset when the compulsion cannot be fully satisfied. This is the precise difficulty with adopting compulsivity as a habit-pattern of reaction. The compulsive individual is fine as long as the compulsion can be satisfied; but when things go wrong and change is required, he suffers greater stress, because his mode of defense has been eliminated.

Depressive reactions are suffered by many individuals at various periods in their lives. The aberrant form of depressive reaction becomes a problem when the condition becomes pervasive. The individual may be mildly or seriously depressed, and his behavior or lack of it reflects the degree of depression. Some depressed individuals internalize their problems for long periods of years, culminating the process with "sudden" suicidal attempts. Many people experience remorse and grief due to family tragedy. In the usual course of events, these causes are overcome and there is a tendency for time to act as a healer. In the deviant personality, however, the depressive state persists long after the cause for the depression has been removed. The depressed individual may harbor feelings of worthlessness, guilt, inadequacy, and rejection. He often feels fatigued, unable to face the world, and has a sense of futility.

Psychosomatic disorders are bodily ailments and afflictions caused by mental and emotional problems. The ailments have real physical symptoms, and the discomfort and pain which the individual experiences are just as intense or even more intense than physically caused and physically related symptoms. If thorough physical examination reveals no underlying physical cause for the individual's problem, it is assumed that the problem stems from emotional and mental factors. Many physicians report that a large number of their patients have psychosomatic disorders; i.e., the physical basis for their difficulties are absent, and their problems stem from psychological factors.

It is possible that future research investigation will uncover psychosomatic relationships between several diseases and illnesses for which there is presently no cure. Carcinoma, in certain forms, may be triggered by psychological factors, but, to date, no research has established any clear pattern. There is also the distinct possibility that certain individuals are "psychosomatic prone"; they may develop physical difficulties as a means of gaining attention, sympathy, and concern.

Psychosomatic disorders include a wide range of physical ailments, such as:

Hypertension	Tics	Ulcers
Headache	Twitches	Coronary attacks
Migraine	Speech disorders	Colitis
Asthma	Somnambulisms	Fainting
Bronchitis	Amnesia	Dizziness
Profuse sweating	Insomnia	Fatigue
Catatonic states	Frequent urination	Sexual frigidity

Palsy	Anxiety reactions	Nervousness-
Affective states	Audio	irritability
Hysterical reactions	disturbances	Sexual aberrations

The problems of the alcoholic and the drug addict have not been satisfactorily resolved to date. That there are psychological factors in their personalities which act as causative factors seems clear, but the exact nature of these factors and the dynamics of their operation are not known. Alcohol addiction and drug addiction represent a form of compulsive behavior over which the individual has lost most if not all control.

The alcoholic is chronically addicted, although he frequently denies his condition, boasting that he can stop at will. The cravings sometimes lead to the intake of such large amounts of alcohol and such frequent indulgence as to cause a condition known as delirium tremens, during which time the alcoholic has tremors, hallucinations, and loses contact with reality. The individual may have symptoms including irrational and uncontrollable fears, twitching of various parts of the body, sweating, nausea, and disoriented, violent kinds of behavior. The condition can last for a few moments to several days.

Drug addiction takes many forms. The habit is one that is very difficult to break by oneself ("cold turkey" is the addicts' term for an individual who can break the habit by himself). Even after extensive treatment, the prognosis for a permanent and lasting cure for many forms of drug addiction is poor. Most psychologists attempt to differentiate between the habitual use of drugs, the frequent use of drugs, and the addiction to drugs. In some cases there is a very fine line of difference. Examples of categories of drugs and the drugs within them are:

Depressants	Phenobarbital
	Plentobarbital
	Amobarbitol
	Secobarbitol
	Chloral Hydrate
	Barbiturates
Stimulants	Amphetamines (Benzedrine)
	Dextroamphetamine (Dexedrine)
	Methamphetamine (Methedrine)
Hallucinogens	LSD (Lysergic Acid Diethylamide)
	DMT (Dimethyltryptamine)
	Mescaline
	Psilocybin
	Psilocyn
	Peyote
Others	Heroin
	Marijuana
	Morphine
	Opiates

Unlike the habitual drug user, the addict has an undeniable and seemingly insatiable craving for the drug. He requires more frequent or more powerful dosage as time goes on. If denied access to the drug, the addict experiences terrible anxieties, cravings, and withdrawal symptoms which include vomiting, cramps, perspiration, headaches, spasms, and other forms of painful muscular contractions. In order to obtain the drug, addicts often turn to a wide variety of crimes, including prostitution, strong-armed robberies, and theft.

Recently some younger persons have indulged in some variations of drug addiction or habituation, including the sniffing of airplane glue, inhaling the odors of turpentines and paint thinners, using nasal inhalants to get "high," and the like. The physical, mental, and emotional dangers to the young individual who embarks upon these activities are profound. Some youngsters do it for "kicks"; others out of curiosity; still others because the group has challenged them and they don't want to appear "chicken."

The overt expression of sexuality has become a trademark of the new morality of the younger generation. A pattern of earlier dating and earlier sexual awareness has become part and parcel of the American culture. Conflicts arise because the fallacy persists that children are supposed to be ignorant of sexual matters, adolescents must refrain from them, while adults can assume sexual responsibilities. Children today, however, are not unaware of sex, and adolescents indulge in overt sexual expression to a much larger degree than in the past. Society remains the judge of sexual behavior, proclaiming certain actions to be "deviant." While times change and judgments and standards change along with the times, certain sexual practices have remained in the category of "unacceptable" behaviors:

Promiscuity	Transvestism
Incest	Masturbation
Prostitution	Rape
Homosexuality	Voyeurism
Fetishism	Necrophilia
Exhibitionism	Nymphomania
Pedophilia	Sadism-Masochism

Promiscuity includes the engaging in an unusual amount of sexual intercourse by either partner of a married couple with others. Incest involves sexual relations between parent and progeny or siblings. Prostitution may be engaged in by either males or females, although the term is generally reserved for females who engage in intercourse for a fee.

The problem of homosexuality is a much discussed concept: having sexual relations and strong emotional attachment for one of the same sex. In England, homosexuals are treated as medical problems; in the United States, they are considered (in several states) as criminal offenders. Homosexuals may be overt (practicing) or covert (latent) individuals; these latter are individuals with inclinations toward members of the same sex who do not openly engage in sexual activity. The problem is thought to be more common among men than women, and homosexuals are generally chastised and ridiculed in the American ethos. Homosexuals cannot be judged by the characteristic mannerisms and behaviors popularized by fiction and the movies. Many "normal" individuals are latent or overt homosexuals.

The background of many homosexuals often reveals unusual parent-child relationships, feelings of insecurity and inadequacy, and self-dissatisfaction. Homosexuals are not impotent, but they do have a very evident desire to avoid heterosexual relationships. The psychosocial aspects of homosexuality remain one of the challenges of today and, in the near future, in all probability the United States will adopt an enlightened attitude toward the problems of these individuals. There is, to date, no satisfactory proof that hormonal lack, organic disturbance, or other physiological factors relate to the problem of the homosexual. Medical treatment has proved unsuccessful, while psychotherapy and other therapies have been only partially successful.

Fetishism concerns sexual arousal and stimulation caused by objects or things, rather than persons. Strong feelings of emotional excitement are induced by articles of underclothing, or by various bodily parts which are not ordinarily included in the sphere of sexuality (e.g., toes or elbows). Fetishists attain sexual pleasure and excitement from touching the object, fondling it, and sometimes sniffing the article. Their perverse satisfactions are usually short-lived, non-satisfying, and are generally regarded as societal taboos.

The exhibitionist is the individual who attains a degree of sexual satisfaction from showing parts of his body to others. He may appear completely or partially nude in public places, or he may enjoy undressing in front of open windows. The general goal seems to be to attract attention and admiration from others. Even when others are repelled by his actions, the exhibitionist obtains a degree of sexual satisfaction because of the excitement which he has caused. Many exhibitionists tend to specialize, exposing themselves only to children or to members of the opposite sex; some exhibitionists can reach a sexual climax from their actions.

The pedophiliac obtains sexual pleasure from fondling children or from engaging in sexual intercourse with children. The transvestite obtains sexual satisfaction and pleasure from wearing the clothing of the opposite sex. The problem seems more acute for men than women.

Many transvestites are married individuals, with families. Others find a solitary existence more suited to their particular sexual behavior.

Masturbation is frowned upon as a sexual practice. The self-stimulation of the sexual organs leading to ejaculation or orgasm has long been associated with many mysterious superstitions. Young adolescents were told they would become diseased, insane, sexually inadequate, deformed, or blind by engaging in masturbation. The practice has religious as well as social taboos. The real evil of masturbation lies in many of the societal taboos surrounding the action, the internalized guilt feelings, and the resultant self-recriminations. Alfred Kinsey found that masturbation is far more widespread than heretofore believed, both among males and females.

Rape is the forcible assault and sexual intercourse with an individual against his will. For the most part, the term has been used in relationship to men attacking innocent and unwilling women. There have been instances, however, where women have raped men. The action is anti-social, illegal, and carries religious sanctions. The penalty for rape is usually a prison term, rather than treatment and rehabilitation. Voyeurism is the act of obtaining sexual stimulation from "looking." The term is synonomous with "peeping tom." Most voyeurs are men. Some enjoy watching women undress, while others look at nude magazine pictures. The voyeur is rarely dangerous in terms of physically attacking others; when discovered he generally tries to flee.

Necrophilia is the sexual stimulation one obtains, in perverse fashion, from an attraction to the dead. Necrophiliacs have been known to habituate funeral parlors and to try to steal bodies. Sometimes they engage in simulated or actual acts of intercourse with the lifeless body.

Nymphomania is the lack of sexual satisfaction which leads to repeated acts of intercourse over a relatively short period of time. The problem is usually associated with women, some of whom marry and divorce with rapidity, while others turn to promiscuity or prostitution in their attempt to find a male with whom they can obtain sexual satisfaction. The nymphomaniac frequently complains that it is impossible to achieve sexual satisfaction or sexual arousal.

The sadist obtains sexual pleasure from inflicting pain upon others. The masochist, his opposite counterpart, enjoys being the object of pain during the sex act. Such individuals engage in beating, hitting, slapping, punching, twisting, or other forms of physical violence. The actions seem to lend a degree of sexual stimulation and pleasure which the sadist-masochist can obtain in no other fashion.

Situational disorders arise unexpectedly. They are unplanned and are characterized by moments of extreme duress. The death of a loved one, a tragic fire, sudden bad news, financial setbacks, loss of a job, marital strain, and the like are in the category of situational disorders. The situation is usually temporary, but for its duration the individual is in a state of emotional shock. He seems to be unable to function normally, cannot think clearly, cannot perform his usual daily routines, and is temporarily withdrawn or lost in a world of his own.

Situational disorders result from traumatic incidents. Their results may persist for a long period of time, although most individuals recover in a relatively short while. For individuals who do recover, regression is possible. Many situational disorders leave permanent psychological scars, so that the individual never again functions in quite the same way. As the result of a traumatic automobile accident, for example, a person may never wish to drive again.

PROBLEMS OF MENTAL HEALTH

The mental hygiene movement began in the United States at the turn of the twentieth century. Today, organizations such as the National Association for Mental Health promote mental health, support programs for the prevention of mental illness, and strive to improve the care and treatment of mentally ill patients. It is largely due to the efforts of local and national mental health organizations that treatment for the mentally ill has improved greatly; antiquated ideas have been discarded, and out-patient treatment has greatly increased. The period of time required for treatment of the mentally ill has shortened considerably in the past decade as new methods, attitudes, and procedures have been promulgated.

Despite the above, we are far from a solution to the problem. It has been suggested that every physical hospital should have a mental or psychiatric unit. One person in ten needs psychiatric treatment at some time in his life. Psychiatric and psychological services should be equated on a plane with the importance of surgical and obstetric services.

There are over eight hundred mental health organizations in the United States today. The movement is local, citywide, statewide, national, and world wide in scope. The World Federation for Mental Health, founded in 1948, now includes over one hundred and twenty-five member organizations located in almost fifty different countries. The aim of the organization is prevention of mental illness, support of research in the field of mental health, and the development of techniques and principles which can be of value and aid to the mentally ill. The organization, and others similar to it, seeks to improve conditions in mental hospitals, encourage enlightened methods of treatment for the mentally ill, and seeks public understanding, support, and acceptance for its programs.

The well-adjusted individual is not mentally ill, nor is he likely to become mentally ill. He has certain characteristics or "vital signs" in terms of mental health. These include a realistic self-concept, self-understanding, a healthy adjustment to his environment, some degree of relationship with others, satisfaction in his work, balanced emotionality, and positive personality characteristics. The mentally healthy individual has insights into his own strengths and weaknesses. He can be fairly objective in terms of self-appraisal, although he may be in error in certain aspects of his analysis. He can adapt to the demands of a changing society and environment, and is flexible and able to maintain a balanced sense of humor through life's stresses.

The mentally healthy person may not be able to adjust under all conditions of stress. Many individuals find certain situations intolerable; they simply cannot adjust under certain circumstances. Mentally healthy persons are not free from anxiety and tension, but they can control their feelings and cope with their problems, even though they may not be able to resolve all of them. Mentally healthy individuals are not fully satisfied with all things, nor do they conform to all aspects of society. They are individuals, with individual tastes, likes and dislikes, opinions, and modes of expression for their feelings.

THE TREATMENT OF THE DISTURBED

The problems of the mentally ill individual and how to treat him are not new problems. References to mental illness can be found in the Old Testament and in the writings of the ancient philosophers. Ancient man believed that evil spirits caused mental disorders. Anthropologists have indicated that primitive societies were cognizant of mental disorders similar to the problems which are recognized today. The usual presumption was that evil spirits possessed the person, and that a hole would need to be drilled into the skull in order to let the evil spirits escape (a process called "trephining").

Most students are probably somewhat familiar with the cruel and unusual forms of treatment of the mentally ill characteristic of those who believed in the supernatural in the early history of our country. Beatings, floggings, imprisonment, starvation, torture, water immersion, and even burning at the stake were once all acceptable patterns of treatment of the unfortunate mentally ill of a bygone era. We pride ourselves today on some of our methods of treatment, but still have a need for enlightenment.

It took the work of many pioneering crusaders to bring an end to the ritualistic thinking and treatment of the mentally ill. The task was not easy; it took several hundreds of years, and some believe it is far from finished today. The first institution for the "insane" in the United States was established in 1773, in Williamsburg, Virginia. At the time, such institutions were commonly called "lunatic asylums."

Handicapped children, including the deaf and blind as well as the mentally retarded and crippled, were often relegated to these asylums; the purpose was not for treatment or rehabilitation, but rather for confinement and concealment. Families of these unfortunate youngsters were made to feel ashamed and attempted to conceal their problem. Remnants of these highly charged emotions persist today, as mental illness is still unfortunately looked upon by some as something which should not occur. Today these youngsters attend special schools and they rarely, if ever, are placed in mental institutions.

It was not until World War II in the United States that a slowly growing public awareness of the problems of the mentally ill reached its peak. The astounding number of young men who were rejected from military service because of mental and emotional difficulties, as well as the number of servicemen who needed psychiatric care, gave impetus to the mental health and reform movement. The National Mental Health Act of 1946 granted financial aid to state and private institutions for the care of the mentally ill. The Act also provided much needed funds for research.

In 1955 a joint commission on mental illness and mental health studied the existing conditions. Its report, first released to the public in 1961, pointed to the imperative need for expanded research programs and improved means of patient care, and virtually condemned many of the antiquated methods which were still being employed at that time.

President John F. Kennedy was instrumental in obtaining the passage of a congressional Act in 1963, called the Community Mental Health Centers Act. It provided for the establishment in each community of local mental health centers for the out-patient treatment of disturbed persons, and lent a new and enlightened approach to the treatment of people and of families with problems. The "bold new approach" initiated by Kennedy in the mid 1960's is beginning to acquire impetus today. New forms of therapy and treatment have been developed and the long-term results of these new approaches should do much to help alleviate the growing problems of a population beset by the pressures of a rapidly changing world.

Modern treatment for the mentally disturbed involves the concept of "therapy." Although many seriously ill (psychotic) individuals still need the confines of an institution, many others are being treated as out-patients. Under these conditions, the individual can receive the help he needs while still functioning effectively as a member of society. Modern treatment includes the concept of treating a "family" as a unit; very few child treatment centers today will accept a child as a patient without also involving either or both of the parents in the process of rehabilitation.

Treatment may and often does involve more than one member of the family. It may include psychotherapy (group or individual), electrotherapy, hydrotherapy, somatic therapy, adjunctive therapy, occupational therapy, milieu therapy, recreational therapy, educational therapy, work therapy, physical therapy, family guidance, specialized treatments for children and adolescents, chemotherapy (drug therapy), out-patient treatment, directive therapy, non-directive therapy, transactional analysis, role therapy, behavior therapy, logotherapy, and other forms of treatment. The process may also include sensitivity training, joining "T" groups, and holding memberships in such organizations as "Recovery, Inc."

THE WELL-ADJUSTED INDIVIDUAL

The well-adjusted individual has a characteristic level of maturity compatible with his stage of development. To a large degree, the college student's adjustment to college is dependent upon his level of maturity. The mature individual, as a young adult, shows characteristics in his behavior which include a certain degree of independence, responsibility, and reliability. He is an autonomous, or self-sufficient, individual, but is dependent upon others for social contact and healthy positive relationships. He has a degree of adaptability, flexibility, and tolerance. He benefits from his experiences, has attainable and realistic goals, and has developed a degree of emotional control. Above all, he has a sense of security and a feeling of belongingness.

The concept of adjustment includes certain recognized and established criteria. The importance of a realistic self-concept is a key factor. Of course, we can never truly see ourselves as others see us; but the college student should have some clear idea of what he can do well and what is difficult for him to do. Continued growth and maturation is a second basic criterion, as is the tendency toward greater integration. A third concept includes the mastery of one's immediate environment. Maladjusted individuals and individuals with lesser degrees of adjustment often describe themselves as being upset or "thrown" by any of the small difficulties one encounters in everyday life. The well-adjusted individual encounters the same difficulties, but seems to be better able to adjust or cope with the problem.

Many individuals face unusual adjustment problems caused by physical deformities, personality problems, or unusual circumstances. These individuals generally adopt patterns of behavior which allow a tolerance level for their particular kind of problem. It is the well-adjusted individual who feels secure, has a feeling of accomplishment or attainment, and generally enjoys life.

COLLEGE RESOURCES FOR THE TROUBLED INDIVIDUAL

More and more colleges have come to recognize the vital role which they must play in helping their students with vocational, academic, social, and personal problems. Colleges today provide a variety of services to help their students with the difficult adjustment problems of college life and young adulthood. Some colleges even provide facilities for non-students; many provide facilities for the families of students as well as for the students themselves. Almost all colleges follow the policy of allowing the student to make the initial request for help on a voluntary basis. Some students are referred by teachers and others are recommended for help by their families. On occasion, various social agencies request the college to provide help for individuals. Many colleges have liaisons with a variety of community agencies, working together to provide psychological and social services for students and their families.

A small percentage of colleges require each student to see a counselor on a regular basis. Most counselors, however, oppose this policy, recognizing that students gain the most when they initiate the request for help voluntarily. A very small percentage of colleges (generally smaller schools) have no psychological or counseling services available whatever.

The kind of help the student needs determines which facility of the college he utilizes. Most colleges today have capable, trained staffs to provide services in the following areas:

Student Personnel Offices	Dean of Men
College Counselors	Dean of Women
Vocational Employment Offices	Dean of Student Affairs
	Dean of Students
Student Financial Aid Offices	Registrar
Psychologists	Treasurer or Bursar's
Director of Student Activities	Office
Director of Student Services	Faculty Advisors

In addition to the above, many progressive colleges have expanded their services to include one or several of the following kinds of help:

Psychiatrists	Health Services Center
Clinical Psychologists	Emergency Small Loans
Psychometricians	Offices
Social Service Workers	Community Services Liaisons

Although most students do well in college, many undergo a period of adjustment due to the difference in pace between their secondary schools and the college atmosphere. In a relatively short time, most students come to feel that they are making satisfactory progress; they have friends, and they have a feeling of belonging. The campus virtually becomes their home away from home; they belong. Many students enjoy campus life so much that they are anxious to return after periods of vacation or weekend trips home. In spite of the above, few students are immune from the anxieties and frustrations, the pressures and demands of assignments, schedules, exams, grades, and the need to achieve. In general, most students are able to tolerate these pressures; they are not crushed; they can adjust. But some students find the process overwhelming; they need help. Often their frustration is compounded because they do not know where to turn for help; for the most part, it is generally available for the asking on their very own campus.

In 1968, at a meeting of the American Orthopsychiatric Association, the role of the colleges in preventing and treating the mental health problems of students was the chief topic of the conference. The conference urged that colleges begin to provide adequate psychiatric and psychological services for their students and for the community. The conference discussed the unique problems of the college student and the community college student, and indicated how these problems relate to the problems of adjustment and mental health.

As more and more students recognize the fact that they can obtain valuable and professional services from their colleges—services which can be of great personal benefit to themselves and to their families—much of the stigma of seeking help has been eradicated. Very few students need feel ashamed or shy about asking for help in today's complex society. In fact, the student who never needs guidance or counseling is becoming the exception rather than the rule.

What We Have Learned

1. The concept of "normality" has changed from a fixed set of standards to the concept of the average or usual mode of behavior.

2. What was once considered "abnormal" may now be considered "normal"; what was once considered "normal" may now be considered "abnormal"; the concepts vary from culture to culture and with the changing times.

3. The concepts of normality and uniqueness are not in opposition to each other.

4. The motivation for adjustment is dissatisfaction; if one is perfectly content with things the way they are, there is little impetus for change.

5. The person who behaves in a bizarre fashion is stigmatized by society; he receives no sympathy, little understanding, and a general lack of acceptance.

6. The concept of "normality" is a changing one.

7. Normality and abnormality form a continuum.

8. There are several different kinds of neurotic individuals; these include the neurasthenic, psychasthenic, anxiety-type, hypochondriac, and the hysteric.

9. Neurotic patterns of behavior generally are most harmful to oneself.

10. Psychosis is a more serious form of mental illness than neurosis; the psychotic often requires institutional care.

11. There are several forms of psychosis, such as schizophrenia, manic-depression, and paranoia.

12. Each form of psychosis has several aspects; schizophrenia, for example, includes varieties categorized as hebephrenic schizophrenia, catatonic schizophrenia, paranoid schizophrenia, simple schizophrenia, and schizo-affective types.

13. Functional psychosis has no organic, genetic, or biological cause; organic psychosis is caused by biological, medical, or genetic factors.

14. Schizophrenia is probably the most common kind of psychosis.

15. There are six stages of manic-depression, ranging from the extremely depressed state known as involutional melancholia to the extremely happy state known as mania.

16. The deviant behavior of the psychopathic personality is among the most perplexing in the entire field of psychology.

17. Each psychopathic personality seems to develop his own unique form of deviancy.

18. The dynamics of psychopathy are not fully understood.

19. There are several forms of personality deviation which cannot correctly be classified as neurosis, psychosis, or psychopathic personality.

20. Phobias are compelling and irrational fears.

21. Psychosomatic disorders are bodily ailments and afflictions which are caused by mental and emotional factors.

22. The problems of addiction have not been adequately resolved.
23. There are numerous forms of sexual deviancy.
24. Situational disorders result from traumatic incidents.
25. The treatment of the mentally-ill individual involves the concept of "therapy."
26. More and more persons who are mentally ill are being treated as "out-patients."
27. The future of mental health care in the United States will probably see the establishment of many more community mental health centers.
28. The mentally healthy individual has a characteristic level of maturity compatible with his stage of development.
29. The concept of adjustment includes certain well-established and recognized criteria.
30. Colleges today are offering more resources for students and for members of the community who need help with mental and emotional adjustment problems.

What We Still Need to Learn

1. All living things must adjust to their environment or perish; man has still not learned to control his atmosphere, his water, and the very air which he breathes.
2. The general public needs to gain a better appreciation of the problems of the mentally ill, so that the stigma and shame can be removed.
3. More effective means need to be found to help the neurotic to control his behavior and to resolve his problems.
4. More community facilities need to be provided for the treatment of the mentally disturbed.
5. The treatment of the psychotic must be refined and delineated so that prognosis for these seriously ill individuals can improve markedly.
6. Much research needs to be done so that the dynamics of psychopathy and other forms of mental disturbance can be better understood.
7. The prevention of suicide among young adults remains one of the important needs of the psychological world.
8. The general populace needs to achieve a better understanding of the mind-body relationship, so that this dualism can help in the understanding and treatment of psychosomatic disorders.
9. We need to find improved means of dealing with such common and serious social problems as alcoholism and drug addiction.

10. We must begin to recognize that many forms of sexual deviancy need psychological treatment rather than social repression and legal incarceration.
11. We have only begun to deal effectively with the problem of the prevention of mental disturbance; mental health should be a top priority item in social affairs.
12. Colleges need to expand the scope of activities in which they are involved with regard to providing community services and student services for those with problems of mental adjustment.

Suggestions for Further Reading

Beers, Clifford W., *A Mind That Found Itself,* New York: Doubleday, 1948.

Bermant, Gordon, and Julian M. Davidson, *Biological Basis of Sexual Behavior,* New York: Harper and Row, 1974.

Candland, D. K., *Emotion: Bodily Change,* Princeton, New Jersey: Van Nostrand Reinhold, 1962.

Garfield, Sol L., *Clinical Psychology: The Study of Personality and Behavior,* Chicago, Ill.: Aldine Publishing Company, 1974.

Horney, Karen, *The Neurotic Personality of Our Time,* New York: W. W. Norton & Company, Inc., 1964.

Jahoda, Marie, *Current Concepts of Positive Mental Health,* New York: Basic Books, Inc., 1958.

Keats, John, *Sheepskin Psychosis,* New York: Dell Books, 1966.

Kleinmuntz, Benjamin, *Essentials of Abnormal Psychology,* New York: Harper and Row, 1974.

Sanford, N., *College and Character,* New York: John Wiley and Sons, Inc., 1964.

Selye, H., *The Stress of Life,* New York: McGraw-Hill, 1956.

Shaffer, L. F., and E. J. Shoben, Jr., *Psychology of Adjustment,* Boston, Mass.: Houghton Mifflin Co., 1956.

Soldwedel, Bette J., *Mastering the College Challenge,* New York: The Macmillan Co., 1964.

Staats, A. W., and C. K. Staats, *Complex Human Behavior,* New York: Holt, Rinehart & Winston, 1963.

Stern, Edith M., *Mental Illness: A Guide for the Family,* New York: Harper and Row, 1957.

Walker, E. L., and R. Heyns, *An Anatomy of Conformity,* Englewood Cliffs, New Jersey: Prentice-Hall, Inc., 1962.

White, R. W., *Lives in Progress,* New York: Holt, Rinehart & Winston, 1966.

Part III

LOOKING FORWARD
Your Future As An Adult

11

Personality Concepts in
Young Adulthood

- The concept of personality
- Personality changes in young adulthood
- Expressing one's personality
- Definitions of personality: Some psychological perspectives
- Personality theories
- Trait theories of personality
- Type theories of personality
- Developmental theories of personality
- Factors in the development of personality
- Intelligence as related to personality
- Methods of personality assessment
- Effects of culture upon the developing personality
- The group personality
- The syndrome concept of personality
- The adult personality
- Personality adjustment mechanisms
- What We Have Learned
- What We Still Need to Learn
- Suggestions for Further Reading

PURPOSE OF THIS CHAPTER

Almost all people talk about the concept of "personality" in one way or another. It is often called a "special something" or it is referred to in positive or negative terms: a person has a "lot" of personality or has a "strange" personality. Do we really know what personality is? Where does personality come from? Can it change? If so, how? These are some of the questions which will be discussed in this chapter, which begins the third major section of the text, "Looking Forward—Your Future As An Adult."

Most people agree that personality develops throughout one's childhood. The concept usually stops there, with the assumption that by adulthood one's personality has been formed. In this chapter, some of the personality dynamics of the young adult will be examined; for personality development does not stop at the end of childhood or adolescence. The various psychological theories offered to explain individual personality differences will be explored, as well as the concept of "uniqueness." Other matters of concern will include how one measures personality, how one assesses each individual, and how one interprets the results of his measurements. The final section of this chapter will explore the personality of the adult, and the concept of "personality modification." Does one's personality change throughout his lifetime? Is there such a thing as a "split" personality? Personality is one of the dynamic areas in the field of psychology. It is a topic of great interest to most people, and it should be of great interest to the college students using this text, as they explore the dynamics of the "Personality Concepts of Young Adulthood."

PERSONALITY CHANGES IN ADOLESCENCE

Personality encompasses the individual's entire range of behavior; it develops from many experiences and situations from pre-natal life through adulthood. Too often, beginning psychology students receive the impression that personality is formed in childhood and, once formulated, remains fixed in adolescence and adulthood. This is not the case. Numerous personality changes occur both in adolescence and young adulthood. In the earlier developmental stages, the influences of genetics, primary groups such as the family, and the immediate culture play an important role in personality formation. In young adulthood, the wider range of cultural activities, peers, and societal influences help to shape the refinements of the basic personality structure.

One of the important developments in young adulthood is the refinement of the self-concept. The concept of "me" as an individual is learned in pre-school years; the meaning of the concept in adult terms of self-worth and achievement potentialities is not learned until much later. An individual's self-concept includes the totalities of all meanings which he believes about himself. These may be overtly expressed, or, as is often the case, internalized expressions. The young adult acquires an awareness of self which includes his goals, his attitudes, his social relationships, and his ambitions. Personality consists, in part, of one's self-concepts.

Personality may be thought of in terms of the stimulus-response pattern of behavior. The stimulus value is represented by the ways in which an individual affects others; the response pattern can be seen in the ways in which an individual usually responds to a given situation.

The development of the personality in young adulthood centers around the breaking of ties with the past and adopting new patterns or modes of expression. As the young adult encounters new value systems, his reactions in terms of acceptance or rejection and in terms of experimentation tend to mold his personality in new ways. He is a maturing person, and must find new ways of expressing his needs, his motives, his wants—in short, himself. Exposure to a wide variety of systems and values forces one to reconsider his own systems and values. As new ideas are internalized and adopted, and as older ideas are rejected or no longer utilized, the individual changes; his "true" personality emerges. Students commonly experience doubts and anxieties about their own beliefs and values. In their search for new identity roles, they often reject the standards of their parents; sometimes they go to extremes and reject many of the values of society.

Psychologists recognize the uncertainties of the young adult as a part of the development indigenous to that age group. Eventually most individuals learn to live with their uncertainties, or to resolve them. Each individual must come to accept himself as he is—with certain weaknesses and with certain strengths. He must come to accept the fact that he can achieve in some areas but not in all. He must recognize his limitations as well as his abilities. These facets of personality development are very important in young adulthood. Some college students find it too difficult to face themselves. They drop out at the end or in the middle of a term; others remain on campus but develop a variety of psychological problems. Some retreat into a phantasy world of their own creation.

DEFINITIONS OF PERSONALITY

The concept of personality is not a concept which is singularly accepted in the same way by all psychologists. Many psychologists express widely divergent opinions as to the nature of personality, its development, and those factors which affect its course of development.

Some textbooks list as many as fifty different uses for the term "personality." The psychobiologists and geneticists hold to the hereditary nature of personality development and cite biological factors as being the most important in terms of personality development. Social psychologists have quite a different point of view, as do the psychoanalytically-oriented psychologists, the behaviorists, and the gestaltists. While we cannot examine all of the finite aspects of the various concepts of personality, the highlights of several differing points of view will be presented.

The most common concept of personality is the popular version which stresses the popularity of the individual and which emphasizes the importance of the individual in the eyes of others. This concept is not satisfactory from the psychological point of view, because it judges the individual largely upon idiosyncratic behavior. The effect an individual has on others varies with a number of factors. The concept that personality is something special which some persons have and others do not is not accepted in psychology. All persons have a personality. Their mode of expression may differ just as the very nature of their personalities differ. From the psychological point of view, the personality of each individual is his total self, expressed in a unique fashion.

The origin of the term "personality" stems from the Latin "persona." The term referred to the theatrical mask which players wore in performing in the ancient theater. The mask hid their true selves and bore a representation to a wide variety of individuals and concepts. Later, the term came to be identified with the person himself rather than with the mask. The term came to be associated with the role which the actor was playing; it referred largely to the outward appearance of the individual. The term, as it is used today, applies to evident characteristics (outward manifestations) and inner qualities of the individual.

Psychologists hold differing points of view as to the nature of personality. There are areas of general agreement and there are areas of wide disagreement, leading to a number of different theories and concepts. Many psychologists define personality in terms of the individual's behavior: that is, what a person does and what he does not do. Most psychologists emphasize the individual nature of personality and its unique aspects. Some emphasize the importance of adjustment to environment to personality development, while others emphasize biological and physical factors.

Many psychologists today emphasize the whole person in defining personality. They point out that one must consider the totality of all behavioral manifestations in assessing personality, rather than any one aspect or any single behavioral event. Other psychologists stress the importance of how the person perceives his environment, and how he organizes these perceptions into meaningful wholes.

The concept of personality is dynamic; that is, it involves a continuously changing structure, one that is never static and one that develops throughout one's lifetime. Still, there are some elements of the personality structure which have come to be regarded as relatively "stable." Certain basic patterns of behavior, likes and dislikes and preferences and attitudes, although subject to modification through learning and experience, tend to remain essentially the same throughout one's adult lifetime. As one gets older, certain traits and aspects of personality stabilize because they become ingrained; through repetition, habit, and individual preference, there is a tendency for certain patterns to persist and to form characteristic behaviors for the individual.

In discussing the normality-abnormality continuum (Section Two, Chapter Ten) the continuity of behavior and the difficulty in assessing the normal-abnormal patterns of behavior was indicated. It was pointed out that there is no sharp line of distinction between the two, but rather a blending from one into the other. The extremes at either end of the continuum are readily discerned, but the various behaviors in between are not so clearly delineated. The extremes of abnormality (i.e., seriously mentally ill individuals) exhibit certain distinct personality deviations with which one can compare the personality patterns of other individuals.

The theoretical orientation of the psychologist himself is a factor in assessing the personality of the individual subject being evaluated.

PERSONALITY THEORIES

There are probably as many variations in theories of personality as there are psychologists. Numerous different theoretical positions have been offered to explain the nature of personality and its ramifications. Each psychologist seems to have his favorite explanation of the wide disparity we see about us in individual personality expression. When each of the theories is examined closely, they tend to fall into one of three categories:

1. *Type Theory:* The earliest theories offered
2. *Trait Theory:* Sometimes referred to as "factors"
3. *Developmental Theory:* Emphasizing the changing nature of personality

Theories which center about body type, or as it is sometimes called, typologies, were the first attempts at an explanation of the basis for personality. According to these early views, one's personality depended upon, for example, his type of body structure or physique. Thus, the endomorphic individual (fat, heavy) was thought to be jolly or good-natured, while the ectomorph (thin body type) was thought to be nervous and quick-tempered. The ideal body type, or mesomorph, was the athletic (perfect body-build) type, which was at that time thought to have the perfect balance in personality. Later still, a dysplastic (mixed) body type with several different personality characteristics was recognized.

Few psychologists today hold to the "pure" concept of type theory. There are too many experiments which point to the obvious fallacies in the theory. Still, popular literature in the form of novels abounds in some of the concepts expounded in type theories of personality. The concept of extroversion-introversion found its roots in type theory. According to this theory, popularized by Carl G. Jung and others, one was either extroverted (outgoing) or introverted (turning inward) in personality. Later, Jung added the concept of the ambivert, the individual who was at times extroverted and at other times introverted. The explanation of personality on the basis of extroversion-introversion is too simple; it does not explain all of the manifestations of personality one finds among people.

Still another offshoot of the type theory of personality are the explanations of behavior based on biological, chemical, hormonal, and endocrine gland activity. According to these theories, the type of behavior found in the individual depends upon the amount of chemicals (usually, endocrines) found in the bloodstream at any given time. While it is certainly true that a lack of hormone of a particular type, or its excess, can have dramatic effects upon an individual's behavior, these theories have been found inadequate to explain a variety of personality manifestations.

The chief criticism of type theories of personality, and the reason that they are not in popular acceptance among psychologists today, is that people simply do not fit into the rather rigid categories which evolve from type theories. The type theory tends to confuse cause and effect; it is generally based on oversimplification, and tends to negate individuality and human variability. In short, typologies fail to explain the dynamics of human personality.

Trait theories of personality differ from type theories in several ways. They are more recent than type theories; they do not categorize the individual as rigidly; they allow for individuality in widely different areas; and they allow for specific traits on the part of an individual. According to trait theories, the individual's personality expression is the sum total of his various traits. Some traits are quite specific, while others are more general. Too, some traits are primary, or more important than others, which are classified as secondary.

While a limited number of prominent psychologists still believe that trait theory is an adequate explanation for personality, it is not the most widely held theory of personality today. The basic assumption that most people share a limited number of traits is subject to criticism on several counts. For one, it leaves too many gaps in the dynamics of personality to be totally accepted as the best possible personality theory. Trait theories also fail to explain the causes of behavior, and often are at a loss to explain the uniqueness of an individual.

Probably the most widely accepted personality theories today in the field of psychology are those which are termed developmental. Although their origins may be found in psychoanalytic theory, not every developmental personality theorist is psychoanalytically oriented. Developmental personality theory attempts to explain the *dynamics* of personality; it attempts to account for individual variation and the effects of culture upon the individual. In its very attempt to be all-inclusive lies its chief drawback: in attempting to do too much, it may not be adequate in any given area.

According to the developmental theory, one's personality is not molded because of a set pattern of inherited traits, nor does one's body type explain all aspects of personality. Personality is molded through a series of changes and experiences which occur from birth (and perhaps even prior to birth) throughout one's lifetime. Personality, then, is seen as a dynamic concept: a changing, ever-structuring, continuous process of development. One's personality is never truly completed, but rather changes with the various modifications of behavior and development which occur throughout one's lifetime.

Other concepts and theories of personality include psychoanalytic theory, cognitive theories, and humanistic personality theories. Each of these have numerous proponents, and each has various meritorious aspects in their postulates. Eclectic personality theory is, frankly, a "borrowing" of the best elements of a variety of personality theories, to combine into a conglomerate theory which is unique in that it cannot be totally supported by any one of the others.

FACTORS IN THE DEVELOPMENT OF PERSONALITY

Personality has been described as the unique and individual organization of behavior. What factors in development contribute to the uniqueness of the structuring of an individual's personality? Would you be the same person you are now if you had been born and raised in a totally different environment, or would some aspects of your personality be different? If you agree that there would be differences, then certainly environmental factors play a key role in the development of one's personality. What about heredity? Doesn't this, too, play a factor in determining what you are today? If you had been born a midget or a giant due to hereditary factors, would your personality be somewhat different from what it is now? If you agree, then heredity, too, plays an important role in personality development. Psychologists recognize that although both heredity and environment are important factors in personality development; more important still is how the individual interprets and perceives himself and his experiences.

Personality, then, is the result of both physiological forces and social forces. Heredity shapes the physical basis, but does not determine which social factors will affect an individual. The environment, factors in learning, intelligence, and training all interact with hereditary factors, as well as with other elements, to play an important role in the formation of what is so broadly termed "personality."

Factors which are missing from the environment of an individual can have negative or positive effects on the developing personality. These factors play a role on the individual's developing personality by the very fact that they are missing. How can something which is not there affect you? Environments such as poverty areas and inner-city ghetto areas exemplify this concept well. The nature of the surroundings contribute to a lack of motivation, a feeling of despair and discouragement, and a lack of the will to achieve. The essential positive elements of the environment are missing, leaving only negative factors. In these circumstances, youngsters soon learn to break accepted social codes in order to survive, or never learn the accepted social patterns at all.

Individuals develop personality patterns in a unique fashion. Some individuals are so different from others than they are classified as "exceptional." Although each person is unique in one or more ways, there are some individuals who are so different in several ways from their peers that we call them "exceptional" with regard to certain personality characteristics and certain behavioral manifestations. An individual may be exceptional in physical, mental, social, emotional, moral, or any combination of these characteristics.

The physically exceptional individual may have obvious problems such as blindness, missing limbs, or a speech impediment. Or he may have less obvious and almost undetectable (by observation alone) problems such as epilepsy, rheumatic heart, or partial deafness. These individuals were formerly classified as "handicapped." Today it is recognized that the degree of handicap of a physical exceptionality is at least partially a function of the psychological attitude of the individual concerned. Some individuals have extreme physical problems which are no handicap at all; they can rise above their problem. Others are almost totally incapacitated by relatively minor physical disabilities.

Mental exceptionality includes both ends of a scale: the very bright and the very slow. Bright individuals may be categorized as those with I.Q.'s above 110; these, however, are rarely categorized as exceptional. The exceptional individual, mentally, is the one who is close to or at the genius level of intellectual functioning. These individuals have unique adjustment problems, just as do those with very low intelligence quotients. Gifted individuals tend to be "out-of-step" with their peers; chronologically, they are the same age as others; mentally they are several years advanced.

Mentally slow individuals are classified as "E.M.H." (Educable Mentally Handicapped) and "T.M.H." (Trainable Mentally Handicapped). These individuals require special kinds of teaching, sometimes in special schools, or at least in special classrooms if within the scope of the regular school plant. They are placed in these categories on the basis of their degree of intelligence, or on the basis of their lack of intelligence.

The Classification of Individuals with Low Intelligence—The E.M.H. and the T.M.H. Categories*

Category	I.Q.	Designation
T.M.H.	0 – 20	Idiot
T.M.H.	20 – 50	Imbecile
T.M.H.	50 – 70	Moron
E.M.H.	70 – 79	Borderline Defective
E.M.H.	80 – 89	Dull normal—backward

*Individuals with less than average intelligence are classified as Educable Mentally Handicapped (E.M.H.) or Trainable Mentally Handicapped (T.M.H.), depending upon their degree of intelligence.

Social and emotional deviation is often found in conjunction with either the mentally or physically handicapped or exceptional individual. These individuals have multiple handicaps, multiple exceptionalities, or multiple learning disabilities. Home conditions, family influences, the immediate neighborhood and the larger general culture, all play a role in shaping the personality of the social-emotional deviate. Sometimes these individuals become psychopathic personalities (their social behavior is so bizarre that they cannot be accepted by society, breaking its laws and regulations at will); often they become neurotic. More often, still, these individuals lead very unhappy, maladjusted lives, never being able to conform, and not being satisfied with themselves when they attempt to do so.

METHODS OF PERSONALITY ASSESSMENT

There is no such thing as a personality "test." The concept of a "test" involves the concept of answering questions in either a "right" or a "wrong" way. Personality testing as such is a misnomer because there are no right or wrong answers when assessing the personality of an individual. The proper terminology is the measurement or the assessment of personality. In this procedure, the individual answers a series of questions or relates in some way to a series of pictures or ink blots, revealing thereby facets of his personality. A skilled examiner (special training is required) records the answers and later interprets them. The answers are subjectively evaluated (which, by the way, is one of the severest criticisms of personality assessment devices).

One method of personality assessment is the case study method. In this technique, the individual is viewed by his peers, family, teachers, associates, etc., and the various reports of these individuals are pieced together to form a composite of his true nature or personality. Case study techniques are not new; they have been in use for many years. The technique is subject to the same criticism as other ways of personality assessment have been criticized: a subjective evaluation must be formulated after all the data has been gathered. Nevertheless, an individual's performance over a long period of time does give clues as to his preferences, his usual mode or pattern of behavior, and his usual way of responding to various stimuli.

Another method of personality assessment involves what is known as the projective technique. Probably the two most widely known personality assessment devices which are projective in nature are the Rorschach (Ink-blot test) and the T.A.T. (Thematic Apperception Test).

Two Widely Used Projective Techniques

Name of Assessment Instrument	Pseudonym	Author	Description
Psychodiagnotik Psychodiagnostiks	Ink Blots	Hermann Rorschach	A series of ten ink blots
Thematic Apperception Test	T.A.T.—Picture-Story Test	Henry Murray	A series of pictures

Attempts have also been made to provide group objective testing procedures for the assessment of personality. The most widely known of these devices is the Minnesota Multiphasic Personality Inventory (M.M.P.I.). In this technique the individual subject answers over five hundred questions in multiple-choice fashion. The test is machine-scored and objectively interpreted according to a predetermined set of standards. One objection to this technique lies in the possibility of the subject willfully distorting his choice of answers to "hide" various aspects of his true self. Another objection lies in the difficulty in assessing the motivation of subjects to perform well under large group testing conditions.

Other aspects of personality have been subjected to critical evaluation in the form of a variety of techniques. Interest inventories, aptitude tests, tests of attitudes and opinions, preferences, and degrees of interests in various vocations, as well as many other evaluation tools are available on the psychological market. Many of these devices are valid and reliable, offering significant information to a trained psychometrist (expert in psychological testing). Others among them are subject to varying degrees of criticism with regard to their value or accuracy.

EFFECTS OF CULTURE ON PERSONALITY DEVELOPMENT

Each person experiences certain events during the course of his development. Since most people view these events in similar fashion, they have been termed "common experiences." For some individuals, however, life is filled with unusual events; these events are known as "unique experiences." For still others, experiences which are quite common become unique by virtue of their interpretation. For example, most children fall and bruise a knee at one time or another during childhood, a "common experience." The child who sustains severe debilitating third degree burns, however, has had a unique experience, one which does not happen to all children, and one which may well leave permanent psychological as well as physical scars. Other youngsters experience common events, but their interpretation of these events tends to place them in the unique category; for example, the child who has a minor cut or bruise and reacts with extreme hysteria.

All of us have observed different patterns of behavior characteristic of individuals who have different cultural backgrounds. Local customs and traditions play a role in the shaping of one's personality. Modes of behavior, manner of dress, colloquial forms of speech, traditions, ethnic backgrounds, group mores, and neighborhood standards all have an effect upon the personality of the developing individual. Patterns of behavior are pre-established for both the masculine and the feminine role. Many of the standards of society for each sex are absurd, fallacious, or hypocritical; nevertheless, they have persisted for many years. The American culture fosters a male image of one who is tall, self-assured, manly, poised, and aggressive. The female is shorter than the male, less dominant, and fits the so-called feminine role. Surely not all males and females can be placed into these rather rigid categories. There are many effeminate men and many aggressive women, just as many men are short and many women are tall. Not all individuals in effect find it either possible or practical to adhere to the pre-established tenets of society.

There are technical terms to describe societies which are male-, female-, or child-dominated or -oriented. A feminine-oriented society is termed a matriarchy; a male-dominant society, a patriarchy; a child-dominated society, a pedarchy; and a society where both males and females play equal roles is termed equalitarian.

Early home and family developmental patterns play a dominant role in the formation of personality. Psychologists have recognized that the effects of early learning (pre-school) are key factors in personality development. Today, we are even concerned about the pre-natal effects upon the yet unborn human of his physiological environment. It is generally agreed that the basic personality structure is largely established in early childhood. Parents transmit to their progeny not only biological heredity, but, by force of example and teaching, moral attitudes, philosophical outlooks, habits, and general interest patterns. Prejudice is learned in the home, generally at a very early age.

Culturally disadvantaged youth are those who belong to minority groups, live in underprivileged or ghetto areas, and whose opportunities for normal or usual environmental stimulus patterns are severely restricted. These youngsters grow up in subcultures whose values and mores differ radically from the mainstream of American society. They include Puerto Ricans, blacks, Indians, and Mexican Americans, as well as southern Caucasians. The common element in the backgrounds of these youngsters is poverty. They generally attend poorer quality schools, and opportunities for wholesome recreation are restricted. Many of these youngsters never reach their full potential, and the waste to American society is tremendous.

THE SYNDROME CONCEPT OF PERSONALITY

Personality manifests itself in complex ways. The patterns of expression of one's individuality cannot be simply analyzed. Clusters, personality types, traits which "go together," and the like form what are termed "syndromes." The layman often refers to these syndromes as the "egghead" type, the "executive" type, the "motherly" type, etc.

Areas of the personality encompass many aspects of the individual, such as:

appearance	ethical practices
aptitudes	day-to-day behaviors
interests	character
intelligence	values
sociability	skills
principles	achievements
attitudes	ideals
moral standards	ambition

Personality, then, is a complex of several factors. Most individuals assess the personality of another by simplistic judgement based largely upon one or two factors or based upon idiosyncratic behavior (certain habits or mannerisms which are either negatively or positively interpreted by others).

How one sees oneself is another aspect of the personality syndrome which should not be ignored. The individual's views of his own self-worth, his abilities, and his capabilities, play an important role in his total personality construct. Part of one's self-concept is derived from the ways in which he is treated by others. Acquired motivations such as the need for esteem and status are important in assessing the self-concept of the individual. Many individuals have self-concepts which are self-deprecating or self-derogatory. Many individuals view themselves with negativism, and some with hostility. Others foster unrealistic self-concepts through strong positive feelings of self-worth.

Because of the syndrome concept of personality, one can understand a little better how difficult it is to modify one's personality structure in adulthood. While not impossible, it requires a modification of several aspects of oneself, rather than just one or another of the areas within the personality structure. The interrelated nature of the various aspects of the personality structure forming the syndrome cannot be ignored. This is one of the reasons why deviant personalities (the mentally ill) take a relatively long time before achieving a modicum of personality alteration.

THE ADULT PERSONALITY

The personality of the adult emerges from childhood, adolescence, and young adult patterns, and is affected by a multitude of developmental and environmental factors. But this does not mean that the personality of the adult is stagnant. Personality in adulthood is not a static, unchangeable commodity, simply by virtue of the fact that one has reached a given chronological age and characteristic level of maturity. True, adults are more set in their ways; their habit patterns have been established for longer periods of time. However, a number of factors are operative in the dynamics of personality which can cause modifications in adult patterns.

There is no arbitrary dividing line between adolescence and young adulthood, between young adulthood and adescence, or between adescence and adulthood. Each stage merges relatively imperceptibly with the next. Each stage of human development has its own unique problems and kinds of adjustments. The stage of adulthood is no different in this respect. Life is a continuous process. While physical growth and development taper off sharply in the adult years, mental, social, emotional, and moral judgments and adjustments are still needed.

In practice, chronological ages have been used to delineate one stage of development from another. This is true in adulthood, where the magic number or chronology seems to be eighteen. At eighteen the young adult has now arrived. Adulthood has begun, at least in a legal sense. At least three distinct phases of adulthood have been recognized:

(1) *Early adulthood:* Ages 18 to 40
(2) *Middle Age:* Ages 40 to 65
(3) *Old Age:* Ages 65 on

Some categorizations of adulthood would add a fourth category, beginning at about age eighty-five, and continuing until the end of one's life. This is termed "senescence." While these categories help in discussing the adult and the problems related to each of the various stages, it should be emphasized that chronology is simply a matter of convenience: there is no sharp line of demarcation between each of the stages; rather, they merge from one into the next with little or no fanfare, and often without recognition by the individual himself.

The American population is increasingly becoming a population of young adults. In 1967, the median age for marriage for men was 22.8 years; for women it was 20.5 years. At the same time, while young people are getting married earlier, there is an increase in the divorce rate (it has doubled in the past fifty years). Other changes in young adults in America are evidenced by the fact that more young women, both married and single, are employed outside of the home, more young married couples are attending institutions of higher learning, and there has been a great trend toward urbanization and suburbanization of life. Each of these factors contribute to the adult personality, causing numerous adjustments and modifications in life-style, in ambitions, goals, attitudes, and beliefs.

Although attainment of the legal age allows the young adult to vote, to obtain credit cards, to buy liquor, to marry without consent, and to sign binding contracts, from the psychological point of view the individual may not, as yet, have attained adult maturity. Adult maturity implies stability, purpose in life, responsibility, capability, seeking worthy goals, the start of a family, and the assumption of civic responsibility. Many individual young adults are ready for these adjustment problems; others are nowhere near ready. In general, adulthood is viewed as the age of greatest potential achievement in one's lifetime; productivity reaches its peak.

The typical adjustment problems faced by adults include:

remaining single or getting married;
continuing school or entering the world of work;
choosing a lifetime's vocation;
slowing of physical capabilities;
economic problems;
the problems of raising a family;
adoption of an individual code of morals, ethics, and religious values; and
facing the realities of life.

A person is never stagnant; life's problems and demands do not end with the achievement of adulthood. One is continually moving from one's past toward one's future, while at the same time faced with the immediate problems of existence. The challenges of adulthood are many, and the adjustments require numerous decisions.

PERSONALITY MODIFICATION

Young adults attempt to change various aspects of their personalities in a number of ways. These attempts and the methods employed have come to be known as "adjustment mechanisms." (A number of these mechanisms were discussed in Chapter Five.) Many of these mechanisms—compensation, rationalization and projection—have their basis in Freudian or psychoanalytically-oriented psychology. In using these devices, the individual is often unaware that he is making an attempt to modify some aspect of his behavior and his personality.

Adults frequently attempt to modify certain aspects of their personality. Physical appearance and habits are among the two highest priority items in adult attempts at adjusting or changing their personalities. By attempting to gain or to lose weight adults are often really trying to improve social relationships, become more attractive to others, and enhance this aspect of themselves and their personalities. Minor habits which are annoying to others may be modified or eliminated completely, although regression and lapses can occur.

WHAT WE HAVE LEARNED

1. Personality development and modification does not stop with adulthood, but is a continuous process operating throughout one's lifetime.
2. Personality encompasses the entire range of an individual's behavior.
3. A fundamental concept of personality stresses the uniqueness of each individual.
4. The development of personality in young adulthood and adulthood centers on breaking ties with the past and developing new modes of expression.
5. Psychologists have recognized the impact of uncertainty upon the personality of the young adult.
6. There are several different definitions of personality.
7. The layman equates personality with idiosyncracy; the psychologist stresses the syndrome nature of personality.
8. Personality is dynamic.
9. Most personality theories can be classified as either type, trait, or developmental.
10. A number of factors operate to shape and to direct the development of the individual's personality, many of which are beyond the control of the individual.
11. Individuals with low intelligence are classified as E.M.H. or T.M.H.
12. Exceptional individuals may differ from others physically, socially, mentally, emotionally, or in any of several combinations of the above.
13. There is no such thing as a personality "test." Personality measurement instruments are properly termed assessment devices.
14. Projective techniques are widely used in personality assessment.
15. Societal structures may emphasize matriarchy, patriarchy, pedarchy, or equalitarianism.
16. There is no definite line between personality development in late adolescence, young adulthood, adescence, and adulthood.
17. Adults have three or four phases of their adult lives: early adulthood, middle age, old age, and senescence.
18. Adults face numerous adjustment problems characteristic of their particular stage of development.

19. Personality modification occurs through a series of adjustment mechanisms.
20. The adult may consciously attempt to modify certain aspects of his personality such as physical attributes or habits.

What We Still Need to Learn

1. We still need to know more about several of the key factors in personality development: how they effect the individual and how the dynamics of these mechanisms operate.
2. The effects of negativism in the environment upon the development of one's personality have been recognized only recently and a start at understanding all of the implications and ramifications in this regard has just begun.
3. We need to find better ways of teaching and training individuals with low intelligence in order to utilize effectively all of the abilities which they possess.
4. Better assessment devices for personality measurement are still needed.
5. A better understanding of the aberrant personality is needed.
6. Modification of traditional societal views such as male aggressiveness and female recessiveness is needed in order to help the personality adjustment of those individuals who do not fit into these pre-established patterns.
7. We need a better understanding of the complexities of personality and of the syndrome concept of personality.
8. There is still much misunderstanding about the problems of adjustment of the adult and the young adult; they have too long been relegated to the category of "completeness." We know now that they too have numerous adjustment problems which must be faced and resolved.
9. We still do not know all of the adult adjustment mechanisms which are operant in the changes we see evidenced in adult personalities.
10. More research is needed into several aspects of the deviant personality in order to prevent these deviancies and to treat more effectively those which occur.

Suggestions for Further Reading

Adams, Donald K., *Anatomy of Personality*, New York: Random House, Inc., 1954.

Allport, G. W., *Pattern and Growth in Personality*, New York: Holt, Rinehart & Winston, 1961.

Bonner, Hubert, *Psychology of Personality*, New York: The Ronald Press Co., 1961.

Brawer, Florence B., *Personality Orientations and Vocational Choice in Community College Students*, Los Angeles, California: ERIC Clearing House for Junior Colleges, 1973.

Brawer, Florence B., *New Perspectives on Personality Development in College Students*, San Francisco, California: Jossey-Bass, 1973.

Cattell, Raymond B., *Personality*, New York: McGraw-Hill, 1950.

Coleman, J. C., *Abnormal Psychology and Modern Life*, Glenview, Ill.: Scott, Foresman Company, 1972.

Endleman, Robert, *Personality and Social Life*, New York: Random House, Inc., 1966.

Gordon, Jesse E., *Personality and Behavior*, New York: The Macmillan Co., 1963.

Kisker, G. W., *The Disorganized Personality*, New York: McGraw-Hill, 1972.

Resnick, William C., and Herbert L. Sachs, *Dynamic General Psychology: An Introduction*, Boston, Mass.: Holbrook Press, Inc., 1971.

Vorrath, Harry H. and Larry K. Brendtro, *Positive Peer Culture*, Chicago, Ill.: Aldine Publishing Company, 1974.

Warga, Richard G., *Personal Awareness*, Boston, Mass.: Houghton Mifflin, Co., 1974.

Whittaker, James K., *Social Treatment: An Approach to Interpersonal Helping*, Chicago, Ill.: Aldine Publishing Company, 1974.

12

The Generation Gap

- The committed student of today
- The role of the group: Differences in points of view
- Individual consistency and stability under group pressure
- Social groups and cultural influences
- The challenge of change: American culture in a changing world
- Group attraction: Kinds of social groups
- The Dyad and the Triad: Kinds of group attraction
- The primary group: Family influences
- Changing social relationships and the new morality
- Life in ghetto areas
- Corruption of the environment
- Psychology and Society: The need for change
- Predictions for tomorrow
- What We Have Learned
- What We Still Need to Learn
- Suggestions for Further Reading

PURPOSE OF THIS CHAPTER

Almost everyone has heard a great deal about the generation gap. Is it real? If so, how great is the generation gap, and what can be done about it? What are the values of the present generation, and how do they compare with those held by previous generations? What are the goals and values of the present generation of college students?

These are some of the questions posed in the present chapter. The role of the group and its influences upon the individual, the kinds of social groups and their effects upon college students, and the influence of the family will also be discussed in this section of the text.

Social relationships and the changes which have occurred and are occurring comprise a part of the subject matter of this present chapter, along with an appraisal of conditions in the ghetto and the contributions which psychology can make to alleviate these conditions, and, perhaps, to prevent them from occurring in the future.

In the final section of this chapter, the needs which have created the demand for change in the present social structure will be examined, and some predictions for the future will be attempted.

Chapter Twelve, "The Generation Gap," is an attempt to bring reality and perspective to the relevant issues of today. While the student may not agree with all of the material presented, he should find it a challenge to his own thinking. Perhaps he will even re-examine some of his own views as he re-evaluates the causes and conditions which have created the "Generation Gap."

THE COMMITTED STUDENT

Since the late 1950's and early 1960's, growing campus activism and militancy have become matters of prime concern to college and university administrators and to government officials alike. While much of the student unrest has been publicized out of proportion by the media, there have been instances where the normal function of the college and university has been brought to a halt. The media have at times indicated that large numbers of students are in open rebellion against university authorities; this is, at best, an exaggeration of the facts. That there is a wave of unrest among today's students is factual, however, and cannot be denied.

Most students do not expect people over the age of thirty to understand them. They feel that this group belongs to what they cynically term the "establishment," the "system," or the "machine." More often than not, their parents are included in this categorization. The wave of discontent and student protest reached a climax in the spring of 1969 as campus demonstrations became common. There is no reliable data to prove that more students today are militant than at any other time because no accurate historical statistics for comparison exist. However, there are large numbers of students today who are sincerely dedicated and committed to social reforms and social causes.

Large numbers of students are not only critical of various aspects of the political, economic, and social systems, but their disenchantment has spread to other controversial areas. Questions of sex, drugs, and almost every conceivable taboo are scrutinized and challenged by these young adults. The differences between the generations are evident; they are even more evident when comparing radical youth with their conservative parents.

The actual number of students who participate in political affairs is relatively small compared with the number of students enrolled in colleges and universities. Most students, while concerned and committed, are neither radical nor revolutionary. Nonetheless, the concept of radicalism and change is neither alien nor novel to them. A survey of the Berkeley, California campus of the University of California revealed that less than 10% of the student enrollment were actively involved in the 1969 campus disturbances.

The committed college student of today is intellectually superior to his predecessor of previous generations. Perhaps this accounts, at least partially, for the fact that he is better informed, more alert, and has a deeper concern and commitment toward his fellow man. For the most part, he comes from a middle-class home rather than the underprivileged or ghetto area home, and is not alienated from society, nor does he choose to be alienated. Alienation implies a withdrawal from the social structure and withdrawal has little to do with the contemporary committed student.

Most students want to have their own campus newspaper; they want control of the budget with regard to collection and dispersement of student fees; they want active participation with voting rights on administrative councils; and they want to share in the solution of community problems. They are not asking for complete control of the college. They are asking that the college administration re-direct many of its priorities.

At a large midwestern state-supported college, the student senate voted to abolish the traditional practice of having a homecoming dance because they felt the expenditure of almost $40,000 could not be justified at a time when students were finding it difficult or impossible to obtain financial aid, scholarships, or loans. The school administration promptly vetoed the suggestion and the festivities were held, accompanied by a wave of student protest, some of which became violent. Violence cannot be justified, certainly, but as the above situation makes plain, its roots often need to be examined.

To sum up, frustration at the seeming impossibility of effecting changes in established practices, youthful impatience, and an articulate minority seem to be the basis for much student dissent.

THE ROLE OF THE GROUP

People are basically social, living in constant interaction. They are born into family groups, often designated as primary groups, and they associate with a wide variety of their fellows in all kinds of human relationships. In this and in other associational relationships they are taught by humans. They acquire social habits, attitudes, beliefs, and goals through a variety of repeated associations. They secure their basic needs for food, clothing, shelter, and other experiences in co-operative efforts with others. From the beginning of history, men have developed systematic methods to achieve their needs and desires and to give meaning to their lives. A vast and complex variety of social relations have emerged to meet the universal needs of man. Social relationships may be relatively simple or exceedingly complex. The social psychologist seeks to understand the relationships which exist between groups of people.

There are a number of ways in which groups have been studied, from differing points of view; each contributes to our further understanding of group behavior. The philosopher seeks to understand the ultimate meaning of life. The biologist examines the physiological responses which make life possible. The novelist examines the dramatic and literary aspects of life, structuring its sorrows and its joys. The sociologist examines the nature of social relationships and tries to delineate the common mode of social expression which binds all of mankind into one entity. The social psychologist explores interpersonal relationships and the systems which emerge from these relationships when groups of people join together for a wide variety of purposes.

The social psychologist works with diverse groups of people. He may study juvenile gangs, segments of a community, the family group, groups in industrial situations, religious and rebellious groups. In each of these studies the social psychologist seeks to explain the underlying dynamics which have led to observable behavioral actions. Often he himself assumes a participant role, in order to more fully appreciate the challenges and demands of various social situations. John H. Griffin underwent such a participant experience in his book, *Black Like*

*Me.** (He travelled through the South disguised as a black man in order to more fully appreciate the treatment accorded black people. His experience was still limited, however, by the fact that he knew he could always return to the non-black world.)

An individual, though he may be part of a group, behaves in ways which he perceives as consistent with his view of what the world should be. Several factors influence this perception, among which are beliefs, values, needs, attitudes, and experiences. Beliefs include faith, knowledge, and superstition. What one believes to be true has much to do with how one acts. Beliefs make up the reality world of the individual. Values are judgments; they include what one feels is important to oneself. Certain values may be changed with maturity and experience, while others persist throughout one's lifetime. Attitudes are more fundamental or basic than beliefs and values; and as such they are more difficult to change and form a more essential component of one's personality. How one feels, in general, about education and its values, comprises an attitudinal posture on the part of the individual which will, partly at least, affect his behavior in the classroom. Needs affect the behavior of the individual in groups. Primary or basic needs, such as food, air, and water, have led to behaviors which could not be included as rational unless the person were known to be starving or dying of thirst. Social needs, such as the need for prestige and status, also affect the behavior of the individual when he is with others. For some, these needs are very strong indeed. Some individuals find these needs are readily met or satisfied, while for others a lifetime is needed. The experiences of the individual as he develops, whether they are common or unique, color and affect the behavior of the individual in groups.

The existence of the social group is not a myth. Indeed, it is an important reality of the complexity of urban and suburban American life. A group is not merely a collection of people; it is a number of people organized with a purpose, a goal, or a common need which they seek to meet. Groups are sometimes loosely organized, and sometimes they have complex and intricate organizational structures. Group leaders emerge, some with vague powers of little note, and others with broad and vast powers which affect millions of people all over the world. Each group has a designated life; the duration of that life depends on how well the group meets the needs of its membership, how it is structured, and how its leadership functions. Some groups last for only a relatively few moments, for example, a group watching an accident in the street, while others, such as church groups, have lasted for centuries.

*Griffin, John H., *Black Like Me*, Houghton Mifflin Company, Boston, Mass., 1961.

THE INFLUENCE OF CULTURE

Man is never alone. He carries his social heritage with him wherever he goes. The influence of culture on the behavior of the individual has been recognized as a very important factor. Social group influences have molded man from his earliest days, furnishing him with a language, a tradition, ways of eating and sleeping, habits of cleanliness, and adults to imitate. The influence of culture is so important that many psychologists have taken the position that whatever the individual is or becomes is a product of the culture from which he has been nurtured. Much of the personal unhappiness which an individual experiences is a result of conflict between himself and the various aspects of culture which he encounters.

For many years in the United States the fact of cultural deprivation was accepted as inevitable. Conventional wisdom had it that there will always be poor people, underprivileged people, and the ghetto. Today, influenced largely by the thrust of the younger generation, these beliefs are being challenged. But the effects of culture have been recognized as being so pervasive one can no longer complacently accept cultural deprivation as an inevitable fact of life, but must seek to remedy these faults. If the individual seeks contentment and happiness as a part of his developmental pattern, then he needs to acquire cultural values which enable him to seek these goals in socially acceptable ways, or he may drop out of society and form a new society based on a different set of cultural values.

People are more concerned today about the effects of the environment upon the individual than at any other time in the history of our nation. A very real change has occurred in the concern of young adults for those who are not receiving the full impact of cultural values inherent in the middle-class American ethic. The poor, racial minorities, the underprivileged, and the derelicts of humanity can no longer be cast aside and ignored. Cultural influences can positively help these people, and young adults want the culture to respond with relevancy to the needs of these people, as it has to those more fortunate economically and socially.

The pattern of life to which a person conforms is no longer dictated by those closest to him: his family, friends, and immediate peers. Patterns of life in the United States are now largely culturally determined. Urbanization, and the advent of the megalopolis, have created new opportunities and values for American youth, as well as new problems. The mass media has played no small role in these changes, as have such factors as the mobility of the population, the anonymity of the city, and the challenge to long-held moral and ethical views.

The challenge of change is the challenge of being alive. Nothing remains the same for very long; existence means adjustment to change. The fertilization of the ovum by the sperm causes a change to take place. The united cells, now one, proceed to rapidly undergo a series of changes into two, four, eight, sixteen, and eventually billions of cells. The birth of the human is a change from an internal, protected environment to that of the external world. All stages of human development face adjustment challenges, requiring changes in behavior and in ways of thinking. New experiences are encountered daily, throughout one's lifetime; each experience changes the individual in small or large ways. Even death itself is a change, requiring numerous adjustments on the part of loved ones.

The challenge of culture is the challenge of change. But along with this challenge comes its opposite force: resistance to change. Pragmatically, the old are more resistant to change than the young; the younger generation offers the challenge of change to the older generation. The older generation views the future in terms of the past and hopes that they will be similar. The young see the future as dissimilar from the past and want them to be different. Culture, like the existence of groups, is a non-tangible entity; but it does exist, and it has power. Culture has the power to coerce, to mold, to enhance, to direct, to enforce, to punish, and to reward. Those who challenge the tenets of their culture have several choices:

1. They can leave the culture and seek other cultures more in keeping with their values.
2. They can try to change the culture.
3. They can form a culture of their own which sometimes, but not always, acts as a challenge to their own previous culture.

KINDS OF SOCIAL GROUPS

Social groups consist of individuals with psychological relationships to each other. The size of the group may vary from two or more to large numbers of people with very indirect relationships. The first and smallest social group consists of the newborn and his mother; one of the largest groups consists of the shareholders in a large corporation, who probably do not know each other at all, but share a common interest. Each social group sets its own standards of conduct of what is acceptable or unacceptable.

Many Americans have come to believe that the American ethic should be *the* standard of behavior for people all over the world. Yet many social groups have standards quite different from ours. The

American standard of ambition, drive, the need to achieve, the importance of status and prestige, and the accumulation of material possessions is not revered throughout the world. Indeed, many other groups find it difficult to understand us because of our values. The standards of the American Zuni Indian tribe, for example, are practically the opposite of those of the usual middle-class American. The Zuni Indians respect individuals who are quiet, unassuming, non-aggressive, and who value the position and sanctity of others. Among the Dobuans, natives on an island near New Guinea, respect accrues to the individual who can perform acts of sorcery and magicianship.

Social groups change as their memberships change. As members grow older and new members take their place, the purpose and intent of social groups can be modified and new directions taken. Group memberships provide meaningful relationships for their members, as well as a sense of identity and security.

As individuals blend together to form groups, they often lose some sense of individuality and personal identity as a result of the group membership and group loyalty. This phenomenon becomes strikingly apparent in mob behavior; the individual subordinates his own identity to the will and pressure of the group. Individuals who ordinarily would never condone acts of destruction and violence may participate in mob actions as a result of group loyalty. Afterward, mob participants often feel ashamed, guilty, and have a sense that it was not themselves who committed these actions.

The smallest group consists of two individuals with an attraction or relationship to each other. This group has been termed a "dyad," and the sense of attraction for each other is termed "dyadic attraction." Three individuals form a triad, and that mutual attraction is termed triadic attraction. Dyadic attraction may occur in one of three ways: positive-positive; positive-negative; or negative-negative.

There is no such thing as a "neutral" dyad for then it would not exist at all. A positive-positive dyad exists when two individuals are mutually attracted to each other (althougl. not necessarily equally so; one individual may be more positively attracted than the other). A positive-negative dyad exists when one individual is attracted to the other (positive) but the other is repelled (negative). The dyad exists by virtue of the fact that the individual who is repelled may be fascinated by the other or may be in a position where he must work closely with the other, regardless of his personal or individual feelings. A negative-negative dyad exists when two individuals, though repelled by each other, must work together or be together by dint of special circumstances. They form a group, perhaps unwillingly, but it is still a group.

It is possible to classify groups in many ways. Size is but one method. The largest possible of all social groups includes all of mankind. Four universally recognized groups which are independent of size are:

> The family
> The community
> The social class
> The nation

Groups have loose or strict ways of structuring themselves. Loose alliances include some social clubs and groups which meet infrequently for discussions, dances, or parties. Strictly structured groups can be found in such organizations as the military, business and industrial corporations, and among certain hospital personnel. Groups normally have a given lifetime or duration of existence. But even those groups which have existed throughout the history of mankind have undergone frequent changes in structure, and in purpose.

A common and widely accepted classification delineates groups into one of three categories: the primary group; the secondary group; and tertiary groups.

Primary groups consist of family group memberships. They are the first groups to which we belong; we have no choice about joining them (although later in life many adults leave the structure of the family group by virtue of starting their own families, while other young adults leave the family group by virtue of rejection or lack of acceptance). Family groups consist of progeny and parents, but can also include a diversity of individuals such as in-laws, cousins, godparents, and even family pets. These groups are termed primary not only because they are the first groups to which we belong, but are also the most influential.

Secondary groups include peers, school chums, club associates, immediate neighbors, friends and acquaintances, and those individuals with whom we choose to associate. They are secondary because we have a choice: we may belong to these groups or we may terminate the association. Some secondary groups become near equal in importance to primary groups, as in the adolescent-peer group, when family is rejected and friends preferred. Other secondary groups are much less influential and often are dissolved in relatively short time.

Tertiary groups include memberships of our choice. They may include many individuals we have never met. Tertiary groups include broad social clubs, world organizations, larger cultural groups, and the like.

THE FAMILY INFLUENCE

The family group as we have stated is the primary group and is the group which has the first and largest influence upon the individual. The family structure evidences the two most characteristic traits of groups which are long-lived: durability and stability. In recent times, however, threats to the fundamental existence of the family group have been directed at both its durability and stability.

Social psychologists stress the importance of family influence as a socializing agency, particularly during the formative years. It has been demonstrated that very young children, separated from their mothers for long periods of time, often suffer severe emotional disorders. There is further evidence that children who suffer emotional deprivation may have trouble later in life with their own families.

Family patterns, including sibling relationships, competition and rivalry among members of the same family, and even the sequence of birth (ordinal position of siblings) have an effect upon an individual's pattern of behavior. The family provides the child with his first and earliest experiences, his values and beliefs, and his orientation toward society. In adolescence and young adulthood, questioning of these patterns and values has led to what has become known as youthful rebellion. Conditions of social deprivation have been shown to have harmful effects upon an individual's development. However, even in families where no discernible psychological or physical deprivation is evident, youthful rebellion probably still takes place as long-held family traditions, customs, and practices are questioned.

CHANGING SOCIAL RELATIONSHIPS

The 1970's ushered in an era distinguished by markedly changing social relationships. Due particularly to the thrust of young adults and college students, a number of social relationships have undergone and are undergoing dramatic change. These include:

Equality of women
New morality and new sexuality
Rapidity of change in social institutions
Questioning of established institutions
Impersonality in social relationships

The new morality and sexuality embrace the concept of equality of sexual experience and practice for both men and women. The old "double-standard" concept has been rejected. Young women today, with the advent of the "pill" and other contraceptive devices, are free to participate in sexual practices without fear of pregnancy. The new sexuality has also changed social relationships. Women today are no longer courted in the fashion of yesteryear. They have become equal partners in a sexual evolution which is unintelligible to some and repugnant to others. To the young adult, however, the sexual changes in today's society are neither of these, but rather a natural sequence of events in a changing world.

While there are still numerous womens' groups organized for the purpose of protesting real or imagined acts of feminine discrimination, women today are freer and have greater opportunity than at any other time in our national history. With this greater freedom of mobility and behavior, women have assumed a new responsibility in society.

The rapidity in change in social values, morals, and social conduct is a part and parcel of today's world. While historically social changes took decades or centuries to evolve, today they occur with startling rapidity. Still, many young adults feel that social change takes place too slowly; that much still needs to be done in this direction before society can begin to realize its full potential.

Young adults throughout the nation have presented challenges to long-established practices in virtually every form of social institution. No social structure is immune from the disturbing, perturbing, and painfully relevant questioning of today's young adult. The church, schools, and governmental institutions have all had values and established practices questioned and threatened; and, as a result, many changes have evolved.

The result of these forces operating in society has been, at least temporarily, an increasingly impersonal society in which the individual is largely subservient to the group. We live in an era of mass transportation, rapid and impersonal communication, and technology whose complexity often overshadows the creativity and needs of the individual. The pendulum has swung dramatically: change is a way of life and stability is of relatively less value.

We also live in an era of the "affluent society." Money is available and the standard of living is rather high—but only for some. In reality, there are many inequalities in our current society. Without a doubt, many of its members *are* affluent, but a great portion of our society lives in poverty or borderline poverty status, while another portion has become embittered, disillusioned, and "dropped out" of the present social order.

As clinical psychologists are faced with disturbed and ill individual patients, the social psychologist too is faced at times with a disturbed and ill society. Values need to be re-designated. Goals need to be more clearly defined. Motives need to be re-examined. Perceptions need definition. Society, as a patient, is a much more difficult patient than an individual. The root causes of the illness lie deeply imbedded in centuries of waste, graft, corruption, and negligence. The task for reform is a formidable task. Some advocate total revolution—starting from the beginning with a new constitution and new forms of government. Others advocate the "bandaid" approach—patching up what we have as best we can. Still others see the possibilities of retaining the essential features of our democratic institutions while instituting realistic, forward-looking, aggressive programs of change.

CONDITIONS IN THE GHETTO

In the list of man's inhumanity to man, the conditions of life in the ghetto surely rank high. It is difficult for non-ghetto residents even to begin to appreciate the bizarre circumstances of life which surround the ghetto resident. Social disorder and disorganization are rife. Severe deprivation in all forms of culture, poor schools staffed by inadequately prepared and poorly motivated teachers, a lack of even the rudiments of the basic necessities in terms of medical care, a total lack of psychological services, constant hunger, rampant crime, oppression, disillusionment and disorder characterize ghetto life. Its effects are far-reaching, pervasive, and possibly affect future yet unborn generations.

Ghetto residents are the socially disadvantaged or culturally deprived of our society. They include the blacks, the Spanish-speaking, poor whites, the impoverished, and the derelict. The offspring of these groups all too often fall into the pattern of ghetto life from which there seems to be no escape. The typical Horatio Alger success story of the past has become less attainable in modern society. The very avenue of escape—increased education leading to realistic employment and economic self-sufficiency—is often the weakest structure within the ghetto. Adding to the confusion, many ghetto schools operate as if they were located in middle-class white or upper-class suburban areas. The methods of fifty to one hundred years ago are simply not adequate in their attempt to deal with social conditions as they exist in the ghetto today.

The report issued by the National Advisory Commission on Civil Disorders points to conditions of life in the ghetto as being strikingly different from those to which most Americans are accustomed. The mortality rate is distinctly higher than that of the national average; there are more incidents of crime; major illness occurs more frequently with less available medical treatment; the rate of admission to mental hospitals is higher in proportion to the overall population; life expectancy is lower; infant mortality is greater; there is generally a total and complete lack of mental health or psychological services facilities.

Educationally, the record of public education for ghetto children is abysmal. Reading rates deteriorate while drop-out rates increase. Students fall further behind in educational progress at a more rapid rate if they are ghetto residents. The result is disillusionment and a lack of motivation. Students drop out rather than persist in their struggles with irrelevant subject matter. But where do they drop out to? The unemployment rate for the ghetto resident is higher than for other people. They often become additions to the welfare roles, a national system which contributes to psychological deterioration by instilling a sense of futility and hopelessness.

PSYCHOLOGY AND SOCIETY

Previously, we have observed the truism that human behavior is socialized behavior; that people exist in groups and that these groups serve to meet the needs of their memberships. Most human learning occurs through a process of socialization; even actions dictated by heredity are channeled through social institutions. Often, however, the social structure denies the individual those things which he sees as necessary to his welfare. In this situation some individuals turn to socially unacceptable patterns of meeting their needs: crime, delinquency, acts of aggression, and various anti-social behaviors.

Some individuals in our society have reached the conclusion that in order to meet their needs as they see them they have to take what they want through illegal action. They may use force, such as armed robbery, or they may use more subtle means, such as a businessman's manipulation of stockholdings. Society views both these actions as hostile. The arrest of the individual and his incarceration in prison is demanded. Crime is of course a psychosocial problem. Its resolution lies in the underlying thinking of the individual and the group which leads them to the conclusion that they must grasp that which is unavailable in more socially acceptable ways. Only through an understanding of the collective thinking of the alienated individual and his group can the prevention of crime be accomplished. Presently, we have only begun to understand the implications of these processes.

Many of the ills of our society have long been recognized. In the past, one of the problems in attempting to eradicate these ills has been the oversimplification of their causative factors. The depression of the 1930's was thought to have been caused by the Hoover administration, if not by Hoover himself; juvenile delinquency is caused by slums; World War II was caused by Hitler alone; these and numerous other oversimplifications simply obscure the real complexity of the causes of psychosocial problems, making attempts at their solution even more difficult. The social psychologist attempts to reduce these oversimplifications to their fundamentals and performs planned experiments to illustrate the true facts in any given situation. Variables are controlled and each individual factor is carefully examined with the support of numerous objective data before conclusions are reached. Still, the conclusions are generally couched in cautious language, being applicable to certain specific situations relevant to the particular investigation, but not necessarily applicable to the broader social spectrum.

Social psychologists have contributed positively to the general understanding of the behavior of man in groups. Eventually the knowledge contributed by the social psychologist may act directly as a positive force in the correction and prevention of social problems. As yet, however, social psychology has not reached this stage of development. It is a relatively young science, and the conditions under which it must operate are of the highest order of complexity.

THE NEED FOR CHANGE

We have examined some of the underlying dynamics of the generation gap, and must conclude that there is a need for change. In a 1970 study, several hundred young adults were asked to indicate which areas of change they considered to be vital. The summarization of their responses indicates that the following aspects of society are in need of change:

1. The restructuring and modernization of the educational system.
2. The termination of cold war hostilities.
3. The reduction in racial discrimination, prejudice, and racial tensions.
4. The effective utilization of national energy resource
5. Ending the still present requirement that young adult males must register for the draft at age eighteen.
6. Making religion more meaningful.
7. Legalization of drugs.
8. Control of inflation.
9. Environmental control.
10. An end to poverty and hunger.
11. Reduction in the power of the federal government.
12. Development of new modes of transportation.
13. An increase in governmental participation by the so-called average citizen.
14. Institutional reform in mental hospitals, hospitals and prisons.

15. More emphasis on the needs of youth.
16. Equality for women.

While many of the suggestions for change are laced with youthful idealism, others point to fundamental inequities in a social system which has contributed to the present generation gap. Many of the suggestions are practical and could be effected immediately without large investments of money; others would require relatively longer periods of time and huge expenditures. Perhaps some of the changes will have been effected by the time the student reads this book; others may not be effected at all, while still others may require the efforts of several generations spanning more than one's lifetime.

It is interesting to note that the interests of young adults have a broad range, from current local matters which affect their immediate lives and the lives of others to worldly matters which are or should be of universal concern. One of the criticisms aimed at the young adult by the older generation is that he offers few suggestions for the improvement of established institutions, while being loudly vocal in his criticism of same. The criticism may have some justification. Nevertheless, the altruism of the present generation in all of its idealism is a positive force which, if properly directed and utilized, can effect vast changes in society for the benefit of mankind.

PREDICTIONS FOR TOMORROW

Whenever one attempts to see into the future, the path is laden with possibility for error. Any attempt in this direction is subject to the test of time. Some of the predictions, no doubt, will seem impossible and impractical to many; others may seem unwarranted or unnecessary. The next generation or two hopefully will see the effective implementation of many, if not all, of the predictions for tomorrow listed below:

1. The obsolescence of school buildings as we know them today.
2. The complete utilization of untapped energy resources.
3. The enhancement of the environment for the benefit of all.
4. An increase in technology and its application in the direction of practicality.
5. An increasing emphasis on the importance of the nation's youth.
6. The development of a new mode of transportation making the gasoline-operated automobile obsolete.
7. Treatment and cures for such illnesses as cancer and heart attacks.
8. The creation of virtually hundreds of new cities comparable in size to Chicago, Detroit, and Cleveland, but as yet unnamed and unplanned.

9. A new form of mass communication which will supplant or replace television.
10. New educational methods utilizing the community as the focus of the college.

Just as the one-room schoolhouse of yesteryear is no longer in existence, except perhaps as a museum attraction, the present structure of school edifices is doomed to obsolescence. They are obsolete now; it is only a matter of time before they are replaced with more modern, office-type structures which will utilize the entire community as a resource for education, rather than centralizing the educational process in one structure with classrooms, corridors, lunchrooms, study halls, and the like.

As the nation comes to recognize the importance of its youth and the potential of their contribution, laws will change giving young adults a greater voice in the various aspects of government and restructuring the society.

A new mode of transportation will replace the automobile as we know it now. The automobile, as we have come to know it, will be as "old hat" as the horse and buggy. Perhaps it will be replaced by airborne vehicles tailored to individual needs, or replaced by pneumatic-computerized forms of transportation; perhaps it will involve belt-linked computerized avenues of transportation or the electric car. But its replacement is a certainty, just as the ox-driven plow has been replaced on the modern farm by the motor-driven tractor. The internal combustion engine has served its purpose; it is doomed to obsolescence.

As technology advances, new forms of communication will appear. The two-square-inch portable television type receiver is a reality. The projection of images without a screen is on the horizon. The potentialities for the utilization of these new means of mass communication for education and for the benefit of mankind challenges the imagination. Students from around the world will be able to communicate instantaneously. Professors in Brussels and Rome will be heard by students in Chicago and New York. The classroom of the future is the world.

WHAT WE HAVE LEARNED

1. There are many relevant and vital issues in society today, to which today's generation of young adults can make, and want to make, positive contributions.

2. Most college students do not expect members of the establishment to comprehend fully what they are trying to accomplish.
3. Large numbers of college students today are extremely critical of established social, political, economical, and educational systems.
4. The committed college student of today is intellectually superior to students of previous generations.
5. Today's college student is properly termed the participant student; to the extent that he is not permitted to participate in those decisions which directly and indirectly affect his life, he is alienated from the social structure and tends to rebel against this non-participant, alienated status.
6. People are basically gregarious; they exist in social groups and seek to express themselves in social groups as a means of gaining both status and security.
7. The social psychologist explores the relationships which exist when groups of people act together.
8. An individual, although he may be part of a group, behaves in ways in which he perceives the world as it should be, directed by the forces and pressures exerted by his group memberships.
9. The existence of the social group is not a myth or a theoretical posit; it is a reality and has the power and force of reality.
10. Young adults enjoy and seek social situations.
11. The pattern of life to which an individual ascribes is no longer dictated entirely by the primary group: the effects of culture are more prominent in these areas than at any other time.
12. The challenge of change is the challenge of being alive.
13. There are numerous kinds of social groups, which can be classified in a variety of ways such as size, interests, primacy, effects, and purpose.
14. Dyads consist of two individuals with psychosocial relationships to each other.
15. Social groups exist when psychological factors bind them together for some agreed-upon or recognized goal.
16. There are three basic kinds of dyadic attraction: positive-positive, positive-negative, and negative-negative.
17. A commonly accepted and widely applied classification of groups places them into categories designated as: primary groups, secondary groups, and tertiary groups.
18. The influence of the family has been recognized as a primary factor in the development of the child.
19. The United States is in the midst of vast social change.
20. The intolerable conditions in the ghetto rank at the top of the list of social disorders with which we are faced.

21. The correction and prevention of the existing conditions of ghetto life is a matter of prime urgency if the nation as we know it is to survive.

22. The contribution of the social psychologist toward the improvement of society is a great potential for the future; its fullest realization and implementation have not as yet been effected.

23. The oversimplification of the ills of society has contributed to the difficulty in attempts at their solution and prevention.

24. The social psychologist can contribute positively to the understanding of the behavior of man in groups.

25. The need for change in many established political, educational, economic, and social institutions has been recognized by the young adult; it is expected that many of these changes will be effected in the future.

WHAT WE STILL NEED TO LEARN

1. We need to find ways to bridge the generation gap by preventing the misunderstandings and by correcting the lacks in communication between the generations.

2. We need to find an effective means of utilizing the energies of the committed student into socially productive directions.

3. Some of the traditional values and practices held on campus need to be modified or abolished; they were effective and served a useful function and purpose in a bygone era; they no longer suffice today.

4. We need a better understanding of the dynamics of the group processes which can be seen in social interaction.

5. The interpersonal relationships of the individual in groups needs to be explored further.

6. Recognizing the importance of culture is not enough; we must act positively to overcome the damaging effects of cultural deprivation upon the underprivileged.

7. We need to find a means of bringing the culturally isolated back into the mainstream of society.

8. The preservation of the family unit in a world of rapid change is a challenge for young adults today who will become the parents of tomorrow.

9. We need to understand better how the effects of world problems and broad social issues (tertiary groups) have changed the behavior and attitudes of today's generation of young adults.

10. The changing social relationships evident in today's society need direction and impetus for positive achievement and purpose.

11. We have not met the problems of the ghetto. We need to learn how to deal with our present problems and how to prevent the further compounding of them in the future.
12. We need to utilize the contributions of the social psychologist with practical applications toward the solution of our pressing social problems.
13. We need to recognize the need for change, instead of resisting this need.
14. We must recognize that there is an urgency about our younger generation which cannot be contained, but must be satisfied through positive social action.
15. Perhaps all of the predictions for tomorrow will not materialize; but we need to have an open mind and perspective to the potentiality for the benefit of mankind for many of these positive forces which drive in the direction of change.

SUGGESTIONS FOR FURTHER READING

Buss, Arnold H., *Psychology: Man in Perspective*, New York: John Wiley & Sons, Inc., 1973.

Butz, Otto, Ed., *To Make A Difference: A Student Look At America*, New York: Harper and Row, 1967.

Feuer, L. S., *The Conflict of Generations*, New York: Basic Books, Inc., 1969.

Freedman, Morris, *Chaos in Our Colleges*, New York: David McKay Co., Inc., 1963.

Fromm, E., *The Sane Society*, New York: Holt, Rinehart & Winston, 1955.

Grinker, R. R., and J. P. Spiegel, *Men Under Stress*, Philadelphia, Pa.: Blackiston, 1945.

Maslow, Abraham H., *Self-Actualizing People*, in C. E. Moustakas, Ed., *The Self*, New York: Harper and Row, 1956.

Pfeiffer, J. William and John E. Jones, *A Handbook of Structured Experiences for Human Relations Training*, Culver City, California: University Associates, 1973.

Sarason, Seymour B., *The Psychological Sense of Community*, San Francisco, California: Jossey-Bass, 1974.

Townsend, Agatha, *College Freshmen Speak Out*, New York: Harper and Row, 1956.

Wolins, Martin, *Successful Group Care: Explorations in the Powerful Environment*, Chicago, Ill.: Aldine Publishing Company, 1974.

Yates, A. J., *Frustration and Conflict,* Princeton, New Jersey: Van Nostrand Reinhold, 1965.

13

The Young Adult as a Revolutionary

- The informed college student of today
- Means of communication—The influence of the media
- Racial problems on the campus
- Problems of poverty
- Inequities in the establishment
- The confrontation: Students vs. the establishment
- Radical student groups: The concept of student power
- The factions of the S.D.S.
- Student militancy—Riotous behavior
- What We Have Learned
- What We Still Need to Learn
- Suggestions for Further Reading

PURPOSE OF THIS CHAPTER

The United States was born amidst a Revolutionary War. Since that time many changes have occurred. Now, a new revolution is taking place: a revolution of young adults rebelling against inequities, real or imagined, in the social framework. The purpose of this chapter is to examine the causes of the revolution, to attempt to understand its goals or purposes, and to try to determine the future direction of the young adult movement across the land.

Are we in the middle of a revolution? Perhaps not. Perhaps a social revolution differs from the usual concept of a revolutionary war or a civil war. Still, the polarization of various groups within the society continues, and covert if not overt hostility exists. The new revolution seems to be a conflict of conservativism vs. radicalism; the new revolutionaries are designated as radicals. In this chapter we will examine some radical concepts and the radicals themselves.

Student militancy is a relatively new phenomenon, making its first appearance in the late 1960's and early 1970's. In the latter part of this chapter we will examine the causes for student militancy and some of the actions which have resulted. It is a simple thing to "write off" the student revolutionaries as immature and irresponsible. In reaction to their outspoken behavior and radical views, many older adults feel harsh punishment, banishment from the campuses, and even imprisonment is fitting. Before making such rash judgments, however, one must consider the important influence of students in nations such as Japan, various parts of Europe, and Latin America. America has begun to mature. Now her people must begin to mature, and the phenomenon we are witnessing, that of The Young Adult as a Revolutionary, may be a part of this process of national maturation and development.

This chapter will present challenging points of view. Not every student will or should agree with each of the various views to be presented herein. Each student should take time to reflect upon his own beliefs and values, to ascertain for himself which position he can successfully "live with" in light of his own individual circumstances. Then, and only then, will the material to follow become meaningful and relevant.

THE INFORMED COLLEGE STUDENT OF TODAY

In periods of relative quiet on the various campuses throughout the nation, many adults sigh with relief and hope for a return to "normalcy." They overlook the fact that today's college student is better informed than students of previous generations; that there will never be a return to complacency as long as students wish to take an active role in the life of their college and community. The fact is inescapable: the college student of today, better informed, more alert, more serious than any of his predecessors, is going to involve himself in the issues of our time. Accepting this, how then can we expect behavior in keeping with the behavior of the relatively complacent students of the 1950's?

Although no two campus demonstrations are alike, one common element in each of the protests was the fact that students were aware of the inequities about which they were protesting. Perhaps they were not fully informed; it is difficult for students to have access to all of the information relative to campus and community operations. But they were informed enough to be able to make a judgment that inequity existed and to move in the direction of expressing their dissatisfaction. We can learn from these demonstrations; indeed, we *must* learn if repetitions of the actions are to be prevented and if escalation of hostilities is to be avoided.

Has the violent action on the nations' campuses subsided, like an earthquake which occurs only every one hundred years, or have we witnessed a hurricane which, though not present now, will return seasonally to vent its fury in many directions? Have the students learned from their protests and from the demonstrations of their fellow students across the nation? Some serious questions need to be answered:

—Will the large numbers of students who participated in campus demonstrations and disorders realize the seriousness of their actions?

—Will students realize that violence can sometimes contribute more to the negation of their cause than the reforms which they seek?

—Will students become aware that repressive forms of tyranny, in any form, including their own, cannot be tolerated?

—Will students learn that denying teachers the right to teach and their fellow students the right to be taught cannot help to improve the institutions to which they must return?

—Will students learn that tearing down existing institutions accomplishes nothing unless better modes of operation are offered in their stead?

THE INFLUENCE OF THE MEDIA

We live in an age of mass and rapid communications. Communication between individuals and large groups of people takes place in a wide variety of ways. Some of these ways involve the use of complex technological equipment; others involve no more than a simple gesture or facial expression. Communication between individuals may take place through: Multi-media; Personal media; Art-form media; or Sense-organ media.

Instant communication via the use of multi-media technology has led to a depersonalization in the relationships between individuals. Empathy between the individual and the television set is difficult to achieve. Realization that virtually millions of people all over the world can be informed about important events at the same time and relatively spontaneously has lessened the sense of personal affiliation and attachment to these events. The media have also had an effect upon the young adult, tending to lead toward passive acceptance of spectacular occurrences. Thus, while the older generation is still fascinated by moon flights and other forms of space travel, the younger generation accepts these occurrences as matter of fact.

Personal forms of communication between individuals are often steeped in the cultural apparatus of local ethnic groups. Various segments of the culture develop signs, gestures, and symbols to communicate non-verbally the meanings which their peer groups fully understand, but which may not be understood or appreciated by those from without the cultural area.

Various art forms have been definitely influenced by the spirit of revolution and change prevalent among young adults today. The theater, motion pictures, and art itself in its various forms have shown the sense of realism, provocativeness, boldness, and frank and candid expressionism characteristic of the young adult of today.

Our sense organs communicate meanings to us which we then perceive individually and interpret according to our backgrounds, experiences, and mental set. Individuals communicate with each other through sensory modes, by the clothing they wear (or do not wear), by the style of their hair and general appearance, by gestures and non-lingual sounds. Even one's poise, bearing, carriage, manner of walking, and posture communicate meaning to other individuals. Certainly the young adult generation has provoked comment from the older generation because of these forms of communication. While the first reaction of older adults was that of general rejection, many of the styles and patterns of the young have since been adopted by them, but without the symbolism or symbolic communicative direction.

Confrontation politics, radical group oratory, campus demonstrations, all have been given wide coverage in the multi-media reporting by the press, radio, and television. Whether the media has served to stimulate groups to greater activity and whether the activists perform many of their more violent actions for the benefit of the media as yet remains unanswered. Factually, however, it can be stated that the various media have had an influence upon young adults. The exact direction of this influence remains to be seen. That the various media will continue to express interest and concern with the expressions of feelings by students is evidenced by the many avenues of reporting of campus events. The Columbia Broadcasting System (CBS), for example, recently produced a series of programs for television, entitled "Generations Apart," in which the attitudes and motivation of campus groups were closely examined and brought to the attention of the nationwide public

RACIAL PROBLEMS ON THE CAMPUS

Racial prejudice and tension in our society are, unfortunately, not new. Their presence on the campuses around the nation, however, is relatively new, and the attempts to deal with these situations are fledgling attempts. The problem never really existed on the college campuses before, largely due to the fact that black students were not present in any sizeable proportion. This situation has changed today in the elementary schools, the high schools, and the colleges. Recent Supreme Court legislation demanding further immediate integration has added many more black students to the college scene; despite this, their numbers are relatively few in proportion to the total black population.

It is not possible to legislate or legally outlaw racial prejudice. Prejudice is learned in early childhood, stems largely from the home, and is greatly a matter of ignorance and lack of factual information. The problem of racial tension and racial violence on the campus is more than a black-white problem. For years prejudice has existed in the direction of virtually every minority group: the Jew, the Oriental, the foreign-born student, and others. The new element in the situation, however, is the increasing attempt to deal realistically and successfully with the problem.

College campuses today, for instance, teach courses which were not heard of a few years ago: Black Literature, Black History, Swahili —all attempts to understand and integrate the black man into the American college and university. The phenomenon is complicated by the fact that black youth today seek a separate identity, and in this quest often segregate themselves purposefully and willfully in order to achieve a sense of camaraderie and to pursue what they see as the common good.

Many college campuses boast of their fully-integrated, peaceful, and well-ordered campus. And indeed a closer examination of the campus reveals that students of many different ethnic backgrounds are attending classes. A still closer look, however, often reveals what may be a deeper and more insidious form of segregation: segregation within a so-called integrated structure. In the lunchrooms, study halls, recreation rooms, even in social events, black and white students tend to cluster and isolate themselves; integration is present only in the sense of the two attending the same physical plant. True social relationships are still lacking.

We have not begun to solve the problem of racial tension and prejudice on the campus. True, in most colleges today, housing and lunchroom facilities, as well as classroom and recreational facilities are open to all students. But does the minority student feel a part of it all, or does he still feel as isolated as if he were not even attending? These key issues have not been resolved, and the problems of the urban areas contribute to the complexity of the problem. Our large cities have not come to grips successfully with the problem of integration. Forced integration has failed. Bussing is questionable in value. Harmonious, social, real-life integration has not been achieved in all but a very few areas.

To make matters worse, the black student is often inadequately prepared for the rigors of the academic world. He is somewhat prepared for the tokenism he often faces in his college classes and among his white peers, but this only contributes to his need to join with other black students as a means of gaining security, status, and acceptance. The number of black teachers and professors is still minimal. Perhaps these problems will never be solved; perhaps their resolution is still a generation away. Nevertheless, the problems exist, and young adults are keenly aware of the bigotry, hatred, and irrational beliefs held by many people in the non-black population. (These feelings often extend to foreign-born students, who complain of impersonal treatment, difficulty in communication, and a general feeling of tolerance rather than warm acceptance).

In the military service, in hospitals, and in some working situations, progress has been made in the racial area. A great deal of work remains to be done in the area of human socialization, but the picture is not one of hopelessness. Elementary schools commonly report few problems in the primary and middle grades where integration has taken place. The children get along well, and the color barrier is non-existent. Their parents, however, often rebel, fight integration, move out of the neighborhood (thus creating more all-black communities), and indoctrinate their children against getting "too friendly."

The trend of the future is clear: the black man and the white man must learn to live together and work together, if either is to survive; anything less than this is self-defeating. As education contributes to the understanding of man, many of these goals may be achieved.

PROBLEMS OF POVERTY

Poor people have many problems; the lack of money is only one aspect of the multitude of complex adjustment situations which they must somehow attempt to resolve. There have always been poor people, and it is probable that there may always be some poor people. The difference is that today these people are faced with the need to provide higher education for their children, just as more well-to-do people are trying to do. The lack of finances creates many more problems than merely the cost of college. The loss of human dignity cannot be measured in dollars and cents; these psychological ramifications are often immeasurable, but of powerful impact.

Denying one's children the basic necessities of life—food, clothing and adequate shelter—has a psychological as well as physical impact upon those who live in poverty. Feelings of futility and hopelessness as well as despair and bitterness are common. Many poor students find that they are virtually eliminated from participation in athletic events, social functions, and other extra-curricular activities because they cannot afford the costs of the clothing, the uniform, or even the time involved in this kind of participation. These students must work; they have no choice. By virtue of this fact, they are eliminated from the kinds of activities in which more wealthy students can participate. Our better-informed students of today are often keenly aware of these situations, and this awareness tends to add to their frustration and conflict.

Present welfare policies and systems for providing for the financially needy are inadequate and in many respects obsolete. Indeed, it has been charged that they create a psychological alienation which is fully as forceful and probably more damaging than the physical slavery of the black man in the nineteenth century. Our present form of welfare programs, aid to dependent children, and support programs in the form of old-age assistance are as dated as the concept of the running board on the automobile.

There is an urgent need for a revitalizing of the entire concept of providing aid to the needy, and particularly for providing funds for the higher education of the children of the indigent.

The rapid rise of the community colleges with their low tuition or tuition-free programs, their open-door policies, their easy accessibility to the cities, and their preparatory-transfer as well as terminal programs has been one recent answer to the problem of educating the children of the masses of people who cannot afford the kinds of higher education offered by the elite, exclusive, highly selective, and economically expensive ivy-league-type private schools. For many, the state schools, although they provide lower tuitions, are becoming prohibitive because of the cost of room and board while living away from home and because of stringent standards of admission.

Present programs for aiding those who need financial help in order to start or to complete their college educations boast of such aspects as scholarships, loans, and work-study programs. Yet in reality the scope of these programs is very limited; students must meet a host of prerequisites in order to qualify for the given type of funding, and then often the funds are unavailable because of too many applicants.

The need is for programs whereby all students may obtain financial assistance with a minimum of "red tape" and as a part of the routine of college admissions.

Some colleges have begun "small loan" or "emergency loan" or "tide-you-over" programs to help students in financial need on a short-term, small-loan basis. Most of these attempts stem from the efforts of counselors and financial aid officers in local institutions. Business and industry need to make a greater commitment in dollars and in personnel to these kinds of programs. The colleges and universities, and the students who attend them, cannot isolate themselves from the community. Nor can the community any longer afford to isolate itself from the problems and issues of the colleges and universities.

INEQUITIES IN THE ESTABLISHMENT

College students recognize many inequities in the establishment. Indeed they are more keenly aware of many of the inequities because they themselves have been subjected to them in the process of education and in the process of gaining college admission. These inequities point to the larger inequities in the social order, and young people today are intolerant of their continued existence and promulgation.

While most colleges have stopped the practice of asking questions about race and religion on college applications, some still require a facial photograph, which is simply another way of identifying those from minority groups, and those who appear too "radical" (this, in spite of the fact that it has been a long-established principle of psychology that judgment of personality attributes from facial photographs is unreliable!). Many colleges, particularly private ones, are highly selective about student admissions. This situation exists even at those private schools which depend for their continued functioning on state and federal funds, funds derived from the tax support of all of the people.

College students want to know why these conditions continue to exist. They want to know why there isn't room for all students who seek to better themselves through higher education. Even the community colleges, which often boast of an "open-door" or "open admissions" policy, have turned away large numbers of students because they applied too late, were from a foreign country, didn't meet some aspect of entrance requirements, or simply because there wasn't enough room to provide for them, despite the fact that they were fully-qualified applicants.

Some of the more common inequities in the educational establishment include:

The system of ranking students
Inequities in grading standards
Selective admissions policies
Limited availability of financial aid
Lack of opportunity to work
The difficulty in being heard

The system of ranking of both secondary school and college students divides them into quarters: the upper quarter (top 25% of their class), the second quarter or quartile (second 25% of their class, or upper half), the third quarter, and the lower quarter (last 25% of their class, or lowest-ranking 25%). This system is used by almost all colleges, at least partially, as a basis for consideration of an applicant's request for admission. It takes no account of the fact that the student has no control over how many students are in his class, or how well prepared academically these students may be. A student ranking in the lower half of his class at one school may have ranked in the upper half in another. Thus some students are selectively rejected because of matters over which they have no effective control.

Class rank is determined by grades. Because of this system some students choose courses in which they believe they can get a good grade, rather than because they feel the course has some educational merit or value for their personal needs and for their academic preparation. Recognizing that some teachers grade more severely than others, students often choose "easy" teachers because they believe they can get a "good" grade. While the grade itself may have little value or meaning to the student, it is a means to an end. However, when we follow this line of thinking we have displaced our value system. A grade should reflect a level of educational attainment or mastery of content material, not the personality or views of the instructor or the competitiveness of the class in which the grade was accomplished.

Colleges justify their selective admissions policies because of lack of facilities, shortages of housing space, limits placed by budgets, and the need to uphold academic standards. Students often question the restrictive nature of these policies, and the underlying truths or realities which fostered many of the policies when they were originally instituted. Students feel they should have a choice of schools for their higher education, rather than coming hat in hand, meek and mild, hopeful of being the chosen one. Many schools compound the problem by notifying students very late that they have been accepted or rejected, thus making it virtually impossible for them to choose alternatives. College administrations have recognized the problem, as indicated by many of the application-for-admission forms which candidly ask the student to list other schools to which he has applied for admission.

Today, many students, if not all, apply to more than one college. Many needy students are effectively restricted from following this procedure because of non-refundable application fees ranging up to twenty-five dollars. Students want to know if it would not be more fair to accept applicants on a first-come-first-serve basis, giving all an equal opportunity to attend the college of their choice, within the limits only of the physical capacity of the institution, and eliminating considerations of grades, rank, race, and ethnic background.

Although many parents and the general public may believe that financial aids are widely available to all students who seek them, this is not always the case. Many students find that no source of financial aid is available, thus forcing a dependency upon their own or parental resources. Adding to the problem, the number of job opportunities both on and off campus is often extremely limited, with students competing for the menial and generally low-paid employment which they can obtain.

Probably the greatest inequity on campus to which students object is their difficulty in being heard. Often, when they are given a voice in institutional matters through organizations such as student government and student senate groups, they complain that the school administration is unreceptive or even hostile to their suggestions.

As this situation has continued for a number of years, the suggestions of the students have become more forceful, leading often to outright demands. When these are ignored, the process leading to direct confrontation is complete.

THE CONFRONTATION

It is not a simple thing to decide to walk the confrontation road. Students are well aware of the risks involved. School administrations can exclude, suspend, dismiss, fine, punish, harass, and arrest students who decide to confront authorities in open defiance of regulations. Yet despite facing such serious consequences as the possible end to their academic pursuits and possible imprisonment, literally thousands of students have chosen to withstand the perils and adopt the course of confrontation. Some may be innocent dupes; others may be swept up by the emotions of crowds of students; still others may have ulterior motives. But all of this cannot explain the behavior of those who knowingly and willingly face the possible penalties of the confrontation.

In its essence, a confrontation consists of one or more students standing in direct opposition to an administrative ruling. In its practical aspects, confrontations have involved hundreds and sometimes thousands of student protesters. These students have faced armed police, soldiers, and the armed might of the federal reserve in their efforts to be heard. Too often confrontations have become violent, assuming the aspects of an out-of-control mob action which seeks vengeance through senseless destruction of both property and innocent bystanders.

Underlying the immediate complaints of the students involved in a confrontation are the larger principles of freedom, equality, and the right to be heard. The deeper social issues of justice and freedom have become so entrenched with the principles underlying some of the recent confrontations that it is difficult if not impossible to separate the two. Student protest marches, classroom boycotts and classroom takeovers, as well as campus demonstrations are a part of the tactics of "confrontation." Powerful forces drive these groups of students to extremes; and once operational, the tactics of confrontation are difficult to slow or to control.

Questions of academic freedom have been raised about student confrontations, as many members of the faculty been forced to choose sides, or have voluntarily made such a choice and have even led student confrontations. Some professors have demanded and obtained greater freedom of expression than is enjoyed by any other employee group, including groups of employed professionals. Others still feel their academic freedom is greatly restricted by obsolete and antiquated administrative dicta.

Groups involved in confrontations need strong leadership. Often these leaders are members of radical student organizations, thus lending credence to the charge that their sole purpose is to subvert and destroy the essence of the concept of the college and the university, of democracy, and of American traditional value systems. In plain fact, most student groups (including the radicals) are rather poorly or loosely organized. Within the student groups themselves there is a wide area of dissent. Organizing a confrontation is a difficult thing for most student groups to achieve. Students are not readily swept up into campus demonstrations, and student participation is often minimal. The actual length of time for the confrontation is generally rather short; students want to return to the business of being students.

Permeating the attitudes of radical student groups are those young adults who are dedicated to action. Most protest does not aim for the complete overthrow of any given institution, but rather to the righting of separate and specific wrongs as the student sees them. Some of the more radical student groups, however, seek complete destruction of the institution, its present leadership, and organizational structure.

RADICAL STUDENT GROUPS

Because of the diversity in attitudes found within student groups, campus activists often find that they cannot organize into one unified student group with an agreed upon platform. They band together to oppose events which outrage them, often dispersing completely when the immediate situation is somehow resolved. Thus student groups on campus are often transient, poorly or temporarily organized, often with unspecified and undefined goals and purposes. Adult critics who feel that radical student groups do not offer positive programs of corrective reform fail to understand the transient nature of many of the radical student protest groups.

Dr. Bruno Bettleheim described some of the characteristics of radical student militants as follows:*

> They have high intellectual ability, developed at an early age.
> There was a lack of full emotional development in their early years.
> They don't want to be students or can't fit into the student role.
> They often want to destroy the university or college.
> They reject knowledge or status as a precondition for action.
> They want action now, not later.
> They are often contemptuous in many areas.

The radical students and the groups to which they belong espouse a long series of virtues. They seek meaningful interpersonal relationships, furtherance of self-development, integrity and responsibility, and a basic philosophy of life. At the same time they reject the ready-made virtues of the establishment. They hold in contempt material values, artificial incentives, status symbols, conformity, repression, suppression, regimentation, and regulation. Many of the radical student groups received their original impetus from political and social protests against the Viet Nam War and Watergate.

There are many different kinds of radical student groups. One such group is composed of black students, who tend to isolate themselves on campus from non-black student groups, and who center their activities about racial injustices and prejudice. Other radical black student groups have formed somewhat tenuous alliances with white students, lending their collective efforts to the eradication of slums and

*Bettleheim, Bruno, "The College Student Rebellion: Explanations and Answers," *Phi Delta Kappa*, May, 1969, p. 513.

ghettos, to the problems of the poor, and to the problems of the environment and other social conditions.

Radical student groups assume many different roles and the diversity of their purposes is illustrated at least partially by the diversity in their nomenclature. Some of the special interest student groups found on campus include: Anti-Junta in Greece Committee; Black Students and Soul Brothers; Militant Students Club; Socialist Students for America; Students for a Democratic Society; Young Americans for Freedom; and the Young Communist League.

How radical are the radical student groups? The answer to the question depends upon each individual's point of view. For some, any change at all is considered radical. For others, progress in the direction of change and reform is developing at too slow a pace. For most people, the use of violence is abhorrent. For others, violence is the only alternative to a lack of social progress. Young adults on college campuses face tremendous psychological pressures when their friends and peers belong to radical groups. Then they must take a stand; they must take a position as a member or non-member of the group. Often failing to join places the student, willingly or unwillingly, in opposition to a group toward which he may feel no opposition at all. In short, attempting to remain neutral today is a difficult if not impossible choice, comparable perhaps to the early organization of labor unions in the United States in the 1930's.

Relatively few of the radical student groups have received any degree of national status and organization. One such group that has achieved this status is the Students for a Democractic Society. Yet even this radical and sometimes militant student group has discovered that unification of purpose, goals, and operational methods is not easy to achieve. In trying to maintain their purpose and goals, some radical student groups find that they must use the very administrative techniques to which they are so violently opposed. Anything less leads to a disintegration of the group, or to its splitting into diverse factions. The Students for a Democratic Society is an example of the latter, where five distinct factions are known to exist, as was discussed in Chapter 8.

STUDENT MILITANCY

Not all aspects of the student revolution are violent or militant. An example of a rather quiet change which has taken place as a result of student demand for action is the change to co-educational institutions by institutions which were formerly restricted to one or the other sex. These institutions have found that admitting members of the opposite sex has positive value for education, causing no visible damage, and creating a better educational atmosphere (as the students themselves report), more in keeping with the realities of life. The co-educationalization of many of the colleges in the United States has received little dramatic publicity, yet it was achieved with virtually no demonstrations, sit-ins, protests, or other kind of public appeals.

On the other hand, there has been a wave of student militancy which has attracted national and international attention. Student militants have closed down campuses, slowed the usual educational process and program, and have been given national attention by the various news media. Student militants are composed of students who are eager for action, want to see changes placed into effect immediately (usually with little concern for possibly more serious problems which some of these changes may create), and who are in their own personal stage of development where they seek independent action.

Colleges, as creative institutions, are naturally receptive to new and somewhat radical ideas. After all, the purpose of the educational process is to foster thinking. Still, many college administrations may not be closely in accord with the radical ideas of the young adults attending their institutions. Students today want to be heard, want to be recognized, want to have their ideas and points of view tried in practice, and want to feel that they are a genuine part of the campus and larger community to which they belong. They seek meaningful relationships, self-satisfaction, self-fullfillment, and social reform.

Today's students make demands covering a wide range of the aspects of their lives as students and encompassing a broad spectrum of social problems. Their complaints may center about such day-to-day matters as cafeteria or dormitory accommodations or the rejection by the school administration of an invited radical lecturer, to the larger problems of world hunger and poverty, the cessation of war, and other such matters which are clearly beyond the control of the local campus heads. As these students become amalgamated or galvanized into a solid force, the older generation becomes the enemy; college officials, police, teachers, and all adults are viewed as suspect.

The direction of student militancy can take several paths. If these students succeed completely, we may find the colleges ruled by anarchy. If they fail completely, the reaction of right-wing conservatives toward suppression of free speech and other freedoms may be equally intolerable. The ultimate course will probably be one of partial acceptance. College administrations will need to recognize that they are not entirely blameless for the social problems of the country, and the militants will need to recognize that college officials are not, conversely, fully responsible.

Campus militants have accused college administrations of a number of violations which have led to violent demonstrations and confrontations. College administrations have been charged with:

keeping their heads in the sand;
not responding to the demands of changing times;
not accepting the new morality;
retaining quota systems in admissions policies;
not recognizing student needs;
clinging to the past;
squelching all forms of protest;
using harsh and repressive forms of discipline;
censoring student publications and student-invited speakers;
viewing all students as problems;
using student fees to help the government in warlike policies and research to be used in war;
unethical real estate practices harming the poor and the underprivileged;
attending to academic matters and ignoring social and emotional needs of students; and
outright acts of prejudice toward minority groups.

The broad range of these accusations encompasses those which do have some basis in fact and those which don't. However, the charges are serious, provoking emotional actions and reactions, and leading to acts of militancy by students who wish to be recognized and wish their demands to receive serious and immediate consideration. Despite hasty and often ill-conceived programs—attempts to demonstrate to students that the college is acting in response to their demands—most colleges and universities today have not succeeded in convincing students that they are truly receptive to their problems.

In the course of time, college students will almost certainly receive a greater degree of autonomy. Indeed, some basic and fundamental changes have already taken place on campuses across the nation. Students are enjoying a more active voice in the formulation of school regulations and practices. They are being invited to sit in on school policy decision-making boards. Even in some relatively conservative institutions, the opinions of the students are being actively sought.

The issues of student militancy and how much of it can be tolerated has led to the broader issue of law and order in the United States. How much power should be entrusted to the police and the military forces? How strict should law enforcement be? What should be done when students actively engage in a riot?

RIOTOUS BEHAVIOR

Although some riots take place spontaneously, triggered by a local inflammatory incident (which is usually of minor significance in itself, and gets lost in the events which follow), most riots develop from long-standing problems, frustration, and the seeming lack of response to issues which students have raised. A number of students have participated in riots on college campuses, and this behavior, like all other behavior, needs to be examined and explained. Since all behavior is motivated, then we must examine the motivation of students who burn property, destroy buildings, overturn cars, and do physical harm to the police, school officials, and any other adults who happen to be in the local area at the time of the riot.

Rebellion in adolescence is a part of growing up, a staple of the developmental process. As one matures into young adulthood, it is natural to want to do more and more things independently, to make decisions, and to take responsibility. Sometimes the rebellion takes place covertly in the form of apathy and passive behavior. It is when the rebellion becomes overtly aggressive that parents and other adults become concerned and alarmed. One form of rebellion occurs when the young adult challenges the fundamental concepts and regulations which have been instituted by parents and by school authorities. Youth is inquisitive and youth must find out for itself. Rebellious behavior becomes harmful when it hurts the individual involved (e.g., apathetic behavior leading to failure) or when it is socially unacceptable (e.g., violent and destructive).

Much attention has been given to riots on college campuses in the past few years. Yet the attention has focused upon the violent and destructive nature of the activities rather than on the underlying causative factors. It is a relatively simple transformation which occurs when a group of youngsters gathering for a sports event, a meeting, or any other kind of assemblage is transformed from an orderly, law-abiding group into an uncontrollable mob. Part of the explanation lies in the sheer force of numbers; individuals feel less responsible for their behavior when everyone in the group is swept up into any form of activity. Part of the explanation lies in the removing of the pressure of being caught; the likelihood of being held responsible for one's actions is tremendously decreased when hundreds or thousands of people are all doing the same thing.

Riots sometimes begin out of stagnation. Police officials experienced in riot control know that as long as groups of people are kept moving, the likelihood of violent action is diminished. It is when crowds are standing still or sitting still, listening to emotion-provoking invective, that riotous behavior is most likely to occur. Once begun, riotous behavior is difficult to control or eliminate; it often provokes more physical violence on the part of police authorites in order to curtail the rioters.

Two factors seem to be present when violence erupts in groups: boredom and specific forms of indignation.

Increasingly students are expressing their dissatisfactions in socially unacceptable ways—through riots and violent demonstrations. Often the target for the violence is the school itself or the community immediately surrounding the school. Recently, however, the riotous behavior of young adults has vented its rage upon innocent bystanders, buildings which are symbolic of institutions, and, in some cases, property and people in no way related, except very indirectly, to the cause of the riot.

In order to attain the impetus needed for riotous behavior, student leaders advocating riots and violence need a cause. The number of potential causes present on college campuses seem limitless. The leaders also need sympathetic groups of students, triggered into action by specific incidents. A part of the problem is centered upon the impersonal nature of educational institutions; their very size, in many cases, lends to this feeling of impersonality in the treatment of students and their problems. As massive educational institutions reach toward the 70,000 and 80,000 student population levels, relatively small numbers of students, feeling isolated and left out, can cause great harm to the physical welfare of the institution as well as to its reputation both locally and nationally.

Strained by the process of rapid growth and by trying to accommodate larger and larger student populations, colleges find that teaching staffs and counseling services are hard-pressed to maintain communications with students. It is partially the lack of communication, lack of understanding of purposes and goals, and general disorientation of students relative to the purposes and goals of the institution which underlie many of the violent actions that have been witnessed nationally in the past several years.

In the past college administrators have been reluctant to admit that there are problems on their campuses. "No trouble" has been too often a preferable slogan to an honest examination of existing problems. Such college administrators often deal with surface problems, handling them ineptly or ineffectively. Others have responded with harsh repression. Wise college officials today understand that these means only serve to drive the problem underground. But as they know, having the problem momentarily out of sight does not mean that it is resolved. The problems fester, and eventually erupt in further violence and riotous behavior.

The young adult is interested in being dealt with honestly and individually. Rising tension and riotous behavior in student bodies can be dealt with effectively when students are treated with respect and with sincerity of purpose. They cannot and will not be "put off." Their problems must be considered, analyzed, and given a chance for genuine operational resolution.

WHAT WE HAVE LEARNED

1. A new social phenomenon is present in the United States: the revolution of young adults against social injustice.
2. Today's college student is better informed, more alert, and more concerned about social problems than students of past generations.
3. Many members of the older generation categorically view all college students with one kind of generalization or another; in fact, students are quite diverse in all aspects of their behavior.
4. Students today protest vigorously in order to achieve what they see as worthy and desirable goals.
5. The influence of the media on college campuses is a relatively new phenomenon; adults are now paying more attention to college students.
6. The various forms of the media include the multi-media, personal media, art-form media, and sense-organ media. Although there are many ways of communicating, the lack of communication between the generations and between individuals is still startling.
7. Racial prejudice cannot be overcome entirely through legislation; one simply cannot outlaw the deep-seated emotional responses of people.
8. Integrated campuses today, on close inspection, are often as segregated internally as they were fifty years ago. The mere presence of minority groups in college institutions does not achieve true social integration.
9. Black and other minority-group students are often inadequately prepared for the rigors of the academic demands of the institutions of higher education.
10. If either is to survive, the black man and the white man must learn to work and to live together in harmony and mutual respect.
11. The problems of poverty are psychological as well as physical; the lack of money to provide the basic necessities of life is but one aspect of the problem of poverty.
12. Present policies and systems for providing for the financially needy are virtually obsolete.
13. College students recognize many of the inequities in the college and university establishment better than many adults, because students must cope daily with these practices.

14. College students find it unacceptable to allow conditions of social inequality to continue to exist.
15. Many students find that sources of financial aid are extremely limited or unobtainable.
16. It is not a simple thing for a student to decide to take part in a confrontation.
17. Most student groups are loosely organized; there are very few carefully and formally structured national student groups of a radical nature.
18. Radical student groups are diverse in organization, purpose, goals, and in the methods used for reaching goals.
19. Many radical student groups find that there is dissent within their own organization.
20. The S.D.S. is one example of a national student group comprised of several diverse factions.
21. Not all aspects of student revolution are violent or riotous.
22. Student militancy, a relatively new form of protest in the United States, has an older tradition in Europe, Asia, and Latin America.
23. Student militancy has been given national attention by the various media.
24. Today's students are more outspoken: their demands cover a broad spectrum from local institutional problems to the larger social problems of the community and the world.
25. Riotous behavior is precipitated by a series of causes which include boredom, neglect, lack of communication, and the pressing need of youth for change.

What We Still Need to Learn

1. We need to recognize the social concerns of today's young adult college student, and to develop means whereby they can individually and collectively contribute their ideas and concepts to the social betterment of mankind.
2. A better means of communication between large institutions and the individuals who comprise these institutions needs to be formulated.
3. Positive steps must be taken to accomplish true racial integration on the college campuses. Simply allowing the minority groups to co-exist does not accomplish true integration and group understanding.
4. People of different racial and ethnic backgrounds must learn to live and work side by side, if the nation and its principles are to survive.

5. A national policy needs to be provided so that all young adults, rich and poor alike, will have the opportunity to pursue higher education.
6. Many of the recognized inequities in the establishment need to be remedied immediately.
7. We need to provide more educational institutions so that students who wish to attend will not be eliminated by lack of facilities.
8. Effective means of curtailing the need for confrontation tactics by students must be developed. These means must not only concern the confrontation itself but the underlying root causes which prompted the action in the first place.
9. Dialogue must be continued effectively with radical student groups.
10. The causes of student riots are known. The means to prevent them must become known as well.

SUGGESTIONS FOR FURTHER READING

Brown, J. S., *The Motivation of Behavior*, New York: McGraw-Hill, 1961.

Califano, J. A., *The Student Revolution: A Global Confrontation*, New York: W. W. Norton & Company, Inc., 1969.

Cohen, Mitchell, *The New Student Left: An Anthology*, Boston, Mass.: Beacon Press, 1966.

Draper, Hal Berkley, *The New Student Revolt*, New York: Grove Press, 1969.

Evans, Dorothy A. and William Claiborn, Eds., *Mental Health Issues and the Urban Poor*, New York: Pergamon Press, Inc., 1974.

Evans, Medford Stanton, *Revolt on the Campus*, Chicago, Ill.: H. Regnery Co., 1961.

Fein, Leah Gold, *The Changing School Scene: Challenge to Psychology*, New York: Wiley-Interscience, 1974.

Hunt, Everett L., *The Revolt of the College Intellectual*, New York: Human Relations Aids, 1963.

Kennan, George Frost, *Democracy and the Student Left*, Boston, Mass.: Little, Brown and Co., Inc., 1968.

Lineberry, William P., *Colleges at the Crossroads*, New York: H. W. Wilson Company, 1966.

Travers, Robert M. W., *Educational Psychology*, Riverside, New Jersey: The Macmillan Company, 1973.

14

Personal Problems of the Young Adult

- Personal problems of young adults
- Feelings and emotions
- Emotional patterns of behavior
- The expression of emotions
- Development of emotions in adolescence
- Cultural effects on the forms of emotional expression
- Emotional syndromes: Complex patterns of emotionality
- The measurement of emotional states
- Motivation as a dynamic of adjustment
- Measuring motivation
- Complex motives
- Social problems of young adults
- Social deviancy: some startling statistics
- What We Have Learned
- What We Still Need to Learn
- Suggestions for Further Reading

PURPOSE OF THIS CHAPTER

Personal problems of young adults cover a wide range of relationships with others, self-evaluation, the family, peers, and inner feelings and emotions. While many of the personal problems are highly unique, just as many seem to be commonly experienced as young adults enter this developmental stage. Chapter Fourteen, "Personal Problems of the Young Adult," seeks to explore these problems and to explain the psychological dynamics which are operative.

Throughout this text, we have studied many aspects of the behavior of young adults. Now we wish to look at the young adult in still another way: as he is, including his personal problems, and as he begins to face the adjustment problems of a vibrant and dynamic society. In order to gain a comprehensive view in these areas, we will examine the emotional state of the individual, including such concepts as the meaning of emotions and feelings, their measurement, ways of expressing emotions, emotional syndromes, and the cultural effects on emotional expression.

Motivation is a fundamental concept in explaining an individual's behavior. In this chapter we will examine the motives of the young adult, and explain some of the ways in which psychologists attempt to measure motivation. The concluding section of the chapter discusses some of the social problems of the young adult, and the concept of "social deviancy"—those behaviors which are not accepted by society at the present time.

FEELINGS AND EMOTIONS

Emotions are powerful forces within man which affect his behavior. The emotional behavior of man involves complex patterns. The term "emotion" itself derives from the Latin "emovere," to stir up, to excite, or to move. Emotional behavior can be disintegrative or integrative, depending upon circumstances surrounding that behavior. In an emotional state, one may become angry, say things he may later regret having said, or behave in any one of several irrational ways. These kinds of behavior are disintegrative. At the opposite pole are integrative emotional states. Consider the example of the mother who, seeing her child pinned under the wheel of an automobile, lifted the car and freed her child. The intensity of the emotional state created a physical energy and stimulus which the mother did not have under normal circumstances. Indeed, she could not even budge the car when the emotional state no longer existed.

Emotional patterns of behavior are usually described by such terms as anger, fear, jealousy, rage, and love. The immediate emotional reaction of the individual may be quite different from his usual pattern of behavior. While experiencing varying degrees of emotion, behavior is altered. The nature of the alteration of behavior depends upon the intensity and duration of the emotion, and the circumstances which surround the emotional state of the individual. Emotions are observable indirectly by their overt reactions produced by the individual. For example, we know that there are physiological and biological states which accompany the emotional state, and the vast majority of these are directly measurable. Thus, while experiencing a strong emotional state, the pulse rate increases and the heart rate and blood pressure accelerate.

Emotional awareness is present in terms of feelings. After experiencing an emotional state, the individual feels either pleasant or unpleasant, depending on circumstances. Apathy and emotion are in direct opposition to each other. Apathy connotes a lack of feeling and responsiveness, while the concept of emotion is closely bound up with feelings and what is termed "affective" reactions or "affective states." To an emotionally aroused, stimulated or excited individual, the part of the emotional experience which he is most able to recall are his feelings. Often such an individual is at a loss to describe his conduct or behavior; but he does remember how he felt at the time, after the experience has passed. The emotional state is one of the most complex aspects of human behavior. Rarely does the individual experience pure "fear" or pure "hate" or pure "love" or indeed any "pure" emotional experience. Emotions combine to form complex patterns, called syn

The Expression of Emotions May Enhance Positive States of Mental Health

Theorist	Important Factors Stressed
Alfred Adler	Social feeling and social interest (Gemeinschaftsgefuhl)
William Blatz	Independent security
Jurgen Buesch	Effective communication
Viktor Frankl	The will to live; the meaning of life
Sigmund Freud	Ability to love and to do productive work
Erich Fromm	Productive and non-productive orientation to others
Carl Gustav Jung	Responsible individuality; self-responsibility
Abraham H. Maslow	Self-actualization: realization of one's potentialities
Otto Rank	Creativity, individuality, assertiveness, and autonomy
Carl Rogers	The fully functioning person
Henry Stack Sullivan	Accurate self-perception and accurate perceptions of others

Various psychologists have stressed the importance of emotional expression as part of their personality theories.

dromes. Thus fear may be accompanied by anger and hostility; love may be accompanied by jealousy and passion.

The individual who can express himself in healthy, wholesome ways, externalizing rather than internalizing his emotions, has a better chance of maintaining a mentally healthy state. Various personality theories have stated that the general emotional state of the individual is caused by a variety of factors, ranging from the culture to biological states. The accompanying table lists several prominent psychologists whose personality theories stress various aspects of emotionality. Each of the theorists stresses a slightly different aspect of human experience in order to insure positive and functionally healthy mental balance in the individual.

THE DEVELOPMENT OF EMOTIONS

Emotions are present at birth, and some current theorists speculate that they may be present prenatally. The emotional state of the new-born infant is one of "generalized excitement." This state, largely undifferentiated at time of birth, begins to be channeled shortly after birth into feelings of pleasantness and unpleasantness. The newborn, for example, can express feelings of pain and discomfort. With learning and maturation, these expressions are further refined to form complex emotional patterns or syndromes. Part of the developmental pattern of childhood lies in learning to express emotions in a socially acceptable manner, and at the right time. Some of the development depends upon parental inclination, while some of the patterns of expression are more broadly culturally determined. Throughout childhood and into adolescence, the normal or usual pattern of emotional development is in the direction of more and more refinement in the way of emotional expression, along with the inhibition, suppression, and the internalization of many less socially-acceptable emotional states.

In our society boys are expected to be brave; they are not to cry, and they are not to exhibit fear. Temper tantrums are tolerated by most parents in the early stages of development; but beyond childhood, such actions or expressions of emotionality are not socially accepted. In adolescence, emotional states are usually discussed in terms of temporary moods, whether they are composed of strong feelings or mild feelings, and how they affect daily patterns of behavior. Moods are temporary; they usually change in short periods of time.

Emotions vary considerably, from mild and fleeting to intense and prolonged experiences. While experiencing strong emotional states, there are often concomitant physical states. These include an increase in blood pressure, accelerated heart beat, muscular in-coordination, disturbances in glandular balance, dryness of the throat, increase in respiration, and many other kinds of temporary physical changes.

While some emotional states can be traced directly to certain physical organs as the source of the sensation and the accompanying reaction, not all can be explained in this manner. For example, seeing others eat may lead to feelings of hunger and the need for food, or it can lead to revulsion and abhorrence, depending on the individual's interpretation. Feeling confident is an important psychological concept which cannot be explained on the basis of physical sensations or, stimuli alone.

Most individuals experience a variety of emotions, often several at the same time and in varying degrees of intensity. The joy of the wedding ceremony is often mixed with feelings of sorrow and sadness. Some individuals find it extremely difficult to experience happiness, joy, or pleasure, and over-react when they do so; others go through life in mixed states of depression and sadness. In one form of serious mental disturbance, the manic-depressive psychosis, the individual fluctuates emotionally from states of extreme joy to states of extreme depression. The accompanying physical reactions are severe, leaving the individual physically and psychologically spent. In the expression of emotional states, the important factors are:

The duration of the emotional state;
The intensity of the emotional experience;
The time of emotional expression; and,
The individual's interpretation of his feelings.

Emotions exist in a state of continuous change. They are not static, and the individual experiencing a variety of emotions responds overtly in some fashion. Some individuals internalize their emotional reactions over prolonged periods of time. The psychological difficulties which may result include psychosomatic reactions of a wide variety, such as ulcers, heart attacks, feelings of weariness and tiredness, pains, and many other physical conditions.

The vigorous forms of protest and demonstrations by young adults in recent years has been viewed by some as overt expressions of long internalized emotions. From the psychological point of view, the expression of emotions is more beneficial for the individual concerned than the internalization of same. However, from the point of view of society, the overt expression of emotions by the individual must be performed in a socially acceptable fashion. There are many forms of overt emotional expressiveness. Clothing and hair styles, speech, gestures, and life-styles are all forms of expressiveness and communication of feelings, attitudes, and degrees of approval or disapproval. While various elements within the society may view the patterns of certain young adult groups as reprehensible, psychologists view these behaviors as forms of overt emotional expression.

CULTURAL EFFECTS ON EMOTIONAL EXPRESSION

Individuals express themselves emotionally in a wide disparity of socially acceptable ways. So too do nations. Maturation and environment each play important roles in this regard. One common emotion experienced by all people are the feelings of joy, pleasure, happiness, and the accompanying physical state of laughter. Anger, too, is an emotion which properly belongs in this category. However, the methods of expression of joy and anger are culturally determined. In some cultures, to laugh out loud is frowned upon at any time; in most cultures, laughing inappropriately (e.g., at a funeral) is looked upon with disdain. Anger may be expressed in physical or verbal terms, or in a combination of the two. In some societies the overt expression of many emotions is discouraged, covert expressiveness being preferred. Consider the wide variety of emotional expressions which are exhibited and which are acceptable with regard to the act of love and the expression of affection.

The complex emotional patterns of adulthood are learned in childhood and adolescence, yet their manner of expression is different from the expressions of the child and the adolescent. Young adults exhibit complex emotional expression in the form of attitudes, preferences, prejudices, hostilities, anxieties, and other more direct and more subtle forms. The adult expression of emotions is highly individual, although the general pattern may be a common one. Groups of people are also affected by the manner of emotional expression. Mob behavior, group violence, and other forms of group activities of a similar nature are the reactions of large numbers of people swept up by emotional states common to the "crowd."

When meeting someone for the first time, the reaction toward that individual is usually based upon emotional feelings rather than on cognitive or intellectual feelings. Our reactions have two basic components:

(1) *Cognitive:* an intellectual reaction based on sound analysis and reasoning; in short, rational judgment.

(2) *Affective:* An analysis of reaction toward others based upon emotions and feelings.

The cognitive and the affective components may be in agreement, or there may be a disparity between the two, as in the case where we dislike an individual based upon feelings (affective reaction) although we can give no exact reason for this dislike (cognitive reaction).

Emotions can act as motivating forces. They cause us to do things, some of which we may regret when the emotional state has passed. In an emotional state, one's thinking becomes unclear; one often says things he would not ordinarily say, and does things he would not ordinarily do. Strong emotional states have also led individuals to perform in unusual ways, sometimes toward the very peak of their capacities. Some emotions which commonly act as motivating factors in behavior include fear, anxiety, jealousy, love, and rage.

Individual and unique adjustment problems entail their own forms of emotional behavior for each person. Some people have worries over money, worries about personal appearance, about progress, or lack of progress in school, family relationships, and the like. Concomitant emotional states become highly individualized for each person. The accompanying behavior patterns, too, become unique, partially conditioned by cultural demands and partly individually determined. Some individuals withdraw from situations, isolating themselves from emotional involvement; others express themselves aggressively or with hostility. Still others internalize their emotional feelings and reactions. The effects upon the personality of the individual who is emotionally distraught, regardless of his unique manner and form of expression, become important to a full understanding of the individual's attempts at the resolution of his adjustment problems.

Emotional reactions can affect the self-concept of the individual. Many outwardly successful individuals harbor feelings of inadequacy, incompetency, and self-destructiveness. Such negative attitudes toward oneself can be debilitating. These reactions can be specific, i.e., feelings of inadequacy and incapability in the sexual realm of behavior, or they may be generalized, i.e., a total overall feeling of helplessness and inadequacy in all areas of behavior. While some individuals can help themselves and overcome the difficulties engendered by these emotional states, others need professional help in the form of counseling, guidance, and therapy in order to better understand themselves in relationship to others and in order to lead a more positive and mentally healthy life.

EMOTIONAL SYNDROMES

Syndromes are complex patterns of several emotions, operating together and at the same time, to cause certain reactions and behavior in an individual. Adults rarely experience "pure" emotional states, but more often experience a combination of emotional reactions simultaneously. The self-analysis of the elements which comprise the emotional syndrome is very difficult, because one can rarely, if ever, be objective about himself. Emotional experiences of adults can rarely be thought of in pure terms of fear, joy, sorrow, grief, excitement, or happiness. For most adults these kinds of experiences involve several emotions at the same time, each acting and reacting with the other, causing a direction of behavior which is guided by a complex combination of emotional forces which is termed a "syndrome."

Syndrome patterns vary considerably in degree of intensity. We may feel cold, but at times we may feel colder than at other times. A chill may be the result of a change in temperature, or a feeling of fear and impending disaster. When we feel happy, the state is a relative one. Degrees of happiness range from wild joy and hilarity to mild feelings of pleasure. Often the state of happiness is accompanied by other feelings, including sadness, laughter, giddiness, silliness, and tears. The syndrome effect of these states upon the individual determines the course of his behavior. The internalization of these emotions often makes judging the state of the individual difficult. The attempt to determine the emotional state of the individual from outward observation and judgment is often deceiving and inaccurate.

The early years of adulthood are often lonely years for both men and women. Emotions are internalized, and their effects tend to contribute to states of nervousness, feelings of lack of accomplishment, and anxiety. The form of social participation of the young adult varies considerably, some young adults being much more outward and social in their behavior and others being inward and withdrawn. Some cling to a relatively few intimate friends, while others embrace a host of acquaintances among their friends. Most friendships are formed on the basis of congeniality of interests, but emotional factors are an essential ingredient if the friendships are to endure.

Young adults who marry relatively early often have two sets of friends, some who merge and become mutual friends of the newly married couple, while others are dropped because of the disparity in relationships between one of the partners. Family relationships, too, in the early stages of marriage, are subject to the emotional reactions of the newlywed couple. A period of adjustment to the needs of each other and the families of the spouses is required.

Emotional reactions affect a wide variety of social areas, including leadership-followership roles, talent and poise, relationships with peers and others, and forms of self-expression. College teachers often find that relatively capable students are hindered by emotional states which prevent their full participation in class discussions and group projects. To the extent that these conditions exist, the progress of the student may be restricted or impeded, resulting in a lower level of academic performance.

MEASURING EMOTIONS

Emotions and emotional states are measured indirectly. They cannot be weighed or measured with the usual kinds of instruments. Their degree and intensity are measured indirectly through evidence concerning physical bodily reactions. During periods of emotional excitement or stress, the individual cannot control all of his physiological reactions. The accompanying bodily changes include the increase in heartbeat; dryness in the mouth; pilomoter response (goose pimples on skin); muscle tension; increased pulse beat; dilation of the pupils; or increased gastrointestinal activity, among others.

Of course, not all of these reactions occur in each individual. The physiological changes which do occur are beyond his willful (voluntary) control. Because of this fact, the "lie detector" or "psychogalvanometer" as it is known in the field of psychology has been useful in determining when an individual is not telling the truth. The theory is that when lying one's emotional reactions are heightened, and these can be measured and recorded. The psychogalvanometer has been useful in the hiring of employees for certain kinds of positions which require bonding, the handling of money, and other positions of trust. The evidence yielded by the psychogalvanometer is still not admissible in most courts, because there is always the possibility that an individual may be able to tell a lie with no emotional reaction whatever, as in the case of a psychopathic liar, who may not be able to tell the truth from a lie. Also there is the further complication of the interpretation of the test results by another person.

Several other kinds of instruments have been devised for the measurement of emotional responses. While most people judge the emotionality of others by their overt actions and by observation, the following instruments have been used in the measurement of various changes in physiological states of the individual:

Electrocardiograph (E.K.G.)	for measuring changes in the rhythm or rate of the heart beat
Electroencephalograph (E.E.G.)	for measuring action of brain waves
Galvanic Skin Response (G.S.R.)	for measuring changes in tactility
Opthalmoscope	for measuring pupillary responses
Pneumograph	for measuring rate of respiration
Sphygmomanometer	for measuring changes in blood pressure

The psychogalvanometer is essentially an instrument composed of each of the above pieces of apparatus. When the individual is asked a series of questions, his "usual" or "normal" responses are graphically recorded. The data are then examined to see where extreme deviations in responses have occurred. Presumably, these areas would be those responses to questions in which the individual was not telling the truth.

Some emotional states are difficult to assess. Such emotions as beauty, wonder, awe, inspiration, and contentment may not necessarily be accompanied by the usual kinds of physical reactions. These complex emotional syndromes are culturally and individually determined. The occasion of their experience is relatively rare, and some individuals may never experience some of these kinds of emotional reactions.

From early childhood, the direction of emotional expression is guided by parents and by societal dicta toward the inhibition of certain emotional expressions. Even in very young children the temper tantrum is frowned upon, crying is quickly stopped, and other forms of emotional release are curtailed. The adolescent has learned much about the need for emotional control, and the adult is expected to be fully in control of his emotions. Yet adolescents and adults both experience times when overt emotional reactions can be of definite psychological benefit to themselves. Such emotional release is known as a "cathartic" reaction, and the person releasing these strong pent-up, inhibited emotions is said to have undergone a "cathartic" experience. The value of cathartic reactions for the preservation of mental health and reduction of tension and anxiety states has been clinically noted for many years by practicing clinical psychologists and psychiatrists.

MOTIVATION

All human behavior is motivated, whether it be caused by biological forces, social forces, psychological forces, or any of the several possible combinatios of these. Regardless of the cause, the important fact is that behavior is caused. Things do not just happen without reason. Motives are powerful forces which propel the person in a given direction. Most of the behavior of students and young adults is goal-oriented behavior. Students attend school, study, take exams, do homework, complete assignments, and strive to perform well in order to achieve a stated goal. This goal may be simple or complex. It may be simply graduation; it may also involve concepts of status, self-satisfaction, or self-improvement. Because of individual differences, the motives and goals of people vary considerably. Often, what the individual states to be his motive and his goal may not be his real motive or his real goal.

In order to succeed in college a student must be capable of achievement. A certain level of intellectual ability must be present. But the mere existence of ability is not enough; the student must want to do well; that is, he must have motivation to succeed. The need to achieve is a psychological motive; it is not innate, but rather acquired or learned. Some individuals are "low-achievement" motivated, while others are "high-achievement" motivated or oriented. The level of achievement for which the individual aims can be measured through various psychological tests. Most of these tests are classified as "personality" measuring devices, and often they are of the "projective" type; that is, they are not of the objective or of the essay type of examination, with required or stated answers. Projective tests which are widely used include the Rorschach (commonly known as the "Ink Blot" test, but technically named Psychodiagnostic Psychodiagnostics, and named after its originator, Hermann Rorschach), and the Thematic Apperception Test (sometimes known as the Picture-Story Test, and often referred to by its abbreviation, T.A.T., and originated by Henry A. Murray). These assessment devices depend upon the honesty and co-operation of the subject; their interpretation is subjective, and various psychologists are proponents of their use.

Many psychologists equate the term "motivation" with the term "drive." In the classification of drives, distinctions are often made between physiological drives (e.g., the need for food and water) and social drives (e.g., the need for companionship, status, and peer-group acceptance). One of the basic drives in human beings is that of curiosity. We have a need to know, often channelized into the need to experiment, to explore, to invent, and to discover. Part of the motivation of young adults today in their quest for something new can be found in the curiosity motive. Young adults, eager to explore, want to know what would happen "if." The "if" may lend itself in the direction of the abolishment of the regular system of grades, a change in college admissions policies, or in any of several other directions.

Most adult motives are complex. We rarely seek food simply as a satisfaction of the physiological need, but, instead, as adults, seek social companionship while we eat, the stimulation of conversation and camaraderie and the satisfaction of our gregarious instincts.

While we sometimes act without conscious awareness of the underlying motivational state, more often than not we are aware of the reasons for our behavior. Motivation makes itself felt in such a way as to initiate activity and to direct that activity. It is also a driving force, sustaining actions, sometimes over a long period of years or over the course of an entire lifetime. The motivation of man is usually goal directed; once the goal is attained, new motives appear. Thus motivation is said to be "cyclical"; that is, cycles are continuous within man, so that, in a technical sense, he is never completely satisfied with all of his physical and psychological states. In the early years of childhood and adolescence, artificial incentives or rewards are used to sustain and create motivation. Thus the gold stars in the elementary school or the praise of the teacher in high school are motivating devices used to sustain the positive direction of the behavior of the child and the adolescent. Some adults require artificial incentives; others can be highly motivated with little or no artificial incentive.

Human motives are not fixed. They move with rhythmic regularity. While the physiological motives are more regulated than the psychological motives, these too are not static. Thus man responds to loneliness by seeking the company of others; to his sexual needs by seeking socially acceptable outlets; to his need for status and recognition by striving to attain a position of worth. Habit and custom affect the motivation of the individual. Some habit-patterns acquired in childhood persist throughout one's lifetime; others can be markedly altered in adulthood.

Motivation is one of the essential dynamics of human adjustment. The term itself means to "move" or to "activate." In this sense, any initiation of activity, internally or externally, is a motivating factor which serves to cause behavior and which in itself is an explanation for that behavior. Motivation is one of the essential sources of human activities. The need for sex is an example of strong motivating forces within man. It directs his energies in numerous directions, causing a wide variety of individual behavior. The sexual motivation in man has a physiological basis, with vast psychological overtones. The unique ways that man has created to satisfy his sex drive illustrate the strength of motivation and the directions of its force in activating, initiating, and causing a wide variety of behavioral actions.

Psychologists have recognized the ramifications of sexual behavior and the need to satisfy the sex drive. Some psychologists classify sexual needs as primary motives, listing them equivalently with the need for food, air, water, and warmth. Such psychological concepts as parental-affiliation, security, submissiveness and dominance, masculinity and femininity, and the feelings of power and control are closely related to the motive for sexual satisfaction. The function of procreation in animals is largely biological; in man the psychological factors are at least of equal importance.

Positive reinforcement acts as important motivational factor for us all. Rewards, praise, approval, acceptance, and encouragement all lead to greater strength of drive. The basic relationship between motivation and reinforcement is found in all learning experiences. Successful adjustment in life is helped by the positive encouragement and reinforcement practices of those who are close to us. Action and activity are encouraged by feelings of pleasantness and acceptance, both in school and in work situations. The individual has a need to feel wanted, to feel important, and to feel that he belongs and is accepted in his role as student or as employee. The amount of motivation in the individual varies from time to time, and varies between individuals. The degree of motivation varies with the goal and with the personality of the individual. Motivational forces can act as strong implements to behavior, and can also act as deterrents to socially unacceptable behavior.

MEASURING MOTIVATION

As in several other areas in psychology (e.g. emotions and personality), the existence of motivation is inferred indirectly, because it cannot be measured by direct means. Motivation cannot be measured in pounds or inches or feet. We measure the state of the individual who is in a motivated condition, and infer the existence of motivation in this way. We cannot see hunger, but we can measure the effects of hunger upon an individual, and observe what he will do in order to obtain food to satisfy his basic needs. Motives have been classified in various ways. One of the most common methods of classifying motives is on the basis of: 1. Primary Motives (food, air, water, warmth, avoidance of pain, sleep, and sex), 2. Secondary Motives (the need for activity, fear, curiosity, and affection); and 3. Complex Motives (the need for status, social approval, the affiliative motive, and the need to achieve).

Some psychologists have classified motivation on the basis of: Physiological Motives (the need for food, air, water, warmth, shelter, and sex) and Psychological Motives (security, autonomy, nurturance, and affiliation, as well as several others). Other categorizations include the concepts of: Survival Motives, Social Motives, and Ego-integrative Motives. Regardless of the system of classification of motivation which one chooses, the problem of the measurement of motivation within the individual remains the same. The problem of the measurement of the motivation of groups is even more complex.

Motivation is measured indirectly. Some of these indirect methods include:

> behavior observation;
> long-term case studies;
> experimental arousal of motives;
> self-reports by individuals;
> retrospective reports;
> imaginative reproduction; and
> animal experimentation.

The observation of the behavior of the individual can give clues as to the motives for his behavior. The method is not infallible, for the observer can err in his analysis, and all forms of motivation are not open to observation. Long-term case studies, too, can combine with observed behavior to yield an analysis of the general mode of behavior or motivational level at which an individual operates. Self-reports by individuals experiencing periods of stress and "fighting for their very lives" have yielded further evidence as to the nature of motivational forces.

Experimentally arousing motives can simulate actual situations, but is still an artificial incentive. In sports, the arousal of the motivation to succeed or to win is a common incentive for the participants to strive to perform at their peak. Animals can be motivated by depriving them of their primary needs for short periods of time. The advantage of animal experimentation is that the possibility exists of a more restricted or controlled environment; the chief disadvantage lies in the fact that evidence from animal experiments cannot be translated and applied directly to human behavior.

Retrospective reports of incidents which have occurred can yield information about the motivation of the individual. This technique is widely used in criminology and sociology. Imaginative reproduction is used with the co-operation of the individual, when he is placed in an imaginary situation such as:

—"What would you do if you had a million dollars?"
—"What one thing would you cause to occur in the world if you had the power to do so?"
—"If you could have three wishes, what would they be?"
—"If you could live your life over again, what would you do differently?"

By using the technique of imaginative reproduction, an estimate as to the motivational level of the individual can be attained. In other experiments, rewards are offered to those individuals who compete successfully in contests whereby those who perform at a low level are gradually eliminated. As the rewards increase, for some people, the level of motivation also increases. Motivating forces direct the behavior of the individual towards goals which he views as worthy or desirable of attainment. To achieve this end, behavior is often modified considerably in many directions.

SOCIAL PROBLEMS

Social pressures and social values have become a part of the life of today's college students. Because students are so involved with numerous social issues, the individual student must make a choice. Whereas in the past his choice centered on whether to become involved or not, today the choice is largely one of degree of involvement. Almost all college students today discuss various aspects of different problems of the society. Their degree of involvement varies from mild interest and a willingness to listen, to wanting to learn more about certain issues, to active protest and violent forms of demonstration.

The young adult seeks social acceptance. He wants to be a part of a group, and must conform to group pressures to a certain degree in order to maintain this acceptance. When the individual does not have full acceptance by the group, he often seeks ways to conform to group standards and group pressures in order to attain acceptance. Adults form close, intimate friendships or "cliques" which are somewhat similar to those in adolescence. Adult friendships generally center around a few "close" or "intimate" friends, a larger sphere of friends, a still larger circle of acquaintances, and business associates. Degrees of social friendships change as the years pass, and the usual pattern is for friendships to change, business acquaintances and lesser acquaintances to be replaced, while a few intimate friends are maintained throughout the adult's lifetime.

Popularity, an important concept in adolescence, is of far less importance in adulthood, and becomes even less important in middle age. Forming new friendships becomes increasingly difficult for adults and those in their middle years. Adults are much more suspicious and less trusting than adolescents. Their habit-patterns are more fixed, and they are reluctant to adjust these habits because of the wishes of newly-formed friends. Many adults attempt to identify with adolescents, mimicking their mode of dress, speech patterns, and even their life style. This is probably a reflection of the reluctance to admit to the aging process as well as a psychological need to maintain virility and vigor.

Many young adult students have virtually withdrawn from the entire social sphere. Faced with difficult choices and alliances, as well as splitting their loyalties and trusts, they have decided to withdraw into their own selves as a means of avoiding social conflict. This solution is less than satisfactory, because the isolated withdrawn world of the self cannot satisfy one's social and gregarious needs. Such an individual finds it increasingly difficult to become a part of the group when his social needs become urgent. Self-ostracization is a form of psychological punishment which most students find intolerable. While self-inflicted, it cannot be readily self-removed, since groups are often reluctant or unwilling to accept the student who has chosen to play the role of isolate.

Enlightened college administrators all over the nation have begun to acknowledge that the social problems of the college student play an important role in his academic life.

Female college students have come to recognize that women are the victims of subtle and not-so-subtle forms of discrimination. Women's groups have been formed on college campuses to fight for the right of equality for women. Among the numerous problems of discrimination faced by women which these groups are attempting to alleviate, are:

> prejudicial admissions policies of graduate and professional schools;
> unequal job opportunity;
> restrictions in professional activities;
> the double-standard of morality;
> unequal rates of pay based upon one's sex;
> the right to self-determination;
> living in the male politically-dominated world; and
> laws regarding abortion and drugs.

Many of these young women have become activists, and some have become militant. Several have become leaders in the fight for womens' rights and for the rights of the ghetto resident, those against whom racial discrimination is aimed, and in the areas of ecology and environmental problems.

Young adults in college whose backgrounds have been typically impoverished face several unique adjustment problems. Today's youth are rebelling against the platitudes that "there will always be poor people" and that the "poor must learn to help themselves." Today's younger generation wants something done about the problems of the poor; wants the ghettos cleaned up and outmoded; wants a higher standard of living for all people, regardless of race, religion, color, or creed.

One of the unique adjustment problems of the underprivileged, the ghetto resident, and the poor, lies in the fact that his teachers, his colleagues, and largely all levels of school administration represent middle-class or middle-upper-class values and standards. Their understanding and comprehension of the problems of the poor are gleaned secondhand from reading and studies. They haven't been "through it." Relating their problems becomes more difficult for these students; often there is no one to whom they can relate; when there is, it is often difficult for the student to discuss his personal problems. The problem for these young adults is that the promise of the future appears to be beyond their grasp, and becomes more and more bleak as they continue on with their educations.

SOCIAL DEVIANCY

The concept of social deviancy is an elusive one. What were considered as acts of deviancy in one era may be perfectly acceptable modes of behavior in another. Social acts of deviancy depend upon one's point of view. It should be remembered that most acts which are termed socially deviant are so termed in retrospect; at the time of their performance, the actions may have generally been considered socially justifiable. Lynch mobs or the burning of the so-called witches in Salem were viewed with a certain degree of propriety by some at the time. On the other hand what is socially deviant today may be considered acceptable tomorrow. The concept is fluid, elusive, changeable, and subject to one's own concept of acceptable and non-acceptable modes of behavior.

Current concepts of social deviancy range from homosexuality to the use of drugs to violent forms of student demonstrations and protest movements. In the future, the use of drugs may not be included in the category of social deviancy, just as attitudes toward homosexuals are changing today. As previously mentioned, in Great Britain today the problem of homosexuality is viewed as one in need of medical and psychological attention, whereas in the United States, the acts of the homosexual are considered to be illegal acts of a criminal nature.

The statistics of social deviancy are startling. Some of the reported figures include the following:

—One out of every six teen-agers becomes pregnant out of wedlock.
—One-third to one-half of all teen-age marriages include illegitimate pregnancy.
—The number of unwed mothers under the age of eighteen has doubled since 1940.
—One teen-age marriage in every two ends in divorce within the first five years of marriage.
—Nearly one-half million adolescents appear in juvenile courts each year.
—It is estimated that as many as fifty per cent of all college students are using drugs in some form.
—Large numbers of young adults have dropped out of society and have attempted to form social structures of their own.

These statistics point to the fact that we need to make a place in society for the adolescent and for the young adult. Methods need to be found whereby young adults can participate in the real fabric of life. Young adults need to be heard with regard to social issues. The development of a concept of service to others needs to be enhanced, and opportunities to give real service need to be made attractively available. The stereotyping of adolescents as young adults should be replaced by genuine attention to the needs of the individual. The present generation's revolution stems largely from resentment of the mechanization and automation of the individual in a society which seems to have lost the values formerly placed upon individual attributes.

The depersonalization of society has contributed heavily to the various forms of social deviancy exhibited by young adults. While the older generation takes the attitude that change must be proved to be for the better, and that changes take time, the younger generation views the lack of response to change as hypocrisy and bureaucratic inefficiency, incompetence, and bungling. One of the big complaints of students today lies in the fact that no one will listen to them; or, if listened to, no action is taken with regard to their legitimate concerns. If action is taken, it is often considered too little and too late.

Many young adults complain that they have been literally forced to rebel. Students have become skeptical. They doubt that the older generation genuinely wants to effect positive social change. In school, irrelevant material is looked upon as a waste of time; teachers who cannot relate their material in a meaningful way to social issues and problems which are currently important to students find that the students are, at best, apathetic. If teachers were still insisting that the world is flat and that one would fall off the edge if he went too far into the ocean, students would be expected to rebel. Some of today's teaching is unfortunately but a step removed from these kinds of antiquated conceptualizations.

WHAT WE HAVE LEARNED

1. Emotions are powerful forces which cause changes in behavior.
2. Changes in behavior caused by emotions depend upon the individual, the culture, the intensity and duration of the emotion, and its mode of expression.
3. Feelings are the usual mode of emotional awareness.
4. Emotional patterns of reaction develop from infancy through adulthood; the adult expression of emotions is usually in the form of syndrome patterns.
5. Emotions vary considerably from person to person and within the same individual.
6. Emotions can act as motivating forces.
7. The early years of adulthood are often lonely years for both men and women.
8. Emotional states are measured indirectly by physiological changes.
9. All human behavior is motivated.
10. Motives to explain adult behavior are usually complex.
11. Human motivation is not fixed or static.
12. Lack of motivation is an important reason for school failure.
13. Motivation is an essential dynamic of human adjustment.

14. Positive reinforcement can be an important motivating factor.
15. Individual motivation is measured indirectly.
16. College students today are keenly aware of social problems and are subject to social pressures themselves.
17. Most young adults seek social acceptance.
18. The social relationships existing today between college students differ markedly from those which existed in previous generations.
19. The problems of certain groups, e.g., women and minority groups, in terms of social relationships, are compounded by artificial rules and standards imposed by society.
20. The concept of social deviancy is elusive.
21. Statistics relating to various forms of social deviancy show marked increases in many areas in the past several years.
22. The depersonalization of society has contributed heavily to the existence of social deviancy.
23. Outmoded forms of teaching and outdated textbooks force students into a posture of rebellion.

What We Still Need to Learn

1. Positive ways of socially accepted emotional expression need to be explored so that tensions and anxieties may be released instead of internalized by young adults.
2. Detailed analysis of the complex syndrome patterns of emotionality in adults is still largely a matter of speculation.
3. Emotional expressiveness in adults needs to be encouraged, rather than inhibited, as a factor which can contribute positively to good mental health.
4. Further investigations are needed as to the development of such complex emotions as prejudice, preferences, and attitudes.
5. Psychosomatic relationships between emotions and physiological states need further exploration.
6. Some of the present cultural and societal inhibitions on the form of emotional expression in man need to be modified.
7. The emotional problems of young adults should be the subject of extensive psychological research.
8. New ways of motivating capable students need to be discovered and introduced operationally into the educational process.
9. New ways of positively reinforcing the academic motivation of adolescents and young adults need to be explored.
10. The effective utilization of the affiliative and gregarious motives of young adults needs to be channeled into positive behaviors.

11. Colleges need to provide social opportunities for students to express themselves in meaningful ways.
12. We must begin to listen to college students in the areas of needed social reforms, and then act meaningfully and effectively with regard to legitimate avenues of change.
13. Many of the highly structured social institutions need to be made more adaptable and flexible for today's youth.
14. Long-standing prejudices toward minority groups and women must become obsolete in the society of today's young adult.
15. It must be recognized that social deviancy is a reflection of great inner turmoil in the young adult.

SUGGESTIONS FOR FURTHER READING

Argyle, Michael, *Social Interaction*, Chicago, Ill.: Aldine Publishing Company, 1974.

Coleman, J., *Abnormal Psychology and Modern Life*, Glenview, Ill.: Scott, Foresman and Company, 1972.

Cook, F. J., *Youth in Danger*, New York: Harcourt, Brace and World, Inc., 1956.

Fromm, E., *Escape from Freedom*, New York: Holt, Rinehart & Winston, 1941.

Gagne, R. M., and E. A. Fleishman, *Psychology and Human Performance*, New York: Holt, Rinehart & Winston, 1959.

Hamsher, J. Herbert and Harold Sigall, *Psychology and Social Issues*, Riverside, New Jersey: The Macmillan Company, 1973.

Horney, Karen, *Our Inner Conflicts*, New York: W. W. Norton & Company, Inc., 1950.

Krasner, Leonard and Leonard P. Ullmann, *Psychology of Behavior Influence*, New York: Holt, Rinehart & Winston, 1973.

Krech, David, Richard S. Crutchfield, and Norman Livson, *Elements of Psychology*, New York: Alfred A. Knopf, 1970.

Lazarus, R. S., *Personality and Adjustment*, Englewood Cliffs, New Jersey: Prentice-Hall, Inc., 1963.

Maier, N. R. F., *Frustration*, New York: McGraw-Hill, 1949.

Resnick, William C., and Herbert L. Sachs, *Dynamic General Psychology: An Introduction*, Boston, Mass.: Holbrook Press, Inc., 1971.

Sokolov, A. N., *Inner Speech and Thought*, New York: Plenum Press, 1972.

15

Becoming an Adult

PURPOSE OF THIS CHAPTER

Everyone talks about becoming an adult and about the importance of preparing in childhood and in adolescence for one's future as an adult. But what, exactly, is an adult? Are there problems associated with adulthood? If so, what are they? Psychology textbooks generally stop short of adulthood, implying that when one reaches adult levels of maturity, the psychological adjustment problems have been satisfacto-. rily resolved. This is far from the reality of the situation, for adults face numerous adjustment problems, and one of the purposes of this chapter is to examine these in detail.

Chapter Fifteen, "Becoming An Adult," is the final chapter in this third section of the text, and completes the section titled "Looking Forward—Your Future as an Adult." In this section some characteristics of early adulthood and the adjustment problems faced in this developmental stage will be examined. The physical, emotional, and social changes which occur in early adulthood will also be described.

The last part of this chapter considers some of the problems one faces as he ages, the problems of marital choice, and the problem of choosing a vocation. Preparing for a career, the concluding section of this chapter, has been described as "what it's all about" by many college students. Becoming an adult and assuming adult responsibilities is the name of the game—the game of preparing for one's entire life as an adult. Many of the students reading this chapter will have some personal familiarity with the problems, for they are already well along on the path toward "becoming an adult" themselves.

CHARACTERISTICS OF EARLY ADULTHOOD

Early adulthood is a period of adjustment to new patterns of life and new social expectations. The young adult is expected to partake in new roles, such as breadwinner, spouse and parent, and to develop new attitudes, interests, and values in keeping with these new roles. The early part of adulthood relates very directly to what has come before in childhood and adolescence. Early adulthood seems much more directly affected by cultural values and determinants, because the young adult is not yet involved in the adult role; he has not as yet become adult-socialized.

As the young adult begins to settle into a pattern in keeping with certain roles, his commitment in behavior and attitudes is formulated in keeping with the choices created by the new roles. The early years of adulthood have more tension and anxiety because of the new responsibilities and the adjustment necessitated by new activities. Too, the unfinished tasks of adolescence do not contribute positively to the adjustment problems, but affect them in a variety of ways and degrees. Early adulthood and adulthood have been termed the "reproductive" age. During the twenties and thirties, parenthood and its concomitant role occupies a great portion of the time of the young adult. By about the age of thirty-five, most adults have developed patterns of behavior and responses which will persist throughout their lives.

One of the unique aspects of early adulthood is seen in the fact that the young adult is faced with numerous adjustment problems that he is expected to meet and resolve successfully without the help, guidance, wisdom, and understanding of parents. He is on his own, as he has wanted to be; often the prospect is frightening. Early adulthood, in short, is a period of emotional tension. The young adult faces problems of courtship, dating, and marriage; problems as to what he wants to be; often he finds himself in a state of indecisiveness with regard to a particular problem, only to be faced with other pressing problems at the same time.

The young adult worries about his personal appearance, about economic problems, about choice of a mate, about being labeled a "failure," and numerous other matters. Sexual problems and questions of sexual morality and indiscriminate sexual behavior still persist; the change from adolescence to adulthood wrought no miraculous solution to many of his earlier questions, but often brought newer, broader, and more pressing ones. The adjustment problems of the young adult can be as intensive and as quantitative as those of the adolescent.

Many young adults are attracted to the more glamorous kinds of occupations. Airline stewardesses, movie stars, stage performers, playing in a band—all such career choices fall into the category of the so-called "glamour" occupations. Often the young adult becomes disillusioned as he realizes that these occupations are not glamorous at all, or that he is unqualified or incapable of performing the required tasks of the given occupation. The process of maturing into young adulthood has entailed a freeing from parental control and supervision. This fact makes the need to seek parental guidance more difficult for the young adult at the very time when such help might be welcomed.

Some parents literally demand that their adolescents, upon reaching a certain chronological age (formerly age twenty-one, but today much more commonly age eighteen), "grow up" and assume adult responsibilities. The reaction of the young adult so challenged may be the reverse of what parents had hoped for; regressive behavior may result. The usual course of development proceeds from dependency upon others to dependency upon oneself. But suppose the individual's view of himself entails inadequacy and incapability; the adjustment problems of such an individual become greatly magnified.

Many adults in the early stages of adulthood feel inadequate, isolated, and incapable of assuming adult responsibilities. These feelings are so common as to be a minor characteristic of the developmental stage of young adulthood. Yet most young adults feel that these inadequacies are exclusively their own; they are reluctant or incapable of discussing their feelings and problems with their parents, and their peer group of high school and late adolescence has disappeared, each pursuing his own self-interest in a diversity of directions. The impetus of adolescent development often culminates in young adulthood; the mature young adult feels responsible and capable and the feelings are manifested in his day-to-day behavioral patterns. While legally the age of young adulthood is eighteen, psychologically the individual may not reach adulthood until much later, or in some cases sooner. The variations are highly individual, dependent upon several personality factors.

Early adulthood extends from approximately age eighteen to age forty. Following age forty, the individual meets new adjustment problems in middle age (approximately ages forty to sixty-five), old age (approximately ages sixty-five to eighty-five) and in senescence (from age eighty-five on). Young adulthood and adulthood are not marked by a specific period of physical or biological change, although primitive groups did have biological landmarks. Young adulthood comes several years after sexual maturity has been achieved (in the biological sense). Adulthood today is a long and poorly differentiated period of life.

The change from adolescence to adulthood is not heralded by any landmarks. Although the young adult has already undergone most of the changes he will incur in his adolescence, there are still several changes which occur both physically, socially, and mentally. The adolescent years generally blend into the adult years with little or no fanfare.

The problems of young adult men and women differ markedly. Young adult women face the possibility of remaining unwed if they do not marry in young adulthood, while others face the problem of choice of career or marriage, or the problem of how to succeed in combining the two. Young adult men face the problem of continued education, thus postponing adult responsibilities, choosing a marital partner or deciding to remain a bachelor, and selecting a vocation for the balance of their adult years. While no period of life is without its adjustment problems, the period of young adulthood has several unique adjustment problems; problems which heretofore were long unrecognized by virtue of the fact that the developing individual had reached the stage of "adulthood."

ADJUSTMENT PROBLEMS OF YOUNG ADULTS

Young adults face numerous adjustment problems. Erik Erikson termed these problems the "identity crisis" of young adulthood. Although Freudian (psychoanalytically) oriented, Erikson felt that the chief crisis in the developmental stages of man was in young adulthood. (Freud emphasized infancy as the chief stage of crises.) Some of the adjustment problems of the young adult include:

Problems of continuing one's education
Lack of economic self-sufficiency
Indecisiveness
Choice of vocation
Choice of marital partner
Religious and moral doubts
The process of "settling down"
Unresolved adolescent tensions and anxieties

As educational demands continue to grow in today's society, the young adult is faced with the decision of postponing the assumption of adult responsibilities and the continuance of education, or terminating education in order to assume these responsibilities, even though the individual may have a firm desire to continue with his educational plans. Graduate schools and post-graduate schools of education, medical and other professional schools, are filled with mature young adults who daily face the anxieties and tensions which accompany this problem. Once having made his decision, the problem is not yet resolved, for the young adult soon realizes that making a choice excludes other possible choices; periods of self-doubt and vacillation are not uncommon. Many young adults wonder if it is "worth it."

Probably more than anything else, the young adult wants to be economically self-supporting. More and more young people today are attempting to achieve this status by working part-time or full-time while maintaining apartments of their own. The economic facts of life are harsh, and often come tumbling down about the young adult who finds himself hard-pressed financially to maintain his status as student and breadwinner. Young married couples commonly both work today, partly as a matter of economic necessity and partly to achieve and maintain this degree of independence and autonomy.

Many young adults are extremely indecisive. Partly this is a reflection of unresolved adolescent problems. Arthur T. Jersild* has stated that every young adult carries over the unresolved problems of adolescence into his early adult years. Successful adjustment in the adult years is usually measured in terms of achievement and satisfaction. But these achievements and satisfactions often must be postponed into the middle twenties and early thirties, depending upon the individual's goals. These decisions are not easy for the young adult to make, and the concomitant indecisiveness is not uncommon.

*Jersild, Arthur T., *The Psychology of Adolescence*, New York: Macmillan Co., 1957.

Deciding upon a vocation is one of the primary decisions of young adults. Many college students find that they must change their major subject, which in effect is a change in future vocational goals. Changing a course of study or curriculum in college often necessitates spending another half-year or longer in college. Too, there is social pressure on young adults from peers and from family. The young man or woman entering college who has announced he intends to become a physician faces many disturbing questions when he realizes that this is not what he wants to be, or that he is not qualified for that particular profession.

Choosing a marital partner is very much a matter of choice by young people today; there is little or no consultation with parents. Two or three generations ago, family approval was considered vital; before that time, families chose partners for their children. Today, young people tend to announce to their parents that they are going to marry a certain person and that's that; parental approval is assumed, or, if not given, is not considered to be a deciding factor. Of course, young adults would like to have the full approval of parents, but, in many cases, there are a variety of parental objections. These objections may be based on race or religion; parents may feel their youngster is too young to be wed; they may have hoped for a choice from another social level. Parental friction in the course of "going steady" and "getting engaged" is a contributory factor to the tensions and anxieties experienced by young adults as one of their several problems of adjustment.

Many young adults today question the moral standards of the previous generation. Young women question the correctness of the so-called double-standard of sexuality. The hypocrisy of the older generation in failing to "practice what they preach" is partly the basis for the moral doubt which the young experience. There is virtually no area which is considered sacrosanct. All established institutions—including school, church, and government—are subject to the moralistic re-evaluation of an alert, responsive, and outspoken group of young adults.

The process of "settling down" does not come automatically in young adulthood. As people mature, they find that some of their earlier interests no longer hold the same degree of attraction for them. New habit-patterns of behavior replace those which, at an earlier stage of development, served their purpose so admirably. Young adults begin to face the need to earn a living, to start a home of their own, to acquire material possessions, and to behave in a way which is in keeping with their own philosophy of life. They want, desperately, to impress others with the fact that they do "have their feet on the ground." Unresolved adolescent tensions and anxieties often interfere, delaying this process and creating conflict. Many individuals live their entire lifetime with unresolved conflicts stemming from childhood and adolescence. Some develop psychosomatic symptoms (bodily difficulties which have no organic basis but which have psychological causes); others develop even more serious forms of behavioral disorders.

THE ADULT AS AN INDIVIDUAL

No period of life is totally free of problems. Yet despite the many problems and adjustments faced in adulthood, most older people remember it as a period of happiness. Women look back on the days of raising children and men look back on their main achievements and satisfactions derived from their work. While childhood rivals young adulthood when one looks back on his happiest days, adolescence is rarely, if ever, a serious competitor. Probably one of the most significant factors accounting for the happy remembrance of young adulthood is the attainment of independence during this stage of development. An individual's independence and self-sufficiency is often judged from the work that he does, the way that he lives (life-style), and the degree of autonomy which he exhibits.

Independence is reflected by employment, financial support of oneself, living apart from parents, and making decisions individually. Independence is a highly valued social state; often the competence and social acceptance of the young adult is judged (by others) by the degree of his attainment of independence. In actuality, however, the adult individual is often tied to the needs of his past adolescent years. These needs have been present for a long time, and they do not disappear automatically with the attainment of a given chronological age. Some of these needs are beyond our control, but we have devised ingenious ways of meeting them. We need food, air, and water, and we have devised helpful "modern" conveniences to satisfy these needs to a degree which encompasses more than the satisfaction of the need itself. Air conditioning, frozen foods, alcoholic beverages, all are a means of satisfying more than the basic need for air, food, and water; they also serve our need for comfort, convenience, and social status.

In the attainment of individuality and independence, some of the things we do are harmful to ourselves. Smoking, the use of drugs, excessive alcoholism, and the like serve to satisfy a basic need but also can destroy the individual in the process. In the process of attaining individuality and independence, the young adult also encounters the fact that he is often reluctant to give up the past. Habit-patterns of adolescence often persist; to some extent they are even indulged in by the young adult. Yet technological advances have made it more difficult to cling to the past, as modern devices have rapidly rendered that past obsolescent. Within the space of a relatively few short years, many of the devices which were so popular a few years ago are no longer in vogue, or even in existence. Other devices have replaced them, and new inventions are constantly challenging the accepted mode or pattern of life.

There is no single, all-encompassing theory as to how young adults attain individuality. There are many different, complex reasons for his behavior, and the variations of particular kinds of behavior are highly personalized and individual. The behavioral action itself, regardless of how simple it may be, is a complex bio-psychological process. We accept the fact that the adult "is"—he is not about to "become." At the same time, we know that he has had a past and will have a future. But the important fact about adulthood is that he has arrived; he is here; his presence is the actuality of all of the development in childhood and adolescence for which parents and teachers have expounded for all of the years which came before.

We accept the fact that adults have come from somewhere and are going somewhere, too. But the young adult is faced with the crucial decision as to where he is going and how he is going to get there. And it is a decision which he, and only he can make—alone. He has passed the stage where he can lean heavily upon parents; even if he could, he is probably reluctant or too proud to do so. For he has been told, all of his growing years, how wonderful it will be to be adult. Now that he has arrived, he cannot shed the cloak of wonderment, lest he be a terrible disappointment to all whom he loves and to himself.

The American myth persists that once one has passed the stage of adolescence, all problems are resolved, because adults are free to do exactly as they please. But is man ever truly free and independent? The answer, with its philosophical and psychological implications, clearly contradicts the persistent myth of adult utopia by virtue of the attainment of adulthood. For the contradictions and inconsistencies surrounding the adult stage of development are many. Surely not all adults are well-adjusted, happy, content, independent, and self-sufficient. The truth of the matter is probably quite removed from this state of affairs.

Most psychologists include the concept of "transition" in their definition of adolescence. In a sense, adulthood and young adulthood, along with all of the other developmental stages of man are also periods of transition. The young adult soon becomes very much aware of the fact that he has not achieved all that he had intended; much yet remains to be done.

PHYSICAL CHANGES IN ADULTHOOD

One of the persistent and fallacious myths surrounding adulthood is that physical development and physical changes cease at the termination of adolescence. Surely nothing could be further from the truth. Physical change and its accompanying biological action and reaction take place throughout one's lifetime. True, the physical changes in adulthood are somewhat less dramatic than those which take place in infancy, childhood, and adolescence; but the reality is probably akin to the Gestalt concept of development: we expect few or no changes in adulthood so we do not perceive them readily; we expect many changes in the childhood years and so we eagerly anticipate their occurrence.

Physiologically, there is a continuing process of change in functioning which slowly but surely changes the outward appearance of the individual. A young man in his twenties experiences a gain in weight, a change in voice, the growth of a heavier beard, and the thinning out of hair on the top of his head. The slim, girlish figure of the late adolescent girl begins to fill out and take on adult proportions. Hip, breast, and leg development occur. Some physiological development reaches its peak in young adulthood. We then say that the individual is in his "prime" in terms of physical capabilities. The highly developed muscular and physical co-ordination needed in athletics seems to reach its peak in the early and middle twenties, followed by a slow, gradual, but definite tapering off toward ultimate decline and weakening of physical attributes. If the individual lives long enough, he may experience total loss of physical prowess.

Young adult males reach the peak of their physical development between the ages of eighteen and twenty-one, with a long and slow decline in succeeding years. The physical prime in young adult females is thought to occur in the middle twenties, with a long and slow decline following thereafter. Many cultural effects are in evidence in the physical development of young adults in different societies. Americans, in general, are better fed than young adults in other nations, but tend to neglect their physical selves in a process of slow deterioration which begins in young adulthood and continues throughout middle and old age. The middle-aged American in general reflects a physique which takes note of years of neglect.

The highly developed fine muscular co-ordination and stamina necessary in athletics seems to reach its peak of development in the middle and early twenties. Again, culture plays a determining role. The American culture downgrades the athletic and physically capable female. Most American females are reluctant to outdistance and outpace their male counterparts, partly because of culturally determined values. We still cling to the fallacy of female shyness, timidity, and lack of physical prowess. In the Soviet Union, on the other hand, the physically strong young adult female is respected and revered. The concept of the male being the stronger sex, while fallacious, is still held in many parts of the United States, contrary to the evidence supplied from a wide variety of sources. Longevity tables of insurance companies indicate clearly the longer life-span of the female.

EMOTIONAL AND SOCIAL PROBLEMS OF ADULTS

The emotional and social problems of young adults have been compounded by the fact that adolescence, in the United States, has become a prolonged and extended stage carrying over into the early twenties and even beyond. Because of this extension, young adults often face the postponement of socialization at the adult level and their emotional problems require greater degrees of control. G. Stanley Hall has stated that adolescence in the United States often extends into age twenty-five. From a psychological point of view the termination of adolescence is not so much a matter of chronology as it is a matter of the kinds of adjustments made by the individual. However, even mature young adults face several emotional and social problems.

The adult years, in general, have been the neglected years of students of the psychology of human development. In our society, which has long been child-oriented, the majority of people living today are under the age of twenty-five. Contrary to many popular beliefs, these young adult years are probably the most productive years from a standpoint of marriage, beginning a family, and starting a life's career. Traditional textbooks concern themselves with the development of personality through childhood and adolescence, but stop at the stage of the young adult. The implication is that personality has been formed by this stage, and that no further development need be discussed. This concept is, to put it mildly, fallacious.

After one has passed through the well-studied and oft-written about stages of adolescence, the individual is termed a "young adult." He is now immersed in a wider ranger of responsibilities—work, the duties of citizenship, marriage, and parenthood—and he is involved in an extremely complex environment and a rapidly changing social world. He must constantly reassess his life and his goals and adjust himself to changing standards of socialization, morality, and economic concerns. In short, he is a very important dynamic human being and he deserves the attention of the behavioral scientist, not in terms of what he was or what he will be, but in terms of what he is now.

Adult socialization largely involves a series of role changes. There are various norms and standards which adults are expected to live up to, to conform to, and to uphold by their own behavior and value systems. Young adults today have particular problems in these areas because so many of them are still students, and, as students, they are expected to conform to the student role, while their chronological age and psychological maturity have pushed them into other roles as well. Adulthood is a series of tasks, accomplishments, and achievements. These tasks, accomplishments, and achievements are challenges which often cause conflict and anxiety. Often the successful adult is the one who has achieved in value systems of his family, his neighbors, and his peer group. The measurement of achievement and happiness is determined by the values of the society in which one lives.

Studies of young adult adjustment have indicated that older people, on looking back to their happiest days, cite most often the period from ages twenty to thirty-five; the next most mentioned period of development is from late adolescence (age eighteen) to early adulthood (age twenty-five). Happiness is often equated to an optimistic and forward-looking outlook on life, along with various measures of achievement and accomplishment. Much of the happiness associated with young adulthood involves the process of "settling down" or adjusting to the circumstances of achieved independence and new family status and security. The realization of one's potential, or the concept of "self-actualization," generally occurs in young adulthood.

Most young adults enjoy a state of good mental health in their twenties and thirties, accompanying their peak of physical stamina. Self-images which are positive, the realization of one's potential, an optimistic feeling of future achievement, and a sense of one's self-sufficiency are all contributing factors toward a positive mental outlook. Later in life, as middle age approaches, new adjustments are necessary. Because of the emphasis on youth in current American society (as contrasted, for example, with Oriental societies, where age is respected and revered), the adjustments necessitated by the approaching middle-age years are difficult for many adults. Good mental health, acquired in adulthood, is a positive asset to the adjustments necessitated by the approaching middle-age years. It is even more necessary in old age and in senescence.

EMBARKING ON A MARITAL STATE

One of the major developmental decisions of young adulthood involves the marital state of the individual. The American ethos moves young adults in the direction of marriage, even though many are not ready for it, and some are unsuited for marriage entirely. Young adult women probably experience the pressures of the drive toward the marital state more than young adult men. In the American society, the young female who is not married by age thirty is likely to remain unwed. While many young adult women choose to remain single, most, regardless of their personality, identification, and level of adjustment, are encouraged to marry.

In previous generations many young adults remained single, either by choice or by dint of circumstance. Today, this is much less likely, although young adults are "single" by virtue of the fact that they have married but are now separated, undergoing the process of divorce, or are divorced. The rate of acceleration toward marriage has been considerable. Many young adults live together in a state of "matrimonial-singleness"; that is, they are unofficially married, or are living together without benefit of wedlock. They consider themselves to be married; however, they know they can separate at the whim or choice of either partner.

In past generations, certain professions which women entered relegated them to the unwed state. School teachers and corporate executives came into this category. Today this is no longer true, as many women have successfully combined professional careers with marriage. Although the opportunity for marriage has been present in all generations, young adults today are getting married at a somewhat earlier age than was true previously. In 1890 the average (mean) age for marriage for young adult females was twenty-two; for males, it was twenty-six. Today the median age for females is twenty, and for males, twenty-two. Current statistics indicate that there is considerably less variation in the age of marriage for the present generation than was true of previous generations. A few more interesting statistics regarding the age of marriage in the United States at the present time are worthy of comment. Today's young adult parents have their children earlier, complete having their children earlier (the siblings are closer together in age), and their own children get married at an earlier age. Today's generation of grandparents are younger and they live longer.

Happiness in marriage is positively related to successful adjustments which have been achieved in other areas of life. A person who succeeds in his marriage must have a degree of certainty with regard to himself and his relationships with others. He or she must know how to share oneself with another, understand the merging and submerging of identities, and be capable of a strong commitment to the needs and welfare of others. Many women enter the marital state with mixed feelings; they marry because society says that this is the thing to do, but they may be less than certain that this is the right time or the right man. Yet the alternatives of remaining single may be equally discouraging. Those who remain single in our society are not necessarily looked upon as "old maids" anymore—that kind of designation was more appropriately suited to a bygone era—yet, the same kind of narrow bigotry exists toward those who do not wed.

Many persons are pushed into an ill-suited marriage because of the tenets of a society which clings to an outmoded bias. Indeed these individuals might have a happier life and be better adjusted if they remained single. In 1900, only 8% of marriages in the United States ended in divorce. Today, the divorce rate is estimated to be as high as 25%. Regardless of percentages, the high divorce rate is indicative of the fact that many of these marriages should not have taken place.

More and more states are beginning to require or to suggest pre-marital counseling, mandatory counseling prior to the granting of divorce or during a period of trial separation, and similar efforts in order to help the young adult make satisfactory marital adjustments. Several studies have indicated that the young age of the couple makes satisfactory marital adjustment more difficult. Problems are further complicated because so often today the young couple is still in college or in graduate school. They soon discover that two cannot live as cheaply as one, and that economic restrictions impose social and emotional adjustment problems. Marriage prior to the completion of the educational process once was rare; today it is a commonplace occurrence on college campuses throughout the nation.

Married students, in general, perform better academically than their single counterparts of the same general age and stage of educational attainment. Perhaps the variable factor here lies in the advanced maturity of the married student as compared to the single student. Similarity of interests and goals is a binding factor in the earlier marriage of young adults while still in college. Too, these young adults have generally known each other for a period of months or years, which has been shown to be a positive factor in predicting marital success and stability. Often the young couple are in basic (prior) agreement on several points which often cause friction in some marriages: the need to economize; the need to postpone having a family; the desire to complete a student role prior to beginning one's own permanent residency.

Psychologists have suggested that the choice of a marital partner is probably the number-one decision in the adjustment process of young adulthood; ranking a very close second is the choice as to vocational goals and direction. Once the marriage has been consummated, and even before, the young couple face numerous problems of sexual adjustment to each other. Sexual attitudes do not begin with marriage; the tone was set many years earlier. Sexual knowledge has been internalized throughout childhood and adolescence from peers, family, the society in general, reading, and numerous other sources. Still, the young adult is now faced with the actuality of sexual performance; performance as a married person. Often sexual disappointments in the early stages of a marriage are several. Inhibiting factors in the society cannot be cast aside overnight; the transformation from the single, perhaps virginal or chaste state to that of a married, sexually active partner does not happen by signing a marriage license.

The need to satisfy the needs, wants, and desires of oneself and of others is a basic concept in maturity. The need exists in many ways other than sexual, but it is often in the realm of sexual relationships that young couples find the most difficult kinds of adjustments to each other. Part of the wave or tide of the new morality is an objection to this state of affairs; many young adults argue that it is important that they get to know each other sexually before marriage if their marriage is to succeed. The moral and religious values and doubts raised by these and related issues have not been satisfactorily resolved to date; their philosophical implications go to the very core of the nature of mankind.

In past generations, marriages were more stable because of the similarity in background of the couple. They came from the same local community and probably settled there; they practiced the same religion; they were of the same general socio-economic class. Today, however, young couples marry inter-racially, inter-religiously, from all social levels, and comprise an American population which has been inadequately described as "highly diverse and mobile." These differences and others are not insurmountable; many young couples have made successful adjustments despite what appears to be incredible difficulties. The differences in the young husband and wife, however, do make adjustment in the early years of marriage more complex, and tend to lengthen the period of time it takes the young couple to adjust to each other's needs, feelings, moods, and background.

Probably the important psychological aspect of marriage is its newness for each of the young adults. Facing new situations, most people rely upon their experiential backgrounds. The young adult couple are facing numerous new situations as they start their marriage. Adjustments are required in areas such as renting an apartment, balancing the budget, agreeing about in-laws, sexual relationships, educational goals, career decisions, and starting a family.

Each of these adjustments, and many more, demand a level of mature behavior by both the young wife and the young husband. As the glamor and joy of the wedding ceremony fade into memory, and as the relatively happy (although sometimes awkward) honeymoon days end, the young couple must face the realities of making decisions related to each of these problem areas. Too, each young couple finds themselves in certain unique situations. Some are faced with parental problems; still others find religious, racial, and philosophical differences which had not been adequately discussed in order to reach a satisfactory agreement prior to marriage.

The unfinished business of adolescence sometimes interferes with the start of a marriage. Marriage is restrictive in several ways; marital partners are expected to devote more time to each other, to remain sexually loyal, and to give up some of their friends to whom the opposite partner objects. These restrictions in freedom sometimes cause a marriage to go "sour." Problems of drinking, gambling, promiscuity, and other such behavior often raise doubts in the mind of one of the married partners. Arguments, dissension, and disagreement appear, where, prior to the marriage, they were not present (or rarely so). Sometimes the period of "making up" becomes prolonged and more difficult. Some young adults want to "run away from it all" and return to their parents, reflecting here again the unfinished adolescent state. While most young married couples make satisfactory adjustments to these and other difficulties, not all are so fortunate or so successful.

BECOMING AN ADULT: MATURITY

Throughout childhood and adolescence young people are admonished to "grow up," to "act one's age," and to become "mature." The goal of maturity is a constant aim throughout the early developmental stages. The concept of maturity, however, is complex, involving more than the chronological attainment of a given number of years. Psychologists continue to consider maturity to be a developmental stage characterized by adult behavior which is both social and emotional, and by actions which reflect a degree of balance within the individual.

Levels of mature behavior vary between different individuals and within the individual himself. At times, one may act very maturely, and at other times, somewhat immaturely or even childishly. The behavior of the individual with respect to maturity and immaturity is a continuum. As one leaves adolescence the degree and frequency of immature behavior normally declines considerably; if one lives to reach the advanced stages of senescence, various kinds of immature behavior may once again recur. Predictions about the exact nature of one's behavior under any given circumstance or in any particular situation are difficult; however, the overall level of maturity can be fairly accurately predicted for the totality of behavior over a long range of time.

Maturity includes the ability to control anger, and the ability to settle differences of opinion with others in a non-violent way. This is one of the reasons some nations are called "immature" and some individuals are termed "unreliable" or "unpredictable." Maturity involves patience, the ability to wait, and the ability to work for long-term goals. The mature individual perseveres until he achieves his goals. He is willing to work with little or no reward or artificial incentives of an immediate nature. Maturity includes too the concept of unselfishness, of giving to others, helping others, and sacrificing self for the benefit of loved ones. It includes the concept of humility. The mature individual can admit errors; he is big enough to state that he is wrong.

The mature individual is able to face unpleasant situations and resolve them with some degree of satisfaction. Maturity in behavioral terms includes the concepts of reliability and dependability. Mature individuals accept the responsibility for their behavior and conduct. The ability to make a decision is a characteristic of maturity, but mature individuals can also modify their positions as circumstances dictate. The concept of maturity includes self-confidence, self-reliance, and economic self-sufficiency. The immature individual is highly dependent upon others; the mature individual depends upon his or her self. The acceptance of people for what they are, as people, is a characteristic of a high level of maturity.

THE PROBLEMS OF AGING

Time is a relative concept. For the adolescent and for the prisoner in jail it moves too slowly. In adulthood, time seems to move much more rapidly, and the approaching middle years and old age create new problems of adjustment for the individual. Population figures indicate that the world and the United States are expanding at a very rapid rate. Predictions for 1980 estimate the population of the United States at over 250 million; by the year 2000 predictions are that the United States will have over 300 million people if the present rate of population growth continues. As the average age of the American population is decreasing, the life-span or life-expectancy of the individual is increasing. In 1950 the average age in America was over thirty; by 1960 it was twenty-eight. Today, the average age is about twenty-five.

Adulthood concerns what people do in a wide variety of roles. It involves a series of activities or roles which are characteristically adult; so too, middle age and old age have their characteristic role expectancies. These activities shape the nature of middle age and old age. They arise from both biological and cultural expectancies. Both biological limitations and cultural expectations are generally accepted as factors in human development. The uniqueness of the individual, however, persists throughout the biological changes which inevitably occur as one ages. Cultural anthropologists stress the impact of society upon the individual, while the psychobiologists stress biological factors as the prime reason for changes in behavior.

Middle age and old age are not static. The biological changes which occur are only a part of the story. Social roles change; interests change; values and attitudes undergo considerable change. The adult is not fixed, but rather quite involved in a stream of changes which occur continuously. Contrary to popular belief, the adult attitude is not as inflexible or fixed as one might suppose. Maturity lends a background of experiences which contribute to changing attitudes and value systems. As individuals, adults seek recreational outlets as well as vocational pursuits. True, the nature of their interests may change considerably; but the interests are still there and their pursuit and fullfillment are part of the adult role.

In middle age and old age, one encounters several unique problems. The problems of health are indigenous to many individuals; others have economic problems, problems with their children, or a combination of any of these plus a wide variety of others. If there is a "generation gap" and a "communication gap," it is at least partly attributable to the fact that the younger generation has little or no comprehension of the problems of the adult generation; nor do they particularly care to become versed with the nature of the problems.

Maturity in middle and old age is reflected in emotional stability, social relationships, intellectual pursuits, physiological changes, cultural expectations, and the overall tenor of the behavior of the individual as his life continues to unfold.

VOCATIONAL CHOICES

One of the most important adjustments in adulthood involves vocational selection. The problem is complicated by a society which holds certain positions in high esteem, relegating other positions to lower rank in the social order. This artificial and arbitrary scale of values makes vocational selection more complex for the young adult. As the goal of a college education for everyone has become a reality, the individual's true choice of vocation and the choices of his parents and peers may be in opposition to each other. Too, the choices of the individual can be restricted by his lack of experience and knowledgeability in many vocational areas.

One's entire adult life is influenced by the kind of work which he performs in his daily life. How much a person earns determines, to a large degree, the kind of life-style he adopts, and the amount of job satisfaction he experiences is a prime factor in his adjustment as an adult. For young women, the problem is complicated by job restrictions which society has artificially imposed. The number of women physicians in the United States remains an infinitesimal portion of the population (a situation not found in other societies) as does the number of high level female executives.

Many young adults have special kinds of vocational problems. The handicapped and people limited in educational opportunity are restricted in unique ways in terms of vocational choices that are available to them. Disadvantaged youth often finds that the struggle for adequate training and educational preparation does not lead to the immediate reward of the position for which they have prepared because of prejudice. While societal attitudes have undergone marked transitions in the past several years, many persistent myths still surround the employability of the underprivileged, the disadvantaged, the handicapped, and members of minority groups.

Expectations of vocational choice in early adulthood are often discarded later in life as the level of aspiration of the adolescent and young adult is found to be out of focus with the reality of his abilities and opportunities. As adults, many of these same individuals experience deep and bitter disappointments and resentments. Even those adults who have all the outward manifestations of vocational success —position, power, status, and material possessions—often express deep inner disappointment, resentments, anxieties, and conflicts caused by the fact that they could not successfully achieve their young adult vocational aspiration.

The prevalent attitude in the American culture is still that the man and only the man should work and support his family. While this attitude has been modified somewhat, as more and more women enter the job market, many men still feel psychologically inadequate and incapable because their wives are gainfully employed. The status of "housewife" is still not of prime importance on the scale of American social values. Many women, not unnaturally, experience deep resentment at their relegation as housewife and mother, when the skills they have acquired in their college and high school days cannot be effectively utilized.

The vocational pursuits of the individual form an important source for self-expression. Erik Erikson has described the adult vocational years as the years of creativity. And certainly work has a far-reaching significance for most individuals. In the present affluent state of American society, the significance becomes even more important. Recent times have seen shifts in job-status appeal. The physician, once held in the highest esteem, has seen his place on the status ladder give way to the space scientist. The automobile salesman and the blue-collar worker remain relatively low on the social-status scale of values.

The adult world of work is a real world. It is important for the adjustment of the individual that he is satisfied with his job, his pay, and his working conditions. Many individuals remain occupied in vocations which are not of their liking, because these vocations are held high in social value. Vocational adjustment is a necessary fact of life adjustment for the adult.

PREPARATION FOR A CAREER

The young adult chooses and begins to prepare for a career at the wrong stage of development. Generally speaking, the choice is made immediately upon graduation from high school as he enters the job market or begins his college career. Because the choice is made so early, many young people find themselves in situations where they are working in jobs which they do not want or enjoy; or they are preparing for careers which they are unsure about entering. Often the discovery is made too late, at graduation or during one's senior year of college.

The nature of most college curricula allows very little, if any, room for experimentation. Once the young adult has entered business school or engineering school, his choice of studies is generally very much restricted within a given area. It then becomes a sticky problem for, say, the young adult who has announced he wants to be a dentist, enters dental school, and then finds he doesn't want this occupation, he is unsuited for the work, or that he cannot master the subject matter.

Many young adults enter the field of psychology with vague notions about therapy, a couch, and helping others. They are often astounded to discover they will need several years of training in research, higher mathematics, and at least a graduate school degree before they can become employable and economically productive. Clinical internships in psychology are a part of the training of the clinical psychologist; but many young adults are totally unaware of the amount and degree of training required. So too, they are often unaware of the diversity of choice within the field of psychology, as is true within the vocational areas of many other fields.

Since adult happiness is partly a matter of vocational contentment, this area should be given more attention at the secondary school and college levels. Many college freshmen, particularly those in community colleges, simply do not know what they want. This situation is not uncommon, since they have not been exposed to the subject areas in terms of content materials and requirements. For these young adults, one or two years, or more, of a general liberal arts education may be the best answer. With a wide exposure to differing subject areas and courses of study, the young adult can make a more realistic appraisal and assessment of those occupations for which he is best suited.

What We Have Learned

1. Early adulthood is a period of adjustment to new social roles and new patterns of life.
2. The young adult is expected to meet new problems and situations and to resolve conflicts independently from his parents.
3. Many young adults often feel alone, isolated, insecure, and inadequate.
4. Early adulthood extends from approximately age eighteen to age forty.
5. The problems of young adult men and women differ.
6. The extension of education into the adult years has meant the postponement of the assumption of adult responsibilities and an increase in accompanying psychological problems.
7. Many young adults are extremely indecisive.
8. Vocational decisions and choice of marital partner comprise two of the main adjustment problems faced by young adults.
9. No period of life is totally free of problems.
10. There is no single psychological theory which satisfactorily explains how young adults achieve individuality.
11. Young adulthood and adulthood are periods of transition.
12. There are several physical changes which occur in young adulthood.
13. The years of adulthood, in general, have been neglected by students of psychology.
14. Adulthood involves a change in role.
15. The challenges of adjustment in young adulthood are multiplex.
16. Happiness in marriage is positively related to adjustments which have been made earlier in life from childhood on into adolescence and young adulthood.
17. Levels of mature behavior differ among individuals and within the behavior of the individual himself.
18. Maturity and immaturity form a continuum.
19. The psychological characteristics of maturity differ considerably from the mere attainment of a given chronological age.
20. Adulthood involves a continuously changing process of adjustment.
21. The life expectancy of Americans continues to increase.
22. Middle age and old age are not static; the process of change and adjustment to change is a continuous process which extends throughout one's lifetime.

23. One of the most important decisions in young adulthood involves the choice of career.
24. The young adult often must choose a career at a time when he is least prepared to do so.
25. The vocational guidance and counseling procedures in most secondary schools leave much to be desired.
26. Many adults are disappointed later in life when they find that they have made an incorrect vocational choice, or that they are unsuited for the occupation for which they have prepared.
27. Prejudice toward women still exists in many vocational areas, including numerous professional areas.
28. The nature of most college curricula allows very little opportunity for the student to experiment with regard to vocational choice.
29. Adult happiness is often largely a matter of vocational contentment.
30. Vocational choice determines the individual's life-style for the major portion of his adult life.

What We Still Need to Learn

1. Many of the problems associated with adulthood have received scant attention from psychological investigators. More research on several aspects of the problems of adulthood is needed.
2. Improved means of vocational guidance must be developed for use at the elementary and secondary school levels.
3. The degree of differences and the directions of these differences in the problems of the young adult male and the young adult female need to be further delineated.
4. Young adults need to be better informed about the adjustment problems which are commonly experienced in this stage of development.
5. The utopian myth that adulthood means the cessation of adjustment problems needs to be exploded.
6. The psychological effects of the physical changes which occur in young adulthood need further exploration.
7. As life expectancies continue to increase, the science of psychology in the areas of senescence and geriatrics needs further refinement.
8. Young adults still need the unobtrusive help and support of parents; parents need to be advised as to the importance of their roles toward their young married children.
9. Pre-marital counseling needs formal institutionalization, perhaps as a legal requirement prior to obtaining a marriage license.

10. Counseling should be a requirement prior to the granting of trial separation or to the obtaining of a divorce.
11. On-the-job guidance, in-service training programs, and continuing vocational guidance for employees needs to be formalized by business and industry, as well as by public institutions.
12. Young adults need to be appraised of the operation of the maturity-immaturity continuum in more realistic terms.
13. Career opportunities which have received relatively little notoriety need to be brought to the attention of the young adult so that he will be enabled to make a more intelligent career choice.
14. The liberation of young adult women needs to gain impetus in the next generation in order to prevent the catastrophic problems which occur when professionally-trained women are virtually barred from obtaining employment because of sex.

SUGGESTIONS FOR FURTHER READING

Douvall, Evelyn M., *Facts of Life and Love for Teenagers*, New York: Association Press, 1956.

Haas, Kurt, *Understanding Ourselves and Others*, Englewood Cliffs, New Jersey: Prentice-Hall, Inc., 1965.

Lipset, Seymour M., and S. S. Wolin, Eds. *Berkeley Student Revolt*, New York: Doubleday, 1965.

McConnell, James V., *Understanding Human Behavior*, New York: Holt, Rinehart and Winston, 1974.

Rogers, Carl R., *On Becoming A Person: A Therapist's View of Psychotherapy*, Boston, Mass.: Houghton Mifflin Co., 1970.

Sachs, Herbert L., *Student Projects in Child Psychology*, Dubuque, Iowa: Kendall Hunt Publishing Company, 1967.

Seymour, Martin Lipset, Ed., *Student Politics*, New York: Basic Books, Inc., 1967.

Slocum, Walter L., *Occupational Careers: A Sociological Perspective*, Chicago, Ill.: Aldine Publishing Company, 1974.

Super, D. E., *The Psychology of Careers*, New York: Harper and Row, 1963.

Teuer, Lewis Samuel, *The Conflict of Generations: The Character and Significance of Student Movements*, New York: Basic Books, Inc., 1969.

Vorrath, Harry H. and Larry K. Brendtro, *Positive Peer Culture*, Chicago, Ill.: Aldine Publishing Company, 1974.

GLOSSARY

The numbers which appear in parenthesis ( ) following each definition in this glossary refer to those chapters where the student can readily locate a more thorough description for each term, and an example of its use in the context of a discussion about the term itself.

A. A. Degree An Associate of Arts degree conferred upon graduates of two-year colleges after completion of prescribed courses of study with a certain level of grades. (2)

Aberrant Deviation from the behavior of normal or typical persons; atypical behavior. (1, 7, & 8)

Abnormal Psychology The study of those behaviors and mental processes which differ from the normal.

Academic Anxiety The fears, tensions, and worries experienced by numerous students during the course of their educational pursuits. (4)

Achievement A demonstrated level of knowledge or skills, usually in a specific subject or content area. (9 & 11)

Achievement Orientation An inclination toward success, accomplishment, and recognition, guided by an individual's high degree of motivation. (9 & 11)

Achievement Test A measure of attainment, mastery, skill, or knowledge, often in a specific subject or content area, as contrasted to the measurement of ability or potential. (3)

Acne A chronic inflammatory condition of the skin, common in adolescence and characterized by the appearance of pimples about the face. (7)

Acquired Needs Those needs which are learned during an individual's development and which serve as a basis for behavior. (6)

A.C.T. American College Test. Over six hundred colleges and universities require that the student take this test prior to acceptance or admission. (2 & 3)

Adaptability The process whereby an organism adjusts to changes in the external environment and to external situations. (1 & 9)

Addict Behavior characterized by an overdependency upon drugs or alcohol and including a craving, need, or desire for the internalization of same. (5)

Addiction A pathological habituation to the use of drugs or alcohol. (10)

Adescence A period in the development of the individual between puberty and maturity; a developmental stage between late adolescence and adulthood during which time the individual maintains many earlier adolescent characteristics. (7)

Adjustment Adaptations in terms of behavior patterns to the demands of the individual's internal (needs, drives, conflicts) and external (society) environment. (1 & 10)

Adjustment Mechanism The kinds of responses an individual makes in attempting to meet the demands of his environment. Some individuals attack the problems which they face directly; others attack other people because of their own problems; some avoid or withdraw from problems, while still others compromise in various ways. (5)

Adult Legally, in most states of the United States of America, any individual who has attained the chronological age of twenty-one; psychologically, the term refers to an individual who is fully grown, developed, or matured. (1 & 6)

Affective State A variety of emotional experiences which are judged to be either pleasant or unpleasant, such as moods, feelings, and emotions. (10)

Affiliation Motive The need to be with others, to associate, and to form friendships. (6 & 14)

Affluence A state of having sufficient wealth to meet one's ordinary needs. (12)

Aggression A bold pursuit toward one's goals, including attacking others who may be in one's way. (4, 7, 9, 11)

Agnosia The inability to interpret sensory impressions; imperfect perception; the loss of ability to recognize familiar objects through the use of a sense organ. (7)

Alcoholic Psychosis A mental disorder resulting in delerium, hallucinations, or paranoia, resulting from excessive use of alcohol. (10)

Alcoholism A state wherein the individual has an excessive need or craving for alcohol, generally resulting in addiction with resulting bodily tissue damage. (10)

Alienation A form of mental disturbance or disorder which estranges one's personality from others. (8)

Altruism Feelings, attitudes, and actions which stress the well-being of others. (9 & 13)

Ambivalence A state wherein the individual experiences conflicting feelings toward the same person or goal. (1)

Ambivert The classification of an individual who has the characteristics of both introversion and extroversion. See, also, "extrovert" and "introvert." (11)

Amnesia A partial or total inability to recall past situations, people, or events. (7)

Anthropologist An individual engaged in the scientific study and analysis of the human species, its bodily forms, evolution, distribution, and culture; a science of anthropology generally divided into Physical Anthropology and Social Anthropology. (8)

Anxiety Apprehension about the future with mixed emotions of fear and hope. (3, 4, & 15)

Anxiety Neurosis A disordered state marked by varying degrees of fear and morbidity. (10)

Apathy The situation wherein an individual lacks motivation or interest or concern with regard to his surroundings or himself. (7)

Aphasia A language defect caused by damage to the brain; loss or impairment in the use of language. (7)

Approach-Approach Conflict A tendency to move toward or in the direction of two goals which are both viewed as attractive or positive. (5)

Approach-Avoidance Conflict The attraction and repulsion by the individual with regard to two goals.

Approval (Need for) The need to be accepted for what one is; the desire for the approval of others. (6)

Aptitude Characteristics of an individual which are symptomatic of an ability to acquire skills and knowledge after suitable training. (11)

Aptitude Test An instrument for the measurement of particular skills which could be developed with adequate training. (3)

Aspiration (Level of) A strong desire to attain a certain goal or standard of achievement which the individual or the society sees as valuable. (1 & 7)

Asthenic A kind of physique (after E. Kretschmer) which is associated as small of trunk, thin, and tall. (7 & 11)

Athletic (Body Type) A well-balanced physique; the perfect physical stage of development (after E. Kretschmer). (11)

Attitude A way of feeling, acting, or thinking about an object, concept, or situation. (8 & 9)

Auto-Eroticism Self-generated and self-stimulated sexual activity wherein the individual uses his own body as a source of sexual gratification. (5)

Autonomous Control over one's own actions; an individual who is self-governing, self-fulfilling, self-regulating, and independent. (35)

Avoidance-Avoidance Conflict A situation in which an individual is faced with making a choice between two negative, or repellent goals. (5)

B.A. Degree Bachelor of Arts Degree. The certificate of graduation from a four-year college or university usually conferred after four years of study which includes certain prescribed courses and the attainment of a certain grade average. (2, 4, & 5)

Behavior Reactions of the whole organism, including overt or observable responses and internal mechanisms such as thinking. (1)

Behaviorism A school of psychology which stresses that behavior can be empirically observed and measured. (7)

Belief Acceptance of an idea, principle, or doctrine as true, real, or of value. (8)

Biological Motives A state of the organism in initiating and regulating behavior with regard to a goal. (6)

B.S. Degree Bachelor of Science Degree. See also B.A. Degree. (2, 4, & 5)

C.A. Chronological Age. The number of years a person has lived since birth; an individual's age. (11)

Catatonia A psychotic condition wherein the skeletal framework and musculature remains fixed in a given position. (10)

Causative Factor The occurrence of a certain event followed by a resultant which assumes a relationship between the former and the latter. (1)

C.E.E.B. College Entrance Examination Board. The agency which produces standardized tests required of many students prior to college admission. (2 & 3)

Chemotherapy The use of drugs in the treatment of mental disorders. See also Drug Therapy. (7 & 12)

Chronological Age A person's age in years and months. See also C.A. (7 & 11)

Claustrophobia A fear of being kept in or locked in a closed place. (10)

Climacteric A period in mature adulthood wherein radical changes occur, such as the menopause in women; usually accompanied by emotional as well as physical trauma. (6 & 7)

Clinical Psychology A branch of psychology devoted to the problems of the individual, and attempting to solve these problems with such techniques as diagnosis, testing, and psychotherapy.

Cognition The process of knowing, beginning with awareness, perception, remembering, imagining, and extending to all forms of reasoning. (14)

Cognitive Needs The change in the behavior of an individual caused by his increased awareness or perceptivity of objects and situations. (6, 7, & 9)

Communication Interaction between two or more persons by the use of language, gestures, or symbols. (7)

Community College A newer term adopted by many two year colleges which formerly called themselves Junior Colleges. The term reflects the commitment to a more comprehensive program aimed at all members of the community in which the college is located. (2, 3, & 4)

Commuter College Colleges wherein the majority, or all of the students, live at home or off-campus; colleges which do not provide resident facilities for students. (2)

Compensation A defense mechanism whereby an individual disguises an undesirable trait by emphasizing a more desirable aspect of his personality. (5 & 11)

Compulsion An irresistible urge to perform or to act in a given manner. (10)

Computer Science A comprehensive term encompassing the entire field of data processing. (3)

Conflict A state of being simultaneously motivated by incompatible tendencies or goals. (1, 7 & 13)

Conformity Being in agreement with the actions, beliefs, and values of a group and following that pattern of behavior. (8)

Consciousness Awareness of something either within oneself or in the surrounding environment. (1)

Construct A synthesis of impression, equivalent to a concept. (8)

Counselor A skilled and trained faculty member of a college or university who works with individual students and small groups in their guidance and in helping them to solve problems. (3)

Cultural Deprivation Refers to an imbalance between a larger cultural pattern and the obvious lacks in a smaller cultural pattern, resulting in personal, social, emotional, and psychological lacks in the individuals in the smaller culture. (8 & 12)

Culture The sum total of the ways of living of a group, including its values, mores, institutional organizations, and patterns of accepted behavior. Within the culture there are smaller subcultures which differ in degrees. (12)

Curiosity Motive A desire to explore or to gain knowledge about events and situations. (1)

Curriculum A prescribed educational program or plan of study. (4)

Daydreaming Wishful, uncontrolled, fanciful imagery which occurs during the waking hours, often in a pleasant context, and sometimes indulged in as a way of adjusting to frustration and anxiety. (7)

D.C.P. Degree Completion Program. A college program for older adults who have finished some college many years earlier, and who now wish to return in order to complete their college education. (4)

Defense Mechanism Any structure used by an individual to avoid unpleasant, stressful, or frustrating events. (5)

Dejection Feelings and moods of sadness and depression. (5)

Delerium Tremens An acute alcoholic psychosis whereby the confused individual experiences hallucinations and illusions. (10)

Dementia Praecox A form of psychosis involving deterioration of intellectual functioning and memory. Often used synonomously with the term Schizophrenia, although Dementia Praecox is an older term in derivation. (10)

Deoxyribonucleic Acid See D.N.A. (17)

Dependency Role A relationship of one person to another or to others involving an excessive degree of reliance. (1)

Depersonalization Loss of a sense of value for self in relationship to others; the desensitizing of the value of the individual. (14)

Depression Feelings of melancholoy, gloom, and hopelessness, which may include individual feelings of inadequacy and self-deprecation. (7)

Development Refers to the maturation and growth processes in organic structure and in psychological maturity. The concept includes the gaining of knowledge through experiences as one grows older. (1 & 11)

Deviant Behavior which varies from the norm or standard patterns which prevail in any group or in any society. (1, 5, 7, & 10)

Dexterity Skillfullness. (11)

Diagnosis Identification of a disorder through tracing its origin, history, development, and symptoms. (3 & 10)

Directive Counseling A form of psychotherapy or treatment for an individual whereby the counselor or therapist attempts to provide specific instructions and definitive solutions for a problem. (10)

Dissociation A defense mechanism which isolates various aspects of an individual's behavior, such as occurs in amnesia or in cases of dual personality aberation. (5, 10, 11)

D.N.A. Deoxyribonucleic acid molecules which are considered today to be the principal element of genes. See also Deoxyribonucleic acid. (7)

Drive A stimulus or condition which motivates an individual to a certain kind of behavior. Often used synonomously with motivation. See also "Primary Motives." (1, 4, 7, & 14)

Drug Therapy See Chemotherapy. The use of drugs to induce a given desired psychological state. (7)

Dyad A couple; a pair; a team; two elements which become strongly identified in a relationship with each other. (12)

Dynamics That which concerns itself with the causes for behavior; that branch of a science which studies motivational factors underlying behavior. (1 & 7)

Dysplastic A body type which is a mixture of several types, hence cannot be classified as any of the main body types (e.g., pyknic or asthenic). After E. Kretschmer. (7 & 11)

Electrotherapy The use of electric shock in the treatment of mental disorders with the aim of alleviating the behavioral disorder of the individual. (7 & 10)

Emancipation Attainment of freedom from control by others; a goal in adolescence. (6)

E.M.H. Educable Mentally Handicapped. Individuals with less than average intelligence who can be educated to a given level of mastery because of limited abilities. (11)

Emotions A complex of responses which heighten the awareness of the individual in a situation, accompanied by physiological and psychological changes in state. These responses often interfere with behavior. (1 & 14)

Endocrine Gland A ductless gland in the body which produces a hormone which is injected into the circulatory system. (7)

Environment All aspects of an individual's surroundings, including the physical, social, chemical, and biological, as well as psychological circumstances in which he finds himself at any given moment in time. (5, 6, & 7)

Establishment Those accepted institutions, economic, political, social, and educational, which regulate the significant aspects of the society. (2, 4, 5, 9, & 12)

Esteem (Need for) The need to have a high regard for self and for others. (6)

Ethics The study of the values, standards, and principles of a group or an individual in terms of attempting to judge right from wrong. (8)

Ethnocentricity The tendency to judge other groups and other ways of life in terms of the standards and values of one's own group. (13)

Ethos (American Ethos) The values, standards, and attitudes which characterize a society and distinguish it from others. (6)

Exhibitionism Exposing or displaying one's sexual organs in order to effect and stimulate sexual excitement in oneself and in others. (5)

Exploratory Motive The need to act resulting from one's curiosity. (1)

Extrovert A type of individual whose interests and attitudes are maintained outside himself, geared to the presence of others in social experiences. See also Ambivert and Introvert. (6 & 11)

Feelings An affective experience resulting from perception or from emotions. (14)

Fetishism An abnormal condition whereby an individual obtains sexual gratification and satisfaction by the attraction of an object, thing, or part of the body, such as clothing worn by another. (5 & 10)

Frustration   A state which results from a blocking or a thwarting of goals so that achievement or attainment of a desired goal is not possible. (3, 4, 9, & 13)

Functional Psychosis   An abnormal condition resulting from behavioral factors such as stress, with no apparent organic basis. A disturbed mental condition with no physiological cause. (10)

General Psychology   That branch of science (behavioral science or sometimes classified as social science) which studies in a general way the behavior of the individual in adjusting to his environment. (1)

Generation Gap   The disparity and misunderstandings which exist between the older (parent and grandparent) generation and their progeny (younger generation) caused by a lack of communication, and by a change in values and standards with the passage of time. (1, 7, & 12)

Geriatrics   The study of the aging process and the problems and adjustments necessitated by growing old. (6, 7, & 15)

Ghetto   An area of residence wherein minority groups are located by virtue of their poverty status, race, or religious differences from the rest of the culture at large, causing deprivation in physical and psychological ways to the residents. (4 & 12)

Goal   An object, situation, or reward toward which an individual directs his behavior and efforts. (4, 5, & 7)

Gregariousness   The tendency to live in groups; the need to associate with others, such as flocks, groups, and crowds. (12)

Group   A social-psychological term including the complex relationship existing between two or more individuals who are in communication with each other. The interaction between two or more people. (12)

Group Therapy   A technique for the treatment of several individuals at the same time in order to alleviate their problems. (14)

Hallucinations   False perceptions; sensory experiences which have no basis in fact, such as seeing things which are not there or hearing voices when there are none to be heard. (5)

Hebephrenia   A form of schizophrenia, or psychotic condition, characterized by silliness, giddiness or laughter, and other forms of bizarre behavior. (10)

Hematophobia   An irrational, excessive, and pervasive fear of blood. (10)

Heterosexual Adjustment   The normal course of development whereby an individual comes to seek the companionship, warmth, and affection of the opposite sex. (5, 6, & 7)

Homosexuality   Sexual attraction between persons of the same sex. (5, 7, & 10)

Hormone   A chemical substance secreted by an endocrine gland and emitted into the circulatory system. (7)

Hostility   Feelings, actions, and attitudes of unfriendliness or hate; negative behavior toward another. (8 & 12)

Hydrotherapy   The use of water (hot baths and other forms) in the treatment of mental patients. (7 & 10)

Hypochondria   A neurotic preoccupation and concern with one's health, physical condition, ailments, and bodily activities. (10)

Hypothesis   A theory or tentative principle formulated in order to explain a given set of data. (7)

Hysteria   A neurotic state associated with amnesia, paralysis, and other forms of dissociation with no apparent organic basis in fact. (10)

Ideal Self   The way the individual would like himself to be, and the way the individual hopes that others may see him. (6)

Identification   A defense mechanism whereby the individual gains esteem through fantasy as if he were someone else. (5, 6, 9, & 11)

Identity   The way an individual sees himself in terms of his assets and his shortcomings and his relationship to the rest of the world. (3, 8, & 11)

Identity-Formation   The part that earlier experiences play in the shaping and the formation of the personality and in one's self-conceptualization. (5)

Idiosyncratic Behavior   Behavior which is characteristic of an individual and is peculiar to that individual. (11)

Idiot   An individual with a mental ability level well below the average; an individual with the mental functioning equivalent to that of a three or four year old. (11)

Illegitimacy   Born out of wedlock.

Illusion   A mistaken or false perception or a misinterpretation of a stimulus whereby what is perceived does not relate directly to the stimulus or to reality. (5)

Imbecile   An individual with below average level of intelligence, functioning at about the four- to seven-year-old level of intellectual competency. (11)

Immaturity   Emotional, social, and psychological behavior by an individual more in keeping and characteristic of behavior of a younger person. A contrast and opposition to mature behavior. (1, 5, & 7)

Immoral   Behavior which violates or contradicts accepted social codes and standards of practice.

Impulsive Behavior   Behavior or actions by an individual without prior deliberation and with little or no regard for the consequences of the actions; often an immediate, ill-conceived, and scarcely thought-out action.

Incest Sexual relations with the members of one's own family. (5, 10)

Independence Self-reliance, including dependency upon one's own thoughts, feelings, and behavior; the self-determined individual pattern of behavior.

Individuality Those traits, individual and collective, which distinguish and differentiate an individual from others. (1)

Ink Blot Test A series of figures (ink blots) which are viewed by an individual who then reports what he thinks he sees, in order to analyze the structure of the personality (Rorschach Test). (11)

Intelligence Generally refers to intellectual functioning, which includes such processes as thinking, problem-solving, reasoning, verbal ability, the ability to conceptualize, perceptivity, etc. (3)

Introvert A turning of thoughts inward, whereby the interests of the individual are motivated toward self rather than toward others; an inclination to recede within the self. See also Ambivert and Extrovert. (6 & 11)

Involutional Melancholia A psychotic condition of mental disturbance characterized by extreme depressive states. (10)

I.Q. Intelligence Quotient. A derived number value obtained by dividing the M.A. by the C.A. (11)

Junior College A two-year college which offers the first half of the programs at senior or four-year institutions. (2 & 3)

Kleptomania An abnormal and persistent desire or impulse to steal without any relation to economic need, value of the object, or usefulness of the stolen object. (7)

Latent Homosexuality The unrevealed presence of an attraction between an individual of one sex and members of the same sex. (5)

Lie Detector An instrument which measures physiological changes of an individual responding to questions, in order to determine if the individual is telling the truth. (4)

Life-Style A particular way of living based upon the individual's perception of the world, his background, and his experiences. (7 & 8)

LSD A chemical substance which produces symptoms of euphoria, hallucinations, and dreams. See also Lysergic Acid. (5)

Lysergic Acid A crystalline alkaloid chemical substance derived from ergot, forming the basis for the drug LSD and producing simulated states of schizophrenia. (5)

M.A. Mental Age. The end product of intelligence testing determines the mental age of the individual, i.e., in relation to one's chronological age, a given state of knowledge at a given stage of development. (11)

M.A. Degree Master of Arts Degree. A graduate college (postcollege) or advanced degree indicating the attainment of knowledge in a given field of specialization. (2)

Maladjustment A state whereby the individual has difficulty in making a satisfactory adjustment to others, to himself, or to his environment. (1, 5, & 10)

Mania A mental disorder characterized by a state of excitment, emotional heightening, or wild behavior; a phase of manic-depressive psychosis. (10)

Manic-Depressive Psychosis A serious state of mental illness which is characterized by alternation between states of excitement and depression in varying degrees. (10)

Marijuana A drug derived from Cannabis Indica which induces a feeling of well-being and a loss of inhibitions.

Masculine Role Behavior which is deemed characteristic of the male sex; this behavior differs in various societies. (6)

Masochism Sexual gratification obtained by an individual through suffering physical pain by one's own hands or through infliction by another. (5 & 10)

Maturation The developmental changes and process of change whereby the physical and psychological state of the adult is achieved. (1, 3, 5, 6, & 7)

Megalopolis A combination of large city metropolitan areas into still larger complexes. (6, 9, & 12)

Menstrual Cycle The monthly discharge of blood from the uterus of a sexually mature woman. (6 & 7)

Mental Health A state of satisfaction derived by the individual from satisfactory achievements and adaptation to his environment. (1 & 10)

Mental Hygiene Refers to mental health and attaining satisfying personal and social adjustment for the purpose of preventing mental illness. (10)

Milieu The setting or environmental circumstances in which an individual finds himself located.

Milieu Therapy A form of treatment whereby a disturbed individual is placed into a new or different environment on a temporary or permanent basis in order to effect desired changes in his behavior. (7 & 10)

M.M.P.I. Minnesota Multiphasic Personality Inventory. A group test designed to measure an individual's attitudes, needs, and other personality factors; a widely used personality assessment device. (11)

Mnemonic Device An aid for remembering; a memory aide which utilizes a puzzle, including the first letter of each word in a sentence, e.g., *Every Good Boy Does Fine* for remembering the lines of a musical staff. (2)

Monogamy The marriage of one person to another, at a time; singularity of marital partners, as opposed to polygamy. (15)

Moods A temporary, mild emotional state such as joy, anger, or elation. (14)

Morality Those customs, values, and standards which a given society has strongly approved as significant behavior patterns. (6 & 9)

Mores The rights and wrongs of a group regarding the welfare of that group; practices which a group regards as important or vital to their well-being.

Moron An individual whose mental capacity (intelligence) is below normal, with an I.Q. range from 50 to 70. Such an individual lacks comprehensive judgment and is deficient in learning ability. (11)

Motivation Goal-directed and goal-seeking behavior by an individual. The process of satisfying felt physical, social, and psychological needs. Directed activity and behavior toward a goal. (1, 4, & 9)

Mythology Accepted beliefs, even though they may have been proven to be incorrect; group faith in a set of beliefs.

Narcosis Therapy The prescribed use of drugs to reduce an individual's normal responses in order to lessen self-destructive responses. (8)

Necromancy An abnormal interest in the dead; magical communication with the dead. (7)

Necrophilia An abnormal attraction to dead bodies. (7 & 10)

Neurasthenia A neurotic condition often characterized by extreme fatigue and lack of vigor, with no apparent organic or physical basis. (10)

Neurotic Sometimes called Psychoneurotic. An abnormal reaction by an individual to problems; the excessive use of defense mechanisms in conflict situations; a form of mental disturbance less serious than psychosis. (1 & 10)

Normal Probability Curve A symmetrical, bell-shaped curve used in statistics, describing the proportion of cases which occur within any given area of the curve. (10)

Normality Close to the average or expected mode of behavior or conduct. (10)

Nymphomania Extreme sexual desire for gratification and sexual relationships by a woman. (10)

Objective Test Contrasts with essay tests; a test which can be impartially scored by anyone, with the same evaluation resulting. (3 & 4)

Occupational Therapy Treatment for disturbed individuals and for mental patients by employing gainful activities and hobbies, such as art, shop work, weaving, knitting, etc. (7 & 10)

Ontogeny The origin, evolution, and development of the individual. (7)

Opinion An attitude formulated by an individual toward an event, condition, or behavior. (8)

Organic Psychosis In contrast to the functional psychosis, organic psychosis has a physiological or biological basis in fact as an underlying causative factor; mental illness traceable to injury or disease. (10)

Over-Compensation Excessive reaction by an individual in an attempt to counteract feelings of inferiority and helplessness. (5 & 11)

Overlearning Learning a given set of material beyond the point of mere recall or minimal competency, so that responses may be elicited at will. (3)

Overt Homosexuality Observable sexual activities and relationships between members of the same sex. (5)

Paranoia A psychotic condition characterized by delusions of persecution or delusions of grandeur. (10)

Pedophilia An abnormal condition whereby the individual adult gains sexual gratification, stimulation, pleasure, or fulfillment through the handling, fondling, or intercourse with children. (5 & 10)

Peers Groups of individuals of the same general age level with common interests and values. (2, 5, & 11)

Perception The ability of the individual to be aware and to recognize stimuli and to differentiate between various kinds and degrees of stimuli. (1)

Personality The total characteristics of the behavior and the traits of any individual which determine his unique adjustment to his environment; traits and attributes of an individual which are of a durable and enduring nature. (1, 4, 5, 8, & 11)

Personality Assessment An evaluation tool (instrument) by which a trained psychologist may make a judgment with regard to the personality characteristics of an individual; a measurement device. (3 & 11)

Perversion Deviation from the normal, often in a sexual sense. (5)

Phobia A pathological or irrational fear of some object or situation. There are literally hundreds of different kinds of phobias. (10)

Phonophobia An abnormal fear of speaking out loud. (7)

Phylogeny The origin and evolution of the species. (7)

Physiological Psychology A branch of psychology which studies the function of the nervous system and other anatomical organs in relationship to the behavior and the mental processes of the individual.

Pneumograph An instrument for the measurement of respiration. (14)

Polygamy Having more than one husband or wife at the same time. In some countries this is accepted practice, legally, or by group sanction.

Postulate A provisional acceptance of a statement of a principle. (1)

Potential Individual characteristics which are not apparent but which can be anticipated at a later time; abilities or behaviors which appear later. (1, 7, & 12)

Pragmatic After William James, Pragmatism. An emphasis of the practical consequences of any action, idea, or concept. (12)

Prejudice A prejudgment, favorable or unfavorable, without adequate evidence and not readily changed by contrary evidence, formulated by an individual and directed at others. (8 & 13)

Prestige A position of high status or importance given to an individual by other members of a society reflecting the importance of that individual in the eyes of the group. (5, 12)

Primary Group The immediate family circle. One's closest and earliest companions and associates, with whom daily face-to-face relationships and encounters are experienced; the primary or earliest molding forces in a society. (12)

Primary Motives See also "Drives." The basic motivating forces which include the need for food, air, water, warmth, shelter, and sex. (1, 4, 7, & 14)

Prognosis Prediction as to the expected course of a particular condition or affliction. (7 & 10)

Projection A defense mechanism whereby an individual places the blame for his own weaknesses or inadequacies upon others. (5 & 11)

Promiscuity Loose participation in sexual relationships with numerous different partners. (5, 9, & 10)

P.S.A.T. Preliminary Scholastic Aptitude Test. A test administered by the College Entrance Examination Board prior to taking the S.A.T. itself (Scholastic Aptitude Test). (3)

Psychasthenia A neurotic condition characterized by anxiety and often accompanied by fixed ideas and a fixed way of thinking. (10)

Psychogalvanometer A measurement instrument which detects the electrical impulses (conductivity) present in the skin: A device for the measurement of the galvanic skin response. (14)

Psychologist A person trained in the theoretical background and in the operational procedures found within the science of psychology. (3 & 7)

Psychiatrist A medical doctor (M.D.) specializing in the analysis and diagnosis, as well as treatment of mental disorders. (3 & 7)

Psychoanalytic Theory A system of psychology embracing a theory and a technique originated by Sigmund Freud, and which emphasizes that behavior is largely caused by repressed factors found in the unconscious; sex and aggressive tendencies of the individual account for a large proportion of his behavior, according to this theory. (7)

Psychometrics The quantitative aspect of psychology which involves tests and measurements of individuals and of groups. (10)

Psychopathic Deviate An individual whose behavior characteristically differs from the socially accepted pattern in bizarre fashion; the behavior often disturbs or disrupts others. (5)

Psychopathic Personality An individual whose behavior is characterized by a pathological instability in which normal modes of conduct are shunned or perverted in some fashion. (10)

Psychopathy A character disorder, with little or no evidence of mental disorder or disturbance, but characterized by behavior which violates the patterns established by society. (14)

Psychosocial (Stages of Development) The impact of social and environmental conditions in the development of the individual toward maturity. (After Erik Erikson) (5 & 12)

Psychosomatic Disorders Bodily symptoms and physiological reactions arising from mental states; such conditions include certain kinds of ulcers, asthma, some heart conditions, etc. (10)

Psychotherapy Various forms of treatments used with individuals who are seriously disturbed, or who have problems in adjustment. (7)

Psychotic Extreme mental disorganization reflecting a serious mental disturbance or illness, characteristically requiring hospitalization or institutional care to effect changes in the bizarre behavioral patterns. (1 & 10)

Puberty Period of sexual maturity in youth. (6 & 7)

Pyknic A body type which is characteristically short, heavy, obese, or fat. (After Kretschmer.) (7 & 11)

Pyromaniac One having a chronic tendency toward incendiarism. (10)

Quack A charlatan; an individual who pretends to have knowledge of the principles of psychology, usually to gain financial reward for himself; an untrained or unqualified practitioner of psychology. (1)

Rationalization A defense mechanism whereby good, although false or inaccurate, reasons are given in justification of various actions. (5 & 11)

Reaction-Formation A defense mechanism whereby an individual separates his real feelings toward a situation and by his actions and behavior strongly denies them, thus channeling his behavior and actions into socially acceptable modes of conduct; behavior in opposition to true feelings. (5 & 11)

Recapitulation Repetition of earlier developmental patterns or sequences later in the life of an individual. (7)

Regression A defense mechanism wherein an individual retreats to an earlier mode or pattern of behavior. (5 & 10)

Rehabilitation Restoring an individual toward successful functioning within the framework of the society; the term is often applied to prisoners and suggests reformatory treatment. (10)

Rejection A negative or antagonistic reaction toward a suggestion or toward an opinion, belief, concept, judgment; usually directed toward another individual or group. (6)

Repression A defense mechanism whereby impulses, thoughts, or memories which provoke anxieties are denied or blocked out, as if they never occurred. (5 & 11)

Role The part played by an individual in conformance with the standards established by society for a given position or situation. (15)

Role Therapy A form of psychotherapy, used in the treatment of the disturbed or maladjusted individual, wherein the individual acts out a part, or plays a role, in order to gain new insights into his own behavioral patterns. (7, 9, & 10)

R.Y.M. Revolutionary Youth Movement. A group or subgroup of college students belonging to the new left, advocating radical, drastic, and immediate changes and reform, to be accomplished, if necessary, by aggressive actions. (8 & 13)

Sadism A sexual perversion whereby an individual seeks and attains gratification and pleasure by inflicting pain upon others. (5 & 10)

S.A.T. Scholastic Aptitude Test. An entrance test used by over eight hundred colleges and universities, devised and administered by the College Entrance Examination Board. (2 & 3)

Scatologic Speech The excessive use of profanity without total awareness of its employment in everyday speech. (8)

Schizophrenia Formerly termed Dementia Praecox. See, also, Dementia Praecox. A serious form of mental illness categorized as psychosis, wherein the individual withdraws from reality; technically, a "split-mind." (10)

S.D.S. An organization of students on college campuses throughout the nation known as the Students for a Democratic Society; the organization has been linked to protest movements and radical forms of campus demonstrations. (5, 8, & 13)

Secondary Group Refers to such groups as school groups, economic and political groups, clubs, and neighbors, where interactions between the group and the individual are carried on in an informal, impersonal fashion. (12)

Secondary Sex Characteristics Biologically transmitted traits such as appear in the course of development, including the lowering of the voice, the appearance of facial hair in the male, and breast development in the female. (6)

Selective Forgetting The purposeful forgetting of events of which the individual wants no recall; often an unconscious mechanism. (5)

Self-Actualization The process of fully realizing one's potential without the barriers or obstacles placed by others; after Abraham Maslow. (5 & 6)

Self-Appraisal An inventory for gathering information about oneself. (40)

Self-Conceptualization The perception of the individual toward himself; including how he sees himself, his role, and his analysis of his own appropriateness of behavior.

Senescence A stage of development in old age wherein the individual experiences mental impairment and physically degenerative changes. (6, 7, & 11)

Senile Psychosis Psychotic symptoms and patterns of behavior including loss of memory which accompany old age or the aging process in some individuals. (10)

Senility The mental and physical changes which accompany the deterioration of old age. (10)

Sensation Excitation caused by the effect of a stimulus upon a particular receptor organ. (1)

Situational Therapy A form of psychotherapy which involves changing an individual's mode of life or life-style, his occupation, or his relationships with others. (10)

Sociability Being agreeable, friendly, and having camaraderie with others.

Social Class A grouping on a scale of prestigious positions in a society whereby positions are ranked according to the amount of income production, location of residency, membership in organizations, etc. (6)

Socialization The process whereby the individual acquires habits, values, and patterns of behavior in accordance with his membership in a given society. (14)

Social Psychologist A trained psychologist who specializes in the area of group processes, group dynamics, the effects of the group upon the individual, and the processes involved in group behavior. (8 & 12)

Social Values Learned behavior in relating oneself to others. (5)

Somatotherapy The treatment of mental illness through the use of drugs, shocks, and surgery. (7 & 10)

Sphygmomanometer An instrument which measures the pressure in the arteries. (14)

Statistician One who uses mathematical techniques in analyzing data and making determinations from groupings of data. (15)

Statistics Mathematical procedures in the collecting and interpreting of data.

Status A position involving a particular role within a social system; achieved level of status. (1, 7, 12, & 13)

Stigma A societal label which brands a person as different in some way from others; e.g., a criminal or a pervert. (10)

Stimuli Internal or external factors which elicit a response from a receptor organ. (7)

Stress A condition of extreme mental tension or anxiety. (15)

Sublimation A defense mechanism used to maintain esteem through the indirect expression of socially approved patterns of behavior; in psychoanalytic-psychological terms, a diversion of sexual energies toward non-sexual activities and pursuits. (5 & 11)

Substitution A defense mechanism by which an individual replaces socially undesirable motives with approved patterns of behavior. (5 & 11)

Surrogate The substitution of one person who becomes an image of another, as when a teacher is viewed as a parental figure of authority, or a policeman as a symbol of authority. (8)

Syndrome A pattern which characterizes a disordered condition; collectively, a grouping or cluster of symptoms in combination to form one pattern. (7)

T.A.T. Thematic Apperception Test. Originated by Henry Murray, a projective technique or personality assessment instrument, often referred to as the picture-story test. (11)

Tension An existing mental state of stress and strain which includes physical reactions, anxiety, tension, and behavioral changes.

Theory A set of principles to explain an event and to enable one to predict what may happen under a given set of circumstances. (1, 7, & 8)

Therapy Treatment of a maladjusted individual in order to effect an improved adjustment. (7)

T.M.H. Trainable Mentally Handicapped. An individual of limited intellectual functioning who cannot be educated in the true sense of the term, but who can be trained to achieve a certain level of self-sufficiency. (11)

Trait Theory A theory of personality which assumes the existence of numerous traits which characterize the individual, and which stresses the importance of the recognition and analysis of these traits. (11)

Transfer of Learning (Training) A method by which earlier learning can be effectively utilized in new learning experiences, in order to make the new learning easier for the learner. (4)

Transvestism An abnormal behavior pattern whereby the individual develops an increasing tendency to want to wear the clothing and assume the appearance of the opposite sex. (10)

Trauma A painful, lasting emotional experience of severe impact upon an individual. (6 & 10)

Triad A psychological relationship between three people. (12)

Trimester A particular organizational structure adopted by some colleges and universities wherein the calendar for the school year has three terms, as contrasted to the usual two (semester). (2)

Type Theory The classification of an individual in terms of kinds of personality characteristics exhibited by that individual. (11)

Unconscious Motivation An unaware motive, involving impulses, desires, and feelings which influence and direct behavior, but of which the individual has no cognizance. (1)

Underachiever An individual whose day-to-day performance does not meet the expectation of his aptitudes and measured ability level. (4)

Unique (Personality) An individual whose characteristics are different from others with whom he might be compared; those traits or characteristics which set an individual apart from others. (8 & 11)

Vacillation To waver between alternative choices; hesitation in making a decision. (15)

Verbalization Articulating feelings and ideas; making oral responses; making one's position known to others. (6)

Vocational Guidance Assisting an individual in choosing an occupation or a career. (3, 5, & 15)

Voyeurism Commonly termed "Peeping Tom," wherein an individual, usually male, obtains sexual pleasure, stimulation, and gratification by watching others undress or by watching the sexual activities of others. (5 & 10)

Weatherman Faction A division or group of students whose parent organization is the S.D.S. (Students for a Democratic Society), and whose membership is prone toward more violent movement in the direction of rapid change. (8 & 13)

Withdrawal A defense mechanism involving escape from conflict and frustration by daydreaming, running away, or evading an issue. (5 & 11)

Work-Study Program A collegiate program whereby students can obtain part-time employment on campus in order to help to pay the costs of their college eudcation; a federally funded program; often the student can earn college credit in addition to salary for his work experiences. (2 & 3)

Y.I.P. Youth International Party. A politically active worldwide collegiate organization which advocates change. (5)

Zoophobia An irrational and pervasive fear of animals. (10)

Bibliography

Adams, Donald K., *Anatomy of Personality*, New York: Random House, 1954.

Allport, Gordon W., *Pattern and Growth in Personality*, New York: Holt, Rinehart & Winston, 1961.

Allport, J. W., *Becoming: Basic Considerations for a Psychology of Personality*, New Haven, Conn.: Yale University Press, 1955.

Aronson, Elliot, *Readings About the Social Animal*, New York: Freeman Books, 1973.

Atkinson, J. W., *An Introduction to Motivation*, New York: Van Nostrand Reinhold, 1964.

Baller, W. R. and D. C. Charles, *The Psychology of Human Growth and Development*, New York: Holt, Rinehart & Winston, 1968.

Becker, Howard S., *Making the Grade: The Academic Side of College Life*, New York: John Wiley and Sons, 1968.

Beers, Clifford W., *A Mind That Found Itself: An Autobiography*, New York: Doubleday, 1948.

Bell, Norman T., Robert W. Burkhardt and Victor B. Lawhead, *Introduction to College Life*, Boston: Houghton Mifflin Company, 1966.

Bennis, Warren, *The Leaning Ivory Tower*, New York: Jossey-Bass, 1973.

Berelson, Bernard (Ed.), *The Behavioral Sciences Today*, New York: Harper and Row, 1969.

Berelson, Bernard and Gary A. Steiner, *Human Behavior: An Inventory of Scientific Findings*, New York: Harcourt, Brace and World, 1967.

Berne, Eric, *The Structure and Dynamics of Organizations and Groups*, New York: Ballantine, 1973.

Bettelheim, Bruno, *A Home for the Heart*, New York: Alfred A. Knopf, 1974.

Bindra, D., *Motivation*, New York: The Ronald Press, 1959.

Blaine, Graham B. and Charles G. McArthur, *Emotional Problems of the Student*, New York: Appleton-Century-Crofts, 1971.

Bonner, Hubert, *Psychology of Personality*, New York: The Ronald Press, 1961.

Boroff, David, *Campus, U.S.A.*, New York: Harper and Row, 1962.

Boroff, Judy, *What I Wish I Knew Before I Went to College*, New York: Pocket Books, 1966.

Bower, T. G. R., *Development in Infancy*, New York: Freeman Books, 1974.

Brammer, Lawrence M., *The Helping Relationship: Process and Skills*, Englewood Cliffs, N.J.: Prentice-Hall, 1973.

Brammer, Lawrence M. and E. L. Shostrom, *Therapeutic Psychology: Fundamentals of Counseling and Psychotherapy*, Englewood Cliffs, N.J.: Prentice-Hall, 1968.

Brown, J. S., *The Motivation of Behavior*, New York: McGraw-Hill, 1961.

Bugelski, B. R., *The Psychology of Learning Applied to Teaching*, New York: Bobbs-Merrill, 1971.

Butz, Otto (Ed.), *To Make A Difference: A Student Look At America*, New York: Harper and Row, 1967.

Byrne, Donn, *Introduction to Personality: A Research Approach*, Englewood Cliffs, N.J.: Prentice-Hall, 1966.

Byrne, John and Katherine Byrne, *You and Your Abilities*, Chicago: Science Research Associates, 1959.

Caeifano, Joseph A., *The Student Revolution: A Global Confrontation*, New York: Norton, 1969.

Candland, D. K., *Emotion: Bodily Change*, New York: Van Nostrand Reinhold, 1962.

Cattell, Raymond B., and Ralph M. Dreger (Eds.), *Handbook of Modern Personality Theory*, New York: Appleton-Century-Crofts, 1974.

Clark, Kenneth B., Behavior today, *The Human Sciences Newsletter*, 1(3), Del Mar, Ca.: March 30, 1970.

Clark, Kenneth B. and L. Plotkin, The Negro student at integrated colleges, in A. Passow, M. Goldberg and A. Tannebaum (Eds.), *Education of the Disadvantaged*. New York: Holt, Rinehart & Winston, 1967.

Cohen, Mitchell and Dennis Hak (Eds.), *The New Student Left: An Anthology*, Boston: Beacon Press, 1966.

Coleman, J., *Abnormal Psychology and Modern Life*, Glenview, Il.: Scott, Foresman and Company, 1972.

Coleman, J., *Equality and Educational Opportunity*, U.S. Department of Health, Education and Welfare, U.S. Office of Education, U.S. Government Printing Office, 1966.

Cook, F. J., *Youth in Danger*, New York: Harcourt, Brace and World, 1956.

CRM Books, *Psychology Today: An Introduction*, Del Mar, Ca.: 1974.

Crow, L., et al., *Educating the Culturally Disadvantaged Child*, New York: David McKay, 1966.

Crowne, Lesle Joan, *Adjustment Problems of College Freshmen*, New York: Columbia University Teacher's College, 1955.

Dennis, L. E., and J. F. Kauffman (Eds.), *College and the Student*, Washington, D.C.: American Council on Education, 1966.

Dennis, Wayne (Ed.), *Readings in Child Psychology*, Englewood Cliffs, N.J.: Prentice-Hall, 1963.

Douvall, Evelyn M., *Facts of Life and Love for Teenagers*, New York: Association Press, 1956.

Douvan, Elizabeth and J. Adelson, *The Adolescent Experience*, New York: John Wiley and Sons, 1966.

Draper, Hal Berkley, *The New Student Revolt*, New York: Grove Press, 1969.

Ellis, Albert, *Humanistic Psychotherapy: The Rational-Emotive Approach*, New York: Pinnacle Books, 1973.

Ellis, Albert, *The Civilized Couple's Guide to Extramarital Adventure*, New York: Pinnacle Books, 1973.

Endleman, Robert, *Personality and Social Life*, New York: Random House, 1966.

Erikson, Erik H., *Childhood and Society*, New York: Norton, 1964.

Erikson, Erik H., *Late Adolescence*, Report of First International Conference on Student Mental Health, Princeton, N.J.: World Federation for Mental Health, 1959.

Evans, Medford Stanton, *Revolt on the Campus*, Chicago: H. Regnery Company, 1961.

Feldman, Kenneth A., *The Impact of College on Students*, San Francisco: Jossey-Bass, 1969.

Feuer, L. S., *The Conflict of Generations*, New York: Basic Books, 1969.

Freedman, Morris, *Chaos in Our Colleges*, New York: David McKay, 1963.

Freeman, Howard E. and Wyatt C. Jones, *Social Problems: Causes and Controls*, New York: Rand McNally Publishing Company, 1973.

Freud, Anna, *The Ego and Mechanisms of Defense*, London: International Universities Press, 1967.

Froe, O., Educational planning for disadvantaged college youth, *Journal of Negro Education*, 33, pps. 290–303, 1964.

Fromm, Eric, *Escape From Freedom*, New York: Holt, Rinehart & Winston, 1941.

Fromm, Eric, *The Sane Society*, New York: Holt, Rinehart & Winston, 1955.

Gagne, R. M. and E. A. Fleishman, *Psychology and Human Performance*, New York: Holt, Rinehart & Winston, 1959.

Gardner, J. W., *Self-Renewal: The Individual and the Innovative Society*, New York: Harper and Row, 1964.

Garrison, Roger H., *The Adventure of Learning in College*, New York: Harper and Row, 1959.

Goldsen, Rose K., Morris Rosenberg, Robin M. Williams Jr. and Edward A. Suchman, *What College Students Think*, New York: Van Nostrand Reinhold, 1960.

Gordon, E., Characteristics of Socially Disadvantaged Children, *Review of Educational Research*, 35, pp. 373–388, 1965.

Gordon, Jesse E., *Personality and Behavior*, New York: Macmillan, 1963.

Gordon, Richard E. and Katherine K. Gordon, *The Blight in the Ivy*, Englewood Cliffs, N.J.: Prentice-Hall, 1963.

Gorlow, L. and W. Katkovsky, *Readings in the Psychology of Adjustment*, New York: McGraw-Hill, 1968.

Greenough, William T. (Ed.), *The Nature and Nurture of Behavior*, New York: Freeman Books, 1973.

Grinker, R. R. and J. P. Spiegel, *Men Under Stress*, Philadelphia: Blackiston, 1945.

Gross, Nancy E., *Living With Stress*, New York: McGraw-Hill, 1958.

Guilford, J. P., *Personality*, New York: McGraw-Hill, 1959.

Haas, Kurt, *Understanding Adjustment and Behavior*, Englewood Cliffs, N.J.: Prentice-Hall, 1970.

Hadden, Jeffrey K., *Psychology Today*, Del Mar, Ca.: 1969.

Hall, C. S. and G. Lindzey, *Theories of Personality*, New York: John Wiley and Sons, 1970.

Hall, J. F., *The Psychology of Learning*, Philadelphia: J. B. Lippincott Company, 1967.

Havemann, Ernest and Patricia Salter West, *They Went to College*, New York: Harcourt, Brace and World, 1952.

Heath, Douglas, *Explorations in Maturity: Studies of Mature and Immature College Men*, New York: Appleton-Century-Crofts, 1965.

Horney, Karen, *Our Inner Conflicts*, New York: W. W. Norton & Company, 1945.

Horney, Karen, *The Neurotic Personality of Our Time*, New York: W. W. Norton & Company, 1957.

Hunt, Everett L., *The Revolt of the College Intellectual*, Chicago: Aldine Publishing Company, 1964.

Hutchins, Robert M., *Education for Freedom*, Baton Rouge: Louisiana University Press, 1943.

Jacob, Phillip, *Changing Values in College*, New York: Harper and Row, 1958.

Jahoda, Marie, *Current Concepts of Positive Mental Health,* New York: Basic Books, 1958.

Janov, Arthur, *The Anatomy of Mental Illness,* New York: Berkley Publishing Company, 1974.

Jencks, Christopher and David Riesman, *The Academic Revolution,* New York: Doubleday, 1968.

Jersild, Arthur T., *In Search of Self,* New York: Columbia University Teacher's College, 1952.

Jourard, Sidney M., *Healthy Personality: An Approach from the View-Point of Humanistic Psychology,* New York: The Macmillan Company, 1974.

Jourard, Sidney M., *Personal Adjustment,* New York: The Macmillan Company, 1963.

Kagan, Jerome and H. A. Moss, *Birth to Maturity: A Study of Psychological Development,* New York: John Wiley and Sons, 1962.

Keats, John, *Sheepskin Psychosis,* New York: Dell Books, 1966.

Keniston, Kenneth, *Radicals and Militants: An Annotated Bibliography of Empirical Research on Campus Unrest,* New York: D. C. Heath and Company, 1973.

Kennan, George Frost, *Democracy and the Student Left,* Boston: Little, Brown and Co., 1968.

Kisker, George W., *The Disorganized Personality,* New York: McGraw-Hill, 1964.

Krech, David, Richard S. Crutschfield and Norman Livson, *Elements of Psychology,* New York: Alfred A. Knopf, 1971.

Lazarus, R., *Personality and Adjustment,* Englewood Cliffs, New Jersey: Prentice-Hall, 1963.

Leeper, R. W. and P. Madison, *Toward Understanding Human Personalities,* New York: Appleton-Century-Crofts, 1959.

Lehner, George F. J. and Ella Kube, *The Dynamics of Personal Adjustment,* Englewood Cliffs, N.J.: Prentice-Hall, 1964.

Lindner, R., *Must You Conform?* New York: Holt, Rinehart & Winston, 1962.

Lineberry, William P., *Colleges at the Crossroads,* New York: H. W. Wilson Company, 1966.

Lipset, S. M. (Ed.), *Student Politics,* New York: Basic Books, 1967.

Lipset, S. M. and S. S. Wolin (Ed.), *Berkeley Student Revolt,* New York: Doubleday, 1965.

Lloyd-Jones, Esther M. and H. A. Estrin, *American Student and His College,* New York: Houghton-Mifflin Company, 1967.

Lundin, R. W., *Personality,* New York: The Macmillan Company, 1969.

Lynes, Russell, *How Good Are Our Colleges?* New York: Harper's Magazine, 1966.

Maier, N. R. F., *Frustration: The Study of Behavior Without a Goal,* Ann Arbor: The University of Michigan Press, 1961.

Martin, W. E. and C. B. Stendler, *Child Development: The Process of Growing Up in Society,* New York: Harcourt, Brace and World, 1953.

Maslow, Abraham H., *Motivation and Personality,* New York: Harper and Row, 1970.

Maslow, Abraham H., *Self-Actualizing People,* in Moustakas, Clark E. (Ed.), *The Self: Explorations in Personal Growth,* New York: Harper and Row, 1956.

May, Rollo, *Man's Search for Himself,* New York: Dell Publishing Company, 1973.

McCann, R. V., Developmental factors in growth of a mature faith, *Journal of Religious Education,* 50, pp. 147–155, 1955.

McClelland, David C., *The Achieving Society,* New York: Free Press, 1967.

McClelland, David C. and Robert S. Steele (Eds.), *Human Motivation: A Book of Readings*, New York: General Learning Corporation, 1973.

McConnell, T. R., The relation of institutional goals and organization to the administration of student personnel work, in *Approaches to the Study of Student Personnel Work*, Martin L. Snoke, (Ed.), Minneapolis: The University of Minnesota Press, 1960.

McGuigan, F. J., *Biological Basis of Behavior*, Englewood Cliffs, N.J.: Prentice Hall, 1963.

McKinney, F., *Psychology of Personal Adjustment*, New York: John Wiley and Sons 1960.

Mednick, S. A., *Learning*, Englewood Cliffs, N.J.: Prentice-Hall, 1973.

Menninger, Karl, *Whatever Became of Sin*, New York: Hawthorn Books, 1973.

Meyers, Lawrence S. and Neal E. Grossen, *Behavioral Research*, New York: The Free Press, 1974.

Michael, D. N., *The Next Generation: The Prospect Ahead for the Youth of Today and Tomorrow*, New York: Random House, 1965.

Monita, Michael V., *The Belching Buddha*, Chicago: The Raven Publishing Company, 1974.

Monita, Michael V., *Zen and the Buddha Mind*, Chicago: The Raven Publishing Company, 1974.

Montagu, Ashley, *The Peaceful Nature of Man*, unpublished manuscript, 1969.

Montagu, Ashley, *The Prevalance of Nonsense*, New York: Harper and Row, 1967.

Morris, Desmond, *The Human Zoo*, New York: Dell Publishing Company, 1971.

Moustakas, Clark E., *Children in Play Therapy*, New York: Random House, 1974.

Moustakas, Clark E., *Portraits of Loneliness and Love*, Englewood Cliffs, N.J.: Prentice-Hall, 1974.

Mowrer, O. Hobart, *Learning Theory and Behavior*, New York: John Wiley and Sons, 1960.

Murphy, G., *Human Potentialities*, New York: Basic Books, 1958.

Murray, E. J., *Motivation and Emotion*, Englewood Cliffs, N.J.: Prentice-Hall, 1964.

Newton, Roy and F. G. Nichols, *How to Improve Your Personality*, New York: McGraw-Hill, 1963.

Palton, A., *Men, Money and Motivation*, New York: McGraw-Hill, 1961.

Pettigrew, T., *A Profile of Negro Americans*, New York: Van Nostrand Reinhold, 1964.

Pikunas, J., *Human Development: A Science of Growth*, New York: McGraw-Hill, 1969.

Quay, H. C. (Ed.), *Juvenile Delinquency: Research and Theory*, New York: Van Nostrand Reinhold, 1965.

Reisman, David, and associates, *The Lonely Crowd*, New Haven, Conn.: Yale University Press, 1950.

Resnick, William C. and David H. Heller, *On Your Own in College*, Columbus, Oh.: Charles E. Merrill Publishing Company, 1969.

Resnick, William C. and Herbert L. Sachs, *Dynamic General Psychology: An Introduction*, Boston: Holbrook Press, 1971.

Resnick, William C. and Herbert L. Sachs, *Student Workbook to Accompany Dynamic General Psychology: An Introduction*, Boston: Holbrook Press, 1971.

Rethlingshafer, D. and D. Dewsbury, *Comparative Psychology: A Modern Survey*, New York: McGraw-Hill, 1973.

Rivlin, Harry N., et al., *First Years in College*, Boston: Houghton Mifflin Company, 1965.

Rogers, Carl R., *Becoming Partners: Marriage and Its Alternatives*, New York: Dell Publishing Company, 1973.

Rogers, Carl R., *On Becoming A Person: A Therapist's View of Psychotherapy*, Boston: Houghton Mifflin Company, 1970.

Rogers, Carl R., *On Encounter Groups*, New York: Harper and Row, 1973.

Rosten, Leo, The World of Leo Rosten: To An Angry Old Man, *Look Magazine*, 33 (9), p. 14, New York: April 29, 1969.

Rubinstein, Joseph, *Annual Editions Readings in Psychology '73/'74*, The Dushkin Publishing Group: Guilford, Connecticut, 1973.

Ruch, Floyd L. and Philip G. Zimbardo, *Psychology and Life*, Glenview, Il.: Scott, Foresman and Company, 1971.

Sachs, Herbert L., *Every Parent Is A Tutor*, manuscript in preparation, 1975.

Sachs, Herbert L., *Student Projects in Child Psychology*, Dubuque, Iowa: Kendall Hunt Publishing Company, 1967.

Sachs, Herbert L., *What Can the Community College Do for You?*, manuscript in preparation, 1975.

Sanford, Nevitt, *College and Character*, New York: John Wiley and Sons, 1964.

Selye, H., *The Stress of Life*, New York: McGraw-Hill, 1956.

Seymour, Martin L. (Ed.), *Student Politics*, New York: Basic Books, 1967.

Shaffer, L. M. and E. J. Shoben, Jr., *Psychology of Adjustment*, Boston: Houghton Mifflin Company, 1956.

Skinner, B. F., *Walden Two*, New York: The Macmillan Company, 1960.

Smith, G. Kerry, *Stress and Campus Response*, San Francisco: Jossey-Bass, 1968.

Smith, P., Some implications for freshman orientation activities with Negro college students, *Journal of College Student Personnel*, 5, pps. 176–179, 1964.

Soldwedel, Bette J., *Mastering the College Challenge*, New York: The Macmillan Company, 1964.

Staats, A. W. and C. K. Staats, *Complex Human Behavior*, New York: Holt, Rinehart & Winston, 1963.

Stern, Edith M., *Mental Illness: A Guide for the Family*, New York: Harper and Row, 1968.

Schutz, William, *Elements of Encounter*, Big Sur, Ca.: Joy Press, 1974.

Super, D. E., *The Psychology of Careers*, New York: Harper and Row, 1963.

Sussman, Marvin B., *Source Book in Marriage and the Family*, Boston: Houghton Mifflin Company, 1974.

Teuer, Lewis Samuel, *The Conflict of Generations: The Character and Significance of Student Movements*, New York: Basic Books, 1969.

Townsend, Agatha, *College Freshmen Speak Out*, New York: Harper and Row, 1956.

Truax, Charles B. and Robert R. Carkhuff, *Toward Effective Counseling and Psychotherapy*, Chicago: Aldine Publishing Company, 1967.

Turkel, Studs, *Working*, New York: Random House, 1974.

University of Illinois, *Handbook*, Student Newspaper Publication, Chicago: January, 1970.

Vogel, Virgil J., *This Country Was Ours*, New York: Harper and Row, 1974.

Von Hoffman, N., *Multiuniversity: A Personal Report on What Happens to Today's Students in American Universities*, New York: Holt, Rinehart & Winston, 1966.

Walker, E. L. and R. Heyns, *An Anatomy of Conformity*, Englewood Cliffs, N.J.: Prentice-Hall, 1967.

Warga, Richard G., *Personal Awareness*, Boston: Houghton Mifflin, 1974.

Watson, Goodwin, *Social Psychology*, Philadelphia: J. B. Lippincott, 1972.

Watson, Robert I., *The Great Psychologists*, Philadelphia: J. B. Lippincott, 1971.

Wechsler, David, *Selected Papers of David Wechsler*, New York: Academic Press, 1974.

Weinland, J. D., *How to Improve Your Memory*, New York: Barnes and Noble, 1969.

White, R. W., *Lives in Progress*, New York: Holt, Rinehart & Winston, 1966.

Whittaker, James K., *Social Treatment: An Approach to Interpersonal Helping*, Chicago: Aldine Publishing Company, 1974.

Williams, Jesse F. and Angela Kitzinger, *Health for the College Student*, New York: Harper and Row, 1967.

Williams, R. and H. Byars, Negro self-esteem in transitional society, *Personnel and Guidance Journal*, 47, pps. 120–125, 1968.

Wise, W Max, *They Came for the Best of Reasons: College Students Today*, American Council on Education, Washington, D.C., 1958.

Wolpe, Joseph, *The Practice of Behavior Therapy*, New York: Pergamon Press, 1973.

Yates, A. J., *Frustration and Conflict*, New York: Van Nostrand Reinhold, 1965.

Index

357

STUDENT SERVICE SECTION

Please print:

Student's Name: _____

College or University: _____

Student's Address: _____
                  Number   Street   City   State   Zip Code

Course Title: _____

Instructor's Name: _____

Student's Question: (Please list only one question below; be specific.)

_____

_____

_____

_____

The question above refers to Chapter ___ Page ___ of the textbook.

Author's Reply:

_____

_____

_____

For a prompt reply please include a stamped, self-addressed envelope

Mail this form to: Professor Herbert L. Sachs, Chairman
                     Counseling and Social Science Department
                     City Colleges of Chicago—Mayfair College
                     4626 North Knox Avenue—Chicago Illinois—
                     60630

STUDENT SERVICE SECTION

Please print:

Student's Name: _____

College or University: _____

Student's Address: _____

                Number   Street   City   State   Zip Code

Course Title: _____

Instructor's Name: _____

Student's Question: (Please list only one question below; be specific.)

_____

_____

_____

_____

The question above refers to Chapter ____ Page ____ of the textbook.

Author's Reply:

_____

_____

_____

For a prompt reply please include a stamped, self-addressed envelope.

Mail this form to: Professor Herbert L. Sachs, Chairman
                      Counseling and Social Science Department
                      City Colleges of Chicago—Mayfair College
                      4626 North Knox Avenue—Chicago, Illinois—
                      60630

STUDENT SERVICE SECTION

Please print:

Student's Name: _____

College or University: _____

Student's Address: _____
                   Number   Street   City   State   Zip Code

Course Title: _____

Instructor's Name: _____

Student's Question: (Please list only one question below; be specific.)

_____

_____

_____

_____

The question above refers to Chapter ___ Page ___ of the textbook.

Author's Reply:

_____

_____

_____

For a prompt reply please include a stamped, self-addressed envelope.

Mail this form to: Professor Herbert L. Sachs, Chairman
                        Counseling and Social Science Department
                        City Colleges of Chicago—Mayfair College
                        4626 North Knox Avenue—Chicago, Illinois—
                        60630

STUDENT SERVICE SECTION

Please print:

Student's Name: _____

College or University: _____

Student's Address: _____
                   Number   Street   City   State   Zip Code

Course Title: _____

Instructor's Name: _____

Student's Question: (Please list only one question below; be specific.)

_____

_____

_____

_____

The question above refers to Chapter ___ Page ___ of the textbook.

Author's Reply:

_____

_____

_____

For a prompt reply please include a stamped, self-addressed envelope.

Mail this form to: Professor Herbert L. Sachs, Chairman
                    Counseling and Social Science Department
                    City Colleges of Chicago—Mayfair College
                    4626 North Knox Avenue—Chicago, Illinois—
                    60630

STUDENT SERVICE SECTION

Please print:

Student's Name: _____

College or University: _____

Student's Address: _____
                    Number   Street   City   State   Zip Code

Course Title: _____

Instructor's Name: _____

Student's Question: (Please list only one question below; be specific.)

_____

_____

_____

_____

The question above refers to Chapter ___ Page ___ of the textbook.

Author's Reply:

_____

_____

_____

For a prompt reply please include a stamped, self-addressed envelope.

Mail this form to: Professor Herbert L. Sachs, Chairman
                     Counseling and Social Science Department
                     City Colleges of Chicago—Mayfair College
                     4626 North Knox Avenue—Chicago, Illinois—
                     60630

BF724   67876
S24
    Sachs, Herbert L.
        Dynamic personal adjustment.